AMERICA
ON TRIAL

AMERICA ON TRIAL

Inside the Legal Battles
That Transformed Our Nation

ALAN M. DERSHOWITZ

WARNER BOOKS

NEW YORK   BOSTON

Warner Books

Time Warner Book Group
1271 Avenue of the Americas, New York, NY 10020
Visit our Web site at www.twbookmark.com

Printed in the United States of America
First Printing: May 2004
10 9 8 7 6 5 4 3 2 1

Library of Congress Cataloging-in-Publication Data

Dershowitz, Alan M.
      America on trial : inside the legal battles that transformed our nation / Alan M.
Dershowitz.
            p. cm.
Includes index.
      ISBN: 0-446-52058-6
      1. Trials — United States. 2. Law — United States — History. I. Title.
      KF220.D37   2004
      349.73'09 — dc22   2003023912

Book design by Giorgetta Bell McRee

This book is lovingly dedicated to the first Dershowitz of the twenty-first century, my great-niece Zara Columbia Dershowitz, and to her parents, Adam and Hanna.

Contents

CONTENTS

Acknowledgments

Although reading classic trial transcripts is a solitary activity, I could not have compiled this book without the assistance of many people. The students in my pass-fail seminar on great trials provided brilliant insights into the trials we studied together, as did my friends on Martha's Vineyard who participated in our great trials movie nights. Special thanks to my student research assistants who helped with the introductions to the various eras in American history. Most particularly my appreciation to: Karen Abravanel (the colonial and early U.S. period and the Nuremberg trials), Holly Beth Billington (European regicides and the 1980s through the present), Jacqueline Cohen (biblical foundations), Alex Gordon (pre–Civil War through Reconstruction periods), Kristy Greenberg (early twentieth century through the interwar period), Mark Sabath (World War II and Vietnam), and Pam Wasserstein (the Cold War and civil rights eras).

In addition to her excellent work on several introductions, Holly Beth Billington helped to organize and coordinate the research and the footnotes. She is a pleasure to work with and always gets the job done.

My assistant, Jane Wagner, provided her usual professional supervision and overall assistance.

Christine Valentine encouraged me to participate in Gryphon's Notable Trials Series and provided excellent editorial assistance to the introductions I first wrote for that series.

My usual thanks to friends and family who encouraged me through this labor of love.

Introduction

The courtroom trial has fascinated human beings from the beginning of recorded history. It has long been a staple of literature, drama, even scripture. The trial also provides a unique window through which to glimpse the narrative of history. Virtually every historical epoch is personified by noteworthy trials. History has been viewed through the window of politics, personality, economics, religion, sociology, culture, art, and ideology. The trial, of course, provides a different vantage point. It generally represents a snapshot of individual litigants rather than a video or panorama of a society. Yet the trial can tell us a great deal about the passions, conflicts, and attitudes of the time, despite — sometimes because of — its narrower focus. *America on Trial* is thus an episodic history of our nation viewed through the prism of our most dramatic and influential public court proceedings.

The trial is drama. Its outcome is often unpredictable. The jurors, in cases where ordinary citizens are chosen to determine the fate of their "peers," are not subject to the control of government. They represent the man and woman on the street, and they return to the street after completing their important but singular task, without being accountable for their verdicts. The judge, whether appointed or elected, is supposed to be the embodiment of the law. Indeed, the traditional wig was designed to highlight the uniformity, rather than the individuality, of judges. Yet he is also a human being with biases, predispositions, and ambitions. The lawyers are the gladiators, facing off against each other in moral combat. And the litigants are central characters in a real-life drama that will determine their own future, and sometimes the future of many others.

In the historically significant trials of any era, more tends to be at stake than the lives, freedom, or fortunes of the litigants themselves. Great issues or events transcend the individual participants in the courtroom confrontation. Sometimes an important precedent is established. Other times, a prominent person or movement is made or broken. Often the verdict of history is determined, or influenced, by the verdict in the case, though sometimes the verdict of history and the outcome of the case may differ dramatically. Nearly always there is something about a memorable case that makes it somehow representative of the passions of its time. The most noteworthy of trials deal with enduring themes that transcend time and place. They reflect the human condition.

Because of the drama and often transcendent character of the trial, it should not be surprising that some of the most memorable trials have served as a basis for books, plays, and motion pictures. They have become part of the popular culture of the day, and on occasion part of the enduring culture of the ages. Sometimes the literary license taken with the actual facts results in a work of great fiction, such as *The Brothers Karamazov* by Dostoyevsky or *An American Tragedy* by Theodore Dreiser; sometimes in semifiction or docudrama, as *In Cold Blood* by Truman Capote, *A Man for All Seasons* by Robert Bolt, or *Inherit the Wind* by Jerome Lawrence and Robert E. Lee. On occasion, the trial that forms the basis of an influential work of literature can be entirely the product of the writer's imagination, as in Kafka's *The Trial* and Harper Lee's *To Kill a Mockingbird*.

In this book, I will present what I believe are among the most important trials in American history. I have selected cases (and occasionally Supreme Court appeals) that I believe are representative of the important eras in our history. Most tell us something about the struggles and passions of the times. Some provide insights into the human condition. Others are noteworthy simply because they involve famous, or infamous, people. They all tell us something about our nation and about ourselves.

In several of the cases in which the trials have been used as the basis for books, plays, or films, I will compare their literary treatments with the actual events. Such a comparison will provide additional insights into how the trials of one era are presented to people living at a different time.

I was involved — as a lawyer, consultant, or commentator — in many of the most notorious cases of the 1970s, 1980s, and 1990s, including the Jewish Defense League murder case, the Dr. Benjamin Spock antiwar conspiracy appeal, the Pentagon Papers case, the Chicago Seven appeal, the *Deep Throat* and *I Am Curious—Yellow* obscenity prosecutions, the von Bülow appeal, the Bakke controversy, the Leona Helmsley appeals, John Lennon's deportation proceeding, Muhammad Ali's appeal, Jeffrey MacDonald's habeas corpus petition, Jim Bakker's sentencing appeal, the John DeLorean case, the attempt to reopen Wayne Williams's serial murder conviction, Michael Milken's sentencing reduction, Mike Tyson's appeal, O. J. Simpson's trial, Bill Clinton's impeachment, the murder appeals of Dr. William Sybers and Sandra Murphy, and *Bush v. Gore*. I was also involved in the several cases involving entertainers such as the David Merrick adoption litigation, the Woody Allen–Mia Farrow custody dispute, the prosecution of film director John Landis, as well as cases involving singers David Crosby, Axl Rose, and Kenny Rogers. As I write these words, I remain involved in several current cases of great interest to the public. I have selected some, but omitted most, of my own cases.

In addition to having read hundreds of transcripts of trials for purposes of preparing appeals, I have also read the transcripts, where available, of many of the great trials throughout history. I believe that I have probably read more trial transcripts than any other living lawyer, and I call on this experience in selecting and analyzing these trials, and in comparing older trials with contemporary ones.*

Several common themes run through many of the great trials. Although history — especially popular history — tends to present these trials as clashes between good and evil, with heroes and villains, the truth is generally less black and white. Shades of gray predominate in the actual trial records. When the media reports on a trial — or when literature fictionalizes it — all the "right" seems to be on one side and all the "wrong" on the other. Real trials, on the other hand, are more complex and often more fascinating. Throughout this book we will see trials that were grossly unfair, but that may well have produced a factually correct result (for example, the Sacco and Vanzetti case). We will also see fair trials that produced factually incorrect results (such as the Central Park Jogger case). We will even see trials that produced both correct and incorrect results (Julius Rosenberg was guilty, but his wife, Ethel, who was executed along with him, was almost certainly innocent — and the FBI knew it!). We will encounter great lawyers who may have helped themselves achieve greatness by improper means (for example, Clarence Darrow), and great cases that have been totally mischaracterized by literature and popular history. (The Scopes "monkey" trial and the Boston Massacre trial are, perhaps, the best examples of this category.)

On the basis of my experience, I can confidently state that actual trial records are almost invariably more interesting than the

*Since the late 1980s I have been writing introductions for books about great trials throughout the world for the Notable Trials Library; some of the material in this book originally appeared in several of those introductions.

fictionalized and popularized renditions of them. Truth is indeed stranger than fiction when it comes to actual trials. Obviously, reading entire trial transcripts is not for everyone. Complete transcripts include highly technical components, much redundancy, and some extremely boring witnesses and arguments. I have tried my best to distill these trials and to present brief accounts that preserve their most interesting aspects, along with the nuances and subtleties that are often airbrushed out in fictional and popular renditions. There are few absolute heroes in real-life accounts, though there are still some absolute villains. Heroism and villainy often reflect the changing of the times, though there are some constants throughout the ages.

The cases that represent the important epochs in American history did not grow out of a vacuum. Their roots were in Western culture, of which they were a part. Most colonial Americans were aware of the biblical accounts of the great trials — whether real or fictional — of the Judeo-Christian tradition, including the trials of the Sodomites, of Joseph, of Tamar, and certainly of Jesus, which led to the central event of Christianity. All these are part of the collective memory of our culture. So, too, were the historic trials of Socrates, Galileo, Thomas More, Joan of Arc, the Spanish Inquisition, and the Star Chamber, as well as the various European prosecutions of kings, queens, regicides — and more.

Yet America was a new land, whose free population consisted largely of people (and their descendants) who had chosen to leave the Old World. (Its slave population, of course, was forcibly removed from Africa, and its Native population was forcibly subdued, killed, dispersed, and placed on reservations.) The American trials were considerably different, in many important respects, from the earlier trials in distant lands. We had no monarchy or established church that the law was designed to protect. Instead, we had a written Constitution designed to protect citizens from the tyranny of governments and churches. We also introduced more democratic elements into our legal system not only by expanding the powers of the lay jury, but also — for better or worse — by electing prosecutors and judges in some of our states and by permitting extensive and contemporaneous media coverage of our trials. We democratized our legal system beyond anything previously known to the common or civil law. We also proved to be a litigious people whose slogans include "so sue me," "see you in court," "tell it to the judge," and "I'm taking it to a higher court." As the French chronicler of the early American experience, Alexis de Tocqueville, observed, nearly every great issue that divides America eventually ends up in a courtroom.

Because the American legal system grew out of the British systems and Western culture, I will begin this book with a brief prologue describing some of the historic trials that directly influenced the development of American law. I will then proceed to the most important trials of the colonial period and the epochs that followed it, culminating in the most significant trials of our current era. Finally, I will end with some informed speculation about what are likely to be the most important trials of the future, particularly in the war against terrorism.

Each of the historical periods will be introduced by a brief overview, placing the trials in their historical setting. The discussion of the trials themselves will begin with an outline of the basic facts — time, place, verdict, sentence, and so forth. I will then provide my own observations concerning the case, including an analysis of the trial, the events surrounding it, its historical significance, and other personal reflections. We will hear (or at least read) voices from the past — the words of the litigants, the lawyers, and the judges. The styles and syntax may be strange to the contemporary ear (or eye), but the substance will often be familiar, since the catalog of deadly sins and crimes has not changed very much over the centuries.

No two lawyers, or even nonlawyers, could ever agree on a definitive list of the greatest trials in history, though everyone's would probably include the trials of Jesus, Socrates, Galileo, and Thomas More. As to American trials, most would probably include those of John Peter Zenger, the Boston Massacre, Aaron Burr, the Lincoln assassination, the Johnson and Clinton impeachments, and the *Bush v. Gore* election dispute. Reasonable people would disagree about whether the O. J. Simpson trials, the Sacco-Vanzetti case, the Rosenberg prosecution, the Scopes trial, and many others belong on the list. In this book I present my own rather idiosyncratic list, based on my personal observations and experiences. For me the basic criterion is passion. Did the trial reflect the passions of the time? Did it engage the passions of the people? Will contemporary readers still feel passionately about the issues, the personalities, and the verdict? If you disagree with my list, you can't sue me, but you can e-mail me with your own suggested additions or subtractions at alder@law.harvard.edu.

AMERICA ON TRIAL

Prologue: The Foundations of American Law

America's legal system is based largely on the British common law, though much of it was a reaction to the abuses against which the American colonies rebelled. To understand American law, we must know something about its traditional sources as well as the unique American reactions to these sources. Among the most important roots of what eventually blossomed into American law were the Bible, the Greek and Roman legal systems, the canon law, and the common law. Among the most palpable outrages against which we reacted were the Inquisition, the Star Chamber, and the "long train of abuses and usurpations" inflicted on the colonists by the king of England and cataloged in our Declaration of Independence.

Most American lawyers, judges, and lawmakers were familiar with the stories of the Bible, with the accounts of famous Greek trials, such as that of Socrates, with the infamous Continental Inquisitions against Joan of Arc and Galileo, with the British prosecution of Thomas More, and with the notorious regicide and treason trials of Europe.

But ours was to be a different kind of legal system, based on a written Constitution, judicial review, and, most important, the separation of church and state. Thomas Jefferson, the primary draftsman of our Declaration of Independence, explained that he intended that document of liberty to be a "signal of arousing men to burst the chains under which monkish ignorance and superstition had persuaded them to bind themselves, and assure the blessings and security of self-government." The "monkish ignorance" to which he referred was the clerical domination that had enslaved European politics and law for so many centuries.

The ancient sources of the common law were viewed by Americans through the prism of their own experiences as religious and political refugees and then as revolutionaries. The historical trials were important not so much as positive precedents, but rather as negative reminders of the regime they had left behind and wanted no part of on their shores.

The American colonists were generally familiar with the stories of the Bible. Some actually regarded the Bible as part of the common law. Sir William Blackstone, the English legal commentator most influential in early American law, believed that all law derived from "[t]he revealed or divine law, and they are to be found only in the Scriptures." Jefferson, Adams, and Franklin — along with other Founding Fathers — disagreed with Blackstone's rigid formulation, but they, too, recognized the influence of the Bible on the way Americans viewed the law.

The Bible is replete with legal confrontations, some of which can aptly be characterized as trials. The earliest narratives of the book of Genesis include God's punishment of Adam, Eve, and the snake following Adam's attempt to shift responsibility to Eve for violating God's commandment not to eat of the Tree of Knowledge. There follows the first recorded murder "trial," after Cain kills his brother, Abel, and denies knowledge of Abel's whereabouts. Shortly thereafter, Abraham becomes the world's first defense attorney by arguing on behalf of the sinners of Sodom and asking God whether He would sweep away the innocent along with the guilty.

More crimes follow. A sleeping Lot is raped by his daughters. Abraham attempts to sacrifice his son. Jacob defrauds both his father and his brother. Joseph is sold into slavery by his brothers and then is falsely accused of sexual improprieties by the wife of his employer. Dina is raped, and her brothers murder in revenge. Tamar becomes a prostitute and is accused of carrying an illegitimate child by her father-in-law, who had impregnated her. On and on it goes, throughout the five books of Moses, with their enduring legal code, and to the story of Susanna and the elders, in a supplement to the book of Daniel, which contains a virtually complete trial that has directly influenced the development of American law. A brief description of this case and a representative quotation from a modern American decision relying on it will illustrate the close relationship between the biblical trials and the trials that took place in our own country. (I have discussed the trials that are described in the first book of the Bible in *The Genesis of Justice*.[1])

Susanna stands accused of adultery by two elders with whom she had refused to have sex. The people of Israel hear the testimony of the elders and act as both judge and jury, sentencing Susanna to death. Susanna cries out to God at the injustice, and He rouses the spirit of Daniel to stand in her defense. Daniel then demands an opportunity to examine each of the elders separately. The elders are brought before the people and isolated from each other. Daniel then asks each elder one question: Under what type of tree did the alleged adultery take place? Each describes a different type of tree, and on hearing this the people of Israel praise God, acquit Susanna, and sentence the elders to death for bearing false witness.

Susanna's case has been cited numerous times by American courts in support of the importance of the rule requiring that witnesses to the same event must be sequestered as other witnesses testify. A 1991 Wisconsin case observed that:

The Story of Susanna and the Elders was relied upon almost from the beginning of recorded trials as justifying the practice of separating witnesses in order to expose inconsistencies in their testimony. The rule of exclusion also aims "to prevent the possibility of one witness shaping his testimony to match that given by other witnesses at the trial." Such shaping may be an unconscious reaction to suggestion rather than a deliberate attempt at collusion. The rule thus has a two-fold goal: to prevent falsification and to uncover fabrication that has already taken place.[2]

Though the Susanna case has had significant impact on procedural rules, the biblical trial that has had the greatest overall influence on Western law is, of course, the trial of Jesus, as recounted in the Gospels. The biblical accounts of this trial are sparse, but they agree that witnesses gave false testimony and that the Sanhedrin (the Jewish court) nonetheless declared Jesus's "blasphemy" to be worthy of death.

The Harvard Divinity School recently invited me to defend Jesus at a moot court conducted before a professor of divinity playing the role of Pontius Pilate and another professor of Bible studies playing the role of prosecutor. There was an advisory jury of divinity school students. Not surprisingly, the verdict was a hung jury (no pun intended). I thought I had done quite a persuasive job in proving the innocence of my client, and so I decided to interview several of the student jurors who had voted to find Jesus guilty. I asked them to explain their votes. They all provided the same explanation: "As believing Christians, we had to vote for Jesus to be convicted and crucified, or else humanity would not have been saved and our religion would not have come into existence." It's hard to argue with that kind of faith.

The point of this anecdote is that everyone writing about the trial and crucifixion of Jesus begins with a point of view. As a lawyer (and as a Jew), I find it difficult to credit the statement in Matthew that the Jews admitted not only their guilt but the guilt of their children as well: "His blood be on us, and on our children." This does not seem typical of a crowd lusting for blood. But it provided a theological justification for anti-Jewish attitudes among some Christians over the past two millennia.

The ancient laws of the Jews and the laws of the Romans both looked unfavorably upon religious dissidents and "blasphemers." Moreover, this was a time of unrest, both politically and religiously. Indeed, at the time of Jesus, the line between the political and the religious was not nearly as sharply drawn as it is today. There is, in fact, no ancient Hebrew word for "religion," since it was an entire way of life. The substantive laws of the Bible punish certain kinds of religious heresy by death, but we know very little about these laws as they were actually applied during that time.

We do know, however, that the Sanhedrin was not empowered to impose the death penalty unless there were two witnesses, advance warning to the defendant, and a variety of other safeguards that made it nearly impossible, in practice, to order anyone executed. Moreover, confessions could not be relied on, and the burden of proof was daunting. A Sanhedrin that imposed a single death penalty in seventy years was characterized as "bloody."

The Romans, on the other hand, had far looser standards of proof, particularly for non-Romans in occupied provinces. It should not be surprising, therefore, that Jews who wanted to be rid of a troublemaking preacher who was urging his followers to renounce wealth, family, and other aspects of "this world" would turn him in to the Roman authorities.

The relationship between the Jewish and Roman authorities, and their relative responsibility for the conviction and crucifixion of Jesus, is among the least trustworthy and most conflicting aspects of the Gospels. During the early days of Christianity, the former Jews who formed the core of the new religion wanted very much to convert their friends and relatives to their faith. It is only natural, therefore, that early accounts may have presented the Jews in a more favorable light. It is also natural that accounts that followed the Roman acceptance of Christianity would favor the Romans at the expense of the Jews.

Now that nearly every branch of Christianity has renounced the anti-Jewish aspects of some of the Gospels, it is easier to read these accounts as an invitation to "love thy neighbor"— which is a central tenet of both Judaism and Christianity — rather than as a justification for hatred. We learn much about justice from accounts of injustice. By any standard — religious, historical, or legal — the conviction and execution of Jesus was a great injustice and thus a great lesson, in justice, for the modern world. The American colonists certainly viewed it as the kind of injustice their laws — both substantive and procedural — should be designed to prevent. It should thus come as no surprise that references to the case abound in American legal history.

In addition to the trials of the Bible, the trials of antiquity most often mentioned by Americans were those conducted by the Greeks. As the "inventors" of democracy, including trial by "jury," the Greeks influenced the American approach to governance. The trial of Socrates (399 BC) was explicitly referenced in the Federalist Papers (No. 55), and James Madison cited "the heroic period of ancient Greece" in the Debates on the Adoption of the Federal Constitution.

Though Roman law was the "most copied system in the west," the recorded accounts of Greek trials fired the imagination of those responsible for adapting ancient legal systems to the needs of the "new republic."

Reading accounts of Greek trials — especially those that took place under the relatively humane laws of Solon, which replaced the harsh Draconian laws of an earlier era — reveals some primitive notions of trial by jury; we also see some early versions of techniques and arguments currently used by defense counsel. Although no "lawyers" were permitted in the Athenian courts, hired speechwriters were an important part of the Athenian justice system. Even without lawyers, the Athenian people were extremely litigious. Indeed, it is fair to conclude from studies of Athenian and other societies that there is a close relationship between the amount of litigation in a society and its commitment to liberty and the rule of law. As Heraclitus put it: "The people must fight to defend their laws as they would their fortifications."[3]

The content of some of the Solonic laws may have been strange to the modern ear, but laws always reflect the culture from which they emerge. The trial of Euphiletus for the murder of Eratosthenes, which occurred sometime between 400 and 380 BC, employed a familiar defense technique: placing the dead victim on trial.[4] The defendant admitted to killing the victim in cold blood after tying the victim's hands behind his back in the presence of numerous witnesses. His defense was that the victim had seduced the defendant's wife, and that killing the man who seduced one's wife was lawful under Athenian law, even if the killing was done in cold blood. A modern variant on this primitive notion of justice is what is colloquially called "Texas self-defense"—a form of jury nullification under which the letter of the law is ignored when a man comes upon his wife committing adultery and "takes the law into his own hands." The verdict in the Greek case was acquittal, and the defendant was deemed free to divorce his wife.

Another classic Greek trial — that of Helos for the murder of Herodes — is much more akin to a contemporary whodunit with a missing body. The defendant, an out-of-towner from an unpopular neighboring state, was accused of murdering an Athenian while on a sea voyage and throwing his body overboard. (I consulted on a similar case in Delaware several years ago.) Helos's speechwriter makes arguments that sound familiar to our contemporary ear, and include our preference for acquitting the guilty to convicting the innocent: "Observe, too, that if a mistake has to be made, it is more pardonable in the eyes of Heaven to acquit a person wrongfully than to destroy him unfairly: the former is merely a mistake, but the latter is a sin."[5]

Despite important and revealing differences between the Athenian justice of old and our current approaches to law and order, such similarities indicate that a passing familiarity with Solonic law is useful in understanding contemporary legal systems. Many colonial American lawyers had this understanding. And nearly all were familiar with the second most famous trial of antiquity, the trial of Socrates, as recounted by Plato.

Socrates, like Jesus, was seen by the authorities as a dangerous provocateur who would have been silenced by virtually every society in history. The reason why this trial is so remarkable is not that the *defendant* was Socrates; it is that the *prosecutor* was Athens. Visionaries such as Socrates were executed throughout history, by every manner of society, left, right, religious, secular, Western, Eastern, black, and white. But Athens was different. "Ancient Athens [was] the earliest society where freedom of thought and its expression flourished on a scale never known before, and rarely equaled since."[6] It was a society that valued ideas, and yet it put Socrates' ideas on trial and tried to execute them, along with him. In this sense, it is Athens that has been on trial in the court of history since Plato chronicled Socrates' martyrdom. The trial greatly influenced our own Founding Fathers in their decision to add to our Constitution a Bill of Rights, with its protections of freedom of speech and religion.

But the religious persecutions that most influenced the development of American law, especially the First Amendment, were trials such as those of Joan of Arc, Saint Thomas More, and Galileo Galilei.

To begin to understand the trial of Joan of Arc, it is essential to go back in time to an age when belief in witchcraft was an essential component of Christian orthodoxy (as it continued to be in late-seventeenth-century New England). As Saint Thomas Aquinas put it, to doubt magic was to doubt the authority of the sacred writings. And witchcraft and magic were the exclusive tools of the devil. Naturally, the devil would use women — or other "weak" or "corrupt" forms of life such as "a Negro an ox or a dog"—to do his evil bidding. The "Jews and the Moslems," of course, also did the devil's work. It took special training to identify the "hounds of Satan," but the churches and universities gave this authority to a select group of experts.[7] These experts determined that the Maid of Orleans was, indeed, the devil's disciple.

Nor was the devil or his disciple entitled to a devil's advocate. Joan had to defend herself against an array of lawyers, clerics, academics, and politicians. How could she prove — and it was the defendant's heavy burden to prove — that she was actually hearing God, when "the greatest ruse of the EVIL ONE is precisely the imitation of Jesus, and the counterfeiting of his miracles"? Catch-22! Not surprisingly, she lost and was declared a witch. The punishment for witchcraft — a punishment used widely during the fifteenth century — was burning at the stake.

In order to fully understand the charges against Joan of Arc, it is also helpful to understand the status of women in fifteenth-century France. Joan was a soldier who wore men's clothing. This was enough to brand her a *putain* (harlot) or a diabolically mad and dangerous disturber of the peace. Though she passed repeated tests of her virginity, administered by noblemen's wives, these physical proofs were not enough to persuade her accusers that she had not joined the troops for "carnal" reasons. Her claim that she had worn the garb of men "to protect her virginity" was answered by the argument that she should never have placed herself in such a position. Like women throughout the ages — not always excluding our own — Joan was condemned for actions that, if engaged in by a man, would have been deemed praiseworthy. And like women throughout the ages, many of Joan's actions were "explained"—by her defenders as well as her detractors — in terms of her "menses," emotions, and glands.

Even accounting for the difference in attitudes over the ages, there is something terribly familiar about the trial of Joan of Arc.

It was a political trial whose stakes (pardon the pun) were quite high. England, France, and Rome all had much to gain and lose by its outcome, as did individual clerics and politicians. Although Joan had her supporters, especially the people of Orleans, the various establishments — political, religious, academic, and social — all had much to fear from an uncontrollable zealot. Her unpredictability (the lack of control over her internal voices) made her dangerous to all who needed to exercise tight control in order to preserve their power. Although the outcome of the trial was preordained, it was important, as it always is in political trials, for the forms of the law to be followed. Justice must be seen to be done, especially if it is not really being done. Accordingly, elaborate measures were taken to create a judicial atmosphere appropriate to the age.

It is in the nature of formal legal proceedings often to disguise substantive injustices. In reading through transcripts even of contemporary trials that we now know were fixed, it is generally difficult to spot the smoking guns of corruption. The fixing generally takes place outside the glare of the official record. Judges know how — and knew how in the fifteenth century — to "due process a defendant to death." As contemporary readers, we are not privy to the worst crimes of the judges — the secret crimes, the unspoken crimes, the covered-up crimes.

In reading the official transcript of Joan of Arc's trial, I found myself wondering what a twenty-fifth-century lawyer (if our profession survives that long) would think about a contemporary trial that we now know produced an unjust result (for example, the trial of the teens falsely accused of raping the "Central Park Jogger" in 1990, which is discussed in Part 13). How much of the injustice would be evident in the carefully selected words of court and counsel? How much would require a look beyond the written record? How much would be impossible to uncover?

Notwithstanding these limitations, the trial of Joan of Arc provides the contemporary reader, as it did the Founding Fathers of our nation, with a unique window into a world and a process that is both so different from ours, and yet so hauntingly familiar. What is truly remarkable is that even with the benefit of this experience, the Puritans of Salem were to repeat the injustices of Rouen centuries later on our own shores.

There were some injustices we were not, however, to repeat — at least not in kind. We never quite had a trial like that of Thomas More, though several trials of the twentieth century — as we shall see — included elements of the sort of "loyalty oath" More refused to take.

Most contemporary Americans know Saint Thomas More either from the classic play and motion picture *A Man for All Seasons* or from Roman Catholic hagiography. The circumstances of his martyrdom were well known among our Protestant Founding Fathers. Catholic, Protestant, and non-Christian historians, of course, see his actions differently. When Henry VIII decided to divorce the barren Queen Catherine of Aragon so as to marry his mistress Anne Boleyn and have legitimate heirs by her, the pope refused to accept Henry's claim that his marriage to Catherine, who had been his brother's wife, was invalid. Henry then created the Church of England, with the king as its head. Parliament enacted a mandatory oath requiring More and other officials to swear allegiance to this new arrangement. But Thomas More, the lord chancellor and a devout Catholic, refused to sign the oath or to explain his refusal.

It was More the religious zealot who refused to sign an oath that, in effect, denied the supremacy of the pope. It was More the lawyer who refused at first to explain his refusal. His theory was that in the absence of an explanation — a confession — he could not be convicted of high treason, since the prosecutor could not prove what everyone inferred from his silence. Quoting a Latin maxim that silence generally means assent rather than dissent, More made a clever lawyer's argument that the only conclusion to be drawn legally from his silence was that he agreed with the contents of the oath.

Notwithstanding this and other arguments, More was convicted on the basis of testimony by a petty official, almost certainly perjured, that More had confided to him his treasonous reason for refusing to sign. Although More argued convincingly that he never would have confided so deadly a secret to so untrustworthy a confidant, he was convicted nonetheless. He really never had a chance, the judges having been handpicked by the prosecutors.

Only after he was convicted and faced certain death did More disclose the reasons for his refusal to sign the oath. He said he had no choice but to refuse, since he was commanded to sign by secular law but commanded not to sign by religious law. When the king commands one action and God commands another, a believer has no choice. This is the way More reportedly put it: "The Act of Parliament is like a sword with two edges, for if a man answer one way, it will confound his soul, and if he answer the other way, it will confound his body."[8]

More followed God's order and gave up his life on earth for the promise of eternal salvation. For his martyrdom, More has been accorded the honor of sainthood by the Catholic Church, which he believed he served in death.

Everyone is entitled to judge More and other religious martyrs by their own criteria. To Catholics, he is the patron saint of lawyers. Even to the Protestant founders of our nation he was something of a hero. Americans admire people who stand for up for their beliefs — in religion, science, philosophy, and politics.

Our First Amendment was designed, at least in part, to free the mind to inquire about such issues. It has not always been entirely successful in protecting this most important of liberties, but we have done better than most. It is sometimes easy to forget that the notion of placing ideas on trial, which is so foreign to current American sensibilities, has been, and continues to be in

THE FOUNDATIONS OF AMERICAN LAW 13

most parts of the world, the norm rather than the exception. We do not have to look to the conviction and death sentence imposed upon Salman Rushdie — was there even a semblance of a trial? — for his *Satanic Verses* to see the absurd lengths to which prosecuting ideas can be taken. Our very civilized northern neighbors in Canada recently put the Holocaust on trial by prosecuting some pathetic neo-Nazis for denying history by claiming that there was no Holocaust. Even on university campuses throughout our own nation, student and faculty censors would conduct disciplinary proceedings against their colleagues for expressing "politically incorrect" ideas about race, sex, and politics, or for violating vaguely drafted "speech codes."

The fight against censorship never stays won. It must begin again every day, because censorship is, and has always been, the human norm. "Freedom of speech for me, but not for thee" is what most people really believe. Indeed, even for many who claim to support freedom of speech, that stand is little more than a tactic calculated to assure that their views are not censored. The great Adam Michnik, a Polish dissident of Jewish descent, observed that when the Communists controlled that country, the church was a champion of dissent and free speech. But as soon as Communism was toppled, the church began to remember the virtues of censorship — as long as it was doing the censoring. Even the former playwright-president of Czechoslovakia, Václav Havel, began to bemoan the "excesses" of free speech when new dissidents began to criticize his regime. And this from a man who had gone to prison for his own dissent just a few years earlier.

Although its history is far more extensive than the history of free speech, contemporary Americans rarely read accounts of systematic censorship. Our Founding Fathers were more familiar with such accounts. The trial of Galileo Galilei for espousing the heliocentric theory of astronomy — that the earth rotates on its own axis and circles the sun — is a classic event in the history of censorship that was well known to our founders.

It must be recalled that at the time Galileo published his arguments, there was no dispositive empirical evidence that he was correct. Despite Galileo's development of a telescope capable of observing far more than the naked eye was capable of seeing, Galileo's "proofs" were far from convincing. He certainly advanced the arguments made by Copernicus a century earlier, but intelligent and objective students of the universe — even secular students — were far from certain that their own senses could fool them into believing that an earth that felt as stationary as our home planet feels was really moving. Even Galileo conceded that until human beings could travel into space and look down on earth, his theories would be open to doubt.

The real question was whether the accepted wisdom, the geocentric theory, would also be open to doubt, or whether it had to be taken as gospel truth, enforceable through Inquisition.

Galileo tried heroically to fit his theory into scripture. His attempt to reconcile the heliocentric theory with the biblical account of God stopping the sun to permit Joshua to vanquish his enemy is a tour de force, if not entirely persuasive.

Galileo also tried to outwit the censor by expressing his views as part of a dialogue, but this heavy-handed attempt to be even-handed fooled no one.

Eventually Galileo was put on trial for his ideas. Unlike Socrates and others throughout history who died for their views, Galileo copped a plea. In exchange for the Inquisition dropping the most serious charge of specifically disobeying a direct order of the church — the religious equivalent of contempt of court — Galileo pleaded guilty to inadvertently transgressing a general order not to defend the work of Copernicus. As is typical of plea bargains, this one did not reflect reality. A reading of Galileo's writings makes it plain that the defendant deliberately and knowingly defended and expanded upon the work of Copernicus and others who believed that the earth traveled around the sun.

The allocution made by Galileo as part of the deal is the

seventeenth-century version of countless allocutions made every day in American courts to resolve litigation. This is part of what the great astronomer swore:

> It dawned on me to reread my printed *Dialogue*, which over the last three years I had not even looked at. I wanted to check very carefully whether, against my purest intention, through my oversight, there might have fallen from my pen not only something enabling readers or superiors to infer a defect of disobedience on my part, but also other details through which one might think of me as a transgressor of the orders of Holy Church. . . . Not having seen it for so long, I found it almost a new book by another author. Now, I freely confess that it appeared to me in several places to be written in such a way that a reader, not aware of my intention, would have had reason to form the opinion that the arguments for the false side, which I intended to confute, were so stated as to be capable of convincing because of their strength, rather than being easy to answer.[9]

Shortly thereafter, Galileo went even farther and abjured "to abandon completely the false opinion that the sun is the center of the world and does not move and the earth is not the center of the world and moves."[10] Galileo not only abjured these heretical views, but also cursed and detested them "with a sincere heart and unfeigned faith."[11] Having thus perjured himself at the request of the church, he was sentenced to house arrest and to having his books banned.

In the end, of course, Galileo's ideas have survived, despite his own compelled abjuration of them. People can be put on trial, imprisoned, and even executed by dictators. But ideas can be destroyed only by a different kind of trial — the trial of history, which no tyrant has yet been able to control.

In addition to the religious trials of the fifteenth, sixteenth, and seventeenth centuries, the European trials that most influenced American law were those involving kings and queens. Among the most dramatic of these were the trials of Mary, Queen of Scots, in 1586, Charles I in 1645, and the French monarch Louis XVI in 1792, just as Americans were adopting our Bill of Rights.

The trial and execution of Mary Stuart, Queen of Scots, has inflamed passion and controversy for more than four centuries. It also influenced the laws of treason and the right to counsel in the United States.

The conflict that led to Mary's beheading grew out of the same events that produced the trial and execution of Thomas More. Mary Stuart was not only the queen of Scotland and the widow of the king of France, but also the Catholic claimant to the English throne occupied by her cousin Queen Elizabeth of the Tudor dynasty. Elizabeth was no stranger to political intrigue and religious strife, since her own mother, Anne Boleyn, had been beheaded by Elizabeth's father, Henry VIII, after a momentous political-religious-romantic conflict that has been immortalized in plays, novels, and motion pictures.

The Catholic Church regarded Elizabeth as an illegitimate child, since it never recognized Henry's brief marriage to Anne, which followed an English divorce that Rome rejected. If Elizabeth was indeed a bastard, then her cousin Mary was the rightful queen, or — at the very least — the next in line to the English throne after Elizabeth. Since Mary was Catholic, and was supported by Rome as well as by other Catholic monarchs in Europe, her claim to the English throne posed considerable dangers to Elizabeth and the relatively new Anglican Church, which had displaced Catholicism as England's official religion after much bloodletting.

The charge that led to Mary's execution was treason. In the anachronistic words of the old common law, she was accused of "compassing, practicing and imagining of Her Majesty's Death."

It is interesting to recall that at this point in the history of the common law, there was no general law of criminal attempts. As Pollock and Maitland put it in their classic treatise on the history of English law: "Harm is harm and should be paid for. On the other hand, where there is no harm done, no crime is committed; an attempt to commit a crime is no crime." And as Jerome Hall, an American authority, reported: "Apparently in those forthright days, a miss was as good as a mile."

There was, quite understandably, one major exception to this general rule: namely, attempting, plotting, planning, or even "imagining" the death of the sovereign. (Kings and queens have always known how to protect themselves, if not their subjects.) And it was under this exception that Mary was charged with treason.

But Mary was not even a citizen of England, and treason is a crime of disloyalty that can be committed only by a subject of the offended sovereign. Mary claimed that as a sovereign herself (of a sister monarchy), she was incapable of committing treason against another queen. She also alleged that, as a foreigner, she did not know English law and could not defend herself against the charges. (According to the English law of the time, persons charged with treason could not have counsel to defend them.)

All of Mary's defenses were rejected, and the political trial proceeded to the predetermined denouement. As the vice chamberlain to Queen Elizabeth responded to Mary: "You protest yourself to be innocent, but Queen Elizabeth thinketh otherwise. . . ."[12] (Sounds a bit like the charge leveled against Martha Stewart: By proclaiming her innocence, Stewart — in the view of prosecutors — engaged in securities fraud.) The vice chamberlain assured the defendant that notwithstanding what the queen "thinketh," she would get a fair trial, but under English law it was a crime to disagree with the queen and thus it was unlikely that the judiciary would conclude that the queen "thinketh" wrong.

Moreover, unlike Henry VIII's contrived case against Anne

Boleyn — members of her entourage were tortured into testifying that she had committed adultery against her "faithful" husband — the evidence against Mary was substantial, if not conclusive. There was documentary evidence that could lead a reasonable person to conclude (though certainly not beyond a reasonable doubt) that Mary was aware of, and perhaps complicit in, a conspiracy against Elizabeth. There can be little doubt that Mary must have often "imagined" the death of her rival. So, of course, did Elizabeth "imagine" the death of Mary. The difference is that Elizabeth accomplished through the legal system what Mary had only imagined or planned.

The Star Chamber proceedings against Mary are well documented. Both the factual and legal arguments are laid out in surviving transcripts, leaving it open to historians to form their own judgments about Mary's guilt or innocence. Under the extremely broad charges brought against her, it seems likely she was guilty, even if she did not participate directly in any concrete plan to murder Elizabeth.

According to contemporaneous accounts, which can hardly be deemed definitive on this score, Queen Elizabeth was reluctant to enforce the judgment of the Star Chamber and actually order Mary's beheading. The idea of a sovereign being executed was not a welcome one, especially since the common law established precedents for the future. But Elizabeth was prevailed upon by her advisers that it would be an "injustice to deny execution"[13] and that mercy would endanger Elizabeth's own crown and cause much bloodshed.

That coldhearted view prevailed and, according to the eyewitness account, Mary, Queen of Scots, "being of stature tall, of body corpulent, round shouldered, her face fatt and broade double chinned and hazell eyed," was taken to the scaffold. The executioner "gave two strookes with an axe before he cutt of her head." The dying queen "made verie small noyse," but her "lipps stirred up & downe almost a quarter of an hower after her head was cut of."[14] So ended the life and times of Mary, Queen of Scots, and thus was preserved the Anglican Church as the official religion of England. But the legacy of this bloody trial carried across the Atlantic and influenced the American law of treason, which was considerably narrowed from its British precedents and included so many safeguards and limitations that it has rarely been invoked on our shores. It also influenced American attitudes toward the right to counsel. Mary Stuart was denied counsel, according to the queen's prosecutor, because "forasmuch as it was a matter of de facto and not de jure, and altogether concerned a criminal cause, she neither needed nor ought to be allowed council in answering thereof."[15] Though this tradition was modified somewhat in England prior to our Revolution, counsel was still denied to treason suspects by the time our Constitution was being formulated. America expressly rejected this tradition. Even before the Constitutional Convention, President Washington signed legislation providing that "in all the courts of the United States, the parties may plead and manage their own causes personally or by the assistance of . . . counsel."

The history of European monarchies is punctuated with regicide. Kings and queens were assassinated and deposed with some regularity by rivals, revolutionaries, and the rabble. Generally, there was no pretense of due process or proper jurisdiction. Power — as a latter-day revolutionary would put it — came from the barrel of a gun. Justification for the regicide, if it was produced at all, came after the fact. And the victor was rarely obliged to produce justification more persuasive than the fact of victory.

This helps explain why those who left England for America brought with them so great a disdain for the divine right of kings. They also brought with them a sense that any constitution must include a mechanism for removing a leader. When our Founding Fathers were debating the contents of the constitutional pro-

visions governing the executive branch, much of the debate centered on impeachment. The trial of Charles I was a key factor in
this debate. As Zechariah Johnson, a member of the Virginia
constitutional ratification convention, noted regarding the trial
and murder of Charles I: "For the want of an efficient and judi-
cious system of republican government, confusion and anarchy
took place. Men became so lawless, so destitute of principle, and
so utterly ungovernable, that, to avoid greater calamities, they
were driven to the expedient of sending for the son of that
monarch whom they had beheaded, that he might become their
master."[16]

Alexander Hamilton, a key member of the Constitutional
Convention, suggested an eerie portent to the Clinton trial during the debates on impeachment procedures. Hamilton argued
that the greatest danger in such proceedings was their ability to
"agitate the passions of the whole community, and to divide it
into parties, more or less friendly or inimical, to the accused . . .
[with] the decision . . . regulated more by the comparative
strength of the parties than by the real demonstrations of innocence or guilt."[17]

The one Continental trial of a king that influenced American
law and sensibilities took place just as we were developing our
own constitutional system. The French revolutionaries decided
to place Louis XVI — called by the revolutionaries "Louis the
Last" — on trial for his life in the winter of 1792. Americans followed the events with great interest, just having won their own
Revolution.

The decision to try Louis was by no means unanimous. Many
Jacobins opposed giving him his day in court, preferring to kill
him without any formality.[18] Robespierre offered the following
typical revolutionary reasoning against a trial: If Louis is to be
tried, then he must be presumed innocent; but if Louis is presumed innocent, then it must follow that the Revolution will be
presumed guilty. As he rhetorically asked the convention, "If

Louis can be presumed innocent, what becomes of the Revolution?"[19]

In the end, cooler heads prevailed and a trial was ordered. Much of the trial was taken up by bickering among revolutionary factions. Indeed, some historians have concluded that although it was Louis who was nominally on trial, the real litigants were the Girondists, the Jacobins, and other claimants to the mantle of postrevolutionary power.

Louis himself appeared at the trial only twice for a total of six or seven hours. His first appearance on December 11, 1792, was largely symbolic, as he listened to the charges against him and made some perfunctory answers. He pleaded innocent and placed blame on his ministers, who were responsible for making all the decisions. He also requested the right to retain a lawyer of his choosing, but that request was initially denied. Revolutionaries have no need for lawyers; Shakespeare's revolutionary character Dick the Butcher reminded us of this long ago, when he advised his fellow rebels "first" to "kill all the lawyers." Despite being denied a lawyer, Louis decided to try to defend himself on legal grounds. He had little choice but to play by the tribunal's unfair rules. As a leading chronicler of the trial outlined the choices available to Louis:

> [H]e could refuse to recognize the competence of his subjects to try him, as did Charles I of England a century earlier; he could throw himself on the mercy of the court and hope for the best; and he could take seriously the offer of a trial and defend himself, thus recognizing the right of his subjects to try him. . . . Disdaining his judges or asking for their mercy offered no hope at all; that way led directly to the guillotine.
>
> So it was with his trial. His choice was noble, perhaps even cunning. He sincerely believed he was innocent, just as he sincerely believed he was not answerable to his subjects. . . . By accepting the offer of a trial Louis sought to force his accusers

to prove him guilty, which he believed they could not do without violating the legal procedures and guarantees created by
the Revolution itself. If his subjects condemned him they
could do so only by exposing themselves as arbitrary, only by
resorting to illegal measure.

He knew he would probably be killed, but he hoped at least
to win a moral victory. By insisting on a fair trial, he would
compel his accusers to live up to their supposed admiration for
the law. *Let them give me a fair trial,* he thought, *and he would
be exonerated.* Unlike Mary, Queen of Scots, unlike Charles I,
Louis thought this moral victory worth fighting for, and he certainly had no interest in the glories of martyrdom. He would
appear in court protected only by the law. He would neither
beg for his life nor try to overawe his judges. He would appear
before the French Convention as a man unjustly charged, as a
man who had not violated the laws of men or God. He was neither a criminal nor a tyrant. He dared his accusers to prove
him guilty.[20]

Louis's decision to recognize the jurisdiction of the tribunal
and to defend himself on the merits was a surprise. It led directly
to the renewed request, initially denied, that Louis be represented by counsel. Louis insisted that under the criminal code
he was legally entitled to a lawyer; his request was ultimately
granted, over the objection of the Jacobins. Louis's first choice
declined the honor of representing the king. His second choice,
François Denis Tronchet, accepted. Several others volunteered
to join the defense team. The lawyers were permitted to meet
with their royal client only after submitting to the most humili-
ating searches "including the most secret places."[21] Nor were
they given adequate time to prepare their defense, despite the
clear requirement of the criminal code.

Although Louis had decided on a legal rather than a political
or divine defense, he realized that the trial was inherently political and that his defense was unlikely to save his life. He was ap-

pealing to the court of history, as other royal defendants before him had done. As he told an interviewer: "I am sure they will make me perish; they have the power and the will to do so. That does not matter. Let us concern ourselves with my trial as if I could win; and I will win, in effect, since the memory that I will leave will be without stain."[22]

On December 26, 1792, Louis XVI was invited to present his defense. One of his lawyers, the flamboyant Raymond de Seze, presented the substantive case for the king. Louis then briefly re-iterated his innocence, stating "my conscience reproaches me for nothing."[23] The defense arguments changed few, if any, votes. Nevertheless, Louis's dignity did apparently have an impact on public opinion. Louis was no longer merely an abstract symbol of tyranny. He was a human being, deserving of human consid-erations. This led those who opposed regicide to call for "the people," rather than the tribunal, to decide Louis's fate. The Girondists favored the proposal, while the Jacobins saw it as a ploy. (Even Tom Paine, the American revolutionary, had a plan for saving the king's life. He proposed that the royal family be ex-iled to America, where the trial was being followed with interest by the American revolutionaries who had been far kinder to their own Tories.)

Eventually, the tribunal rejected any appeal to the people by a vote of 424–283. It was ironic, though not surprising, that the most radical revolutionaries voted against any role being played by the masses. They knew they had enough votes for regicide within the tribunal, and they did not want to take any chances with any democratic mercy. Free to impose its will, the tribunal voted to execute the king. The vote was very close on the death penalty, but there was no appeal to a higher authority. On Janu-ary 21, 1793, Louis XVI was beheaded. Shortly thereafter his queen, Marie Antoinette, followed him to the guillotine.

The tangled history of postregicide France — the Jacobin vic-tories, their overthrow, the Napoleonic era, the restoration of the

monarchy, and its eventual replacement by a series of re-
publics — is well known. The trial of Louis XVI influenced these
events in many subtle ways, though most historians focus on the
execution itself rather than on the legal proceeding that led to it.

On January 21, 1993, the French commemorated the two
hundredth anniversary of their regicide. Five thousand royalists
gathered at the Place de la Concorde in honor of the executed
king. Many in that crowd believed that Louis XVI had won his
historical trial and that his memory, though not necessarily the
memory of the monarchy, had prevailed in the tribunal of history. In the United States, the French Revolution had considerable influence on the evolution of American democratic theory
and practice. The fear of "mobocracy" in the United States led
to the creation of institutions designed to check the influences of
majority popular opinion. Similar fears also led to the enactment
of the alien and sedition laws during the presidency of John
Adams. These laws were directed primarily at the alleged "Jacobin" sympathies among supporters of Thomas Jefferson. Grad-
ually this fear abated, and "Jacksonian democracy" resulted in
the popular election of a wide array of public officials, including — for better or worse — even judges and prosecutors in many
states. (My own view is that the election of judges and prosecutors has contributed to the politicization of justice in this country, and has generally produced more bad than good.) The
execution of Louis XVI had a significant impact on Thomas
Paine, author of *The Age of Reason* and *The Rights of Man*. For
years to come, these two books would exert considerable influence on the hearts and minds of academics, lawyers, and politicians. Paine had been a member of the French Convention,
which voted to execute Louis XVI over Paine's vociferous objections. Paine was no monarchist. But he also believed that the execution of the former king would leave an indelible stain on the
morality of the cause. Paine was one of the first and most outspoken members of the anti–capital-punishment movement and

believed that clemency toward Louis XVI would afford global respect for the new French regime.[24] The convention did not listen
to him, and the lawlessness that ensued gave the French the dubious title of being the creators of the modern conception of
state terrorism. Our own Revolution, and the constitutional experiment that followed it, was far more successful and enduring
in part perhaps because of lessons learned from the excesses of
the French Revolution, which produced continuing instability.
But we were not without our own problems, as we shall now see
by turning to the great trials of the colonial period that influenced American law and history.

1. Alan Dershowitz, *The Genesis of Justice* (New York: Warner Books, 2000).

2. *James v. Heintz*, 478 N.W. 2d 31, 36 (Wis. Ct. App. 1991).

3. Cited in Kathleen Freeman, *The Murder of Herodes and Other Trials from the Athenian Law Courts* (New York: The Notable Trials Library, 1995), p. 30.

4. *Ibid.*, p. 43.

5. *Ibid.*, p. 83.

6. I. F. Stone, *The Trial of Socrates* (New York: The Notable Trials Library, 1994), p. x.

7. Pierre Champion, "On the Trial of Jeanne d'Arc," trans. Coley Taylor and Ruth H. Kerr, in W. P. Barrett, *The Trial of Jeanne d'Arc* (Birmingham: The Notable Trials Library, 1991), pp. 484–86.

8. Cited in E. E. Reynolds, *The Trial of St. Thomas More* (New York: The Notable Trials Library, 1993), p. 67.

9. *Ibid.*, pp. 277–78.

10. *Ibid.*, p. 292.

11. *Ibid.*

12. A. Francis Steuart, ed., *Trial of Mary Queen of Scots* (Birmingham: The Notable Trials Library, 1989), p. 41.

13. *Ibid.*, p. 71.

14. *Ibid.*, p. 205.

15. *Ibid.*, p. 29.

16. Jonathan Elliot, ed., *The Debates in the Several State Conventions on the Adoption of the Federal Constitution* 2nd ed., vol. 3 (Philadelphia: J. P. Lippincott, 1836), p. 649.

17. Alexander Hamilton, "The Powers of the Senate Continued," *Federalist* no. 65 (March 7, 1788), as quoted in Jacob E. Cooke, ed., *The Federalist* (Middletown, CT: Wesleyan University Press, 1961), pp. 439–40.

18. David P. Jordan, *The King's Trial: Louis XVI vs. the French Revolution* (New York: The Notable Trials Library, 1993), pp. 56–59.

19. *Ibid.*, p. i.

20. *Ibid.*, pp. 113–15.

21. *Ibid.*, p. 119.

22. *Ibid.*, p. 127.

23. *Ibid.*, p. 136.

24. R. B. Bernstein, "Rediscovering Thomas Paine," *New York Law School Law Review*, 1994, p. 888.

PART I

Colonial America

THE BRITISH LEGAL SYSTEM (with some modifica. was prevalent throughout the colonies prior to the Re olution. The forms of the law — the adversary system, trial by jury, and an independent judiciary — resembled the English procedures ultimately incorporated into our Constitution and Bill of Rights. The substance of the law — the conduct that was prohibited — was, however, quite different. Blasphemy, witchcraft, adultery, sodomy, and sedition were capital crimes. Censorship was prevalent. The slave trade was encouraged. Most colonies had established churches. And the British army — the Redcoats — kept the peace.

Professor Lawrence Friedman has suggested that for most contemporary lawyers and laypeople, the years between the settlement of Jamestown in 1607 and the signing of the Declaration of Independence in 1776 represent "the dark ages of American law."[1] Legal historians have traditionally defined the formative era of American law as extending from independence until the time of the Civil War. According to this view, colonial legal history was seen as little more than a series of anecdotes, of no importance to the current system of American law.[2] The trials of that era, though important to the people involved, are commonly perceived as of little relevance to today's law.

Yet a study of colonial legal history reveals much about the use of law in the colonization of America, and about the society that drove this process. It also tells us something about why we eventually created a legal system designed to prevent recurrence of some of the evils of colonial law. Colonial charters recognized that colonial law had to conform to English law,[3] but recent scholarship has debunked the old misconception that the law of the colonies was essentially the law of England. Unique conditions in America made divergence from English law inevitable,[4] and the cases and statutes of the colonial period reflect an ongoing attempt to adapt the English legal procedures to the very different realities of American life. The colonists used the law to create a new country, but at the same time they used it to make this country feel more like home.[5]

Each of the thirteen colonies had its own legal system, reflecting the colony's particular needs. The four trials I have chosen to represent this period of American history are all from Northern states — two from Massachusetts and two from New York. They represent different stages in the transition from colony to country: the Salem witchcraft trials of 1692, the freedom of press case involving John Peter Zenger in 1735, the New York slave revolt case of 1741, and the Boston Massacre trials of 1770.

Many colonists knew something about the law before arriving in America — some had been involved in local legal proceedings, had sat as jurors in the courts of the English countryside, or had even visited the royal courts at London's Westminster Hall — but only a handful of the earliest colonists had received formal legal training.[6] Although the early colonial codes implied a right to some kind of legal representation, they were quite hostile toward the legal profession. Massachusetts Bay prohibited pleading for hire, Virginia and Connecticut excluded lawyers altogether from the courts, and the first constitution of the Carolinas described the legal profession as "a base and vile thing"[7] — a view still shared by some Americans.

As a result, while the judges and lawyers in England were full-time professionals with many years of experience, the colonial courts were filled with untrained laymen.[8] The colonial codes created a court system that preserved the basic structures of the English system — the adversarial process, trial by jury, and an independent judiciary — but the colonists' lack of legal training produced a system of legal procedure that was far less formal than that of the English courts. Legal historian Peter Hoffer describes this situation:

> In the seventeenth century an educated visitor in a colonial
> court might well hear many technical legal "terms of art," but
> a plain style of pleading suits predominated. . . . In the records
> one occasionally finds a term of art, but often as not it is mis-
> used and almost always misspelled. Most often litigants did not
> even bother to use the English formulas. They simply went to
> the clerk of the court; paid for a summons, which the sheriff
> delivered to the opposing party; came to court; and made a
> declaration of the facts.[9]

The lay judges and attorneys in the colonial courts were familiar with the language of English law, but not with its underlying concepts or practices.

This lack of legal training, combined with the harshly moralistic nature of early colonial legal codes, produced a jurisprudence that differed considerably from the English system. In developing the early legal codes, the colonial governments viewed the enforcement of moral law as a primary obligation.[10] The Puritan governments in New England took this obligation seriously, and used the colonial legal codes as a means to enforce their strict religious values. For example, the *Laws and Liberties of Massachusetts* (1648) blended English legal procedures with selected provisions in the Bible, imposing the death penalty for crimes such as idolatry, adultery, witchcraft, and sedition. There were few actual prosecutions for these capital crimes — the most commonly punished crimes in the seventeenth century were the less serious offenses of fornication and drunkenness.[11] The Sunday "Blue Laws" promulgated throughout the New England colonies, some of which remain in force today, further represented the colonial governments' attempts to control and correct sin by prohibiting certain activities on the Lord's day.

In some cases, these two factors combined to produce terrifying consequences. Lay judges presided over the Salem witchcraft trials of 1692. Eager to rid the colony of the perceived influence of the devil, the Salem judges ignored the practice of the English courts and allowed into evidence every accusation of participation in witchcraft, no matter how unfounded.[12] English jurists had uncovered several instances of fraud and perjury in witchcraft cases, and had grown skeptical of testimony about assaults by spirits.[13] But the judges in Salem — educated and respected, but not learned in the law — seemed less interested in the possible falsity of the accusations.

By the eighteenth century, the dramatic economic and social expansion of the colonies made the use of trained lawyers inevitable. The colonial marketplace was large enough to accommodate both professionally educated lawyers and laymen with some legal knowledge, although the line between them grew more distinct. Friedman writes:

> As soon as a settled society posed problems for which lawyers had an answer or at least a skill, lawyers began to thrive, despite the hostility. Courts were in session; merchants were drawn into litigation; land documents had to be written, and the more skilled the better. Men trained in law who came from England found a market for their services; so did laymen with a smattering of law; there were semiprofessionals, too, with experience for sale.[14]

By 1750, there was a professional bar in all major communities in the colonies, dominated by highly skilled and successful lawyers.[15]

The colonial codes eventually recognized the need for lawyers, at least in criminal cases. By the time of John Peter Zenger's trial for seditious libel in 1735, the defendant's right to legal representation was widely recognized.[16] Zenger, a member of a political opposition group, launched the *New York Weekly Journal* to stir up criticism of New York governor William Cosby.[17] Zenger's attorney, Andrew Hamilton, argued the case eloquently and the jury returned a verdict of not guilty. Legal historians celebrate the case not only as a symbol of the freedom of the press in early America, but also as a demonstration of the power of juries in the colonial court system.[18]

The importance of juries marked yet another colonial divergence from the English legal system. In England, juries rarely disagreed with government prosecutors; they often served as mere window dressing for the judges' decisions. But in America, beginning in the colonial period, juries had the power to disregard the law. Since juries were composed of laymen, they balanced out the increasingly professional nature of the courts. Their verdicts reflected both the community's sense of morality and the jury members' understanding of the laws. The unjust jury verdicts in the slave revolt trials of 1741 — convictions of thirty African slaves and four whites for arson, treason, and conspiracy — demonstrated the corrupting effect of slavery on the law in general and on the jury system in particular.[19] American juries would likely not have convicted whites of comparable crimes on similar evidence if the context of the crimes had not been that of the much-feared slave uprising.

Many of the founders of the American republic were lawyers — such as John Adams, Thomas Jefferson, and John Marshall — but on the eve of the American Revolution, most lawyers in the colonies were loyalists.[20] John Adams holds a special place in the mythology of the American Revolution for agreeing to defend the English army officers for their role in the Boston Massacre of 1770. In his memoirs, Adams justified his participation in the trial as an attempt to uphold the rule of law in the colonies: "To depend upon the perversion of the law, and the corruption or partiality of juries, would insensibly disgrace the jurisprudence of the country and corrupt the morals of the people," he wrote.[21] Yet it now seems that Adams's participation in the trial may also have reflected his disdain for the lower-class zealots who had provoked the British officers. By the end of the eighteenth century, law had become a lucrative profession, and lawyers readily counted themselves among the elites of colonial society. These lawyers, by shaping our great trials and basic laws, were soon to play a crucial role in our transformation from colony to constitutional democracy.

The Salem Witchcraft Trials

Date: 1692
Location: Salem, Massachusetts
Defendants: Approximately twenty-five in 1692, but several hundred men and women were arrested and imprisoned on charges of witchcraft between 1648 and 1706
Charge: Witchcraft
Verdict: Guilty
Sentence: Thirteen women and six men hanged; one man pressed to death with heavy stones; at least four others imprisoned (two dogs were also executed as suspected accomplices)

Although the Inquisition never reached the colonies — Catholics were a tiny minority among the colonists — the Salem witchcraft trials bore some striking resemblances, writ small, to what had roiled the Continent two centuries earlier. They paralleled, in some ways but not in others, the trial of Joan of Arc in 1431. The pre-Enlightenment church was a dominant influence in the Bay Colony during the seventeenth century, but other influences were also at play against the women who were accused — primarily by other women — of the capital crime of witchcraft.

As is typical with most episodes of legal persecution, a small kernel of truth may have provided an early explanation, if not justification, for the concerns that led to the prosecutions. In a society that believed in the power of the devil and in the phenomenon of witchcraft, it should not be surprising that some young girls may well have experimented with magic spells and other aspects of the occult. Nor should it be surprising that some of the girls may have experienced the functional equivalent of psychosomatic symptoms of being bewitched — symptoms that were manifested by convulsions, fits, screeching, and pain. A doctor, summoned by the minister, diagnosed affliction by the devil, and before long dozens of "witches" were arrested and prosecuted. Informers named names, including those of a former minister and several young children. Nineteen people were hanged, others imprisoned. Several of the condemned were of Native American heritage. This, too, should not be surprising, since warfare between the Puritans and Indians was wreaking havoc among the Northern settlements. In a recent account of the trials, a distinguished historian found that "the key affected accusers in the Salem crisis were frontier refugees whose families had been wiped out in the wars. These young women said they saw the devil in the shape of an Indian."[22] The Puritans needed a scapegoat to explain why "God's chosen people" were being slaughtered by the Indians. They decided that "their Indian enemies had the Devil on their side."[23]

In reading accounts of the witchcraft trials of three centuries ago, a modern-day lawyer's mind naturally turns to the roles played by the seventeenth-century lawyers, prosecutors, judges, and defense attorneys — and how they used the forms of the law to perpetrate such injustice. One courtroom observer criticized the magistrates' contributions to the increasing hysteria in Salem: "The chief Judge is very zealous in these proceedings, and says, he is very clear to all that hath as yet been acted by this Court, and, as far as ever I could perceive, is very impatient in hearing any thing that looks the other way."[24] (I've certainly encountered judges like that!) Indeed, on several occasions, the Salem magistrates dispensed even with any pretense of impartiality. During one trial in May 1692, the accused said that she felt faint, and she asked the court if she might lean against her husband. "She had strength enough to torment those persons," the magistrate replied, "and she should have strength enough to stand."[25]

In his play and motion picture *The Crucible*, Arthur Miller apparently intended his audience to think about the McCarthy prosecutions of contemporary "witches" and those who refused to testify against them. *The Crucible* certainly made me think, as a young man interested in the law, about the relationship between legal procedures and justice. The descriptions of the legal proceedings by which citizens charged with witchcraft were tried make numerous references to justices, judges, and magistrates. There are prosecutors as well, though the roles of magistrate and prosecutor often seem to be merged. The Salem magistrates viewed themselves as inquisitors eliciting confessions and repentance, rather than interpreters of a body of law.[26] Deodat Lawson, a courtroom observer, recounted an episode from the proceedings against Martha Corey: "On Monday the 21st of March, the Magistrates of Salem appointed to come to Examination of Goodow C. And about twelve of the Clock, they went into the Meeting-House, which was thronged with Spectators. . . . The Worshipful Mr. Hathorne [the magistrate] asked her, Why she Afflicted those Children? She said, she did not Afflict them. He asked her, who did then? She said, 'I do not know.'"[27]

As Justice Hawthorne vigorously pursued a confession, Corey was confronted with the live testimony of some ten "afflicted persons," including three young girls. With the interaction among Corey and her accusers, the proceedings grew chaotic. Lawson "observed several times, that if she did but bite her Under lip in the time of Examination the persons afflicted were bitten on their armes and wrists and produced the Marks before the Magistrates, Ministers and others."[28] One accuser "complained of grievous torment in her Bowels as if they were torn out," and hit Corey on the head with a shoe.[29] Corey still did not confess, but she was convicted and hanged, along with six other persons, in September 1692.

There are few references to defense attorneys, certainly not in the way we have come to know them over the past two centuries. It is clear that the principal legal officers in these notorious proceedings are the "honorable" and "distinguished" judges who conducted the trials, rendered the verdicts (sometimes with the assistance of a special jury), and imposed the death sentences.

As I read about the judges, I could not help wondering how our own Supreme Court and lower courts would react if a hysteria comparable to the witch trials were to occur today. I also could not help wondering whether the presence of a vigorous defense bar would not have made, and would not now make, a difference in the processes and outcomes of the cases.

There is, of course, some relevant history to look to for guidance. The Salem travesty was neither the first nor the last of its kind. The Spanish Inquisition employed the forms of the law and the legitimation of judges. Even in Hitler's Germany and Stalin's Soviet Union, "good" and "decent" judges went along to get along. During the McCarthy period in our nation, many judges willingly participated in the Red-baiting and career-destroying paranoia of the time; and during the Jim Crow era in the South, most of the judges perpetuated a system of apartheid that not only kept the races separate but also imposed a double standard of justice on blacks and whites. Although some of these ignoble judges believed in the "justice" of the cause they were serving, most were motivated by simple opportunism, careerism, and a need to please those in power.

Today's "witches" may be those suspected of complicity with terrorism, especially if they are not citizens. Terrorism, unlike witchcraft, poses real dangers to vulnerable citizens, but what must be recalled is that in seventeenth-century Salem, many good people honestly believed that witches posed a real danger. Too many of today's judges are prepared to ignore — or manipulate — the law to assure that no one they release becomes the next Mohammed Atta or Osama bin Laden.

It is possible, of course, that, even without the complicity of the judiciary, people would have hanged witches, burned heretics, gassed Jews, shot "cosmopolitans," imprisoned fellow travelers, subjected blacks to apartheid, and denied due process to Muslims suspected of terrorism. Nevertheless, that the imprimatur of the judges legitimized entirely illegitimate undertakings becomes clear in reading these accounts of the witchcraft trials and seeing how the trials relied on the forms of the law. (It also becomes clear when one reads, as every judge should, the record of the Nuremberg trials of Nazi judges.)

Throughout history, some judges have had the courage to stand up to the abuse of the legal system. A few paid with their lives, others with their careers. In some instances, most notably McCarthyism, dissenting judges had an impact on slowing down and finally halting the evil. (During the McCarthy period, as distinguished from the others, vigorous defense attorneys also played an important role in vindicating the rights of the accused.) Even so, too few judges have risked going against powerful and popular tyrants.

When I look at our current judiciary, especially the Supreme Court, I see some judges in the mold of those who went along with the excesses of tyrants. Oh, sure, today's judges would find some contemporary rationale for their unwillingness to intercede on behalf of the victims of tyranny: judicial restraint, executive and legislative prerogative, separation of powers, original intent, national security, and many other catchphrases can be selectively invoked to justify inaction. Nevertheless, the real reason why the Rehnquists, Scalias, and Thomases of today's judiciary

would not intercede is that they are *statists* rather than true conservatives: Conservatives believe in limited governmental power
over individuals; statists believe in virtually unlimited governmental power and limited individual rights (except, in some instances, when it comes to property rights or the right to bear
arms).

Consider what former chief justice Warren Burger had to say
in 1986 about the "crime" of private homosexual activity between consenting adults — a "crime" akin to witchcraft in many
ways, including its biblical source and its lack of actual victims.
In the case of *Bowers v. Hardwick*, Chief Justice Burger, in a concurring opinion, approvingly quoted Blackstone's characterization of "'the infamous crime against nature' as an offense of
'deeper malignity' than rape, a heinous act 'the very mention of
which is a disgrace to human nature,' and 'a crime not fit to be
named.'"[30] The judges in Salem might also have quoted Blackstone on the evils of witchcraft (had his book, which was published a few decades later, been available to them): "The civil
law punishes with death not only the sorcerers themselves, but
also those who consult them; imitating in the former the express
law of God, 'thou shalt not suffer a witch to live.' And our own
laws [rank] this crime in the same class with heresy, and condemn both to the flames." (In June 2003, the Supreme Court reversed *Bowers v. Hardwick*, striking down a Texas law that
prohibited private consensual sex between same-sex couples.
"The petitioners are entitled to respect for their private lives,"
wrote Justice Anthony Kennedy for the majority. "The state cannot demean their existence or control their destiny by making
their private sexual conduct a crime."[31] The Court concluded
that "*Bowers* was not correct when it was decided, and it is not
correct today."[32] Chief Justice Rehnquist, along with Justices
Scalia and Thomas, dissented. You can read an account of the
Texas sodomy case starting on page 551.)

Burger's successor, Chief Justice Rehnquist, has rendered similar decisions, nearly always siding with claims of governmental power over individual rights. This is especially true when rights have been claimed by weak and unpopular, even despised, minority groups. I can picture Rehnquist as a German judge during the 1930s and 1940s. (Indeed, when he was nominated to be an associate justice in 1971, I learned from several sources who had known him in the 1940s that as a Stanford Law School student, he had outraged Jewish classmates by imitating Adolf Hitler and goose-stepping around the campus with brown-shirted friends.) The German judges who were tried at Nuremberg included several distinguished jurists and professors with an authoritarian bent not so different from Rehnquist's. This is not to deny that Chief Justices Burger and Rehnquist have sometimes sided with unpopular individuals and against the prosecution, but the judges of Salem and Germany also occasionally acquitted persons accused of witchcraft or of violating the Nuremberg laws. Indeed, when challenged about their complicities in a system of injustice, many judges rationalized their participation by pointing to the ameliorative role they played in helping some victims of injustice. I have little confidence that most current Supreme Court and other federal and state court judges would act courageously and independently in the face of witchcraft trials today, especially if the atmosphere of the country were such that it would require personal and career risks to do so. Despite lifetime appointments, too many judges seek popularity and acceptance by the powers that be.

It seems more likely that several of our current justices and judges would become part of the problem, going out of their way to give an imprimatur to the evil at hand, as former chief justice Burger did in the homosexuality case and as numerous judges did during the McCarthy period. Nor is this an issue that falls neatly on any right–left continuum. In today's world, left-wing zealots on the bench — of which there are, thankfully, very few — also pose a danger of using the imprimatur of the law to exorcise their devils. For example, some feminist extremists regard sexual crimes — rape, pornography, and child molestation — as so heinous that even innocence should not be regarded as a valid defense![33] But the dominant contemporary danger still does come from the extreme right for two reasons: There are far more right-wing ideologues on the bench today than left-wing ideologues; and extreme right-wingers are more likely to be statists, especially during times of political right-wing domination.

Former justice Robert Jackson, who took a leave from the Supreme Court to serve as our nation's chief prosecutor at the Nuremberg trials of Nazi war criminals, wrote of the role of judges and law in legitimating tyranny, "[t]he most odious of all oppressions are those which mask as justice."[34] Jackson was echoing the caution of Lord Coke, expressed even before the Salem witch trials: "It is the worst oppression that is done by colour of justice." And Justice Brandeis warned us, three-quarters of a century ago, that even good intentions are no protection against zealotry: "Men [and women] born to freedom are naturally alert to repel invasion of their liberty by evil-minded rulers. The greatest dangers to liberty lurk in insidious encroachment by men [and women] of zeal, well meaning but without understanding."[35] We should keep the words of these great judges in mind as we recall the judges of Salem and as we assess our own Supreme Court.

Most importantly, we should recall the cautionary words of Learned Hand about the limited role that judges can play in preserving our liberties: "Liberty lies in the hearts of men and women; when it dies there, no constitution, no law, no court can save it; no constitution, no law, no court can even do much to help it. While it lies there it needs no constitution, no law, no court to save it."[36]

This history should warn us never to abdicate to any branch of government — indeed to government at all — the job of keeping liberty alive. That is a full-time job for all citizens, especially those of us who carry the proud title of lawyer.

The Trial of John Peter Zenger

Date: 1735
Location: New York City, New York
Defendant: John Peter Zenger, a printer
Charge: Seditious libel
Verdict: Not guilty

John Peter Zenger was no Galileo — in at least two significant ways. First, the political lampoons published by Zenger were, for the most part, drivel. Nobody today remembers his amateurish attacks against the then governor of New York. In contrast, the heliocentric theory for which Galileo was placed on trial remains an enduring truth. Second, Zenger was prepared to risk his freedom for his right to publish, whereas Galileo copped a plea and publicly renounced his own truthful ideas.

The trial and acquittal of publisher John Peter Zenger in 1735 has become part of the folklore of American freedom. Though some recent historians have downplayed the actual significance of the event in transforming the law of press freedom, it is impossible to overestimate its impact on American attitudes toward speech and censorship.

As is typical with great cases expanding our liberties, the political cause immediately at stake in Zenger's trial now appears trivial, if not petty. The *New York Weekly Journal* appears to have been a somewhat amateurish political magazine comprising an assortment of essays, lampoons, and other provocative items directed primarily against the governor of New York.

Not surprisingly, the offended officials set out to silence the offending publication. The method of censorship they selected was a criminal prosecution of the printer. Zenger was arrested, bail was set in an amount calculated to keep him in jail, his chosen lawyers were disbarred, and Zenger was advised that he had no defense since even the "truth" of the publication would not justify a "libel." The chief justice publicly announced that "if a jury found Zenger not guilty, they would be perjured."[37] The stage was set for an open-and-shut kangaroo court proceeding.

Despite these formidable odds, Zenger would eventually prevail, but only after serving eight months in pretrial detention. He won not because the law was on his side, but rather because the people — as represented by the jury — were on his side. The lawyer who eventually was able to argue on Zenger's behalf, a brilliant orator from Philadelphia named Andrew Hamilton, understood the political dynamics of the colonies and realized that his client's only chance was to get the jury of Zenger's peers to overrule the judge on the issue of whether the truth was a defense to libel. Such jury nullification would not be easy, since the governing English law was apparently clearly to the contrary. The prosecutor put it this way:

> [A]s Mr. Hamilton has confessed the printing and publishing these libels, I think the jury must find a verdict for the King; for supposing they were true, the law says that they are not the less libelous for that; nay indeed the law says their being true is an aggravation of the crime.[38]

Hamilton quickly focused on the last part of his opponent's argument as support for his attempt to introduce evidence of the truthfulness of his client's publications. Hamilton offered the following brilliantly ironic response:

Well, suppose it were so, and let us agree for once *that truth is a greater sin than falsehood*: Yet as the offenses are not equal, and as the punishment is arbitrary, *that is*, according as the judges in their discretion shall direct to be inflicted; is it not absolutely necessary that they should know whether the libel is *true* or *false*, that they may by that means be able to proportion the punishment? For would it not be a sad case if the judges, for want of a due information, should chance to give as severe a judgment against a man for writing or publishing a lie as for writing or publishing a truth? And yet this (with submission), as monstrous and ridiculous as it may seem to be, is the natural consequence of Mr. Attorney's doctrine *that truth makes a worse libel than falsehood*, and must follow from his not proving our papers to be *false*, or not suffering us to prove them to be *true*.[39]

Although the presiding judge did not allow Hamilton to introduce evidence of truth, Hamilton nonetheless argued the truth of the printed material, reminding the jurors that they were, in effect, witnesses, since they came from the neighborhood where the alleged offense occurred:

Then, gentlemen of the jury, it is to you we must now appeal for witnesses to the truth of the facts we have offered and are denied the liberty to prove; and let it not seem strange that I apply myself to you in this manner, I am warranted so to do both by law and reason. The law supposes you to be summoned *out of the neighborhood where the fact is alleged to be committed*; and the reason of your being taken out of the neighborhood is *because you are supposed to have the best knowledge of the fact that is to be tried*.[40]

It was a brilliant ploy, calculated to arouse the jury's anger at the court for seeking to deny it its proper role. Hamilton went

even farther, inviting the jurors to take the law into their own
hands and out of the courts:

> A proper confidence in a court is commendable; but as the
> verdict (whatever it is) will be yours, you ought to refer no part
> of your duty to the discretion of other persons. If you should be
> of opinion that there is no falsehood in Mr. Zenger's papers,
> you will, nay (pardon me for the expression) you ought to say
> so; because you don't know whether others (I mean the Court)
> may be of that opinion. It is your right to do so, and there is
> much depending upon your resolution as well as upon your
> integrity.[41]

It took the jury only "a small time" to agree and render its popular verdict of not guilty. The verdict, according to the reporter,
was greeted by "three huzzas" in the crowded hall,[42] and the next
day Zenger was freed.

But Zenger's freedom did not end the controversy. The jury's
verdict may have been popular with the crowd, but it was much
criticized within the bar as lawless. There ensued an exchange of
pamphlets between defense lawyer Hamilton and a more conservative lawyer who wrote under the pseudonym "Anglo-
Americanus." These extraordinary pamphlets contain some of
the most interesting eighteenth-century arguments I have encountered concerning the limits of free speech and the role of
the jury. "Anglo-Americanus" even anticipated Holmes's famous
aphorism about shouting fire in a crowded theater. In arguing
against the right of a citizen to complain "to the neighbors" as
distinguished from complaining to the proper authorities, he observed that speech ". . . is a two-edged weapon, capable of cutting both ways and is not therefore to be trusted in the hands of
every discontented fool or designing knave. Men of sense and address (who alone deserve public attention) will ever be able to
convey proper ideas to the people, in a time of danger, without

running counter to all order and decency, or crying fire and murder through the streets if they chance to awake from a frightful
dream."[43]

Eventually Hamilton's view of popular speech — speech to be
judged in the marketplace of ideas — prevailed in America, but
not without long intervals of rejection. It was not until the twentieth century that Hamilton's view received the approval of the
Supreme Court, first in the dissenting opinions of Justices
Holmes and Brandeis, and then eventually as the majority holding. Although it is Peter Zenger's name that has achieved im-
mortality in the Pantheon of Freedom, it is his brilliant and
innovative lawyer, Andrew Hamilton, who deserves to be remembered as one of the architects of our structure of liberty.

The Slave Revolt Trial

Date: 1741
Location: New York City, New York
Defendants: Approximately 175 men and women, blacks and
             whites
Charges: Assorted property crimes, arson, conspiracy to
             kill, and in one instance "being an ecclesiastical
             person," namely a Catholic priest
Verdict: Guilty
Sentence: Seventeen blacks and four whites hanged, thir-
             teen blacks burned; many banished

New York is not generally thought of as the city of slavery, and
yet at the mid–eighteenth century it was second only to
Charleston, South Carolina, as "an urban center of slavery." At
the time, New York consisted of what today lies below Washington Square and Lower Manhattan, and its eleven thousand residents included approximately two thousand black slaves. In the
late spring of 1741, thirty blacks and four whites were executed — by hanging and burning — for seditious planning and
conspiratorial actions.

These alleged crimes were part of a developing pattern of
slave uprisings including the Stono Rebellion of 1739 in South
Carolina, in which between twenty and twenty-five whites were
killed; and Nat Turner's famous rebellion of 1831 (popularized
by William Styron's The Confessions of Nat Turner), which re-

sulted in the deaths of fifty-five white people. Although the
New York conspiracy was not nearly as violent (or perhaps as
heroic) as some of these other uprisings, it is an important part
of the history of black efforts, sometimes assisted by whites, to
resist the horrors of slavery.

The story begins with a rash of fires. No one was sure of the
source, but accusing fingers pointed at the slaves, especially
those of Spanish background, since Spain was engaged in hostilities with England, and Spanish authorities were constantly stirring up rebellious feelings among the slaves.

The response of the New York aldermen to this outbreak of violence will be familiar in the post–September 11 world. War-
rantless searches were authorized. Strangers and other suspicious
persons were stopped. Armed men halted all traffic under orders
"to stop all suspected persons that should be observed carrying
bags or bundles. . . ."[44] After a series of frustrating searches uncovered little, "some things were found in the custody of Robin,
Mr. Chambers' African slave, and Cuba his wife which the al-
derman thought improper and unbecoming the conditions of
slave, which made him suspect they were not come by honestly."[45] Mr. Chambers was the city clerk, but that did not protect
his slaves from arrest, along with numerous other slaves who
were carted off to jail.

Despite the mass jailings and rough interrogation of black
men, no evidence was produced, and most of the slaves were released after two weeks. Some slave owners were upset that their
property was being taken from them without just cause, while
other prominent white citizens, who held no slaves, sought more
crackdowns and roundups of blacks in an effort to drive them
from the city.

There was little doubt among the citizens that the fires were
part of a conspiracy. As the leading law-and-order councilman
put it in his formal legalese, "Taking notice of the several fires
that had lately happened in the city the manner of them, the fre-

quency of them, and the causes of them yet being undiscovered, [we] must necessarily conclude that they were occasions and set on foot by some villainous conspiracy of latent enemies among us."[46] But beyond suspicion, there was little hard evidence upon which to base a formal prosecution. Some suspected the Spanish; others concocted a "Catholic conspiracy hatched by the Pope."[47] But the primary focus remained on the slaves.

In an effort to secure evidence, the town fathers convened a grand jury. The first witness subpoenaed was an indentured servant, Mary Burton. When she refused to answer any questions, she was sentenced to jail for contempt. The prospect of imprisonment loosened her tongue and she agreed to talk, first about several burglaries and then about the fires. She recounted hearing conversations among several black men threatening to "burn the whole town."[48]

A grand jury quickly indicted those incriminated by Mary Burton, and the stage was set for the jury: "the king against . . . slaves and others."[49] The "others," who were white, were entitled by law to a jury; the slaves could be tried before a judge. The authorities preferred trial by jury, however, secure in the knowledge that justice would not only be done but be seen to be done.

The first trial was against two slaves for burglary. Being slaves, they were not allowed to testify in their own defense. Guilty verdicts were quickly returned. More convictions followed, but to this point only for burglary. Finally, an indentured servant facing trial for theft became a jailhouse informer: Some things never change! The dominoes were beginning to fall. Eventually, a conspiracy to burn down buildings was brought to court. In making the case against the black defendants, the prosecutor talked about their ingratitude for being benignly enslaved:

> The monstrous ingratitude of this black tribe is what exceedingly aggravates their guilt. Their slavery among us is generally softened with great indulgence: they live without care and

commonly better fed and clothed and put to less labor than the poor of most Christian countries. They are indeed slaves, but under the protection of the law, none can hurt them with impunity. They are really more happy in this place than in the midst of the continual plunder, cruelty, rapine of their native countries.[50]

The two slaves were convicted and sentenced to be chained to a stake and burned to death. Before the execution, they confessed their guilt, hoping to receive a gubernatorial pardon. The governor, in fact, agreed to a conditional delay. But the crowd demanded death, and the burnings proceeded despite the governor's order.

More trials were commenced, and with similar outcomes. Although the fear of the community was directed primarily against the black slaves — witnesses claimed that the defendants planned to "kill the white men and have the white women for our wives"[51] — there was also considerable prejudice against Catholics. John Ury, a white man, was indicted for "being an ecclesiastical person, made by authority pretended from the See in Rome, and coming into and abiding in this province."[52] He was also charged with conspiring with the black slaves to cause insurrection. He, too, was convicted and hanged despite the lack of any evidence to support the charges.

The difference between the New York trials and the Salem witchcraft trials is that there actually was some kind of a conspiracy to burn buildings, but for those — both black and white — who played no part in this conspiracy and were convicted simply because of prejudice, the two travesties were similar. John Ury was as much a victim of religiously inspired paranoia as were the witches in Salem. Being an "ecclesiastical person" of the Catholic faith was the functional equivalent of being a witch. He could not possibly prove his innocence to a jury that was predisposed against him and essentially directed by the judges to convict him. Nor could those blacks who were falsely accused, especially since they could not even testify on their own behalf.

The "great Negro plot" in colonial New York is an important part of the underside of American colonial history, which is rarely recounted in the patriotic textbooks assigned to our schoolchildren. It was also a prelude to other slave revolts, and to the John Brown attack against slave owners that would later play such a great role in the events leading up to the Civil War.

The Boston Massacre Trials

Date: 1770
Location: Boston, Massachusetts
Defendants: Captain Thomas Preston, Corporal William Wemms, and seven British soldiers
Charges: Murder, accessory to murder
Verdict: Captain and corporal acquitted; two privates convicted of manslaughter
Sentence: Branding

The manner by which an event is characterized by history often determines our collective attitudes toward the culpability of the participants. The so-called Boston Massacre is a case in point. Every American schoolchild learns that British soldiers "massacred" several Bostonians by shooting into a crowd of patriotic protesters. It was the "real" beginning of the American Revolution, the first shots heard round the world.

A review of the actual trial records — there were two trials, the first of the commanding officer, the second of the soldiers — shows anything but an unprovoked massacre. It was much closer to an instance of arguable self-defense by a handful of frightened soldiers, cornered by a violent mob threatening to injure or kill them. Situations like this have arisen throughout history — most recently in Israel and Iraq — where soldiers fire on provocateurs who engage in, or threaten, violence. The term *massacre* should be reserved for cases of unprovoked mass killing against innocent people. To be sure, the Boston case was a close one, but close cases are supposed to be resolved in favor of the defendants — at least by a court of law. The verdict of history may well be different, as it was in this case. History, especially patriotic history, thrives on mythology. And the "Boston Massacre" emerged as one of the canonical myths of prerevolutionary America.

Another myth — this one perpetrated by lawyers at bar association conventions and in Law Day speeches — is that it took enormous courage for the defense lawyers, led by future president John Adams, to defend the hated British soldiers. The evidence suggests that this was not true. The community was divided, and many upstanding citizens of Boston understood that the "rabble" that gathered in Dock Square on that cold March night with cudgels, ice balls, and other makeshift weapons comprised provocateurs who invited the violence that ensued. Maybe the soldiers overreacted; perhaps they shot too soon and did not stop quickly enough. But reasonable people could, and did, disagree as to whether this was murder, manslaughter, or self-defense. Judges and juries decided these complex factual and legal issues only after listening to the dozens of witnesses called by each side.

The trials themselves were exemplars of civility and due process, conducted professionally and brilliantly by all the lawyers. The true hero of this tragedy was the legal system — the British legal system, as administered by colonial Americans — which managed to turn a potentially explosive incident into a civics lesson about the rule of law.

Every American, especially lawyers and law students, should study this trial. The reality is far more interesting than the mythology. The closing arguments of counsel are classic instances of the advocacy of the day. Listen to John Adams:

May it please your honors, and you, gentlemen of the jury:
I am for the prisoners at the bar, and shall apologize for it

only in the words of the Marquis Beccaria: "If I can but be the instrument of preserving one life, his blessing and tears of transport, shall be a sufficient consolation to me, for the contempt of all mankind." As the prisoners stand before you for their lives, it may be proper, to recollect with what temper the law requires we should proceed to this trial. The form of proceeding at their arraignment, has discovered that the spirit of the law upon such occasions, is conformable to humanity, to common sense and feeling; that it is all benignity and candor. And the trial commences with the prayer of the court, expressed by the clerk, to the supreme judge of judges, empires and worlds: "God send you a good deliverance."

We find, in the rules laid down by the greatest English judges, who have been the brightest of mankind; we are to look upon it as more beneficial, that many guilty persons should escape unpunished, than one innocent person should suffer. The reason is, because it is of more importance to the community, that innocence should be protected, than it is, that guilt should be punished; for guilt and crimes are so frequent in the world, that all of them cannot be punished; and many times they happen in such a manner, that it is not of much consequence to the public, whether they are punished or not. But when innocence itself, is brought to the bar and condemned, especially to die, the subject will exclaim, it is immaterial to me whether I behave well or ill, for virtue itself is no security. And if such a sentiment as this should take place in the mind of the subject, there would be an end to all security whatsoever.[53]

Not everything Adams said should be praised. He played an early version of what has come to be known as the "race card." One of those killed by the soldiers was a black man named Crispus Attucks. Adams told the all-white jury that Attucks was the one to blame for the confrontation:

Bailey "saw the mulatto seven or eight minutes before the firing, at the head of twenty or thirty sailors in Cornhill, and he had a large cord-wood stick." So that this Attucks, by this testimony of Bailey compared with that of Andrew and some others, appears to have undertaken to be the hero of the night; and to lead this army with banners, to form them in the first place in Dock square, and march them up to King street with their clubs; they passed through the main street up to the main-guard, in order to make the attack. If this was not an unlawful assembly, there never was one in the world. Attucks with his myrmidons comes round Jackson's corner, and down to the party by the sentry box; when the soldiers pushed the people off, this man with his party cried, do not be afraid of them, they dare not fire, kill them! kill them! knock them over! and he tried to knock their brains out. It is plain the soldiers did not leave their station, but cried to the people, stand off; now to have this reinforcement coming down under the command of a stout mulatto fellow, whose very looks was enough to terrify any person, what had not the soldiers then to fear? He had hardiness enough to fall in upon them, and with one hand took hold of a bayonet, and with the other knocked the man down: this was the behavior of Attucks: to whose mad behavior, in all probability, the dreadful carnage of that night is chiefly to be ascribed. And it is in this manner, this town has been often treated; a Carr from Ireland, and an Attucks from Framingham, happening to be here, shall sally out upon their thoughtless enterprises, at the head of such a rabble of Negroes, &c., as they can collect together, and then there are not wanting persons to ascribe all their doings to the good people of the town.[54]

Adams also played the "God card." He consistently invoked the law of God and the Bible in support of his claim of self-defense:

As the love of God and our neighbor, comprehends the whole
duty of man, so self-love and social, comprehend all the duties
we owe to mankind, and the first branch is self-love, which is
not only our indisputable right, but our clearest duty; by the
laws of nature, this is interwoven in the heart of every individual; God Almighty, whose laws we cannot alter, has implanted
it there, and we can annihilate ourselves, as easily as root out
this affection for ourselves. It is the first and strongest principle
in our nature; Justice Blackstone calls it "the primary canon in
the law of nature." That precept of our holy religion which
commands us to love our neighbor as ourselves, doth not command us to love our neighbor better than ourselves, or so well,
no Christian divine hath given this interpretation. The precept
enjoins that our benevolence to our fellow men, should be as
real and sincere, as our affections to ourselves, not that it
should be as great in degree. A man is authorized, therefore,
by common sense, and the laws of England, as well as those of
nature, to love himself better than his fellow subject: if two
persons are cast away at sea, and get on a plank (a case put by
Sir Francis Bacon), and the plank is insufficient to hold them
both, the one hath a right to push the other off to save himself.
The rules of the common law therefore, which authorize a
man to preserve his own life at the expense of another's, are
not contradicted by any divine or moral law.[55]

Finally, when two of the soldiers were convicted of
manslaughter — the officer and the other soldiers were all acquitted — the defense team pulled the ultimate God card from
the bottom of the deck. They invoked "the benefit of the clergy,
which was allowed them, and thereupon they were each of them
burned in the hand, in open court, and discharged."[56] This "benefit" originally protected Christian clergymen from criminal
prosecution in England's secular courts. The privilege developed over time to protect "clerks," or literate persons, from prosecution for felonies punishable by death. Here it was applied to

soldiers in service of the king. It seems quite anachronistic that just a few years before the enactment of our First Amendment, a British colonial court in Boston would have allowed this archaic, religiously inspired resolution to a great political case. No wonder we fought a revolution and built a wall of separation between church and state!

1. Lawrence M. Friedman, *A History of American Law* (New York: Simon and Schuster, 1985), p. 33.

2. Christopher Tomlins, "Introduction: The Many Legalities of Colonization," in *The Many Legalities of Early America*, ed. Christopher L. Tomlins and Bruce H. Mann (Chapel Hill: University of North Carolina Press, 2001), p. 7.

3. Friedman, p. 46.

4. Maldwyn A. Jones, *The Limits of Liberty: American History 1607–1992* (New York: Oxford University Press, 1995), p. 31.

5. Tomlins, pp. 19–20.

6. Peter Charles Hoffer, *Law and People in Colonial America* (Baltimore: Johns Hopkins University Press, 1998), p. 4.

7. Friedman, p. 94.

8. Hoffer, p. 41.

9. *Ibid.*, p. 35.

10. David Flaherty, "Law and the Enforcement of Morals in Early America," in *American Law and the Constitutional Order*, ed. Lawrence Friedman and Harry N. Scheiber (Cambridge, MA: Harvard University Press, 1978), p. 53.

11. Friedman, p. 72; Hoffer, p. 22.

12. Hoffer, p. 41.

13. *Ibid.*, p. 43.

14. Friedman, pp. 96–97.

15. *Ibid.*, p. 97.

16. Hoffer, p. 118.

17. Stanley Nider Katz, "Introduction," in James Alexander, *A Brief Narrative of the Case and Trial of John Peter Zenger*, ed. Stanley Nider Katz (Birmingham: The Notable Trials Library, 1963), pp. 6–7.

18. *Ibid.*, p. 34.

19. Hoffer, p. 124.

20. Friedman, p. 101.

21. Cited in Frederic Kidder, *History of the Boston Massacre, March 5, 1770* (Delanco, NJ: The Notable Trials Library, 2001), p. 19.

22. Mary Beth Norton, "They Called It Witchcraft," *New York Times*, Oct. 31, 2002.

23. *Ibid.*

24. "Letter of Thomas Brattle, F.R.S., 1692," in *Narratives of the Witchcraft Cases, 1648–1706*, ed. George Lincoln Burr (New York: The Notable Trials Library, 1992), p. 184.

25. Cited in Frances Hill, *The Salem Witch Trials Reader* (New York: Da Capo Press, 2000), p. 70.

26. *Ibid.*, p. 34.

27. Deodat Lawson, "A Brief and True Narrative Of Some Remarkable Passages Relating to sundry Persons Afflicted by Witchcraft, at Salem Village

Which happened from the Nineteenth of March, to the Fifth of April, 1692," in Burr, pp. 154–55.

28. *Ibid.*, p. 156.
29. *Ibid.*
30. *Bowers v. Hardwick*, 478 U.S. 186, 197 (1986) (Burger, C.J., concurring).
31. *Lawrence v. Texas*, No. 02-102, slip op., 18 (June 26, 2003).
32. *Ibid.*, p. 21.
33. Richard Gardner, MD, letter, "Child Sex Abuse Cases Can Be Witch Hunts," *New York Times*, June 19, 1992.
34. *Krulewitch v. United States*, 336 U.S. 440, 458 (1949) (Jackson, J., concurring).
35. *Olmsted v. United States*, 277 U.S. 438, 479 (1928) (Brandeis, J., dissenting).
36. Judge Learned Hand, speech at "I Am an American Day," Central Park, New York (May 20, 1945).
37. Katz, p. 18.
38. *Ibid.*, p. 62.
39. *Ibid.*, p. 71.
40. *Ibid.*, p. 75.
41. *Ibid.*, p. 96.
42. *Ibid.*, p. 101.
43. Anglo-Americanus, "Remarks on the Trial of John Peter Zenger, Printer," reprinted in *ibid.*, p. 176.
44. Cited in Thomas J. Davis, *A Rumor of Revolt: The "Great Negro Plot" in Colonial New York* (Delanco, NJ: The Notable Trials Library, 2002), p. 40.
45. *Ibid.*, p. 41.
46. *Ibid.*, pp. 37–38.
47. *Ibid.*, p. 45.
48. *Ibid.*, pp. 50–51.
49. *Ibid.*, p. 59.
50. *Ibid.*, p. 92.
51. *Ibid.*, p. 100.
52. *Ibid.*, p. 194.
53. Cited in Kidder, p. 232.
54. *Ibid.*, pp. 257–58.
55. *Ibid.*, pp. 234–35.
56. *Ibid.*, p. 285.

PART II

The Early History of
the United States

THE THIRTEEN ORIGINAL COLONIES declared their independence from England in 1776, and enacted new constitutions to become sovereign states.[1] These new states sent representatives to a Continental Congress, where they produced the Articles of Confederation and joined together to fight the British army. The Revolutionary War proved a bitter, transformative struggle, which lasted until the British army surrendered at Yorktown in 1781. American and British representatives signed a preliminary peace treaty in 1782, and the British army evacuated by 1783.[2]

In many ways, however, the real challenges were yet to come. The American victory produced a new nation, but it also posed a fundamental question: How would the new nation — comprising sovereign states — govern itself? It had been obvious to the leaders of the American Revolution that national unity was required to achieve independence,[3] but now that independence had been achieved, could these very different sovereignties maintain any semblance of unity? How would the thirteen states be incorporated under a national body of government and law? What would be the structure of this government? What would be the nature of this law?

The Articles of Confederation, which had created a loosely connected national union without a strong executive, soon proved ineffective. While some called for revision of the articles, most leaders and lawyers quickly turned their attention to the development of a new federal constitution. Ratified in 1787, the American Constitution established the framework for the new republic, allocating the powers and functions of government among three branches: executive, legislative, and judicial. With the addition of the Bill of Rights in 1791, the Constitution also institutionalized (at least insofar as the federal government was concerned) several provisions of the English common law, such as the right to trial by jury, and added others, such as the prohibition against Congress making any law "respecting an establishment of religion."

In 1776, the Continental Congress had declared that the colonies were "entitled to the common law of England."[4] After overthrowing the authority of the English king, however, it was not certain that the thirteen states would uphold the lingering authority of English law. Alternatives included replacing the common law with a rival system (such as the civil law system of Continental Europe) or creating a new system from scratch, based on natural principles of justice.[5] Yet in the end, as during the colonial period, familiarity proved the chief asset of the English common law. "In hindsight," explains legal historian Lawrence Friedman, "the common law had little to fear. It was as little threatened as the English language. The courts continued to operate, continued to do business; they used the only law that they knew."[6] Reversing the "Anglicization" trend of the late colonial period, the common law now embarked on a process of "Americanization."

The political future of the new nation remained the subject of intense and ongoing debate. By creating a centralized federal government and a single, unified republic, the U.S. Constitution seemed to violate many of the ideals that had driven the American Revolution. During the debates over the ratification of the Constitution in 1787–88, the Anti-Federalists argued that the new government resembled a monarchy, which would have to act tyrannically to govern the diverse populations of the thirteen states.[7] Yet the Anti-Federalists lacked the influence of the Federalists, and they proved little match for the arguments that the Federalists gathered in support of the Constitution.[8] In 1789, with the first election under the new Constitution, the Federalists gained control of the new national government.[9] Federalist leaders such as Alexander Hamilton used their positions in the government to promote a political and economic program that aimed to fill the gaps left by the Constitution.

Anti-Federalist leaders such as James Madison and Thomas Jefferson called for a strict interpretation of the Constitution as a protection against the Federalist program. By 1792, Madison and Jefferson had become the spokesmen for the newly formed Republican party, which established itself in opposition to the Federalists and their attempts to expand the national government.[10]

The debate over the nature of the American republic intensified after the success of the French Revolution in 1789, and the subsequent outbreak in 1792 of a war between Great Britain and the new French Republic. Believing that the French Revolution demonstrated the tendency of popular government to degenerate into mob rule, the Federalists generally sided with Great Britain as the symbol of order, property, and religion; the Republicans saw Great Britain as the enemy of liberty and generally sided with France.[11] In 1794, responding to a British naval blockade of American ships, President Washington sent Chief Justice John Jay to London to negotiate a settlement. The Republicans were outraged by the resulting treaty, which granted more favorable trading conditions to Great Britain than to any other nation.[12] Jay was burned in effigy,[13] and every aspect of American life, from business to religion, became highly politicized. After only two decades of independence, America was in crisis. This chapter examines two legal dramas that unfolded in the politically charged atmosphere of the early Republic: the trials under the Alien and Sedition Acts in 1798–1800, and the 1807 treason trial of the Republican former vice president, Aaron Burr.

The Trials of Aliens and Seditioners

Date: 1798–1800
Location: Vermont, Pennsylvania, and Massachusetts
Defendants: Approximately twenty-five assorted publishers,
             politicians, and public figures
Charge: Seditious libel
Verdict: Ten convicted; others acquitted
Sentence: Short jail terms, fines, and surety bonds

While Ecclesiastes may be charged with exaggeration for proclaiming that there is nothing new under the sun, Santayana was
surely correct when he warned that "those who cannot remember the past are condemned to repeat it." The enactment and enforcement of the Alien and Sedition Acts in the final years of the
eighteenth century are among those terrible historical events
whose lessons have not been understood adequately by most
Americans. We have seen these lessons repeated over and over
again during our history, and I fear we are once again failing to
understand their important implications for our current national
security crisis.

Times of crisis test a nation's commitment to basic freedoms,
and most nations fail that test most of the time. The year 1798
was surely a time of crisis for the new republic. John Adams, a
conservative Federalist, was president. Thomas Jefferson, a Republican, was vice president and was planning to run against the
incumbent president in 1800. France had supported America's

independence from Great Britain, and tensions were high between the two European powers, and between France and the
United States. The Federalists feared the revolutionary and antireligious fervor of France. They were more comfortable with the
stable and conservative nation they had recently defeated in the
War of Independence. The Republicans, on the other hand,
were more closely aligned with the philosophy of the French
Revolution, though they, too, abhorred its excesses.

It was against this background that President John Adams and
his fellow Federalists prepared for a possible war with France,
as well as a certain challenge to his presidency from Jefferson.
Exaggerating the threats posed by a French invasion and the
"Jacobin" sympathies of some Americans, especially recent
immigrants, they decided to enact federal laws that would
weaken their enemies, both foreign and domestic. These laws
came to be known as the Alien and Sedition Acts, and their aim
was to suppress seditious speech, particularly that which was critical of the administration. The pro-Federalist press remained free
to exaggerate the dangers, as the following excerpts illustrate:

> [R]emove your wives far from the Infernal Fraternal embrace,
> or you may prove witnesses of their violation and expiring ag-
> onies, or if reserved for future infamy, may increase your fam-
> ilies not only with a spurious, but with a colored breed. . . .
> Remove your daughters, unless you would be silent spectators
> of their being deflowered by the lusty Othellos. Remove your
> infants! unless you shall deem it more merciful and humane
> to shorten their agonies, by plunging your paternal daggers
> into their innocent bosoms.[14]

• • •

Was it not known that Jacobins were everywhere and that
"even the nursery is not exempt from the unremitting efforts of

these disturbers of the human race"? Even children's books must be scanned: by planting seditious principles in the primers, Jacobins were seeking to corrupt the younger generation and "to make them imbibe, with their very milk, as it were, the poison of atheism and disaffection."[15]

Strong stuff in the view of the Federalists that warranted the equally strong medicine of censorship, imprisonment, and deportation! As one supporter of the Alien and Sedition Acts put it: "Surely we need a sedition law to keep our own rogues from cutting our throats, and an alien law to prevent the invasion by a host of foreign rogues to assist them."

The interesting point, one not easily accepted by modern sensibilities, is that almost everyone favored the censorship of newspapers and the imprisonment of journalists who published seditious material. George Washington strongly supported the Alien and Sedition Acts. Even Jefferson, who has come to stand for the absolute freedom of the press, believed that the press ought to be restrained "within the legal and wholesome limits of truth."[16] (This itself was a departure from British law, under which even truth did not protect against prosecution, as will be recalled from the discussion of the Zenger case.) After Jefferson became president, he expressed the view that "a few prosecutions of the most prominent offenders would have a wholesome effect in restoring the integrity of the presses."[17] Every journalist can quote the stirring words of the young Jefferson: "Were it left to me to decide whether we should have a government without newspapers, or newspapers without a government, I should not hesitate a moment to prefer the latter."

Few reporters, however, are familiar with what the older Jefferson said about newspapers after he had experienced scathing attacks on his presidency: "The man who never looks into a newspaper is better informed than he who reads them, insomuch as he who knows nothing is nearer the truth than he whose mind is filled with falsehoods and error."

Calling for the prosecution of those who abused freedom of the press, Jefferson was not so different from the very conservative Blackstone who wrote that "to censure the licentiousness is to maintain the liberty of the press." Jefferson's primary objection to the Alien and Sedition Acts was that they authorized *federal* prosecutions of offending journalists, rather than *state* prosecutions. Indeed, under his presidency "prosecutions were instituted in the state courts against federalist (and against some Republican) editors for seditious libel. In most of these cases, the charge was libeling the Chief Magistrate"[18]— that is, the president. Jefferson, the Virginian, was a strong believer in states' rights and a staunch opponent of expansive federal jurisdiction. Indeed, the Bill of Rights, whose First Amendment protects freedom of speech and press, by its terms grants these freedoms only in relation to the federal government ("Congress shall make no law respecting an establishment of religion, or prohibiting the free exercise thereof; or abridging the freedom of speech, or of the press"). Today we view the great battle over the Alien and Sedition Acts as a conflict between freedom and censorship. The protagonists themselves saw it largely as a conflict between the powers of the states and those of the federal government.

At a deeper level, however, there were certainly adumbrations of liberty in the opposition to these censorial laws. Although freedom of religion was not explicitly at issue in the debate, the fear of atheism was certainly part of the animating force behind these acts. As one grand jury announced in support of the Sedition Act: "We feel ready, by our example, to defuse the laudable spirit and determination of repelling the abominable principles of French politics, and the horrible doctrine of Atheism by prostrating ourselves this day before the altar of our religion and our liberties, and in the all-seeing Eye of Heaven, make a Solemn Vow to defend with our Lives and our Interests our Religion and our Country." (This attack on "French politics" and "atheism" was also a not-very-subtle attack against Jefferson, who was regarded as a Francophile and an atheist, though he was critical of French excesses and was a deist who strongly believed in a non-intervening god of nature.[19])

The divisive issue of slavery also played a role in the Alien and Sedition Acts. Southern supporters of slavery opposed the laws, fearing that the Northern proponents of these laws might use them to deport African slaves. Southerners also feared the increasing powers of the federal government at the expense of the states.

Two dozen prosecutions were brought under the acts; the first, and perhaps the most notorious, victim was U.S. representative Matthew Lyon of Vermont. Lyon, a Republican who frequently denounced his Federalist opponents in the House as "warmongers," was indicted in 1798 under the Sedition Act for publishing an article that harshly criticized the policies and character of President Adams.[20] Undaunted by his indictment, Lyon responded by establishing his own magazine dedicated to encouraging widespread resistance against the Federalists. He believed that he was conducting a loyal political opposition, and based his defense on arguments about the unconstitutionality of the Sedition Act. As a result, the outcome of Lyon's trial — a conviction and a sentence of four months' imprisonment in federal jail — took him quite by surprise. "It is quite a new kind of jargon to call a Representative of the People an Opposer of the Government . . . because he does not, as a Legislator, advocate and acquiesce in every proposition that comes from the Executive."[21] Lyon became a martyr to the freedom of the press, and that fall he was easily reelected to the House.[22] Yet the Vermont authorities continued to threaten him after his release from federal prison, announcing that they were prepared to arrest him for violating state libel and sedition laws.[23]

Other prosecutions were directed against supporters of Jeffer-

son, including Benjamin Franklin's grandson, Benjamin
Bache. Bache published an Anti-Federalist newspaper called
The Aurora, which was so inflammatory that it earned its publisher the nickname "Lightning Rod Junior." He attacked
George Washington with special venom, contributing to his decision not to seek a third term as president. Bache was arrested
two weeks prior to the enactment of the alien and sedition laws,
on common law charges of libeling President John Adams. Before he could be brought to trial, Bache died of yellow fever in
the epidemic of 1798. But others did face trial and conviction.
When Jefferson was elected president, he allowed the laws to
lapse and ended all federal prosecutions commenced under
their provisions.

To Santayana's dictum that we must "remember the past"
should be added the caveat that in seeking to understand the
past, we must not view it narrowly through the lens of the present. We must understand the passions of the time. Most people
employ conceptual and abstract arguments as support for practical results they seek to achieve. It is important to understand the
particular agendas, both open and hidden, that animated the arguments made in support of and opposition to the Alien and
Sedition Acts. Today's agendas may well be different, though
similar arguments are offered in support of them. We live today
in a time of crisis. Although the Patriot Act of 2001, and its legislative and judicial progeny, are in no way comparable to the
Alien and Sedition Acts, we must be on our guard to protest
against an administration that is willing to use fear to justify repression. The following frightening criticism of opponents of the
Patriot Act by Attorney General John Ashcroft could easily have
been uttered by John Adams against those opposed to the Alien
and Sedition Acts: "To those who scare peace-loving people with
phantoms of lost liberty, my message is this: Your tactics only aid
terrorists, for they erode our national unity and diminish our resolve. They give ammunition to America's enemies and pause to

America's friends."[24] The difference is that, despite his support for the Alien and Sedition Act, John Adams had a long history of support for individual liberty and basic human rights. Ashcroft can point to no such history, and for that reason, his comments are potentially far more ominous.

The Trial of Aaron Burr

Date: 1807
Location: Richmond, Virginia
Defendant: Former vice president Aaron Burr
Charge: Treason
Verdict: Not guilty

The defeat of John Adams and the Federalists in the election of 1800 did not end the criminalization of political disagreements. Thomas Jefferson, the newly elected Republican president, felt threatened by his own vice president, Aaron Burr; Jefferson and Burr had tied in the number of electoral votes for the presidency, leaving it up to Congress to break the tie in Jefferson's favor. President Jefferson granted little power to his vice president and blocked Burr's nomination for a second term. It was thus during Jefferson's second term, when Burr was only a private citizen, that he had his now infamous duel with Alexander Hamilton. Much hated for killing Hamilton in that confrontation, Burr was later charged with treason — for actions unrelated to the killing of Hamilton — and brought to trial.

In his standard biography of Chief Justice John Marshall, Albert J. Beveridge characterizes the proceedings against Aaron Burr as "the greatest criminal trial in American history." Although many subsequent trials lay claim to this title, Beveridge's conclusion is certainly plausible. Most other Western nations have experienced numerous great treason trials. The United

States has been spared such transforming legal events because there have been few attempts to seize power by force.

The dramatis personae alone would qualify the Burr case as among the greatest in American history. The presiding judge was Chief Justice John Marshall, probably the most influential jurist in our nation's history. Burr's attorneys included Charles Lee (who had been attorney general of the United States), Edmund Randolph, and Luther Martin — among the most prominent lawyers and patriots of the day. At an earlier stage, Burr had been represented by Henry Clay. Among his supporters was the future president Andrew Jackson. The prosecuting attorney was George Hay, son-in-law of James Madison. He was assisted by William Wirt, a future presidential candidate. The prosecutors took their orders directly from President Thomas Jefferson, who tried to manage the prosecution from Washington, declaring publicly that Burr's guilt was "beyond question." As Winfield Scott put it: "It was President Jefferson who directed and animated the prosecution."

The political stakes were high for everyone involved. Jefferson let it be known that "if Marshall should suffer Burr to escape, Marshall himself should be removed from office." And Marshall acknowledged that "it would be difficult or dangerous for a jury to acquit Burr, however innocent they might think him."

Aaron Burr was a person of considerable stature. He will always be remembered in American history as the man who killed Alexander Hamilton in a duel in Weehawken, New Jersey, in July 1804, and also as the subject of the most notorious treason trial in U.S. history. It is easy to forget that prior to these events, he was an authentic American hero, on the scale of Jefferson, Madison, and Hamilton. Born into the best of families — his father was president of Princeton University and his mother's father was Jonathan Edwards — Burr had distinguished himself during the Revolutionary War. Following his one term as vice president, however, Burr had little money or political influence.

Further, his duel with Hamilton had led authorities in New York and New Jersey to issue arrest warrants against him, which rendered him a fugitive and an exile from his home area.[25]

Between 1805 and 1806, Burr traveled through the South on a mysterious journey that became the subject of the controversial treason charges. Spending considerable time in the newly acquired western territories of Louisiana and Mississippi, Burr met with several different individuals with whom he allegedly hatched a conspiracy to conquer some of the territories — perhaps even Mexico — and thereby regain his lost political power. At the beginning of 1807, based on information gathered from Burr's correspondence allegedly showing that he had begun preparations for a large-scale military expedition, the former vice president was arrested in Louisiana and indicted on the charge of "wickedly devising and intending the peace and tranquility of the . . . United States to disturb, and to stir, move, and excite insurrection, rebellion and war against the said United States." The indictment focused on a particular meeting "at a certain place called and known by the name of Blannerhassett's island [sic]," a private piece of land in the middle of the Ohio River where Burr allegedly made plans and contracted for supplies for a large-scale military expedition.[26]

Burr's trial opened in Richmond, Virginia, in August 1807 amid considerable fanfare. It was certainly the greatest trial the new republic had so far experienced. The court proceedings against Burr could constitute an entire course in criminal law, constitutional law, or early-nineteenth-century American history. The opinions of Chief Justice Marshall, on subjects ranging from the definition of treason to the power of the judiciary to subpoena the president, are among the formative judicial decisions of our nation's history. The proceedings from beginning to end comprised a political trial in the most literal meaning of that much-overused term. This trial was motivated by politics; it was about politics; it was argued as politics; the sides were chosen along political lines; and it was decided on political considerations. Yet the law — at least the structure of the law — played a central role.

In light of the political nature of the case and the president's declaration of Burr's certain guilt, it was obviously difficult to select an unbiased jury. Burr acknowledged that it would be nearly impossible to find twelve jurors who did not come to the case with prejudgment. He was prepared to accept jurors who believed he was guilty, as long as they were open to persuasion. In fact, he accepted jurors who stated the following under oath:

JOHN M. SHEPPARD	I, too, feel myself disqualified for passing impartially between the United States and Aaron Burr. From the documents that I have seen, particularly the depositions of Generals Wilkinson and Eaton, I have believed, and do still believe, that his intentions were hostile to the peace and safety of the United States; in short, that he had intended to subvert the government of the United States. It would be inflicting a wound on my own bosom to be compelled to serve under my present impressions.
MR. BURR	Notwithstanding Mr. Sheppard's impressions, I could rely upon his integrity and impartiality.[27]

When the prospective juror Henry E. Coleman was called, he stated that he had conceived and expressed an opinion that the designs of Colonel Burr were always enveloped in mystery, and inimical to the United States; and when informed by the public prints that he was descending the river with an armed force, he had felt as every friend of his country ought to feel:

MR. BURR	If, sir, you have completely prejudiced my case —
MR. COLEMAN	I have not. I have not seen the evidence.
MR. BURR	That is enough, sir. You are *elected*.²⁸

As it turned out, the most important rulings of the court were those excluding evidence of a treasonous conspiracy. A few weeks into the trial, Burr interrupted the prosecution's case with a motion to preclude any testimony about Burr's actions and conduct in the days following the alleged meeting on Blennerhassett's Island. He argued that the prosecution had "utterly failed to prove any overt act of war had been committed," and had even admitted that Burr "was more than one hundred miles distant from the place where the overt act is charged to have been committed."²⁹ After hearing eight days' worth of argument, Chief Justice Marshall granted Burr's motion, holding that evidence of Burr's subsequent actions was inadmissible "because such testimony, being in its nature merely corroborative and incompetent to prove the overt act in itself, is irrelevant until there be proof of the overt act by two witnesses."³⁰

This ruling — and others along the same line — may explain the jury's unusual verdict, which was delivered the following day: "We of the jury say that Aaron Burr is not proved to be guilty under this indictment by any evidence submitted to us. We therefore find him not guilty."³¹

Burr objected to the verdict as "unusual, informal, and irregular," and Chief Justice Marshall agreed to enter the formal verdict as one of "not guilty," despite the jury's unwillingness to change its particular wording.³²

Aaron Burr remained active in public life for several decades following his acquittal. He was instrumental in Andrew Jackson's ascension to the presidency. Until his dying day, Burr denied any treasonous intent, but the verdict of history is more in accord with the jury's carefully phrased verdict than with Burr's own assertion of total innocence. Despite Chief Justice Marshall's several opinions defining what constitutes treason, that quintessentially political crime remains very much a matter of degree — especially in cases like Burr's, where the line between ideas and actions is certain to be blurred.

1. Paul Johnson, *A History of the American People* (New York: Harper-Collins, 1997), pp. 157–58.
2. Jones, p. 56.
3. *Ibid.*, p. 63.
4. Friedman, p. 109.
5. *Ibid.*, p. 108.
6. *Ibid.*, p. 109.
7. Bernard Bailyn et al., *The Great Republic: A History of the American People* (Lexington: D. C. Heath and Co., 1985), p. 236.
8. *Ibid.*, p. 237.
9. Jones, p. 76.
10. Bailyn, p. 246.
11. Jones, p. 82.
12. Bailyn, p. 248.
13. Jones, p. 83.
14. Cited in John C. Miller, *Crisis in Freedom: The Alien and Sedition Acts* (Delanco, NJ: The Notable Trials Library, 2002), p. 6.
15. *Ibid.*, pp. 12–13.
16. *Ibid.*, p. 231.
17. *Ibid.*
18. *Ibid.*, pp. 231–32.
19. See Alan Dershowitz, *America Declares Independence* (Hoboken: John Wiley and Sons, 2003).
20. Miller, pp. 102–06.
21. Cited in *ibid.*, p. 109.
22. *Ibid.*, p. 107.
23. *Ibid.*, p. 111.
24. "Ashcroft: Critics of New Terror Measure Undermine Effort," CNN.com (Dec. 7, 2001), www.cnn.com/2001/US/12/06/inv.ashcroft.hearing/.
25. J. J. Coombs, *The Trial of Aaron Burr for High Treason* (New York: The Notable Trials Library, 1992), pp. v–vii.
26. "Indictment Against Aaron Burr," reprinted in *ibid.*, pp. 140–41.
27. Cited in *ibid.*, pp. 136–37.
28. *Ibid.*, p. 138.
29. Cited in *ibid.*, p. 209.
30. Cited in *ibid.*, p. 352.
31. *Ibid.*, p. 352.
32. *Ibid.*, pp. 352–54.

Part III

From Jacksonian Democracy to the Pre–Civil War Period

THE PRESIDENTIAL ELECTION of 1828 marked a major transition in the life of the new republic. The incumbent president was the last of an old breed. John Quincy Adams represented the elitists who had founded the new nation, created its political and legal structures, and defended it against Great Britain in two wars. They were from Massachusetts and Virginia, well educated, and still connected to the European continent.[1]

In contrast, Andrew Jackson had been born in poverty on the Carolina frontier and had received little formal education. He appeared closer to the American people than any of the six presidents who had preceded him, and this image proved extraordinarily effective; the newly formed and aptly named Democratic party was to control the White House for most of the three decades following Jackson's election.

America, now secure against external threats, could turn inward and deal with its own domestic problems. Instead of always looking over the ocean to the east, it could look over the prairies and mountains to the west, with the opportunities for expansion and the great challenges that would be posed by its "manifest destiny."[2]

Echoing the Jacksonian emphasis on individualism, political and religious leaders warned that America's fate rested on the moral character of its people. The desire to shape individual character gave new social importance to educators, religious revivalists, cultural figures, and other reformers, yielding a variety of movements for change that targeted all aspects of American society.[3] Concerned by the rise of juvenile delinquency in the larger cities, educational reformers advocated a system of formalized, mandatory, and publicly funded schools. Religious revivalists presented the church as the only means of preserving a sense of unity and shared purpose among America's widely spread communities. Cultural reformers promoted the creation of uniquely American art forms and encouraged the birth of a national literature. Appalled by the categorization of slaves as personal property, the abolitionist movement promoted the recognition of universal human rights. In a similar vein, early feminists began to seek some degree of gender equality. New scientific claims — some enduring, others passing fads — also became influential.

These developments led to a reconsideration of the purpose of criminal justice, shifting the general aim of the system from punishment to deterrence and rehabilitation. Seeking to reduce the number of crimes that carried the death penalty, several states, led by Pennsylvania, distinguished among different degrees of murder. Only murder in the first degree, which involved willful, deliberate, or premeditated killing, was punishable by death.[4]

In practice, however, these reforms of the criminal law had only a marginal effect. The courts handled most criminal cases in a quick and summary fashion. Almost all defendants charged with petty crimes were tried before a judge alone; juries, which had enormous power to decide the law and facts, were impaneled only in cases involving serious crimes. And when they were impaneled, juries tended to convict: One analysis suggests that between 1833 and 1859, 85.9 percent of criminal defendants in Massachusetts were found guilty.[5] Furthermore, the criminal justice system of the early to mid-1800s continued to suffer from a lack of professionalism. There were no detectives, probation officers, public defenders, or forensic scientists, and in many communities even the prosecutor worked only part time.[6]

This chapter examines three early American trials that were characteristic of the lack of professionalism and the influence of the populism of this period: two "ordinary" murder trials, and a fascinating mini-trial for the attempted assassination of President Andrew Jackson. The murder trials are notable primarily because of the passions they engendered at the time. The attempted assassination case is notable because it was a portent of violence to come in the politics of our nation.

The Boorn-Colvin Murder Mystery

Date: 1819
Location: Manchester, Vermont
Defendants: Jesse and Stephen Boorn
Charge: Murder
Verdict: Guilty; but verdict overturned in 1820
Sentence: Death by hanging; overturned in 1820

Lawyers tell a tall tale about the case of a man on trial for murdering his wife. No corpse had been found, but the circumstantial evidence was convincing. During his closing argument, the defense lawyer told the jurors that they were in for a surprise: When he counted ten, the allegedly murdered wife would walk through the courtroom door. "One, two," the lawyer began. By "seven" every juror's eyes were riveted upon the door. "Eight, nine, ten," the lawyer counted. The jurors waited expectantly, but the door remained closed. The defense attorney smiled and explained to the jurors, "See, each of you turned your eyes to the door. You each must have had a reasonable doubt about whether the wife was really dead. . . . My little experiment," the lawyer declared victoriously, "proved that you had a reasonable doubt and that you must acquit the defendant." Despite this logic, the jury convicted the defendant. Afterward, the disappointed defense lawyer asked one of the jurors how she could have voted for conviction after the jurors had all looked at the door. "Yes, we all looked to the door," the juror explained, "but we noticed that the defendant did not look to the door. He knew his wife was not going to walk through it."

A variation on this apocryphal tale actually took place in Vermont during the early history of this country. Jesse Boorn and his brother, Stephen, were accused of murdering their sister's husband, Russell Colvin. Colvin had disappeared several years earlier following an altercation; at first, his disappearance was treated as innocent, since Colvin had a history of wandering and instability. Yet seven years after the disappearance, Amos Boorn, an uncle of the suspects, claimed that Colvin had appeared at his bedside during a recurring dream. Like Hamlet's father, the ghost revealed that he had been murdered. It even told the dreamer where the body had been buried — in a cellar hole in a potato field on farmland formerly owned by the Boorn family.[7]

Remember, this was early-nineteenth-century rural America, when ghosts were as real to many people as angels are today. Dreams, too — even in this pre-Freudian era — were taken seriously (recall Joseph and Pharaoh), especially when related by men of substance. Even in those days, the hearsay dream of a ghostly victim would not be admissible in a court of law, but it was enough to open an inquiry — as well as an alleged grave. Guided by Amos Boorn, the court of inquiry and a crowd of inquisitive onlookers went to the field to examine the old cellar hole. It contained no human remains, but it did produce a series of artifacts — pieces of broken crockery, a button, a penknife, and a jackknife — which Colvin's wife quickly identified as belonging to her husband.[8] Mrs. Colvin had a particular interest in having her husband proven dead: She had given birth to a child several years after her husband's disappearance, but because the law presumed a child born to a married woman to have been fathered by her husband, she could not get child support from the actual father.[9] If it were to be determined that her husband was, in fact, dead at the time she conceived her child, her chances of receiving some payment would improve.

Called to testify before the court of inquiry, an agitated Jesse Boorn testified to a conversation in which his brother, Stephen, said that he had given "Russel [sic] a blow, and laid him aside, where no one would find him."[10] Jesse's testimony tipped off a widespread search for Colvin's bones; a boy and his dog uncovered a cache of bones in a stump on the old Boorn property, which three area physicians pronounced the remnants of a human foot. A rumor quickly spread about the chain of events: The brothers had buried Colvin in the cellar hole, but for some reason had moved his remains a couple of years later.[11] In jail, Jesse Boorn allegedly confessed to a cellmate, a man charged with perjury who had been promised leniency if he could elicit an admission. (Some things never change!) Stephen, who had moved to New York, returned to Manchester to give a long-awaited confession. Thus, the stage was set for the October 1819 trial of Jesse and Stephen Boorn.

Before trial, one physician decided to test the hypothesis about the bones by comparing the largest of them with an actual human leg bone that had been preserved after an amputation. This bit of primitive empiricism proved that the bones were not human. Yet it was too late to reverse the influence of the physicians' earlier, unfounded, opinion; furthermore, the Boorns' confessions provided much better evidence than animal bones and ghostly dreams.

The jury was quick to convict, and the brothers were sentenced to hang. Yet the real story was only beginning. The Vermont state legislature and governor agreed to commute Jesse's sentence to life imprisonment, but Stephen was sentenced to hang within a few weeks. There being no appellate process in Vermont and no federal issue to bring to Washington, little legal hope remained for Stephen. The desperate Stephen asked his friends and lawyers to place an advertisement in newspapers seeking information on whether the alleged murder victim had been seen alive. This tactic is reminiscent of the ploy commonly used by accused or convicted murderers to offer a reward for the "real killer." Even his own lawyer was skeptical of Stephen's plan. Perhaps he knew something he couldn't share with the public. The lawyer agreed, however, to prepare an ad that read as follows:

> Printers of newspapers throughout the United States are desired to publish, that Stephen Boorn, of Manchester, in Vermont, is sentenced to be executed for the murder of Russell Colvin, who has been absent about seven years. Any person who can give information of said Colvin may save the life of the innocent by making immediate communication. Colvin is about five feet five inches high, light complexion, light coloured hair, blue eyes, about forty years of age.[12]

Stories — many with a sensational bent — also appeared in newspapers around the country. One such story produced a letter in response from a minister, which disclosed the existence of a New Jersey man who fit the description of the murder victim. The New Jersey man was found and questioned. Sure enough, he was from Vermont and used to have the same name as the purported victim. But he was in "a state of mental derangement." Despite this state, he knew the names and characteristics of many of the people in the area of the alleged murder. He was brought to Vermont and subjected to an inquiry, which he passed with flying colors. All agreed that he was the "dead man," and the convicted murderers were set free. Justice triumphed, lessons were learned about the questionable nature of alleged confessions to cellmates, and the case became part of the folklore of the American legal system.

But wait! It wasn't over yet. Forty years later, one of the brothers allegedly confided to a fellow counterfeiter — who was really an undercover marshal — that the man from New Jersey was an imposter who bore a striking resemblance to the man who had

actually been killed. This new "confession" was rife with exag-
gerations, such as that he and his brother were about to be
hanged, and that they "ascended the scaffold, and the noose was
placed around their necks, when the supposed dead man appeared in the crowd."[13]

Some historians believe it probable that the amazing appearance of the man from New Jersey was the result of a carefully orchestrated conspiracy by the condemned man and his family.
The conclusion is certainly plausible, though not conclusive.
We will probably never know the truth. The verdict of history always remains open to revision, even after a case has been long
closed by the law.

The Richard Lawrence Case

Date: 1835
Location: District of Columbia
Defendant: Richard Lawrence
Charge: Assault upon the president of the United States, with an intent to murder him
Verdict: Not guilty by reason of insanity
Sentence: Lifetime imprisonment; later transferred to a mental hospital

Richard Lawrence, the first — but tragically far from the last — person to make an armed assault upon a president of the United States, had tried to kill Andrew Jackson. Approaching the president with two well-loaded pistols, he fired — the first shot from a distance of about thirteen feet, and the second from point-blank range. The percussion caps of both pistols exploded, but neither succeeded in igniting the powder. The pistols, which were both in excellent working order and properly loaded, fired successfully in hundreds of tests conducted after the attempted assassination. It was never determined why they had misfired at the critical moment, though some observers attributed the fortuity to unusual dampness in the weather.

Having been observed by dozens of prominent witnesses and "arrested in the very act," Lawrence was immediately "brought before the chief judge at his chambers." He was accused of "an assault upon the President of the United States . . . with intent to murder him" — a common law charge that, implausible as it may sound, was "not a penitentiary offense, there being no actual battery. . . ."[14] The maximum penalty that could have been imposed under the indictment was a "fine and imprisonment"; and although the precise range of punishments for this "misdemeanor" was not clear, it was probably in the area of a year in jail and a fine of less than a thousand dollars.

It may sound strange to the modern ear that an attempt to kill the president — prevented solely by the chance misfiring of two properly loaded pistols — should be regarded so lightly by the law. In part, this reflects the early result-focus of the criminal law, both in this country and in England. Felonies — with the exception of treason-type crimes — were defined, for the most part, in terms of the harm actually caused, rather than the risk created. Thus, since there had been "no actual battery" upon the president — he literally had not been touched — the crime committed was "inchoate" (that is, incomplete). Though the law of "attempts" had its origins many centuries prior to Lawrence's crime, it was still not well developed in the United States. There was an attempt statute in the District of Columbia, but apparently few, if any, cases had been brought under it at the time of the Jackson episode. Also, there must have been some question whether conviction for an attempt would be possible in the circumstances of the case. Nor could there have been a statutory indictment for assault with intent to kill, for the applicable statute punished "assault and battery with intent to kill" (two to eight years), and there had been no battery — actual touching — upon Jackson. Thus, the prosecution was relegated to bringing a "common law" indictment against Lawrence for assault with intent to kill. (There is even some question whether this common law indictment would have been sustained by the Supreme Court, since in 1812 a unanimous Court had held that the circuit courts of the United States could not "exercise a common law jurisdiction in criminal cases." The applicability of this landmark decision to the District of Columbia was not certain at the time of the Lawrence indictment, but there surely must have been some doubts about the legality of a common law charge.[15]) It is against this background that certain important aspects of the Lawrence case can best be understood.

The first judicial decision reached in the case involved bail. It may sound strange that bail would even be considered for a thwarted presidential assassin, but since the crime with which Lawrence was charged was not a capital one, it was thought that bail had to be set. Even the prosecutor — Francis Scott Key (a part-time poet and songwriter) — acknowledged this, and limited his argument to raising the bail amount from the thousand dollars proposed by the chief judge to fifteen hundred. The report of the case indicates that Mr. Key at first acquiesced in the judge's proposal, "but having conversed with some of the president's friends who stood around him, he suggested the idea that it was not impossible that others might be concerned, who might be disposed to bail him, and let him escape to make another attempt on the life of the president; and therefore thought that the larger sum should be named."

The judge responded that "there was no evidence before him to induce a suspicion that any other person was concerned in the act; that the constitution forbade him to require excessive bail; and that to require larger bail than the prisoner could give would be to require excessive bail, and to deny bail in a case clearly bailable by law."[16]

This statement by the respected Chief Judge Cranch of the District of Columbia Circuit Court has considerable relevance to the debate over the constitutionality of pretrial detention and other forms of preventive confinement now being employed against suspected terrorists and other dangerous people. If the words stood alone, outside the context in which they were delivered and apart from the actions that accompanied them, they would make a powerful case against the constitutionality of such detention in noncapital cases. After all, it was acknowledged by all concerned that the judge could not refuse to set bail, even if there had been evidence of a continuing conspiracy to kill the president. He could, in such a situation, raise the bail; but there were limits even to that. Had the offense been a capital one, bail could have been denied — even if there were no continuing danger. This strongly suggests that the underlying reason why bail was denied in capital cases was not because capital offenses, as a class, were thought to be the most dangerous, but rather because, as a class, they provided the greatest incentive for flight since the prospect of execution was so grave.

The words of the chief judge also seem to suggest that he believed pretrial release could not be denied on economic grounds; that the maximum bail that could properly be set was the highest sum that the defendant was capable of raising. If this were in fact the original historical understanding, then it would pose considerable questions about current bail practices and judicial pronouncements. The chief judge went on, however, to say — and more significantly, to do — various things that diminish the importance of his quoted statement. First, he decided to set bail at fifteen hundred dollars, reasoning as follows: "This sum, if the ability of the prisoner only were to be considered is, probably, too large; but if the atrocity of the offense alone were considered, might seem too small, but taking both into consideration, and that the punishment can only be fine and imprisonment, it seemed to him to be as high as he ought to require."[17]

Although the judges asserted that "the prisoner had some reputable friends who might be disposed to bail him," Lawrence was not, in fact, "able to find bail to that amount [and] was committed for trial, by warrant of the Chief Judge."[18] Thus, despite the judge's statement of the law that "to require larger bail than the prisoner could give would be to require excessive bail," the net result of the case was that the prisoner was denied pretrial release because of his inability to raise the bail money. It is interesting to speculate whether a man who almost succeeded in killing the president would really have been set free — actually released to the street — if he had been able to raise the bail money. There are some suggestions in the case that Lawrence might not have obtained his freedom even if he had posted the fifteen hundred dollars.

These suggestions appear in that portion of the opinion devoted to the habeas corpus petition brought on the prisoner's behalf. This petition alleged that Lawrence was insane and requested that: "he may be discharged from imprisonment 'for the cause for which he is now confined,' and that you honor do them in the premises what belongs to humanity and the unfortunate Richard Lawrence, and also to secure the public peace by proper restraint." In other words, the petition did not seek outright release for the prisoner; instead, it requested the court to confine him not as a suspected criminal awaiting trial, but as a dangerously insane man. The place of confinement would not be different, since in those days the dangerously insane in the District of Columbia were confined in the same jail as indicted criminals. (There was no insane asylum in the district until 1852; between 1841 and 1852 the dangerously insane from the district were accommodated in the Maryland Hospital in Baltimore, and before then they were left in jail.) Counsel for the prisoner intimated, however, that the court could "meliorate his condition, or change his custody."

Despite the prosecutor's agreement that the writ should issue, the court denied the petition on grounds that clearly show the close relationships among the various mechanisms of preventive confinement:

> I would remark, here, that if the prisoner is a dangerous maniac, the only manner in which I could secure the public peace (or rather secure the public safety) would be, to remand him to the prison where he now is. His imprisonment then

would be interminable; he would have no day in court; no
means to compel a trial, no right to apply for a discharge for
want of trial, and no right to bail. He could not be bound to
keep the peace. If sureties should be bound for his keeping the
peace, it is doubtful whether they could ever be liable upon
their recognizances, whatever acts he might do; as I appre-
hend, a madman cannot be guilty of a technical breach of the
peace. I have said that I could only remand him to the prison
where he now is?[19]

Here we have a paradigm case of an allegedly insane man who
has caused no actual harm (other than, perhaps, psychological,
which was not well protected at common law), but who might
well have been quite dangerous. The first problem was what to
do with him in the interim between his arrest and the final disposition of the case. There were a number of possibilities: (1)
The court could refuse to set bail; (2) bail could be set in an
amount higher than he could raise; (3) bail could be set in an
amount that he could raise; (4) he could be required to post a
peace bond — a financial guarantee that he would not breach
the peace by committing a future crime; or (5) he could be confined as dangerously mentally ill. Pragmatically, the basic choice
is twofold: confinement or release. In this kind of case, despite
the rhetoric of liberty, it is extremely unlikely that any defendant
would have actually been released pending final disposition of
the case.

The next problem was how to dispose of the case on the merits. Again, there were a number of possibilities: (1) The defendant could be charged with an inchoate crime, such as assault
with intent to kill, attempted murder, or treason; (2) he could be
found incompetent to stand trial and remain in confinement
awaiting the restoration of his competency; or (3) he could be acquitted by reason of insanity and confined as criminally insane.
Pragmatically, the first alternative is the one least well designed

to protect the community (at least at the time of the Lawrence case). Punishment for inchoate crimes was of relatively short duration. (It was not deemed treason to attempt to kill an American president.) If convicted of an attempt or assault, Lawrence would have had to be released within a few years, at most. Moreover, as previously suggested, there may have been considerable doubts whether, on the facts of the case, a conviction would have been upheld by the Supreme Court.

The second alternative — incompetency to stand trial — requires no trial, and therefore no public disclosure of the government's evidence. It might well have been employed if the government's case were weak or embarrassing. In the Lawrence situation, however, there was every reason for the government to put on its case to prove that the attempted assassination was the work of a solitary deranged individual.

The third alternative — acquittal by reason of insanity followed by confinement as mentally ill — has been widely employed in attempted political assassinations. (This is by no means to imply that these defendants have not, in fact, been mentally ill. It is to suggest that other defendants, who have been as seriously deranged, have probably been convicted when their crimes were not of a political nature.) Acquittal by reason of insanity followed by indefinite confinement is ideally suited for an attempted assassination. The government can prove the facts (especially that the crime was the act of a madman). It can obtain a jury verdict that "closes" the case, and it can secure the defendant's safe confinement for an indefinite time.

It is not surprising, therefore, that the prosecution in the Lawrence case did not vigorously contest the plea of not guilty by reason of insanity. Robert Donovan, who chronicled the trial of Lawrence in a series appearing in *The New Yorker*,[20] takes the common but naive view that the prosecution, in not contesting the insanity "defense," was necessarily acting with "magnanimity, humaneness and liberality." Donovan observes that "a relentless prosecution" was possible, and considering the political climate of the trial, it seems that Key (the prosecutor) could have waged "a very strong prosecution along the lines that Lawrence knew right from wrong." But Donovan fails to understand that a "strong" prosecution that resulted in a misdemeanor conviction was less to be desired by the government than a "weak" prosecution that culminated in lifetime confinement. Accordingly, Key acquiesced in a very broad instruction on insanity — one that would never be given today. It took the jury five minutes to conclude that Lawrence had "been under the influence of insanity at the time he committed the act."

The judge then concluded, from the evidence, that it would be extremely dangerous to permit him to be at large while under this mental delusion and remanded him to jail. In 1855, after twenty years in jail, Lawrence became one of the first inmates confined in the new Government Hospital (now Saint Elizabeths), where he died in 1861. Had he been convicted of the crime for which he was charged, he might have lived the last twenty years of his life at liberty — and at risk of trying to kill again.

The Harvard Medical School Murder

Date: 1850
Location: Boston, Massachusetts
Defendant: Professor John Webster, MD
Charge: Murder
Verdict: Guilty
Sentence: Death by hanging

It was the most notorious murder of the day. It shook the foundations of the ivy-covered buildings at Harvard. One distinguished professor at the Harvard Medical School was accused of killing and dismembering the body of another distinguished Harvard Medical School professor. The Harvard community split right down the middle: The president of Harvard, Jared Sparks, testified for the defendant; the great poet, essayist, and medical doctor Oliver Wendell Holmes testified for the prosecution. Virtually all the participants in the trial — the judges, the prosecutors, the defense attorneys, and many of the witnesses — were sons of Harvard. Though the university survived, its reputation for *veritas* was tarnished by the trial and the sordid revelations testified to by the witnesses.

The victim of the crime was an old curmudgeon named Dr. George Parkman. At the time of his death, Parkman had all but abandoned his career in medicine and become a real estate speculator. His penchant for hounding those who owed him rent and mortgage money had earned him a reputation as a money-hungry and merciless predator. But with his vast wealth — he was a true "Boston Brahmin," and among the city's richest — Parkman purchased powerful friends and honors. He endowed The George Parkman Professorship of Anatomy and bestowed it on his friend Dr. Oliver Wendell Holmes, who delivered the eulogy at Parkman's memorial service. It is revealing that Holmes, the great word master, could come up with no better characterization of the dearly departed than that he was a "man of strict and stern principle with never a flagging energy, simple and frugal."

The man accused of killing Parkman was Professor John White Webster, the author of *Webster's Chemistry*, a standard medical school text of that era. Webster was as outgoing as Parkman was stern; a colleague described him as "a great asset at every Cambridge party." He was witty, charming, well read, musical — and utterly irresponsible in his financial dealings. It was these very differences that originally brought Webster and Parkman together. Webster borrowed money from Parkman, and the creditor began to hound the debtor for payment. Parkman demonstrated his "never flagging energy" by bursting into Webster's lectures, family dinners, and social events in quest of the several hundred dollars that he was owed. Unfortunately, Webster had no way to repay the debt.

On the morning of November 23, 1849 — a few days before Thanksgiving — Parkman set out to take care of some of his outstanding accounts. Many people saw and spoke with him that morning, and had reason to remember their encounters; one woman who owed Parkman money ran from him when he demanded she hand over the dollar he had seen in her hand as she tried to pay for food.[21] Parkman was last seen at 1:30 PM on his way to meet with John Webster at the medical school.

When the fastidiously punctual Parkman failed to appear for dinner on the night of November 23, his family became concerned. The following morning, when he still had not returned, the family commenced an official search, distributing thousands of circulars and offering thousands of dollars in exchange for any information about Parkman's whereabouts. But Parkman was not found alive.

A week after Parkman's disappearance, the janitor at the medical school, Ephraim Littlefield, made a grisly discovery. Acting on a suspicion, Littlefield dug up a secret chamber below the toilet in Dr. Webster's laboratory, where he found several large pieces of a human body. It appeared that the body had been dissected and dismembered by an experienced hand and deliberately hidden. Medical experts, including Dr. Holmes, deemed the bones consistent with Professor Parkman's physique. A subsequent search of Webster's laboratory produced additional parts, including an armless, headless, hairy torso. Mrs. Parkman identified the torso as her husband's based on markings near the penis and the lower back; the victim's brother-in-law said that the torso must have belonged to Parkman, based on the extreme hairiness of Parkman's body.[22] On the basis of this evidence, Webster was arrested and put on trial for the capital murder of his colleague.

The trial began on March 19, 1850. It lasted twelve days, and was conducted by the entire Supreme Judicial Court of Massachusetts, presided over by its dour and harsh chief justice, Lemuel Shaw. (Shaw, who was Herman Melville's father-in-law, is believed to have been the real-life prototype for Melville's Captain Vere, who reluctantly ordered the execution of the morally innocent Billy Budd.) The jury was composed of eleven tradesmen and one merchant — all of whom must have favored the death penalty, since three prospective jurors were excused for "having such opinions against capital punishment as would forbid them to convict the prisoner."[23]

The prosecutor was an experienced criminal lawyer, selected and paid for by the Parkman family. As for the defendant's counsel, the Webster family had, according to some reports, attempted to secure the services of Daniel Webster (no relation) and Rufus Choate, but both had refused to take the case. Thus, the Websters settled for a lawyer who had represented the defendant in several civil matters, but who had little criminal experience. His co-counsel was a lower court judge. The result of this matchup was predictable, and palpably one-sided. One member of the bar evaluated the performance of the defense as follows: "We have no acquaintance with either of these gentlemen, but have been informed that they are worthy and useful citizens in other spheres. If this be so, we trust that their lamentable failure at this may not impair that usefulness. But sure we are that should they live to be as old as Methuselah, their services as criminal lawyers will never again be put in requisition."

The prosecution's case relied heavily on medical testimony. First, Dr. Jeffries Wyman, a Harvard anatomy professor, presented to the jury a life-size drawing of a skeleton that indicated which parts had been recovered.[24] Dr. Holmes testified that the person who dismembered the body seemed experienced in the art of dissection, because "there is no botching about the business."[25] And Dr. Nathan Keep, the victim's dentist, testified that false teeth fitted into the jawbone recovered from Webster's laboratory matched the teeth he had made for Parkman's "very peculiar mouth."[26] Such testimony, if believed, gave rise to a circumstantial inference of Webster's guilt.

But guilt was not the only reasonable inference. The defense vigorously challenged the expert evidence suggesting that the body parts belonged to Dr. Parkman. Indeed, decades before the advent of forensic science technology, the experts were capable of little more conclusive testimony than Dr. Holmes's statement that he "did not see any particular similarity between the parts and Dr. Parkman, or anything dissimilar."[27]

Aside from the medical testimony, several of the witnesses who swore that they had sighted Parkman after the alleged time of his death were upstanding and credible. And there was another plausible suspect. Littlefield, the janitor who had originally discovered the body parts and who had become Webster's principal accuser, was himself engaged in the illegal business of providing cadavers to medical school students for exorbitant payments. Littlefield was a self-taught expert in dissection. The defense never directly accused the prosecution's star witness of committing the murder, although it did try to suggest that Littlefield was motivated by a desire for the reward money. "I have never made any claim to any reward," Littlefield insisted. "I have said that I never made any claim and never should. I say now that I never shall claim it."[28] Eventually, though, Littlefield accepted three thousand dollars from Parkman's family.[29]

On the basis of such inconclusive evidence, the jurors could have had a reasonable doubt, and many observers believed they would. But the jury was not told simply to decide the case. It was given a lengthy, and highly controversial, set of instructions by Chief Justice Shaw. The instructions were controversial for two reasons: The first is that, by all accounts, they were weighted heavily in favor of the prosecution; the second is that the official published version of the instructions — as distinguished from the ones actually given to the jury — was toned down considerably to create the misleading impression that they had been fair and balanced.

In those days, private "reporters" published accounts of the trial based on their notes. The reporter for this trial portrayed the chief justice in a negative light. Instead of responding to the criticism, or ignoring it, Shaw set out to rewrite history. He arranged for another reporter to publish a new report "to vindicate the character of our state judiciary" against accusations of a "harsh and unwarranted charge of the judge." According to the new reporter's diary:

I spent two mornings with the Chief Justice in part (after having first spent a week or so in correcting his manuscript) in which the Chief honored me with the greatest freedom of suggestion & alteration & then spent nearly another week in recorrecting the manuscript & revising proof. Nearly every correction made on this latter occasion was adopted bodily and in some instances previously I had stricken out whole sentences as repetition, & recast others as disconnected or of doubtful expediency.

The portions of the charge that had been most criticized were simply omitted or recast. The "docudrama" version of the trial was then published as the "authorized" account. This version is still used as the standard instruction for homicide in Massachusetts, despite the historical fact that it was not the one actually delivered to the Webster jury.

Nor did this overt revisionism end the controversy over the Webster trial. After Webster's conviction, death sentence, and appeal (which was rejected by the same judge who presided at his trial), efforts were undertaken to have the sentence commuted to life imprisonment. A pastor named John Putnam, who had allied himself with the Parkman camp, claimed to have elicited a solemn confession from Dr. Webster. The alleged confession was published, but immediately denounced as a fraud. John Webster went to his death by hanging on August 20, 1850, still proclaiming his innocence. To this day, Webster's guilt or innocence continues to be debated along Brattle Street in Cambridge, at Harvard reunions, and in law school classes. What is beyond dispute is that Chief Justice Lemuel Shaw was guilty of putting his thumb on the scales of justice and then rewriting history to make his thumbprint disappear from the official record.

1. Jean V. Matthews, *Toward a New Society: American Thought and Culture, 1800–1830* (Boston: Twayne Publishers, 1991), p. 150.

2. Maldwyn A. Jones, *The Limits of Liberty: American History 1607–1992* (New York: Oxford University Press, 1995), p. 139.

3. Bernard Bailyn et al., *The Great Republic: A History of the American People* (Lexington: D. C. Heath and Co., 1985), p. 312.

4. Lawrence M. Friedman, *A History of American Law* (New York: Simon and Schuster, 1985), p. 281.

5. *Ibid.*, p. 286.

6. *Ibid.*

7. Rob Warden, "The Murder That Wasn't," Center on Wrongful Convictions (2002), www.law.northwestern.edu/depts/clinic/wrongful/documents/TheMurder.htm.

8. *Ibid.*

9. Gerald W. McFarland, *The "Counterfeit" Man: The True Story of the Boorn-Colvin Murder Case* (Delran, NJ: The Notable Trials Library, 2000), p. 39.

10. Cited in *ibid.*, p. 58.

11. Warden.

12. Cited in McFarland, p. 117.

13. *Ibid.*, p. 183.

14. *United States v. Lawrence*, 26 F. Cas. 886, 887–88, 891 (C.C.D.C. 1835).

15. See *United States v. Hudson*, 11 U.S. (7 Cranch) 32 (1812).

16. *Lawrence*, 26 F. Cas., 888.

17. *Ibid.*

18. *Ibid.*

19. *Lawrence*, 26 F. Cas., 889.

20. This series was later published as a book. See Robert Donovan, *The Assassins* (New York: Harper, 1955).

21. Katherine Ramsland, "Missing Person," in *All About George Parkman* (2003), www.crimelibrary.com/notorious_murders/classics/george_parkman/2.html?sect=13.

22. Ramsland, "Not as Simple as It Seems," www.crimelibrary.com/notorious_murders/classics/george_parkman/6.html?sect=13.

23. James W. Stone, *Report of the Trial of Prof. John W. Webster* (1850) (Birmingham: The Notable Trials Library, 1990), p. 4.

24. *Ibid.*, pp. 54–59.

25. *Ibid.*, p. 59.

26. *Ibid.*, pp. 50–51.

27. *Ibid.*, p. 59.

28. *Ibid.*, p. 77.

29. Ramsland, "The Star Witness," www.crimelibrary.com/notorious_murders/classics/george_parkman/8.html?sect=13.

PART IV

The Prelude to the Civil War

THE TWO HISTORIC CASES that led up to the Civil War were the Supreme Court's notorious decision in the Dred Scott case, which said that black slaves were "ordinary articles of merchandise" without any rights, and the trial of John Brown, who decided to oppose slavery by force rather than by law. The *Dred Scott* decision made the Civil War almost inevitable, since it virtually assured that the issue of slavery would not be resolved by law. It may be the only American court case to have caused a war — though, of course, no single event can ever be said to cause so momentous a conflict as the Civil War. Other forces — economic, political, ideological — were at work as well. The conflict between the abolitionists and those who represented the continuation of slavery seemed intractable, despite efforts at compromise. The Fugitive Slave Act — a law that had the effect of requiring even those strongly opposed to slavery to "return" fugitive slaves to their owners — was enacted as part of one such compromise, but it only generated greater tensions. It was an invitation to conflict, and ultimately to violence of the sort engaged in by John Brown.

James Buchanan, a Democrat from Pennsylvania, won the 1856 presidential election, defeating the first Republican candidate, John C. Frémont, and former president Millard Fillmore, who ran as the nativist Know-Nothing candidate. In his inaugural address, Buchanan characterized the slavery issue in the territories as follows:

[I]t is a judicial question, which legitimately belongs to the Supreme Court of the United States, before whom it is now pending, and will, it is understood, be speedily and finally settled. To their decision, in common with all good citizens, I shall cheerfully submit, whatever this may be, though it has ever been my individual opinion that under the Kansas-Nebraska Act the appropriate period will be when the number of actual residents in the Territory shall justify the formation of a constitution with a view to its admission as a State into the Union.[1]

The pending case to which Buchanan referred was that of the former slave Dred Scott, which the Supreme Court decided two days after Buchanan took office. Buchanan was more than a bit disingenuous in his tone and implication, because he had been secretly pressuring Justice Robert Grier, his friend and political ally, to side with the Southern justices, urging them to issue a broad decision in the case, which they did.[2]

The geographic makeup of the Court bears noting: Five of the justices were Southerners (Taney, Wayne, Catron, Daniel, and Campbell), all of whom ruled against Scott; of the four "Northerners" (McLean, Curtis, Nelson, and Grier), only one (Grier of Pennsylvania, Buchanan's home state) voted with the majority and agreed with its reasoning.[3]

In the famous senatorial race between Abraham Lincoln and Stephen Douglas in 1858, Lincoln sought to shift attention from the policy issues of slavery to its philosophical aspects.[4] Whereas Douglas touted popular sovereignty for states and territories as the only "national" solution to the slavery issue, Lincoln sought to undermine this "middle ground and force a single, sectional solution on the entire Union."[5] Following the Dred Scott decision, Lincoln feared that the Supreme Court might hold that there was a constitutional "property" right to own slaves and that no state could abrogate that right by abolishing slavery within its own borders.[6]

Although Lincoln considered slavery immoral, he was a strong advocate of keeping the Union intact; thus, he supported leaving slavery undisturbed in the states where it already existed, and he accepted the principle behind the fugitive slave laws.[7] Indeed, like Jefferson before him, Lincoln believed there was a "physical difference between the white and black races [that would] forever forbid the two races from living together on terms of social and political equality. . . . The superior position [is] assigned to the white race."[8] For a while, he also proposed colonization of blacks in Liberia — "What I would most desire would be the separation of the white and black races"— but he came to support gradual emancipation after recognizing the impracticalities of colonization.[9]

Where Lincoln and Douglas focused the attention of the American public on the philosophical aspects of slavery, John Brown's violent actions forced Americans to confront its emotional aspects.[10] Brown's mission culminated in his 1859 seizure of the federal arsenal at Harpers Ferry, where his eighteen-man army — among them five blacks — killed four people and wounded nine; ten of Brown's men (including two of his sons) were killed, five escaped, and seven were captured.[11] Brown himself was wounded and captured. He expressed no regrets about his action, though he was disappointed that Northern free blacks and Southern slaves had not rallied around him at Harpers Ferry.

Interestingly, Brown earned the admiration of many Virginians, including Governor Henry Wise, for his courage in captivity. Upon refusing to order Brown examined for insanity, Wise remarked: "I know that he was sane, and remarkably sane, if quick and clear perception, if assumed rational premises and consecutive reasoning from them, if cautious tact in avoiding disclosures and in covering conclusions and inferences, if memory and conception and practical common sense, and if composure and self-possession are evidence of a sound state of mind."[12] A devout Calvinist, Brown believed his mission at Harpers Ferry was divinely inspired — a belief so deep he thought it unnecessary to make battle plans, examine the surrounding mountainous terrain, get word to slaves nearby, or draw up escape plans.[13]

Brown was arraigned promptly, then indicted and brought to trial within a week of his capture and while still suffering from his wounds. After a weeklong trial, he was sentenced to hang for the crimes of murder, inciting slaves to insurrection, and treason against the state of Virginia (though he was not even a citizen of that state).[14] At his sentencing, Brown averred: "I feel entirely satisfied with the treatment I have received on my trial. Considering all the circumstances, it has been more generous than I expected. But I feel no consciousness of guilt."[15] At his trial and in his final days in jail, Brown actually maintained his innocence — insisting dishonestly that he had never intended to trigger an insurrection. He told the Charleston court that at Harpers Ferry he had planned only a localized operation to liberate the slaves and send them to the North.[16]

Many in the North made a martyr of Brown, honoring his mission, while most of the South regarded him as a terrorist and loathed his canonization.[17] Typical of the reverence for Brown was this verse penned by Louisa May Alcott: "No breath of shame can touch his shield / Nor ages dim its shine. / Living, he made life beautiful, / Dying, made death divine."[18] Brown's attack at Harpers Ferry and subsequent execution only sank the North and South deeper into sectional conflict. As the *Richmond Dispatch* proclaimed: "The Harper's Ferry invasion has advanced the cause of Disunion more than any other event that has happened since the formation of the Government."[19]

Meanwhile, in his annual message to the Senate at the opening of Congress in 1859, Buchanan called the *Dred Scott* decision "the final settlement . . . of the question of slavery in the Territories . . . [which protects] the right . . . of every citizen" not only "to take his property of any kind, including slaves into the common territories," but also "to have it protected there under the Federal Constitution."[20] In response, Senator Jefferson Davis, future president of the Confederacy, introduced resolutions demanding a federal slave code for the territories.[21]

Such was the backdrop of the 1860 election, in which protection of slavery in the territories caused a rift in the Democratic party.

The 1860 election was a four-way contest that illustrated the intense sectional strife gripping the nation. Lincoln, campaigning on the Republican platform that slavery must ultimately be abolished, was elected with 180 electoral votes and 1.86 million popular votes (39 percent)— he did not win a single Southern state, nor did he even campaign in the South.[22] Douglas, the Northern Democratic candidate, garnered twelve electoral votes and 1.38 million popular votes; John C. Breckenridge, the Southern Democratic candidate, and John Bell, the Constitutional Union candidate, shared the remaining votes.[23]

White Southerners recoiled at Lincoln's presidential victory and grew increasingly resistant toward acknowledging him as the nation's president and his platform as the nation's path. The purely sectional Republican triumph brought white Southerners to a crossroads between their loyalty to the nation and their loyalty to their regional identity— characterized most prominently by slavery.[24] South Carolina became the first state to secede from the Union in December 1860, followed within the next two months by six other Lower South states— Mississippi, Florida, Alabama, Georgia, Louisiana, and Texas. Together, they formed the Confederacy.[25] But eight Southern states, from the Upper South, did not secede at this time.[26] Although the Confederacy elected Jefferson Davis as its president in February 1861, the South still remained divided.

Lincoln took office amid this great tension. In his first inaugural address, he struck a deliberate tone: "In *your* hands, my dissatisfied fellow-countrymen, and not in *mine*, is the momentous issue of civil war. The Government will not assail *you*. You can have no conflict without being yourselves the aggressors. *You* have no oath registered in heaven to destroy the Government, while I shall have the most solemn one to 'preserve, protect and defend it.'" Lincoln closed by imploring Americans to be friends, not enemies, and to reach this point by appealing to "the better angels of our nature." One month later, in April, the Confederacy shelled Fort Sumter and the bloodiest of American wars had begun.

The Dred Scott Case

Date: 1847–56
Location: District of Columbia
Plaintiff: The former slave Dred Scott
Defendant: The executor of his former owner's estate
Claim: Scott was entitled to freedom
Decision: Scott remained a slave

The *Dred Scott* decision presented the Supreme Court with the most contentious issue dividing the "slave" states from the "free" states in the years leading up to the Civil War: whether it was within the power of the federal government to prohibit slavery in its territories. Scott argued that his long stay in the free state of Illinois, as well as in the Wisconsin Territory, gave him legal standing to sue for his freedom.

The Supreme Court's majority opinion in this infamous case should be required reading for every American. Indeed, it should be reread periodically, if for no other reason than to remind us of what we once were as a nation. It is difficult to believe that we, as a civilized country, once *officially* regarded people of "the enslaved African race" as "ordinary articles of merchandise . . . ," "a subordinate and inferior class of beings," "beings of an inferior order, and altogether unfit to associate with the white race . . . and so far inferior, that they had no rights. . . ." To revisit this blight on our history is not only to make us feel ashamed of our past; it is also to give us pause about our present and future. The *constitutional methodology* by which the Supreme Court reached its decision in 1856—a rigid and static focus on the original intent or understanding of the Constitution's framers — bears a striking similarity to the methodology currently espoused by several members of the Supreme Court. Indeed, it is fair to say that at least three of our current justices — if they were to remain true to their professed philosophy of constitutional interpretation — would have to have joined Chief Justice Taney's majority ruling that the framers of the U.S. Constitution intended to disqualify freed African slaves from U.S. citizenship, even if a state awarded them full state citizenship. Ironically, one of them would have been disqualified for membership on the Supreme Court by his own logic.

The "logic" of the *Dred Scott* decision is familiar to readers of current Supreme Court opinions. Chief Justice Taney begins by stating the question before the Court:

Can a negro, whose ancestors were imported into this country, and sold as slaves, become a member of the political community formed and brought into existence by the Constitution of the United States, and as such become entitled to all rights, and privileges, and immunities, guarantied by that instrument to the citizen?[27]

He then quickly distances himself personally — and the Court institutionally — from the "justice or unjustice" of what the framers intended:

It is not the province of the court to decide upon the justice or injustice, the policy or impolicy, of these laws. The decision of that question belonged to the political or law-making power; to those who formed the sovereignty and framed the Constitution. The duty of the court is, to interpret the instrument they have framed, with the best lights we can obtain on the subject, and to administer it as we find it, according to its true intent and meaning when it was adopted.[28]

This formulation of the role of judges — to apply existing law rather than to make new law — is the essence of "judicial restraint," as contrasted with "judicial activism." A contemporary Roger Taney could be nominated today to the Supreme Court.

Chief Justice Taney then proceeds to blame the unjust result on the "state of public opinion" at the time the Constitution was ratified:

> In the opinion of the court, the legislation and histories of the times, and the language used in the Declaration of Independence, show that neither the class of persons who had been imported as slaves, nor their descendants, whether they had become free or not, were then acknowledged as a part of the people, nor intended to be included in the general words used in that memorable instrument.
>
> It is difficult at this day to realize the state of public opinion in relations to that unfortunate race, which prevailed in the civilized and enlightened portions of the world at the time of the Declaration of Independence, and when the Constitution of the United States was framed and adopted. But the public history of every European nation displays it in a manner too plain to be mistaken.
>
> They had for more than a century before been regarded as beings of an inferior order, and altogether unfit to associate with the white race, either in social or political relations; and so far inferior, that they had no rights which the white man was bound to respect; and that the negro might justly and lawfully be reduced to slavery for his benefit. He was bought and sold, and treated as an ordinary article of merchandise and traffic, whenever a profit could be made by it. This opinion was at that time fixed and universal in the civilized portion of the

white race. It was regarded as an axiom in morals as well as in politics, which no one thought of disputing, or supposed to be open to dispute; and men in every grade and position in society daily and habitually acted upon it in their private pursuits, as well as in matters of public concern, without doubting for a moment the correctness of this opinion.[29]

In light of these widespread attitudes — which Taney carefully documents by citing state legislation throughout the nation, even in the abolitionist states — it would be inconceivable, Taney argues, for the framers, especially the "great men of the slaveholding states who took so large a share in framing the Constitution,"[30] to have intended the parade of horrible results that he believed would ensue from granting citizenship to blacks. Taney believed such an unintended result would

give to persons of the negro race, who were recognized as citizens in any one State of the Union, the right to enter every other state whenever they pleased, singly or in companies, without pass or passport, and without obstruction, to sojourn there as long as they pleased, to go where they pleased at any hour of the day or night without molestation, unless they committed some violation of the law for which a white man would be punished; and it would give them the full liberty of speech in public and in private upon all subjects upon which its own citizens might speak; to hold public meetings upon political affairs, and to keep and carry arms wherever they went. And all of this would be done in the face of the subject race of the same color, both free and slaves, and inevitably producing discontent and insubordination among them, and endangering the peace and safety of the State.[31]

As an empirical matter, it is difficult to quarrel with Taney's assessment of the mind-set of the framers — at least most of them — at the time the Constitution was ratified. But his normative constitutional conclusion does not simply flow uncontroversially from his simple-minded factual recitation. It is surely possible that "the great men" who framed our perpetual charter of liberty understood that attitudes change over time and that by using open-textured language they would not bind future generations to the primitive racism of the past. Perhaps the very openness of the language was intended — at least by some — as a farsighted compromise capable of differing interpretations over time. Taney rejects this view out of hand, without serious consideration:

> No one, we presume, supposes that any change in public opinion or feeling, in relation to this unfortunate race, in the civilized nations of Europe or in this country, should induce the court to give to the words of the Constitution a more liberal construction in their favor than they were intended to bear when the instrument was framed and adopted. Such an argument would be altogether inadmissible in any tribunal called upon to interpret it. If any of its provisions are deemed unjust, there is a mode prescribed in the instrument itself by which it may be amended; but while it remains unaltered, it must be construed now, as it was understood at the time of its adoption. It is not only the same in words, but the same in meaning, and delegates the same powers to the Government, and reserves and secures the same rights and privileges to the citizen; and as long as it continues to exist in its present form, it speaks not only in the same words, but with the same meaning and intent with which it spoke when it came from the hands of its framers, and was voted on and adopted by the people of the United States. Any other rule of construction would abrogate the judicial character of this court, and make it the mere reflex of the popular opinion or passion of the day. This court was not created by the Constitution for such purposes. Higher and graver trusts have been confided to it, and it must not falter in the path of duty.[32]

This ringing language sounds familiar to the modern ear. We hear it spoken by senators and judicial nominees at virtually every confirmation hearing. We hear it espoused by presidents in the making of judicial appointments, and we read it — albeit selectively — in judicial opinions at every level of the judiciary culminating in the Supreme Court.

Contemporary judicial nominees who glibly recite the expected formula of original intent or understanding should read the above paragraph and be asked whether they would have joined the majority decision in Dred Scott — and if not, why not? I have yet to hear a persuasive explanation of how honest "originalists" could have wiggled their way out of the majority conclusion in Dred Scott or how they could have agreed with the Supreme Court's unanimous decision, a century later, interpreting the equal protection clause as forbidding the kind of "separate but equal" public school education that was indisputably prevalent at the time the Thirteenth, Fourteenth, and Fifteenth Amendments were ratified.

Reading and rereading the justices' opinions in the most divisive case in American history, originally publicized by the Supreme Court itself "in consequence of the general desire of the public to have access to these opinions," is an important exercise of citizenship with striking relevance to our own times. Even the dissenting justices, who found that Scott's "negro ancestry" should not prevent him from claiming the rights of U.S. citizenship (including the right to sue in federal court), nonetheless conceded that a slave could be sold, reclaimed, and given as inheritance "where he is legally held to service."[33] Historian David Blight has commented that the Dred Scott decision thus signified that "to be black in America in the late 1850s was to live in a land that said you didn't have a future."[34]

But African Americans did have a future. The post–Civil War

amendments — the Thirteenth, Fourteenth, and Fifteenth — overruled the *Dred Scott* decision, assuring the former slaves their freedom and promising all people the equal protection of laws. It would be a long time, however, before this promise would be kept.

The John Brown Case

Date: 1859
Location: Charleston, Virginia
Defendant: John Brown
Charges: Murder, insurrection
Verdict: Guilty
Sentence: Hanging

During the Civil War, the most popular anthem of the Union army was: "John Brown's body lies a-mouldering in the grave / But his soul goes marching on," set to the tune of the "Battle Hymn of the Republic." The John Brown of this stirring song was the zealous abolitionist who resorted to violence — even against innocent bystanders — in what he regarded as his divinely mandated efforts to free the slaves and initiate a slave revolt.

In the decade preceding the Civil War, Brown led a series of guerrilla raids against proslavery forces, killing several people in the process. Following the Supreme Court's notorious decision in the Dred Scott case, many abolitionists became convinced that only armed struggle would end slavery. Even some pacifists contributed to Brown's efforts, which culminated in his abortive effort to capture the U.S. arsenal at Harpers Ferry, Virginia, in October 1859. Leading a band of thirteen white men and five former slaves, Brown seized control of several buildings. The revolt was quickly crushed by a company of U.S. Marines under the command of Colonel Robert E. Lee. Brown was immediately put on trial for "treason to the Commonwealth" and "conspiracy with slaves to commit treason and murder."

The trial itself, which was open and shut on its facts, is best remembered for Brown's eloquent final address to the court, which included the following:

> I am yet too young to understand that God is any respecter of persons. I believe that to have interfered as I have done — as I have always freely admitted I have done — in behalf of His despised poor, was not wrong but right. Now if it is deemed necessary that I should forfeit my life for the furtherance of the ends of justice and mingle my blood further with the blood of my children and with the blood of millions in this slave country, whose rights are disregarded by wicked, cruel, and unjust enactments — I submit; so let it be done!

It is also remembered for what was not presented. It was widely believed that Brown, whose family had a long history of mental illness, might plead insanity. But he did not. Nor would the governor commute his death sentence, despite reviewing seventeen affidavits from neighbors and relatives attesting to his insanity. Six weeks after the raid on Harpers Ferry, John Brown was hanged.

But Brown's execution did not end the controversy over who Brown really was and whether his violent actions deserved commendation or condemnation. In his famous Cooper Union speech of 1860, Abraham Lincoln characterized Brown as an assassin:

> That affair, in its philosophy, corresponds with the many attempts, related in history, at the assassination of kings and emperors. An enthusiast broods over the oppression of a people till he fancies himself commissioned by Heaven to liberate them. He ventures the attempt, which ends in little else than his own execution. Orsini's attempt on Louis Napoleon, and

John Brown's attempt at Harper's Ferry were, in their philosophy, precisely the same.

Ralph Waldo Emerson, on the other hand, believed that Brown's execution would "make the gallows as glorious as the cross." And the abolitionist Wendell Phillips argued that history would date the beginning of slavery's abolition from Harpers Ferry.

Brown's execution did not end the legal and political controversy over what had transpired at Harpers Ferry. Since the state criminal trial of John Brown was not deemed a suitable vehicle for exploring the larger issues surrounding the attempted uprising and treason, the U.S. Senate decided to appoint a select committee to inquire into that event. Hearings were held, and testimony was taken. A three-man majority — which included Senator Jefferson Davis, soon to become president of the Confederate States — concluded that the invasion of Harpers Ferry was

> simply the act of lawless ruffians, under the sanction of no public or political authority — distinguishable only from ordinary felonies by the ulterior ends in contemplation by them, and by the fact that the money to maintain the expedition, and the large armament they brought with them, had been contributed and furnished by the citizens of other States of the Union, under circumstances that must continue to jeopardy the safety and peace of the Southern States.

Davis and his colleagues tried to place the blame for Brown's actions on Northern radicals, and especially on those in Massachusetts, who had supported Brown even after becoming aware of his willingness to employ violence against innocent civilians.

The minority saw the event in a somewhat broader historical context:

So long as Congress, in the exercise of its power over the Territories, is invoked to exert it to extend, perpetuate, or protect the institution of slavery therein; so long as the policy of the government is sought to be so shaped as to aid to extend its existence or enlarge its power, in any way, beyond its present limits, so long must its moral, political, and social character and effects be unavoidably involved in congressional discussion. Hence, it is equally unavoidable that the people in all parts of the Union will discuss this subject, as they are to select those who are to represent them and their sentiments in congressional action. So long as slavery is claimed before the world as a highly benignant, elevating, and humanizing institution, and as having Divine approbation, it will receive at the hands of the moralist, civilian, and theologian the most free and unflinching discussion; nor should its vindicators wince in the combat which their claims invite. In this discussion, it is true, as in other topics of exciting debate, wide latitude and license are, at times, indulged, but it seldom or never exceeds in severity the terms of reprehension on this subject which were long since indulged by Washington, Madison, Jefferson, Mason, and, in later times, by McDowell, Faulkner, and their worthy compeers, all of Virginia, whose information and opinions, on this as well as other subjects, the people of the free States have not yet learned to disrespect. We insist, however, that there is no such matter presented in the testimony or existing in fact, as is more than intimated in the report, that even the abolitionists in the free States take courses intended, covertly, to produce forcible violations of the laws and peace of the slaveholding States, much less that any such course is countenanced by the body of the people in the free States. We cannot join in any report tending to promulgate such a view, as we regard it unfounded in fact and ill calculated to promote peace, confidence, or tranquility, and a departure from the legitimate purpose for which the committee was appointed.[35]

The proceedings of the Senate select committee really consti-tute the trial of John Brown, especially since the issues in dispute were not of the whodunit nature, but rather of the broad ideo-logical and religious motivation behind what was done. The proceedings provide the most complete record of the events leading up to the raid on Harpers Ferry. They are historically skewed by the biases of the participants and they are far from complete, but their contemporaneity provides a unique window into a transforming event in American history — an event that continues to be disputed almost a century and a half after its bloody denouement. Sometimes a trial takes place in committee rooms rather than in a courthouse. Sometimes it takes place in the history books and in the court of public opinion over time. John Brown's trial is still not over, though the Civil War resolved the contentious issue of slavery, which had motivated Brown's murderous actions.

1. James Buchanan, "Inaugural Address," Mar. 4, 1847, reprinted in *Inaugural Addresses of the Presidents of the United States: From George Washington 1789 to George Bush 1989* (Washington: GPO, 1989), pp. 126–27.

2. David Herbert Donald et al., *The Civil War and Reconstruction* (New York: W. W. Norton and Co., 2001), p. 103; James McPherson, *Ordeal by Fire: The Civil War and Reconstruction* (New York: Alfred A. Knopf, 1982), p. 99.

3. David M. Potter, *The Impending Crisis* (New York: Harper and Row, 1976), pp. 273–74. (Nelson [NY] concurred only in the result.)

4. *Ibid.*, p. 338.

5. Eric Foner, *The Story of American Freedom* (New York: W. W. Norton and Co., 1998), p. 46.

6. Stephen B. Oates, *Our Fiery Trial: Abraham Lincoln, John Brown, and the Civil War Era* (Amherst: University of Massachusetts Press, 1979), pp. 68–69. According to Oates: "The train of ominous events from Kansas-Nebraska to *Dred Scott* shook Lincoln to his foundations" (p. 68).

7. Potter, p. 343.

8. Quoted in *ibid.*, p. 344.

9. Quoted in *ibid.*, pp. 345–46.

10. *Ibid.*, p. 356.

11. *Ibid.*, pp. 371–72; Oates, pp. 9–11. The precise count of Brown's army seems to vary in different texts — Donald writes that Brown led a band of eighteen followers (p. 114).

12. Quoted in Potter, p. 376.

13. Oates, p. 11.

14. Potter, p. 376; Oates, p. 11.

15. Quoted in Potter, p. 377.

16. Oates, pp. 49–50.

17. Potter, p. 378.

18. *Ibid.*, p. 376.

19. October 25, 1859. Quoted in Oates, pp. 19–20.

20. Quoted in Potter, p. 403.

21. *Ibid.*

22. *Ibid.*, p. 477.

23. *Ibid.*, pp. 430, 444.

24. *Ibid.*, pp. 52–53.

25. Potter, p. 498.

26. States from the Upper South — Virginia, Tennessee, Arkansas, and North Carolina — all seceded after the Confederate attack on Fort Sumter. The border slave states — Maryland, Delaware, Kentucky, Missouri, and West Virginia (which became its own state in 1862) — remained in the Union. Donald, pp. 128, 179–82.

27. Cited in Benjamin C. Howard, *A Report of the Decision of the Supreme Court of the United States, and the Opinions of the Justices Thereof, in the*

Case of Dred Scott versus John F. A. Sandford (New York: The Notable Trials Library, 1995), p. 403.

28. *Ibid.*, p. 405.
29. *Ibid.*, p. 407.
30. *Ibid.*, p. 417.
31. *Ibid.*
32. *Ibid.*, p. 426.
33. *Dred Scott*, 60 U.S. 531, 548 (McLean, J., dissenting).
34. David W. Blight, "David Blight on the Dred Scott Decision," in *Africans in America*, part 4, www.pbs.org/wgbh/aia/part4/4i3090.html.
35. See *Report of the Select Committee of the Senate Appointed to Inquire into the Late Invasion and Seizure of the Public Property at Harper's Ferry* (New York: The Notable Trials Library, 1993), p. 25.

PART V
The Civil War

WARTIME TRIALS are rarely typical of a nation's legal system, but they often tell us something interesting about the capacity of its institutions to deal with the passions of the time. The three great trials of the Civil War frame the crisis. The first — the piracy trial of privateers operating on behalf of the Confederacy — marked the beginning of the war. The second — the trial of the commanders of a notorious Confederate prisoner-of-war camp — represents the brutality of the war itself. And the third — the trial of Lincoln's assassins — signaled the end of the Civil War and the birth of Reconstruction.

Naval operations were an important element of the war from the outset, when Lincoln announced a blockade of the South four days after the attack on Fort Sumter.[1] To compensate for its own naval deficiency Davis began issuing, on behalf of the Confederacy, letters of marque and reprisal, which authorized private ships to hunt down and attack Union shipping vessels.[2] Such letters were recognized by international law and are explicitly authorized by the Constitution — if issued by the United States or another sovereign nation. Refusing to recognize the Confederacy as a legitimate government, Lincoln responded by issuing a proclamation declaring the crews and officers of Confederate warships and privateers to be pirates — that is, they would not be treated as prisoners of war.[3]

The tense exchange of words came to a head in June 1861, when the privateer *Savannah*, captained by Thomas Baker and armed with an eighteen-pound swivel gun, captured a brig laden with sugar and sent it into a South Carolina port.[4] The next day, a U.S. Navy brig, the USS *Perry*, captured the *Savannah* outside Charleston Harbor after a brief exchange of fire.[5] A Union prize crew boarded the *Savannah* and arrested its crew, the first privateers to be captured by the North.[6] They were taken to New York City and incarcerated in the infamous Tombs Prison.[7]

In October 1861, thirteen members of the *Savannah* went on trial, over which Justice Samuel Nelson of the Supreme Court presided.[8] True to his threat, Lincoln had ordered the defendants charged with and tried for piracy on the high seas, which meant that they faced likely death sentences if convicted.[9] An infuriated Davis insisted that the *Savannah* crew had operated lawfully as a Confederate warship. He countered Lincoln's order by directing that thirteen of the highest-ranking Union prisoners, chosen by lot, be executed if the *Savannah* defendants were executed.[10] Indeed, in a letter issued shortly after seizure of the *Savannah*, Davis had warned Lincoln that the Confederate government would "deal out to the prisoners held by it the same treatment and the same fate as shall be experienced by those captured on the *Savannah*."[11]

The trial of the *Savannah* crew lasted one week and then went to the jury, which was hopelessly deadlocked.[12] The court declared a hung jury; the defendants were never tried again and were later exchanged for Union prisoners. Judges and juries were generally reluctant to convict captured Confederate privateer crews, but following the capture of the *Savannah*, the crew of the *Jeff Davis*, "the most notorious of the privateers," was convicted and sentenced to death in Philadelphia.[13] With Lincoln and Davis still in a staredown over treatment of captured crews — the hung jury in the *Savannah* trial left the question unresolved — Davis ordered lots drawn among Union prisoners, and those selected (including a grandson of Paul Revere) were held for execution if the death sentences of the *Jeff Davis* crew were carried out.[14] Lincoln ultimately backed down, announcing in early 1862 that privateer crews would be treated as prisoners of war.[15]

The prisoner-of-war issue became prominent as the conflict wore on. By war's end, according to official reports, the Confederacy captured 211,000 Union soldiers and took 195,000 prisoners, while the Union captured 247,000 Confederate soldiers and took 215,000 prisoners.[16] Prisoner-of-war camps were certainly an undesirable venue in either North or South, but the shortage of resources and decimated supply system in the South contributed to the harsh conditions endured by prisoners there.[17] Particularly notorious was Andersonville Prison in southwestern Georgia, where "mosquito-infested tents, myriad maggots, a contaminated water supply, unbaked rations, inadequate hospital facilities, and lack of sanitation led to high death rates."[18] When Union prisoners attempted to escape by tunneling, prison officials sent bloodhounds to hunt them down.[19] In the first six months of 1864, there were 130,000 prisoners at Andersonville; in one month, nearly 3,000 prisoners had reportedly died — a rate of 100 per day. In total, approximately thirteen thousand prisoners are believed to have died there.[20]

Both the Union and Confederacy used the reports of conditions at these prison camps as propaganda during the war.[21] Sentiments of outrage and vengeance lingered for some time. Henry Wirz, commander of Andersonville, was later convicted of war crimes and hanged — the only Confederate to be tried and executed after the war.[22] Historians disagree as to whether Wirz's conviction and execution were warranted or rather "a miscarriage of justice resulting from the North's need for a scapegoat."[23]

The imprisonment of soldiers at Andersonville and other wartime prisons persisted, at least to some degree, because of the breakdown of the prisoner exchange program between the Union and Confederacy. The Confederacy rejected the program in response to the Emancipation Proclamation and to the Union army's enlistment of black soldiers — Davis called these measures "the most execrable recorded in the history of guilty man."[24] The Confederacy ordered, and its Congress approved, the permanent detention of captured black soldiers and all Union officers captured in the Confederacy; they would be turned over to state governments for likely execution.[25] Lincoln

halted all exchanges of Confederate officers and in July 1863 issued an executive order declaring that the Union would treat
Confederate prisoners correspondingly — either execution or
hard labor — to Confederate treatment of Union prisoners.[26]
Nevertheless, the Confederacy executed black soldiers. The
most brutal such episode occurred in April 1864 at Fort Pillow,
Tennessee, where Nathan Bedford Forrest — who later became
"Grand Wizard" of the infant Ku Klux Klan — led the massacre
of nearly three hundred black soldiers, as many as thirty after
they had surrendered.[27] Evidence from Fort Pillow shows the
burying alive of the wounded and the deliberate burning of hospital tents.[28] Finally, during the winter of 1864–65, the Union
and Confederacy exchanged thousands of sick and wounded
prisoners, both black and white.[29]

The first years of the Civil War were difficult for Lincoln; he
struggled to maintain cohesion and morale within the Union as
each month brought more bloodshed and less hope that an end
to the conflict was imminent. The Democrats scored great victories in the 1862 congressional elections and were anticipating
success in the 1864 elections.[30] Lincoln's prospects for reelection
were uncertain when he faced the Democratic challenger, General George McClellan, with whom Lincoln had clashed repeatedly when McClellan commanded the Army of the
Potomac. By the time the 1864 election took place, momentum
had swung to the Union side and the Democrats were running a
poorly organized campaign around a weak, unrealistic peace
platform. Lincoln defeated McClellan soundly, winning 55 percent of the popular vote and the electoral votes of every state but
three (221–12).[31] The country had spoken on war and emancipation: Lincoln's victory crushed any Confederate hopes for a
negotiated peace and ensured that the Union would continue to
fight until it achieved military victory.[32]

As Lincoln looked toward the end of the war, he insisted on
reunion and limited black suffrage, as well as a generous recon-

struction with no persecution of the South after the war.[33] In his second inaugural address, Lincoln famously articulated these sentiments: "With malice toward none, with charity for all, with firmness in the right as God gives us to see the right, let us strive on to finish the work we are in, to bind up the nation's wounds, to care for him who shall have borne the battle and for his widow and his orphan, to do all which may achieve and cherish a just and lasting peace among ourselves and with all nations."[34] The Union had overwhelmed the Confederacy in material superiority — manpower, weapons, and resources — by mid-1865. The Confederacy was tired and beaten; the glory of fighting for its way of life had ended in defeat and desolation.[35]

More than 620,000 Union and Confederate soldiers died during the Civil War, a ratio of 182 of every 10,000 Americans.[36] On April 9, 1865, Lee surrendered to Grant at Appomattox Court House, Virginia. Less than a week later, Lincoln was assassinated by John Wilkes Booth while watching a play at Ford's Theatre in Washington. The Union troops tracked down Booth nearly two weeks later and shot him to death. Booth had apparently plotted for months to kidnap Lincoln and to hold him hostage in exchange for concessions to the Confederacy, but the end of the war ruined Booth's plan.[37] Booth then decided to murder Lincoln. He recruited accomplices to kill Secretary of State William Seward (who was stabbed but survived) and Vice President Andrew Johnson (whose supposed attacker lost his nerve to carry out the assignment).[38]

A military court convicted eight accomplices of conspiracy in the assassination, sentencing four to death by hanging and the rest to imprisonment at hard labor.[39] Two of the accomplices, notes historian James McPherson, were likely convicted unjustly: "Mary Surratt, keeper of a boardinghouse where Booth planned the kidnapping, was part of his original kidnapping plot but probably unaware of the revised plans for assassination; Dr. Samuel Mudd, who treated Booth's broken leg, was at most an accessory after the fact."[40] Surratt was hanged; Mudd was convicted and sentenced to life in prison, but was eventually pardoned by President Johnson in 1869, along with the other imprisoned conspirators (one conspirator had already died in prison, two years after his conviction).[41] The nation at once clamored angrily to avenge Lincoln's death and mourned deeply its former president, whom it now likened to the martyred Jesus.[42]

The most deadly war in American history was over, but its legacy was to continue well beyond the termination of military hostilities.

The Savannah *Case*

Date: 1861
Location: New York City, New York
Defendants: Captain Thomas Baker and crew members
Charge: Piracy
Verdict: Hung jury

The piracy trial of the officers and crew of the ship *Savannah* reflects the passions and conflicts of the early stages of the American Civil War. Within days of the attack on Fort Sumter, the stage was set for a great legal confrontation that could determine whether soldiers and sailors of the Confederacy would be treated as belligerents, entitled to the protection of the law of warfare, or common criminals subject to punishment for their "crimes." This controversy has recurred throughout the history of warfare, most recently in the war against terrorism, the status of which is also subject to reasonable dispute.

Following the capture of the *Savannah* by a Union warship, it was towed to New York, where its officers and crew were placed on trial for piracy. The punishment, if convicted, was death by hanging. Their defense was that they were acting under the authority of the Confederacy, which had granted a letter of marque and reprisal, and that they must therefore be treated as prisoners of war. The prosecution countered by arguing that the United States did not recognize the Confederacy as a legitimate government capable of issuing letters of marque and reprisal.

There was no real dispute over the facts, especially since one of the crew made a deal to have the charges against him dropped in return for his testimony. The case turned on issues of law, but the defendants, probably in the hope that some jurors might be sympathetic to their claims that they were not acting as common criminals and that there was a difference between Captain Baker and the notorious British pirate Captain Kidd, demanded a jury trial. The prosecution was obviously concerned that jurors might not want to see sailors hanged as pirates, and it addressed this issue of punishment in its opening argument:

> The crime of those who have acted as the agents and servants of these leaders is also a grave one — a very grave one — mitigated, no doubt, by ignorance, softened by a credulous belief of misrepresentations, and modified by the very air and atmosphere of the place from which these prisoners embarked. It is, undoubtedly, a case where the sympathies of the jury and counsel — whether for the prosecution or the defense — may be well excited in reference to many, if not all, of the prisoners at the bar, misguided and misdirected as they have been. But it will be your duty, gentlemen, while allowing these considerations to induce *caution in* rendering your verdict, to disregard them so far as to give an honest and truthful return on the evidence, and on the law as it will be stated to you by the Court. This is all the prosecution asks. As to the policy of ultimately allowing the law to take its course in this case, it is not necessary for us to express any opinion whatever. That is a question, which the President of the United States must determine if this trial should result in a conviction. It is for him, not for us.[43]

The suggestion was plain: President Lincoln might well commute any death sentences resulting from the conviction of the "pirates" because they were dupes of the Confederate leaders. But that was far from certain at that time.

The defense was concerned as well that the inflamed passions of war might turn the jury against defendants and defense lawyers. It argued forcefully that the acts committed by the defendants were not intended to be covered by the law of piracy, but rather by the law of war. The defense sounded this theme in its opening statement:

I think that we have proceeded far enough in this case for you to have perceived that it is one of the most interesting trials that ever took place in the continent of America, if not in the civilized world. For the first time, certainly in this controversy, twelve men are put on trial for their lives, before twelve other men, as pirates and — as has been well expressed to you by the learned District Attorney who opened this case on behalf of the prosecution — as *enemies of the human race* [emphasis added].

. . . These prisoners have the misfortune, as I say, of being placed on their trial far from their homes. They have been now in confinement and under arrest on this charge for some four or five months. During that whole period they have had no opportunity whatever of communicating with their friends or relatives. Intercourse has been cut off. They have had no opportunity of procuring means to meet their necessary expenses, or even to fee counsel in their defense. Without the solace of the company of their families, immured in a prison among those who, unfortunately, from friends and fellow-countrymen have become enemies, they are now placed in this Court on trial for their lives. You will certainly reflect, gentlemen, that it was not for a case of this kind that any statute punishing the crime of piracy was ever intended to be enacted. [I]t is a monstrous stretch of the provisions of those statutes to ask for a conviction in a case of this kind.[44]

Although there was little room for adversarial passion in the presentation of the facts, the defense lawyers certainly pulled out all the stops in their advocacy regarding both the law and the right of the jury to engage in nullification.

Indeed, the defense suggested that the law of piracy was inapplicable altogether to the case. In the mid–nineteenth century, piracy was defined at international law as "the offense of depredating on the seas without being authorized by any sovereign state, or with commissions from different sovereigns at war with each other."[45] Drawing upon this definition, the defense argued that it was impossible to convict the defendants of piracy when "they honestly believed that there was a valid Government called the Confederate States, and that they had a right to act under it."[46] To that end, the sole witness for the defense — a lieutenant in the Confederate navy — testified that he had seen the *Savannah* "with the Confederate flag flying," and that Captain Baker appeared to be dressed in a Confederate uniform.[47]

Perhaps the most remarkable argument came from the leading criminal defense lawyer of the day, James T. Brady. He began by questioning the legitimacy of the U.S. goals in fighting against the secessionist states of the Confederacy:

A war carried on for what? What is to be its end, gentlemen of the Jury? The war to which you like myself, and all classes and all denominations of the North have given a cheerful and vigorous support — pouring out treasure and blood as freely as water — what is it for? Not to look at the result which must come out of it is folly; and it is the folly that pervades the whole American people. Suppose it were now announced that the entire Southern forces had fled in precipitate retreat before our advancing hosts, and that the American flag waved over every inch of American soil — what then? Are we fighting to subjugate the South in the sense in which an emperor would make war on a rebellious province? Is that the theory? Are we fighting to compel the seceded States to remain in the Union against their will? And do we suppose such a thing practicable? Are we fighting simply to regain the property of the Federal Government of which we have been despoiled in the Southern States? Or are we fighting with a covert and secret intention, such as I understand to have been suggested by an eloquent and popular divine in a recent address to a large public audience, some of them, like himself from the Bay State, "that Massachusetts understands very well what she is fighting for"? Is it to effect the abolition of slavery all over the territory of the United States? I will do the Administration justice to say that, so far as it has given the country any statement of its design in prosecuting the war, it has repelled any such object as Negro emancipation. Who can justify the absurd aspect presented by us before the enlightened nations of the Old World, when they find one commander in our army treating slaves as contraband of war; another declaring that they belong to their masters, to whom he returns them; and another treating them all as free. I am an American, and feel the strongest attachment to my country, growing out of affection and duty; but I cannot see that we present before the world, anything like a distinct and palpable theory. But I tell you, and I stand upon that prophecy, as embodying all the little intelligence I possess, that if it be a war for any purposes of mere subjugation — that if it be for the purpose of establishing a dictatorship, or designedly waged for the emancipation of all the slaves, our people never will sustain it at the North.[48]

Strange as the argument may sound to the contemporary ear, it apparently resonated with at least some New Yorkers, as evidenced by the statement in the court transcript that there was "applause, which was checked by the court."[49]

Brady went even farther, defending, if not the institution of slavery itself, certainly the bona fides of those who believed in it:

And the South says: "If you undertake to abolish slavery in any fort, any ceded place, any territory that we have given you for the purposes of a National Government, we will regard that as a breach of faith; for whether you abhor slavery, or only pretend to abhor it, it is the means of your life. I, a Southerner, whose mother was virtuous as yours — whom I loved as much as you loved your mother — received from her at her death, as my inheritance the slaves whom my father purchased — whom I am taught, under my religious belief to regard as property, and whom I will so continue to regard as long as I live." That is the argument of the South; and if men at the South conscientiously believe that, from the knowledge of the sentiments, factions or agitations at the North, such as these, there is an intention to make a raid and a foray on the institution of slavery, deprive them of all the property they have in the world, and condemn them to any stigma — is it any wonder they should express and act upon such an opinion?

Brady then reminded the jurors that they were proud sons of revolutionaries who had seceded from Great Britain by acts of violence that even the British had never deemed crimes:

When the British took possession of this city, they had at one time in custody five thousand persons. That was before any formal declaration of independence — before the formation of a Government *de jure* or *de facto* — and yet, did they ever charge any of the prisoners with being robbers? Not at all.[50]

By turning the case into a debate over the Civil War itself, Brady obviously hoped for a jury deadlock. He could not expect unanimous acceptance of his dissident political views, but he knew that the official antislavery views of the Union were not universally shared by New Yorkers. The gamble paid off, and the jury was unable to reach a verdict. Eventually these defendants were traded for Union prisoners. This turned out to be very fortunate for them, considering the ill treatment suffered by prisoners of war on both sides.

The Trial of Captain Henry Wirz

Date: 1865
Location: District of Columbia
Defendant: Confederate captain Henry Wirz
Charges: Murder, battery, torture
Verdict: Guilty
Sentence: Hanging

Throughout the ages, there have been those who have attempted to rewrite history, especially the history of human atrocities. Some Turks are seeking to erase from the pages of history the attempted genocide of the Armenian people. Holocaust deniers — calling themselves "revisionists" — are now trying to rewrite the most awful episode in modern history. Not surprisingly, there have been repeated efforts to "revise" the history of the American Civil War, especially its most barbaric aspects.

The American Civil War was one of the most brutal internecine struggles in history. It was fought on battlefields, in cities, and, most disturbingly, in prisoner-of-war camps. The savagery of the war is difficult to understand by the usual racial, linguistic, nationalistic, or religious explanations. When different races, religions, or nations engage in combat, each side generally dehumanizes the other. They are killing not merely their enemies, but rather "savages," "heathens," or "inferiors."

Not so in the Civil War. The combatants were, if not brothers, certainly cousins. They shared a common religion, national origin, language, and race (except for the black soldiers of the Union). They also shared a common destiny and future. Yet they killed with the ferocity of eternal enemies.

Perhaps the most inexplicable manifestation of this fraternal hatred was the treatment of prisoners of war, particularly by the Confederacy, and most especially in the "rebel prison" at Andersonville, Georgia, where nearly thirteen thousand prisoners died.[51] Though the prison was originally designed to hold ten thousand prisoners, the Andersonville population swelled to more than thirty-two thousand by August 1864 as a result of the Confederacy's dwindling resources and the breakdown of the formal prisoner exchange system.[52] Reading the record of mistreatment, brutality, and outright murder of the Union prisoners at Andersonville — many of whom were only teenagers — shocks the conscience of any civilized person.

The keeper of the prison was a Swiss émigré named Captain Henry Wirz. Under Wirz's stewardship of the prison camp, which lasted only thirteen months, more Union soldiers died than were killed in action in the combined battles of Gettysburg, Antietam, Second Bull Run, Charlottesville, and the Wilderness. According to witnesses, Wirz boasted that he "could kill more Yankees there than they were killing at the front."[53] But Wirz's victims were unarmed and imprisoned. Most died of malnutrition, disease, exposure, and other preventable causes aggravated by the overcrowded conditions. Some prisoners were hanged, others shot, and still others beaten to death.

Wirz, like other camp commanders later in history, sought to defend himself on the ground that he was simply "obeying the orders of his superiors." And indeed, the Union prosecutors lent some credence to this argument by originally naming as unindicted co-conspirators Jefferson Davis and other leaders of the Confederacy. Subsequently, new charges were prepared that eliminated these leaders as co-conspirators. But after hearing the evidence, the court-martial restored the names of Jefferson Davis and several of the other leaders.

The evidence of Wirz's barbarity and gratuitous cruelty was overwhelming. Dozens of witnesses — Union prisoners, Confederate soldiers, doctors, local farmers, ministers and priests — testified as to the general condition of the camp. One Union soldier from New York described his experience in the prison stockade:

> When I was first put into the stockade I tried to find a place to lie down, but it was a pretty hard matter; I went to two or three places, but it was of no use. One man said that I could not lie down there. Pretty soon I had to fight for a place to lie down on. There was no room there, and they said we had no business there. Of course I got a place after a while. The men were perfect skeletons where I lay. They were in the worst kind of a state, half-naked, filthy, lousy, too sick to get up; I lay on the ground many a night when I couldn't sleep; sometimes on account of men around me groaning in agony. When I would wake up in the morning I would see men dead all around me, perfect skeletons. One man died and lay there so long that he could not be taken out, and they had to bury him where he died.[54]

Several witnesses recalled the particular brutality of Captain Wirz, who used packs of hounds to hunt down fugitive prisoners, and directed the prison sentries to shoot any man who crossed a wooden railing around the camp (called the "dead-line"). One witness described the cold-blooded murder of a defenseless Union prisoner:

> As I came near the gate I saw a cripple — a man with one leg, on crutches; he had lost one leg above the knee. He was asking the sentinel to call Captain Wirz. He called him, and in a few minutes he came up. I stopped to see what was going to be done. . . . This cripple asked him to take him out; he said his

leg was not healed, and that he had enemies in camp who clubbed him. Captain Wirz never answered him, but said to the sentinel, "Shoot that one-legged Yankee devil." I was there and heard the order, and saw the man turn on his crutches to go away. As he turned the sentinel fired, and the ball struck him on the head and passed out at the lower jaw. The man fell over, and expired in a few minutes. . . . The sentry was relieved. . . . Report says that he got a thirty days' furlough.[55]

After a sixty-three-day trial, Wirz was found guilty and hanged.

But the controversy over his court-martial and hanging did not end with his burial in Washington, DC. Several years after Wirz's inglorious death, partisans of the Confederate cause — led by Jefferson Davis himself — tried to revise the history of Andersonville and its barbaric commander. Jefferson Davis published an influential article in which he blamed the "despondency" of the Union soldiers, rather than starvation and execution, for the extraordinary death rate at Andersonville.[56] Eventually, a monument was erected to the memory of Captain Wirz at Andersonville, declaring his innocence and the guilt of those who convicted him. Wirz was officially proclaimed "a martyr" of the Confederacy by the Georgia Division of the United Daughters of the Confederacy, who put the entire blame for the deaths at Andersonville on "causes wholly unavoidable," as well as on Union refusal to arrange prisoner exchanges.

This attempt to "revise, reverse [and] discredit the findings and judgment" of the court-martial and of history stimulated General N. P. Chipman to publish a counterattack in 1911. Chipman acknowledges that he published it "more [in] the spirit of the advocate than of the judge."[57] And indeed, he was an advocate — specifically, the judge advocate who prosecuted Wirz at the court-martial. But he assures the reader that he has presented the testimony and evidence on both sides without having "suppressed any fact which would have tended to strengthen the defense of the accused. . . ."[58]

A reading of Chipman's book supports the author's assurance, since considerable testimony is presented on Wirz's behalf. For example, Chipman reprinted much of the testimony given for the defense by the Reverend Peter Whelan, a priest from Savannah who attended to Catholic prisoners at Andersonville. The Reverend Whelan offered a favorable portrayal of Wirz and attributed many of the problems in the camp to "great moral depravity" among the prisoners:

> Captain Wirz afforded me every facility to visit the prisoners and afford them any relief that was in my power. He never put any obstacles in my way, whether physical or spiritual. . . .
>
> I administered to five of the prisoners who were hanged. There was one of them who was not a Catholic. They were arrested as raiders in the stockade, together with several more who were not condemned. There was a court-martial of the prisoners held on these men and six of them were condemned. They were put in the stocks. I visited them the evening before they were hanged and gave them all the consolations of religion that it was possible for me to do. The next morning Captain Wirz came down to carry them to the stockade to be delivered to the prisoners there. I asked him to delay their execution for another day. He said to me that it was out of his power. They were prisoners who were plundering or robbing and using violence on other prisoners. . . . Captain Wirz said something like, "Boys, I have taken these men out and now I return them to you, having taken good care of them. I now commit them to you. You can do with them as you see fit." Then turning around to the condemned men he said, "May the Lord have mercy on your souls."[59]

Yet the totality of the evidence speaks for itself, and it speaks convincingly of Wirz's moral and legal guilt.

We must never forget, of course, that military history is generally written by the victors rather than the vanquished. This is even truer of postwar military trials. No Union camp commander was placed on trial for the killing of Confederate prisoners, nor was any Union general tried for the destruction of civilian cities.

The trial, conviction, and execution of Captain Wirz make up an important episode in the development of the laws of warfare. Tragically, it did not prevent other atrocities in subsequent wars.

The Trial of the Lincoln Assassins

Date: 1865
Location: District of Columbia
Defendants: Mary Surratt, Lewis Powell, George Atzerodt,
             David Herold, Dr. Samuel Mudd, Samuel
             Arnold, Michael O'Laughlen, and Edman
             Spangler
Charge: Conspiracy to assassinate
Verdict: Guilty
Sentence: Death (Surratt, Powell, Atzerodt, and Herold);
             imprisonment—later pardoned (Mudd, Arnold,
             O'Laughlen, and Spangler)

Criminal trials — particularly those that grow out of highly publicized crimes — are theater. Often the outcome is known in advance. The defendants play to the galleries. And the transcript
reads like a melodrama. The trial of the conspirators who were
convicted of plotting the assassination of President Abraham
Lincoln had an added element of theatrical drama. The central
event — the shooting of the president — actually took place in a
theater. The assassin was himself a well-known actor as well as
the brother of America's most celebrated actor. He was eventually caught and killed because he broke his leg after it became
entangled in the American flag during his escape. The victim
was the most beloved and hated figure of his time. The conspirators were an assortment of characters right out of Dickens.

The trial itself was conducted not by a court of law, but rather by a military commission convened by President Andrew Johnson. It was far from a model of justice, and contemporary jurists will squirm with discomfort at the process as well as some of the outcomes, especially in light of the military tribunals currently proposed for some terrorist suspects. Since the Civil War was essentially over by the time of the assassination — Lee had surrendered to Grant on April 9, 1865, and Lincoln's murder took place a week later — there is a grave doubt about the jurisdiction of a military tribunal to try the civilian defendants. But the trial went forward under tight security and military rules. There was no jury.

The evidence was overwhelmingly against those who actually took part in the shooting of Lincoln, the assault on Secretary of State Seward, and the planned assassinations of Vice President Johnson and General Grant. The verdict of history has sustained these convictions. But the evidence against the alleged accessories — especially Mary Surratt, who ran the boardinghouse in which some of the conspirators roomed, and Dr. Samuel Mudd, who set Booth's broken leg after the assassination — was far less compelling. Doubt persists to this very day about whether Surratt and Mudd knew of the planned assassination plot in advance, or whether Mudd knew it had taken place when he attended to Booth shortly after the shooting. Evidence that would have tended to exculpate the accessories — for example, diary entries by John Wilkes Booth — was suppressed by the military. Other questionable evidence pointing to guilt was accepted uncritically by a commission determined to justify the actions of the military in arresting a large number of conspirators.

This was also a political trial, designed to paint the conspirators — and the Confederacy in general — in the worst possible light. Jefferson Davis was named as an unindicted co-conspirator on the ground that he "incited and encouraged" the actual conspirators.[60] Evidence was introduced about plots by terrorist groups, acting on behalf of the Confederacy "to demoralize the Northern people in a very short time."[61] Witnesses described plans to destroy vessels and public buildings, poison New York City's public water supply, and give Union troops and leaders, including President Lincoln, suitcases of goods that had been "carefully infected in Bermuda with yellow fever, smallpox, and other contagious disesases."[62]

The evidence itself was fairly straightforward, consisting primarily of eyewitness testimony and physical items. The story told by several of the witnesses was full of drama and excitement.[63] (Interestingly, the trial transcript from this Northern court meticulously identified each black witness as "colored," as if to detract from his or her credibility.[64]) Many witnesses described the circumstances of the fatal shot fired in Ford's Theatre, and the subsequent pursuit of Booth; others testified about the simultaneous attempts by Booth's colleagues and co-conspirators to assassinate members of the president's cabinet. At the same moment that Booth fired, for example, defendant Lewis Powell viciously attacked U.S. Secretary of State William Seward as the secretary lay in his bed recovering from a serious injury. Armed with a knife and a pistol, Powell (who was tried under his alias, Lewis Payne) forced his way into Seward's bedroom. Seward's bodyguard described the attack:

That man [pointing to the accused, Lewis Payne] looks like the man that came to Mr. Seward's house on that Friday night. I heard a disturbance in the hall, and opened the door to see what the trouble was; and as I opened the door this man stood close up to it. As soon as it was opened, he struck me with a knife in the forehead, knocked me partially down, and pressed by me to the bed of Mr. Seward, and struck him, wounding him. As soon as I could get on my feet, I endeavored to haul him off the bed, and then he turned upon me. . . .

I saw him strike Mr. Seward with the same knife with which

he cut my forehead. It was a large knife, and he held it with the blade down below his hand. I saw him cut Mr. Seward twice that I am sure of; the first time he struck him on the right cheek, and then he seemed to be cutting around his neck. . . .

Mr. Seward had received all his stabs in bed; but after the man was gone, and I went back to the bed, I found that he had rolled out, and was lying on the floor.

After he was gone we picked up a revolver, or parts of one, and his hat.[65]

The arguments of counsel varied, depending on the nature of the evidence against their particular client. The lawyer for Lewis Powell argued in mitigation of his client's guilt that the young Floridian, who had deserted his post in the army to join the Confederate Secret Service, believed he was acting patriotically. The attorneys for Mary Surratt (whose boardinghouse was the site of several key meetings among the conspirators) and Dr. Samuel Mudd (a country doctor and advocate of slavery, who aided Booth's escape by providing shelter and treatment for his broken leg) challenged both the jurisdiction of the military commission and the sufficiency of the evidence. David Herold's attorney recognized the insurmountable challenge of saving a man who was found with the president's assassin, and who appeared to have masterminded the conspiracy to destabilize the federal government.[66] As such, Herold's attorney made a last-ditch attempt to convince the military commission that his client was no more than "a weak, cowardly, foolish, miserable boy," who was "only wax in the hands of a man like Booth."[67]

The prosecutor insisted that the jurisdiction of the military commission was proper because the insurrection had not yet been completely crushed. He maintained that Jefferson Davis himself was behind the conspiracy, and devoted a considerable part of his argument to making this political point — irrelevant as it was to the trial of the defendants in the dock. His legal arguments, which were eventually rejected by the Supreme Court as well as the court of history, would impose no limitations on military jurisdiction during wartime (or anything resembling wartime):

> How can there be trial by jury for military offenses in time of civil war? If you can not, and do not, try the armed enemy before you shoot him, or the captured enemy before you imprison him, why should you be held to open the civil courts and try the spy, the conspirator and the assassin, in the secret service of the public enemy, by jury, before you convict and punish him? Why not clamor against holding imprisoned the captured armed rebels, deprived of their liberty without due process of law? Are they not citizens? Why not clamor against slaying, for their crime of treason, which is cognizable in the civil courts, by your rifled ordnance and the leaden hail of your musketry in battle, these public enemies, without trial by jury? Are they not citizens? Why is the clamor confined exclusively to the trial by military tribunals of justice of traitorous spies, traitorous conspirators, and assassins hired to do secretly what the armed rebel attempts to do openly — murder your nationality by assassinating its defenders and its executive officers? Nothing can be clearer than that the rebel captured prisoner, being a citizen of the republic, is as much entitled to trial by jury before he is committed to prison, as the spy, or the aider and the abettor of the treason by conspiracy — and assassination, being a citizen, is entitled to such trial by jury, before he is subjected to the just punishment of the law for his great crime. I think that in time of war the remark of Montesquieu, touching the civil judiciary, is true: that "it is next to nothing."

But this open-ended argument, which was ultimately rejected in this nation — but still has some resonance today, as we battle terrorism — carried the day during the frenzied period following the Lincoln assassination. The frenzy persisted even after the guilty verdicts were rendered. Four of the conspirators, including Mary Surratt, were sentenced on July 6, 1865, to be "hung by the neck until . . . dead." The president ordered these death sentences to be carried out two days later, with no appeal or other review. Surratt's lawyers immediately applied to the federal court for a writ of habeas corpus. The court issued the writ and commanded Surratt's jailer to produce her so that the court could consider the legality of her detention and capital sentence. But President Johnson "especially" suspended the writ of habeas corpus for this case, and the court declared itself powerless to act. The executions were carried out as scheduled.

The trial of the Lincoln conspirators was not a bright episode in the history of American jurisprudence. The fact that doubt still persists about the guilt of some of those convicted is a reflection of the rush-to-judgment attitude manifested by the military commission, which — like other such commissions throughout history — seemed more concerned about efficiency than due process. As we once again live in an age of military commissions to try foreign terrorists, we should remember the history of past commissions and the questionable justice they provided during earlier conflicts and times of crisis.

1. David Herbert Donald et al., *The Civil War and Reconstruction* (New York: W. W. Norton and Co., 2001), p. 394.

2. *Ibid.*, p. 404.

3. James McPherson, *Ordeal by Fire: The Civil War and Reconstruction* (New York: Alfred A. Knopf, 1982), p. 174; Donald, p. 405.

4. The Editors of Time-Life Books, *The Blockade: Runners and Raiders* (Alexandria: Time-Life Books, 1983), p. 28.

5. *Blockade*, p. 28; Webb Garrison, *Civil War Hostages: Hostage Taking in the Civil War* (Shippensburg, PA: White Mane Books, 2000), p. 14.

6. *Blockade*, p. 28.

7. Lonnie Speer, *Portals to Hell: Military Prisons of the Civil War* (Mechanicsburg, PA: Stackpole Books, 1997), p. 33.

8. Garrison, p. 14.

9. *Blockade*, 28; Garrison, pp. 14–15.

10. *Blockade*, p. 28.

11. Quoted in *ibid.*

12. Garrison, p. 15.

13. McPherson, pp. 174–75.

14. *Ibid.*, p. 175.

15. *Ibid.* McPherson notes that, by this time, the Union blockade and the refusal of neutral ports to admit prizes taken by privateers had effectively ended privateering. Confederate naval cruisers replaced the privateers in commerce raiding.

16. Donald, p. 244.

17. *Ibid.*

18. *Ibid.*

19. *Ibid.*

20. *Ibid.*, p. 245; McPherson, pp. 450–51 (noting that both modern historians and Northerners at the time questioned why Union prisoners at Andersonville were not permitted to build huts out of wood from the abundant pine forests surrounding the prison — instead, the prisoners were relegated to ragged tents with little space in between them).

21. Donald, p. 245.

22. McPherson, p. 450; Donald, p. 245.

23. McPherson, p. 450.

24. *Ibid.*, p. 455. The Confederacy refused to recognize black troops as legitimate soldiers. Donald, p. 243.

25. McPherson, p. 455.

26. *Ibid.*, pp. 353, 455.

27. Donald, p. 243.

28. *Ibid.*

29. McPherson, p. 456.

30. *Ibid.*, p. 416.

31. Donald, pp. 424–27.

32. McPherson, p. 456; Donald, p. 427.

33. Donald, p. 472.

34. Abraham Lincoln, "Second Inaugural Address," Mar. 4, 1865, in *Inaugural Addresses*, p. 143.

35. Donald, p. 449.

36. *Ibid.*, p. 475 (as compared to 30 out of 10,000 in World War II).

37. McPherson, p. 483.

38. *Ibid.*

39. *Ibid.*

40. *Ibid.*

41. Douglas Linder, "Trial of the Lincoln Assassination Conspirators," in *Famous American Trials* (2000), www.law.umkc.edu/faculty/projects/ftrials/lincolnconspiracy/lincolnconspiracy.html.

42. McPherson, p. 484.

43. Cited in A. F. Warburton, *Trial of the Officers and Crew of the Privateer Savannah, on the Charge of Piracy* (New York: The Notable Trials Library, 1997), p. 19.

44. Cited in *ibid.*, pp. 66–67.

45. Cited in *ibid.*, p. 239.

46. Cited in *ibid.*, p. 241.

47. Cited in *ibid.*, pp. 112–13.

48. Cited in *ibid.*, pp. 237–38.

49. *Ibid.*, p. 238.

50. *Ibid.*

51. National Park Service, *Andersonville National Historic Site* (2003), www.nps.gov/ande/.

52. National Park Service, Southeast Archaeological Center, *Conditions at Andersonville Prison*, www.cr.nps.gov/seac/andecon.htm.

53. Testimony of O. S. Belcher, cited in General N. P. Chipman, *The Tragedy of Andersonville: Trial of Captain Henry Wirz* (Birmingham: The Notable Trials Library, 1990), p. 258.

54. Testimony of Thomas H. Horne, cited in *ibid.*, p. 177.

55. Testimony of Samuel D. Brown, cited in *ibid.*, p. 332.

56. Cited in *ibid.*, p. 21.

57. *Ibid.*, p. 500.

58. *Ibid.*

59. Testimony of the Reverend Peter Whelan, cited in *ibid.*, p. 194.

60. Cited in Benn Pitman, ed., *The Assassination of President Lincoln and the Trial of the Conspirators* (Birmingham: The Legal Classics Library, 1982), p. 19.

61. *Ibid.*, p. 48.

62. Testimony of Godfrey Joseph Hyams, cited in *ibid.*, p. 55.

63. *Ibid.*, pp. 47–57.

64. See, e.g., *ibid.*, p. 75.

65. Testimony of Sergeant George F. Robinson, cited in *ibid.*, pp. 155–56.

66. Douglas Linder, "Biography and Images of David Herold, Assassination Conspirator," *Trial of the Lincoln Assassination Conspirators* (2002), www.law.umkc.edu/faculty/projects/ftrials/lincolnconspiracy/herold.html.

67. Argument of Frederick Stone, cited in Pitman, p. 274.

PART VI

The Post–Civil War Period

THE END OF THE CIVIL WAR and the assassination of Abraham Lincoln, less than a week apart in April 1865, brought Vice President Andrew Johnson — a Tennessee Democrat who had served as a state legislator, governor, congressman, and senator — into the White House barely one month into Lincoln's second term.[1] Johnson, like Lincoln, was a "self-made man of humble background" who had opposed Southern secession.[2] With the war over, Johnson and the nation faced the issue of what sort of reconstruction policy to impose on the economically devastated South. Union victory in the war brought hope to the freed slaves, bitterness to white Southerners — and uncertainty to both.[3] Thus, the main tasks of a reconstruction policy were to keep peace, reintegrate the former Confederate states into the Union, and secure basic rights for the newly liberated slaves.[4]

From the outset, Johnson and the Republicans, who controlled Congress at the time, locked horns over the proper course of Reconstruction, becoming publicly embroiled in a bitter struggle for control.

To preserve the newly won freedom of blacks in the South, the Republicans passed the Fourteenth Amendment in June 1866, making its ratification by the former Confederate states a requirement for reentry into the Union and thereby preventing Democrats from easily repealing a statute if they later regained control of Congress.[5] The amendment endowed all Americans with the rights of citizenship and guaranteed them "the equal protection of the laws."[6] Johnson publicly denounced the Fourteenth Amendment, and white Southerners vehemently objected to it; white mob massacres of blacks in Memphis and New Orleans in mid-1866 killed more than eighty people.[7] Interestingly, Susan B. Anthony, Elizabeth Cady Stanton, and other leaders of the women's suffrage movement — who had vigorously opposed slavery — felt betrayed by the amendment's focus on black males and its silence on women; they demanded the same legal recognition and rights.[8] Angered that their political rights had been subordinated to those of black men, writes historian Eric Foner, "[w]omen's leaders now embarked on a course that severed their historic alliance with abolitionism and created an independent feminist movement."[9] The Fourteenth Amendment became the Republican platform for the 1866 congressional elections, in which the Republicans retained two-thirds majorities in both chambers with sweeping victories.[10]

The enmity between Johnson and Congress boiled over in late 1867 and early 1868 when Johnson decided to test the constitutionality of the Tenure of Office Act, which provided that all federal officials whose appointment required Senate confirmation could be removed only with the consent of the Senate. Johnson's decision to fire the secretary of war triggered the Republican-led impeachment against him. Johnson had never gotten along with Edwin Stanton, the secretary of war appointed by Lincoln in his first term; the breaking point was Stanton's active role in helping the Republicans frame the laws that imposed Reconstruction on the South. When Congress adjourned in 1867, Johnson demanded Stanton's resignation. Stanton refused, and Johnson offered the post to General Ulysses S. Grant (who would succeed Johnson as president); Grant accepted the post, a move that angered Radical Republicans.[11] When Congress reconvened, it passed a resolution in January 1868 ordering Stanton's reinstatement; Grant turned the office back over to Stanton.[12] Determined to test the constitutionality of the Tenure of Office Act, which prohibited the appointment of an interim cabinet officer while Congress was in session, Johnson violated the act by appointing General Lorenzo Thomas as the new interim secretary of war.[13] At the urging of Republican senators, Stanton disobeyed Johnson's order, barricaded himself in his office, and refused to surrender the keys.[14] The stage was set for one of the nation's most dramatic political confrontations.

The House of Representatives impeached Johnson 126–47 in February 1868, three days after Johnson's appointment of Thomas — and before even discussing or drafting articles of impeachment.[15] Every Republican voted for impeachment; all the opposition came from Democrats.[16] Johnson would now be tried before the Senate acting as a jury, with Chief Justice Salmon Chase presiding as judge; conviction required a two-thirds majority vote.[17] House Republicans adopted eleven formal articles of impeachment, the majority of which dealt with Johnson's violation of the Tenure of Office Act — the eleventh was the "omnibus" article, encompassing all the charges of the previous ten.[18] But the engine driving the impeachment effort, even if tacitly, was Johnson's unyielding opposition to the Republican Reconstruction program.[19]

Historian James McPherson has noted that Johnson's lawyers "demonstrated a good deal more legal acumen than did the impeachment managers," who relied on emotional appeals and political passions in their arguments for Johnson's removal.[20] During the trial, Johnson — whom Supreme Court justice David Davis had described as "obstinate, self-willed, combative" and entirely unfit for office — behaved with dignity and restraint, refraining from any public denunciation of Congress.[21] In the end, the Senate voted 35–19 for Johnson's removal — one vote short of the necessary two-thirds majority. Johnson owed his survival to seven moderate Republicans (known as the recusants) who voted against his removal.[22]

Ulysses S. Grant, the famed war hero of the Union, won the 1868 election as a Republican, over Democrat Horatio Seymour, the wartime governor of New York.[23] Four years later Grant was reelected over Horace Greeley, but his second term was highlighted by graft and corruption, which fed into the economic depression. Even though historians generally agree that

Grant himself was personally honest, according to David Herbert Donald, he "displayed abysmal judgment in picking advisors and indefensible laxity in overseeing their activities."[24]

The 1872 election also occasioned the trial of Susan B. Anthony for voting without a legal right to do so. Anthony went on trial in federal district court in Canandaigua, New York (Ontario County), in June 1873, before a jury of twelve white men and a packed courthouse; former president Millard Fillmore and two U.S. senators attended the trial.[25] The judge, Ward Hunt, was an opponent of female suffrage, and he treated Anthony with contempt throughout the trial. Hunt refused to allow Anthony to defend herself because, as a woman, she was not competent as a witness on her own behalf.[26] Holding that neither the Fourteenth nor the Fifteenth Amendment gave women the right to vote, Hunt determined that Anthony had knowingly violated the law.[27] Incredibly, he ordered the jurors to deliver a guilty verdict without allowing them any deliberation, an obvious violation of Anthony's right to a trial by jury — prompting Anthony to call the order "the greatest judicial outrage ever recorded."[28] Hunt fined Anthony one hundred dollars, but she refused to pay it. Even though Anthony was supposed to remain imprisoned until the fine was paid, Hunt did not apply this rule; he knew that if he did, Anthony could bring her case to the Supreme Court under a writ of habeas corpus.[29] Anthony later submitted a request to Congress to have the fine remitted, which would have undercut the judge's decision, but that failed. Nevertheless, Anthony's trial received prominent national attention and press coverage, which included much criticism of her prosecution — she herself printed and distributed three thousand copies of the courtroom proceedings.[30]

Two years after Anthony's trial, another well-known woman went on trial, but under starkly different circumstances. Mary Todd Lincoln had been a widow for just over a decade when her son, Robert, swore out a warrant for her arrest on a charge of insanity in May 1875.[31] Mary Todd Lincoln was brought to trial in the Cook County Courthouse; the trial lasted three hours and involved seventeen witnesses, including Robert Lincoln.[32] The spectacle of a former first lady standing trial for insanity — on charges brought by her own son — shocked the nation. Mary Todd Lincoln's lawyer did not contest the case, nor did he call any witnesses, including the former first lady.[33] The all-male jury deliberated ten minutes before finding her insane.[34] She was forced to surrender the valuable bonds she had sewn into her petticoat, and the court appointed a conservator to take control of her money; she was ordered to confinement at Bellevue, a private asylum forty miles outside Chicago.[35] She spent nearly four months in the asylum and in September 1875 returned to Springfield, where she lived with her sister and battled Robert for control of her property.[36] In June 1876, Mary Todd Lincoln petitioned the court for a jury to judge her condition — the jury found her sane and mentally and legally capable of managing her own estate. She died in July 1882, and for her funeral the mayor of Springfield declared a holiday, as thousands of people lined the streets to bid farewell.[37]

Following the scandal-plagued Grant presidency, the parties turned to more politically reputable candidates in the 1876 election. The Republicans ran Rutherford B. Hayes, a Civil War general and three-term governor of Ohio, against the Democrat Samuel Tilden, the New York governor who helped bring down Boss Tweed.[38] Tilden won the popular vote by a slim margin, but controversy surrounded the electoral vote. Tilden led Hayes in the electoral vote count, 184–165, one vote short of the necessary majority; an additional 20 electoral votes (19 of which came from Florida, Louisiana, and South Carolina) were in dispute due to voting fraud.[39] Congress created a special electoral commission, comprising five congressmen, five senators, and five Supreme Court justices, to investigate the matter.[40] The commission voted along party lines to award the twenty disputed electoral votes — and with them, the election — to Hayes. (Sound familiar?) In exchange for the White House — as part of the so-called Compromise of 1877 — Hayes had promised the withdrawal of federal troops from Louisiana and South Carolina, and no further federal intervention in the South.[41] Hayes pledged and carried out a generous policy to help the South rebuild with internal improvements and appropriations, supporting its self-government and the removal of the "carpetbaggers" — Northern politicians who had traveled south with their "carpetbags" to occupy the defeated states.[42] In his inaugural address, Hayes announced an unofficial end to Reconstruction. This, of course, also meant the unofficial end of black voting rights in the South.

Following Hayes's relatively uneventful term in office, James A. Garfield, the Republican candidate, won the 1880 presidential election. A self-made man born in a log cabin (like Lincoln), Garfield had served as a major general during the Civil War and later as an Ohio congressman in the House for eighteen years before becoming president.[43]

But in July 1881, after barely four months in office, Garfield was assassinated by Charles Guiteau in a Washington railroad station. Guiteau's trial, which one author has called "the biggest event in Washington since the impeachment of Andrew Johnson," opened in November 1881.[44] Represented by his brother-in-law, Guiteau frequently interrupted the court proceedings.[45] Guiteau thought his most effective legal strategy was a defense that argued medical malpractice by the doctors who operated on Garfield: "the doctors killed the President, not I, they were guilty of murder."[46] (A similar defense recently worked in the prosecution of Limerick Nelson, a young black man charged with murdering a Chasidic Jew during a race riot in Brooklyn.) Instead, Guiteau's lawyers argued an insanity defense. Guiteau testified for nearly a week, rambling on about his life story.[47] Guiteau's defense team sent a set of questions to the White House for President Chester A. Arthur, who succeeded Hayes, to answer, regarding his knowledge of or contacts with Guiteau.[48] The defense also called as a witness then-senator (and future president) Benjamin Harrison, who testified that Guiteau had unsuccessfully sought his help in obtaining a job.[49] In total, the prosecution called twenty-three doctors to testify, and the defense called thirteen.[50] Guiteau was convicted in January 1882 by the jury, which had deliberated less than one hour; the judge set Guiteau's execution date for June of that year.[51] In the meantime, 160 doctors sent a petition to Arthur stating that they believed Guiteau was insane and asking for clemency. Arthur denied the plea, and Guiteau was hanged on June 30, 1882.[52]

The assassination of Lincoln and the end of the Civil War marked the beginning of a long era of conflict based on regionalism, race, gender, and national origin. Several of the important trials that represent the period between 1865 and the end of the nineteenth century reflect the continuing influence of Lincoln and the violent circumstances of his death. The first case involved the impeachment of Lincoln's successor, Andrew Johnson; the next marked a transition to our future of women's suffrage; the third revolved around the mental status of Lincoln's widow; and the fourth concerned the man who assassinated one of Lincoln's successors, James A. Garfield. The final trial, that of Lizzie Borden, demonstrated that women sometimes benefited from their legal status as weak and docile followers who had been neglected when the Thirteenth, Fourteenth, and Fifteenth Amendments granted equality and the vote — at least in theory — to African American males.

The Trial of Andrew Johnson

Date: 1868
Location: District of Columbia
Defendant: President Andrew Johnson
Charge: High crimes and misdemeanors
Verdict: Not guilty

President Nixon's resignation in 1974, to avoid almost certain impeachment, and the impeachment and acquittal of President Clinton in 1998–99 renewed interest in the constitutional mechanism for removing a president of the United States. The events also revived historical interest in the earlier presidential impeachment and removal trial in the United States against President Andrew Johnson in 1868.

The process of impeachment and removal is inherently political, despite the constitutional requirement of an "impeachment for, and conviction of, treason, bribery, or other high crimes and misdemeanors." *Conviction* refers to the process by which the Senate decides, by a two-thirds vote, that the president is guilty of the crimes for which the House has impeached him. Thus, a president may not properly be impeached for incompetence or political failure. (The Twenty-fifth Amendment, ratified in 1967, provides a mechanism for temporarily replacing a disabled president.) The Constitution seems to contemplate the availability of impeachment and removal as an extraordinary remedy to be used only against corrupt criminals who hold high office. The electoral process is the ordinary remedy for expressing dissatisfaction with incompetent officeholders.

The impeachment of President Andrew Johnson violated both the letter and the spirit of the Constitution. It was a thoroughly political action, motivated entirely by the raging dispute over Reconstruction that followed the end of the Civil War and the assassination of President Abraham Lincoln. Lincoln's vice president was a lifelong Democrat from Tennessee who had owned slaves, but who had opposed the secession of the Southern states and fought against the Confederacy. Notwithstanding his loyalty to the Union during the Civil War, Johnson opposed the so-called radical approach to Reconstruction advocated by many Republican lawmakers, who feared that Democratic domination of Southern politics would deny any hope of equality to the newly freed slaves, and might also threaten Republican control of national politics.

The provoking event was President Johnson's decision to fire Secretary of War Edwin M. Stanton in the face of the Tenure of Office Act. Johnson, along with many others, believed that the Tenure of Office Act — passed over his veto — was an unconstitutional constraint on the power of the executive. Even some who eventually supported Johnson's impeachment had earlier expressed doubts about the constitutionality of the act. It was a complex and controversial issue about which reasonable people could, and did, disagree. But it was not, by any stretch of the imagination or of the language of the Constitution, a legitimate basis for impeachment and removal of a president.

Nevertheless, President Johnson was impeached by the House after a prior impeachment attempt had failed. Much of the debate centered on general complaints against the president, unrelated to the specific charge.[53] As one congressman candidly put it: "It is true the removal of the Secretary of War is a relatively small matter, and I believe it would be regarded as scarcely a sufficient ground for this proceeding, if not considered in the light of greater previous offenses." Another chastised Johnson as a "despicable, besotted . . . accidental President."

The trial of the president in the Senate was no less political than the impeachment in the House of Representatives, despite the judicial appearance of the tribunal. The Senate was presided over by the chief justice of the United States. The fifty-four senators were anything but impartial jurors. Forty-two of them were Republicans, and most of those had already declared Johnson guilty. But a two-thirds vote was needed to convict.

Retired Supreme Court justice Benjamin Curtis, who had achieved fame by dissenting in the notorious Dred Scott case, represented President Johnson. The prosecutor was an equally illustrious lawyer named Benjamin Butler. This was not, however, a case that would be won or lost on advocacy skills. It would be decided by backroom politics and bargaining for votes. Hyperbole was the order of the day during the debates, as Johnson's opponents declared his actions to be unprecedented in their baseness. For example: "Never in the history of any free government has there been so base, so gross, so unjustifiable an attempt upon the part of the executive, whether Emperor, King or President, to destroy the just authority of another department of the government."

Johnson's champions had equally overstated criticisms of the Tenure of Office Act, declaring it to be "the most offensive law that has ever been passed since the government was organized." Extreme pressure was placed on senators to change their votes. In the end, thirty-five senators voted to convict, nineteen to acquit. President Johnson was, therefore, acquitted.

It was plainly the correct result. A conviction would have established a terrible precedent. As one senator perceptively argued:

Once set the example of impeaching the President, for what, when the excitement of the hour shall have subsided, will be regarded as insufficient causes, as several of those now alleged against the President were decided to be by the House of Representatives only a few months since, and no future President will be safe who happens to differ with a majority of the House and two-thirds of the Senate on any measure deemed by them important, particularly if of a political character. Blinded by partisan zeal, with such an example before them, they will not scruple to remove out of the way any obstacle to the accomplishment of their purposes, and what then becomes of the checks and balances of the Constitution, so carefully devised and so vital to its perpetuity? They are all gone.

This was not only a transforming political event but also a great trial, even though it took place on the Senate floor rather than in a courtroom. It was a great trial because, in the end, it preserved — perhaps even strengthened — our system of checks and balances. Impeachment is a part of that delicate system, and following the Johnson debacle it was widely believed that it would never again be used improperly. But as we shall see, it almost certainly was, a century and a quarter later.

The Trial of Susan B. Anthony

Date: 1873
Location: New York State
Defendant: Susan B. Anthony
Charge: Voting
Verdict: Guilty
Sentence: Fine

The trial of Susan B. Anthony, for the "crime" of voting, is one of the most remarkable events in American legal and political history. The great suffragette decided to test the male-only voting laws of New York and so, in 1872, she registered to vote. By a 2–1 decision, the election inspectors accepted her registration, and she was allowed to cast her ballot. Then she and the election inspectors were indicted and brought to trial before the district court in Canandaigua, New York. Her trial was conducted by Judge Ward Hunt, a cantankerous and rigid jurist who was utterly unsympathetic to women's suffrage in general and Ms. Anthony in particular. Anthony's lawyer, Judge Henry R. Selden, was an eloquent supporter of women's suffrage. He — it had to be a "he," since women could not practice law — presented her case brilliantly, arguing that various provisions of the U.S. Constitution, including the privileges and immunities clause and the equal protection clause of the Fourteenth Amendment, forbid discrimination in voting based on sex:

The only alleged ground of illegality of the defendant's vote is that she is a woman. If the same act had been done by her brother under the same circumstances the act would have been not only innocent, but honorable and laudable; but having been done by a woman it is said to be a crime. The crime therefore consists not in the act done, but in the simple fact that the person doing it was a woman and not a man. I believe this is the first instance in which a woman has been arraigned in a criminal court, merely on account of her sex.[54]

Selden then went on to argue that even if he and his client were mistaken about her right to vote, that mistake would be a reasonable one, based on legal advice she had been given. She could not be convicted of a crime because she did not have a guilty state of mind:

Miss Anthony believed, and was advised that she had a right to vote. She may also have been advised, as was clearly the fact, that the question as to her right could not be brought before the courts for trial, without her voting or offering to vote, and if either was criminal, the one was as much so as the other. Therefore, she stands now arraigned as a criminal, for taking the only steps by which it was possible to bring the great constitutional question, as to her right, before the tribunals of the country for adjudication. If for thus acting, in the most perfect good faith, with motive as pure and impulses as noble as any which can find place in your honor's breast in the administration of justice she is by the laws of her country to be condemned as a criminal, she must abide the consequences. Her condemnation, however, under such circumstances, would only add another most weighty reason to those which I have already advanced, to show that women need the aid of the ballot for their protection.[55]

The judge ruled, as a matter of law, that women did not have the right to vote and that a good-faith belief that they did was not a defense to the crime of unlawful voting. Then, in a remarkable act of judicial tyranny, he directed the jury to enter a verdict of guilty. The jury sat mute. The judge then directed the clerk to enter the jury's verdict of guilty. The defense attorney asked that the jury be polled. The judge refused and ordered the jury discharged. Several jurors were apparently ready to acquit Anthony, but the judge gave them no opportunity to express their views. In Judge Hunt's view, a woman not only had no right to vote, she had no right to a jury verdict that might not find her guilty.

Susan B. Anthony was then asked whether she had "anything to say" before her sentence was imposed. She made an impassioned speech denouncing the verdict. The judge repeatedly tried to stop her, but she would not be silenced. The judge, not wanting to make a martyr of her by imprisoning her for contempt, had no choice but to let her continue. In the end, he sentenced her to pay a fine of one hundred dollars. Anthony refused:

> May it please your honor, I shall never pay a dollar of your unjust penalty. All the stock in trade I possess is a $10,000 debt, incurred by publishing my paper — *The Revolution* — four years ago, the sole object of which was to educate all women to do precisely as I have done, rebel against your man-made, unjust, unconstitutional forms of law, that tax, fine, imprison and hang women, while they deny them the right of representation in the government; and I shall work on with might and main to pay every dollar of that honest debt, but not a penny shall go to this unjust claim. And I shall earnestly and persistently continue to urge all women to the practical recognition of the old revolutionary maxim, that "Resistance to tyranny is obedience to God."[56]

Again, the judge refused to make a martyr of her: "Madam, the Court will not order you committed until the fine is paid."[57]

And so the case ended, but the cause continued unabated until women were finally given the right to vote by constitutional amendment.

This case demonstrates that political cases, like hard ones, often make bad law. The courts are not suited to dealing with great issues of policy, such as women's suffrage. What we get are speeches, posturing, and politics — both from the litigants and from the judge. The trial of Susan B. Anthony was a political milestone on the long road to sexual equality, but the inequity perpetrated in that case remains a legal millstone around the neck of justice.

The Trial of Mary Todd Lincoln

Date: 1875
Location: Chicago, Illinois
Defendant: Mary Todd Lincoln
Charge: Insanity
Verdict: Guilty
Sentence: Served four months

The very idea that a former first lady of the United States could be railroaded into an insane asylum by family members seeking to gain control of her money seems ludicrous, even to contemporary sensibilities jaded by conspiracy theories. But the conventional wisdom for generations was that Robert Lincoln — the last surviving child of the assassinated president — conspired with lawyers, doctors, and others to commit his mother and take her money. In 1975, a file was discovered in Robert Lincoln's home that appears to support the opposite conclusion — that Mary Todd Lincoln was, in fact, insane, and that her son acted in her interest.[58]

There is little doubt that Mary Todd Lincoln was a disturbed and eccentric woman, especially following the death of her husband and three of her four sons. Even while she was serving as first lady, her husband saw signs of peculiarity, especially when it came to money. After Abraham Lincoln's death, she carried the family fortune — some fifty-six thousand dollars in negotiable securities — sewed into her petticoat. The securities were forcibly removed from her person when the jury reached its verdict that she was insane. These facts — plus the disturbing realization that her own lawyer was handpicked by the Lincoln family to prevent her from securing "some mischievous lawyer to make us trouble"— led many Americans to the conclusion that the commitment of Mrs. Lincoln was yet another instance, among many, of venal men using the insanity laws of the day against vulnerable women.

During the post–Civil War period, reformers focused public attention on patriarchal laws that made it easy for a husband to commit his wife to an asylum. Typical of those laws was the following: "Married women and infants who, in the judgment of the medical superintendent are evidently insane or distracted, may be entered or detained in the hospital at the request of the husband, of the women, or parent, or guardian of the infants, without the evidence of insanity or distraction required in other cases."

In an age when divorce was difficult, commitment sometimes served as a convenient surrogate. Dr. Phyllis Chesler, in her classic work *Women and Madness,* documented the scandalous misuses to which such statutes were put. This was part of the larger pattern of medical discrimination against women. "Womankind had no worse enemy in the nineteenth century than the medical doctor. This is among the principal findings of the modern literature on woman's history. Medical 'science' in Mrs. Lincoln's era merely endorsed and reinforced the dominant view of woman's frailty, low intellect, and restricted social destiny. Medical school lectures and gynecological manuals provide impressive evidence of woman's degraded condition in that era."

It is noteworthy that the law of Illinois, where the Mary Todd Lincoln commitment occurred, provided greater safeguards, including trial by jury, than most other states. Nonetheless, it was an easy matter for the well-connected Robert Lincoln to hire the foremost lawyer and expert of the day and to convince a jury that his eccentric mother was insane and needed to be put away for her own good. The asylum to which she was sent was a far cry from the snake pits to which the indigent insane were sometimes sent, or even from the large public asylums, which claimed staggeringly high cure rates. (These rates were largely a function of the fact that many marginally ill and relatively healthy wives, paupers, and other disenfranchised people were originally misdiagnosed as insane and were quickly "cured" after a few days of rest, relaxation, and hot baths.) Bellevue — not to be confused with New York's large public asylum — was a small, private home for the wealthy elite. Mrs. Lincoln was permitted carriage rides, croquet games, and other amenities not typically accorded mental patients around the country. Nonetheless, she was determined to gain her release, and she had some powerful allies who knew which buttons to press. Judge James Bradwell and his wife, Myra, were friends of Mrs. Lincoln. Even more significant, they were ardent reformers and early feminists who were in the forefront of the movement for reform of the commitment laws. They threatened legal action, orchestrated press coverage, and made it plain that they would not relent until their friend was released. Mary Todd Lincoln was released and taken to Chicago in early September 1875, after a relatively brief confinement. The conservatorship over her continued. Within three months, she was carrying a pistol and threatening to kill her son. Nonetheless, by June 1876, Robert Lincoln agreed to end the conservatorship and a jury was quickly impaneled to find that Mrs. Lincoln was now "restored to reason and is capable to manage and control her estate."

Shortly after she was declared sane, Mrs. Lincoln embarked to Europe, apparently out of fear that her son would once again try to have her found insane. When her health began to deteriorate, she traveled back to the United States. On the trip back, she nearly stumbled down a steep flight of stairs, but her life was saved by the famous actress Sarah Bernhardt, who caught hold of her clothing. Mrs. Lincoln thanked the actress, but Bernhardt later observed that she had "done this unhappy woman the only service that I ought not have done her — I had saved her from death." In less than two years, Mrs. Lincoln was dead. She had reconciled with her son — by then secretary of war in the Garfield administration — shortly before her demise.

There is a darker, more conspiratorial theory of what happened to Mrs. Lincoln: "A popular book, *The Trial of Mary Todd Lincoln,* by James Rhodes and Dean Jauchius, weaves a tale of political conspiracy into the case, suggesting that David Davis and other Liberal Republicans maneuvered Robert into committing his mother in order to ruin his promise as a politician with the magical vote-getting name of Lincoln. Robert was a staunch adherent of the more conservative wing of the Republican Party, the faction that stalwartly supported Ulysses S. Grant."[59]

On the opposite side from the conspiracy theorists are the Lincoln hagiographers. To them, no Lincoln could do wrong. Several books were written from this perspective, arguing that Robert did nothing improper in temporarily committing his mother, but that Mary was not really insane, just a grieving widow.

In the end, history is often the victim of negligence in failing to preserve records. Because so much of the primary evidence no longer exists, we will never know for certain how sick Mary actually was, what Robert's motives really were, or whether the judicial proceedings were fair. What we can say with some degree of confidence is that cases of this kind are rarely black and white. The shades of gray that dominate in familial matters involving marginal mental illness, especially following personal tragedy, make it impossible to point a finger of blame at any one target. It is interesting to note in this regard that a quarter century after his mother's problems, Robert himself suffered what he called a "nervous breakdown" following the death of a close friend.

The available evidence would seem to contradict both the "political conspiracy" and the "Lincolns can do no wrong" theories. What seems to have been at issue was a combination of legitimate filial concern about a disturbed mother, family embarrassment over her public displays of eccentricity, and, perhaps, a desire to preserve the family wealth.

The discovery of the "MTL Insanity File" in a locked closet in Robert's summerhouse allowed the case to be reopened in the court of history. The file contained many documents — legal, medical, and financial — relating to the commitment of Mary Todd Lincoln, and closed many, but not all, of the gaps deemed significant by conspiracy theorists. Yet it failed to answer the human question of why Robert, who went to such great efforts to destroy so many of his father's and his own documents, would have preserved this file for half a century after his mother's death. Perhaps he believed that it would vindicate him in the court of public opinion, though it contained much material from which critical judgments about his own conduct could be reached. Perhaps he never got around to destroying them. If so, this would be one instance of negligence helping history.

In any event, this was an important trial, both in the history of commitment of the mentally ill and of the rights of women, because it involved one of the most famous women of the day, and thereby focused public attention on serious abuses in our legal system. In the decades — and the trials — that follow, we will see these abuses addressed by advocates, scholars, and legislators, and we will see them come to court again and again.

The Trial of the Assassin Guiteau

Date: 1881
Location: District of Columbia
Defendant: Charles Guiteau
Charge: Murder
Verdict: Guilty
Sentence: Hanging

Whenever I read accounts of great old trials, I marvel at how little has really changed over the years. Had Charles Guiteau — the
madman who assassinated President James A. Garfield — been
on trial today, and had his lawyers invoked an insanity defense,
the case would have played itself out quite similarly to the way it
did in 1881.

Guiteau, like many assassins of prominent figures, was clearly
suffering from some mental illness. His views of politics, religion, and life were bizarre. But he was not a totally dysfunctional
psychotic. He was capable of planning and executing his plot, as
well as articulating a plausible, if unconventional, explanation
for his conduct. Guiteau was, he insisted, God's messenger who
was merely carrying out the Lord's command. The governing criteria of the M'Naghten Rule (the British test for insanity employed throughout the United States during the nineteenth
century) limited the insanity defense to those mentally ill defendants who did not understand the nature or quality of their actions or did not know they were legally wrong. It was a close

question whether Guiteau fit this description, but the public was demanding his neck, and the legal system gave short shrift to his lawyers' claims of insanity. Nor did Guiteau himself want to raise the excuse of mental illness, since that would deflect attention from his messianic mission. "I would rather be hung as a man than acquitted as a fool," he shouted to the jury. (Guiteau was repeatedly threatened with removal from the courtroom, but he persisted in his outbursts.)

As it is today, "the defense of insanity was bitterly controversial" in the 1880s and was popularly referred to as the "insanity dodge."[60] And like today, the psychiatric community was divided over the issue: "More conservative physicians, committed to a relatively rigid interpretation of the M'Naghten rule, found its rejection of the emotional and behavioral manifestations of mental illness quite satisfactory. Liberals, on the other hand, more hospitable to innovation and deterministic explanations of behavior, placed a far greater emphasis on the importance of emotional symptoms in the diagnosis of mental disease."[61]

As there is today as well, there was criticism of the role of experts for hire:

The role of expert witnesses was a problem disturbing to conservatives and innovators alike. All disapproved of the existing advocate system in which experts appeared for both sides, leaving the public with a somewhat cynical view of the integrity of those involved. For some time before 1881, concerned American physicians had been urging the appointment of court-designated commissioners to evaluate the responsibility of criminals, serving not as witnesses for either defense or prosecution, but as servants of the state and the judiciary.[62]

Yet the trial of Guiteau did become a duel of experts, with conservatives favoring his execution and liberals favoring his hospitalization.

The essential facts of the case were never in dispute. Guiteau, a sometime lawyer, theologian, and political hanger-on, was a disappointed office seeker who decided that President Garfield's elimination would save the Republican party and the nation from ruin. He stalked the poorly guarded president and shot him in a railroad station. Garfield lingered for several weeks before he succumbed to his wound (which was further aggravated by incompetent medical treatment). Guiteau did not deny the act, but he did deny his culpability on the ground that he was God's instrument. His lawyers argued that this belief made him insane in the eyes of the law.

One of the interesting ironies of the case is that as a politician, Garfield himself had railed against the insanity defense, writing a congratulatory letter to a Cleveland judge back in 1871 for rejecting an insanity plea: "The whole country owes you a debt of gratitude for brushing away the wicked absurdity which has lately been palmed off on the country as law in the subject of insanity. If the thing had gone much further all that a man would need to secure immunity from murder would be to tear his hair and rave a little, and then kill his man."

Most Americans, including many psychiatrists (then called alienists), shared this view. The medical establishment rallied behind the prosecution, attributing Guiteau's bizarre conduct to "depravity" rather than illness. He was bad, not mad, and there was too much method in his madness, as one doctor put it. Another prominent expert declared him "a perfectly sane man, as bright and intelligent a man as you will see on a summer's day."

A group of young Turks within the psychiatric profession supported the insanity defense. The influence of phrenology was rising in America, and as one of the defense experts put it, "while I had no other evidence than the expression on his face, I should have no doubt that he was also a moral imbecile, or rather a moral monstrosity." Another expert attributed his insanity to his "abuses of the sexual organs," which are the causes of "much insanity."[63] (Justice Antonin Scalia missed this tidbit of information when he worried — in his dissenting opinion in the 2003 Texas sodomy case — that if the Supreme Court took that decision to its logical conclusion, it might have to strike down state laws prohibiting masturbation.)

There was considerable discussion of the role of heredity on insanity and debate about Guiteau's family history, which included a father who believed that people with sufficient faith in Jesus — including himself — "might never die."

In the end, the presiding judge left little room in his instruction to the jury for an acquittal. He saw his job as leaving "no grounds for the reproach that Guiteau had been hurried to the gallows without a fair trial." The jury did not seem similarly concerned, rendering their verdict of guilt in a little more than an hour.

The second trial of Guiteau began after he was hanged and his body subjected to autopsy. An examination of his brain showed evidence of syphilitic paresis, as well as "chronic degeneration of grey cells and small blood vessels." As a result of the autopsy report, many doctors changed their opinions of Guiteau's condition and agreed that he was mentally ill and probably legally insane. This led to an increase, at least over the short term, in the respect accorded to physiologically oriented psychiatrists. But it produced no immediate change in the legal definition of insanity. There were some changes in the middle of the twentieth century, but following the insanity acquittal of the man who tried to assassinate President Ronald Reagan in 1981, the situation was returned essentially to what it had been a century earlier. The letter written by Garfield in 1871 condemning the insanity defense could be written today by politicians flexing their muscles in search of law-and-order support.

The Trial of Lizzie Borden

Date: 1893
Location: Fall River, Massachusetts
Defendant: Lizzie Borden
Charge: Murder
Verdict: Not guilty

We generally think of a miscarriage of justice as involving the conviction of the innocent. But despite our historical bias in favor of innocence — "better that 10 guilty be freed than even one innocent convicted" — the acquittal of a guilty murderer may also constitute a miscarriage of justice.

This is especially so when the erroneous verdict results not merely from a jury mistake, but rather from the heavy hand of a biased judiciary on the scales of justice. That is what occurred in the infamous case of Lizzie Borden. Though she was acquitted by a Massachusetts jury in 1893 of murdering her stepmother and her father, the verdict of history is aptly summarized by the most famous ditty ever composed about an American murder: "Lizzie Borden took an ax / And gave her mother forty whacks / When she saw what she had done / She gave her father forty-one."

Actually, the total number of whacks administered by the murderer was twenty-nine, but the rest of the ditty seems far more historically accurate than the verdict reached by the twelve men who heard a heavily edited version of the available evidence against the thirty-three-year-old "spinster."

Judicial bias does not simply occur in a vacuum. The social, political, and economic attitudes of the community and the times tend to be reflected by the judiciary, despite its theoretical independence. The Lizzie Borden prosecution was a case in point. Had Borden been an Irish or Italian immigrant working as a domestic, she surely would have been convicted — on the basis of the evidence presented at trial — of the double murder. The circumstantial case was compelling. Borden had the classic motive, means, and opportunity. She had difficulties with her parents, with whom she lived, and she had access to an ax. She was also the only actual person other than the perennial "outside intruder" who could have administered the fatal blows. There was evidence that she burned one of her dresses as soon as she learned that she was a suspect and that the authorities would be searching for bloodstains. There were also witnesses to the fact that shortly before the ax murders, Borden went to a pharmacy in an adjoining town in an unsuccessful effort to purchase prussic acid, ostensibly to clean a sealskin fur. But despite expert testimony that this acid does not clean furs but does kill people, the court excluded the entire episode, including evidence that the victims had experienced a mysterious stomach ailment the night before they were butchered.

The judges also excluded Borden's testimony during the inquest proceedings, which took place before Borden was formally charged. Borden's inquest testimony was filled with incriminating inconsistencies. For example, Borden gave a series of different answers when the district attorney asked her simply to describe where she was and what she was doing when her father came home. When asked for the first time, Borden said she was "down in the kitchen. . . . Reading an old magazine that had been left in the cupboard, an old *Harper's Magazine*."[64] The district attorney then asked Borden if she was certain that she was in the kitchen when her father returned; she replied that she was "not sure whether I was there or in the dining room."[65] When the question arose for a third time, a few minutes later, Borden now responded that she was "in my room upstairs."[66] Trying to get a straight answer, the district attorney confronted Borden with these inconsistencies. "I don't know what I have said," she responded. "I have answered so many questions and I am so confused I don't know one thing from another. I am telling you just as nearly as I know."[67]

The decision to exclude Borden's inquest testimony, particularly since Borden did not testify during her trial, would have surprised even the most fastidious adherent of modern-day *Miranda*-type exclusionary rules. Yet this decision was rendered in the absence of such modern rules or precedents. "The common law regards this species of evidence with distrust," explained the court. The court concluded that the circumstances of the inquest testimony constituted an arrest in substance, if not in official form, because Borden was "as effectually in custody as if the formal precept had been served."[68]

Why then were the judges — and eventually the jurors — so generous to the defendant in their interpretations of the law and the facts? The answer lies not in the nature of the crime, but in the character and the background of the alleged criminal. Lizzie Borden was a churchgoing woman of virtue, a product of old New England Puritan stock. She had the support of church and community leaders, who regarded it as inconceivable that one of their own could have done so dastardly a deed. Moreover, in a perversion of feminism, many women's groups, including those battling for suffrage, championed her cause, arguing that no woman was capable of such brutality.

The trial pitted some of the leading political figures of the day against each other. The defendant was represented by a former governor of Massachusetts (who had appointed at least one of the presiding judges). One of the prosecutors would later become a justice of the U.S. Supreme Court. But despite the talent of the advocates, the real "stars" of the media show — it was one of the most widely covered trials in American history — were the three presiding judges. They clearly determined the outcome of the case, by their one-sided evidentiary rulings and, even more important, by their instructions to the jury, which virtually directed a verdict of innocence. For example, the judges noted the prosecution's concession that "defendant's character has been good; that it has not been merely a negative and neutral one that nobody had heard anything against, but one of positive, of active benevolence in religious and charitable work."[69] The judges also offered a lengthy discussion on the elements of proving a case by circumstantial evidence, suggesting that "some special considerations need to be borne in mind: Inasmuch as the conclusion of guilt, if reached at all, must be inferred or reached from other facts that are proved, every fact which in your judgment is so important and essential that without it the conclusion of guilty could not be reached must itself be proved beyond reasonable doubt, must be proved by the same weight and force of evidence as if it were the main fact in issue." Indeed, one of the journalists covering the trial characterized the instruction as a *"plea for the innocent."*

Not surprisingly, it took the jurors less than an hour to reach their verdict. Nor should it be surprising that the public, fed by a frenzied pro-Lizzie press, would welcome the verdict. But the experts reacted with extreme skepticism to what many of them regarded as a trial that was unfair to the prosecution.

Dean Wigmore, an early-twentieth-century legal expert who wrote extensively about the trial, concluded that "the conduct of the accused after the killing was such that no conceivable hypothesis except that of guilt will explain the inconsistencies and improbabilities that were asserted by her." Wigmore was apparently referring to Borden's inquest testimony — which, although officially excluded from the evidence presented at trial, was printed in the local newspaper under the title "Lizzie's Story."[70] Other Massachusetts judges and commentators agreed. As one of them put it: "Within the profession there is a general dissatisfaction with the law of evidence administered at the trial." The case was retried many times, in law reviews and classrooms across the country. The general consensus seems to be that on the basis of the incomplete picture presented to the jury, there may well have been a reasonable doubt of Lizzie Borden's guilt. But it is also widely believed that the evidentiary rulings that excluded much of the incriminating evidence were highly suspect and reflected the judges' bias in favor of the defendant.

History, of course, has no exclusionary rules, and its evidentiary criteria are different from those employed in the courtroom. We have a right, as citizens, to reject the verdicts of the court — whether they have convicted or acquitted — and to decide the historical truth for ourselves. We must always keep in mind the limited, though important, role of the jury in Anglo-American law. Its verdict decides the case before it on the basis of the admissible evidence. But it does not decide historical truth. The Lizzie Borden case is an excellent example of a divergence between the verdict of the jury and the verdict of history.

1. James McPherson, *Ordeal by Fire: The Civil War and Reconstruction* (New York: Alfred A. Knopf, 1982), pp. 495–96.

2. *Ibid.*, p. 495.

3. David Herbert Donald et al., *The Civil War and Reconstruction* (New York: W. W. Norton and Co., 2001), p. 494.

4. *Ibid.*, p. 477.

5. Donald, p. 544. The Fourteenth Amendment was ratified in 1868. Eric Foner, *The Story of American Freedom* (New York: Harper and Row, 1976), p. 105.

6. McPherson, pp. 516–17 (noting that the Fourteenth Amendment has been the basis of more litigation than all the rest of the Constitution combined).

7. Donald, pp. 549, 551–53.

8. Eric Foner, *Reconstruction: America's Unfinished Revolution, 1863–1877* (New York: Harper and Row, 1988), p. 255. The women's movement experienced similar sentiments about their rights being ignored with passage of the Fifteenth Amendment in 1870. *Ibid.*, p. 447; Foner, *American Freedom*, p. 108.

9. Foner, *Reconstruction*, p. 255.

10. McPherson, p. 518; Donald, pp. 553–55.

11. Donald, p. 566.

12. *Ibid.*

13. *Ibid.*

14. McPherson, p. 531.

15. Donald, pp. 566–67, 571.

16. *Ibid.*, p. 567.

17. *Ibid.*

18. Donald, p. 571; McPherson, p. 531.

19. McPherson, p. 532.

20. McPherson, p. 532; Donald, p. 572.

21. Foner, *Reconstruction*, p. 335; McPherson, p. 533.

22. Donald, p. 573.

23. Donald, pp. 575, 608.

24. *Ibid.*, p. 607.

25. *Ibid.*, p. 231.

26. *Ibid.*

27. *Ibid.*

28. Kathleen Barry, *Susan B. Anthony: A Biography of a Singular Feminist* (New York: NYU Press, 1988), p. 255.

29. Barry, pp. 256–57.

30. *Ibid.*

31. Jean H. Baker, *Mary Todd Lincoln: A Biography* (New York: W. W. Norton and Co., 1987), pp. 316–17. Baker is very sympathetic toward Mary Todd Lincoln and treats Robert Lincoln quite unfavorably.

32. *Ibid.*, p. 319.

33. *Ibid.*, p. 321.

34. *Ibid.*, p. 325.

35. *Ibid.*, p. 326.

36. *Ibid.*, pp. 336, 341.

37. *Ibid.*, p. 368.

38. Donald, p. 629; McPherson, p. 597.

39. Donald, pp. 632, 634.

40. *Ibid.*, pp. 636–37.

41. *Ibid.*, p. 638.

42. *Ibid.*

43. McPherson, p. 606.

44. James C. Clark, *The Murder of James A. Garfield: The President's Last Days and the Trial and Execution of His Assassin* (Jefferson, NC: McFarland and Co., 1993), p. 121.

45. *Ibid.*, pp. 116, 123.

46. *Ibid.*, pp. 126–27, 130.

47. *Ibid.*, pp. 128–29.

48. *Ibid.*, pp. 132–33. In written answers, Arthur acknowledged that he had seen Guiteau on a few occasions and only briefly; Guiteau had apparently sought employment by the Republican party in the 1880 campaign.

49. *Ibid.*, p. 133.

50. *Ibid.*, p. 137.

51. *Ibid.*, p. 139.

52. *Ibid.*, p. 142.

53. See David Dewitt, *The Impeachment and Trial of Andrew Johnson* (New York: The Notable Trials Library, 1992).

54. Beverly Jones et al., *An Account of the Proceedings on the Trial of Susan B. Anthony, on the Charge of Illegal Voting, at the Presidential Election in November 1872* (New York: The Notable Trials Library, 1997), p. 17.

55. *Ibid.*, pp. 58–59.

56. *Ibid.*, pp. 84–85.

57. *Ibid.*, p. 85.

58. Mark E. Neely and R. Gerald McMurtry, *The Insanity File: The Case of Mary Todd Lincoln* (Delran, NJ: The Notable Trials Library, 1999), p. 133. Apparently, the documents were made public in the 1980s. *Ibid.*, p. xi.

59. *Ibid.*, p. 78.

60. Charles E. Rosenberg, *The Trial of the Assassin Guiteau* (New York: The Notable Trials Library, 1996), p. 53.

61. *Ibid.*, p. 63.

62. *Ibid.*, pp. 66–67.

63. *Ibid.*, p. 135.

64. Edmund Pearson, *Trial of Lizzie Borden* (Birmingham: The Notable Trials Library, 1989), p. 404.

65. *Ibid.*

66. *Ibid.*, p. 405.

67. *Ibid.*, p. 406.

68. *Ibid.*, p. 199.

69. *Ibid.*, p. 378.

70. *Ibid.*, p. 394.

PART VII

The Early Twentieth Century

THE FIRST GREAT TRIAL of the twentieth century, for the murder of the most celebrated American architect of the day, grew out of the excesses of the so-called Gilded Age. More than the guilt or innocence of the pathetic killer of Stanford White was on trial. New York society — and especially "the New York four hundred," who were given notoriety by Mrs. William Astor of New York's high society[1]— stood in the dock, accused by the yellow journalists of being "naughty millionaires"[2] who did not feel bound by the rules applicable to ordinary people. So when one of the more ordinary "blue bloods" was charged with murdering a member of the elite who had "ruined" his glamorous wife, there was considerable sympathy for the defendant. By taking the law into his own hands, he was enforcing a morality that was too often left unenforced against privileged characters such as Stanford White.

The president of the Society for the Suppression of Vice, Anthony Comstock, who denounced Stanford White, viewed "ruining" a woman as worthy of death. The views of "moralists" such as Comstock on the murder of Stanford White are best summarized by the Reverend Charles A. Eaton, pastor of John D. Rockefeller: "It would be a good thing if there was a little more shooting in cases like this."[3] It is not clear, however, that all Americans agreed that Nesbit was "ruined"; in fact, some believed she was a loose woman who was telling magnificent lies.[4]

The stage was thus set for a culture war fought on the battlefield of the law. Other culture wars were being fought as well: between labor and corporations, between old Americans and newer immigrants, between rural and urban residents.

Theodore Roosevelt, who served as president from 1901 through 1908, advocated a New Nationalism, which sought to use the government to regulate industry and finance so as to protect against the abuses of privilege.[5] Roosevelt sympathized with the workers' plight, but he resisted union recognition for fear that organized labor would "become powerful and monopolistic."[6]

Labor achieved little success in the courts and legislatures, as employers used their political power to impede progress for workingmen and -women.[7] Thus, a large percentage of workers lived in actual poverty and suffered from low wages with little protection from the hazards of labor.

The war between organized labor and corporate America turned quite violent during the early years of the twentieth century. Although there had been previous episodes of violence between labor and capital, it was now threatening to become more systematic and sustained. These battles, too, ended up in the courtroom, with famous lawyers — such as Clarence Darrow and William E. Borah — representing the litigants.

The trial of labor organizer "Big Bill" Haywood for conspiracy to murder in 1907 intensified the class warfare between labor and management. Labor and socialist groups actively supported Haywood. For them, Haywood was not on trial; the Mine Owners Association was in the dock. Labor and socialist groups sought to use the Haywood trial as a means of exposing the inhumane working conditions of the miners.[8] Management also found powerful supporters, among them President Roosevelt, who "tacitly intervened on behalf of the prosecution" of Haywood and referred to him as an "undesirable citizen."[9] Conservative and progressive politicians alike condemned Haywood, some calling "for his execution in the name of law and order."[10] The prosecution's detailing of the murders and dynamitings committed by the "inner circle" of the Western Federation of Miners served as an indictment of the violence employed by some in the labor movement.[11]

The trial of the McNamara brothers in 1911 reminded the

public yet again of the "class warfare" between labor and management.[12] The labor movement rushed to the defense of the McNamaras, just as it had for Haywood.[13] Unlike the Haywood case, where the labor movement was vindicated, the obvious guilt of the McNamara brothers, as well as the finding of guilt against thirty-eight officers of the International Association of Bridge and Structural Iron Workers, resulted in an assessment of collective guilt against the labor movement among much of the public.[14]

There were significant questions, however, about the fairness of the courts that had ruled against labor. Corruption and influence peddling were rampant, especially in big cities such as Chicago, Los Angeles, and New York. The great labor trials pitted corporate America, which controlled the prosecutors and the judges, against organized labor, which often sought to influence the jurors. The end result was massive corruption and a loss of respect for the legal system.

Finally, cities and towns, especially in the South, had their own forms of corruption. Racism and bigotry were rampant, not only against blacks, but also against Jews, Catholics, and outsiders. The trial of Leo Frank, a Northern Jew, for murdering a young Southern girl, brought together all the prejudices of the South. Leo Frank was seen not only as a Northern capitalist exploiting Southern women and children, but also as a Jew who was "public[ly] upright but privately perverse and dishonest."[15] Moreover, Southern conceptions of Jews as wealthy and "above the law" were prevalent. Leo Frank was rumored to have influential Jewish friends who would buy the jury and witnesses with "Jew money."[16] Such discussions of Leo Frank reflected "traditional stereotypes of financial wiliness with the time-worn southern prejudices."[17]

The Leo Frank trial also reflected the Southern disillusionment with the social upheaval generated by industrialization and urbanization.[18] Atlanta's public outcry against Leo Frank was about more than avenging Mary Phagan's death; it was an outcry against "modernization, family dissolution, foreign influence in the South, and the possible collusion of Jew and African American for the benefit of Jews."[19] The Jew, rather than the African American, was the scapegoat for the infiltration of industrial capitalism and urbanization in the new South.[20] Leo Frank was a symbol for everything that Southerners resented: Northern (particularly Jewish) capitalist entrepreneurs, employment of minors in factories, work for women. Factories, which became known as places of ill repute and sexual immorality, "where working women were vulnerable to the advances of their bosses," violated Southern values of female purity and male protection of their women.[21] The tragic ending to the Frank case reflected the bigotries and frustrations of certain elements of Southern society near the beginning of the twentieth century.

Bigotry and frustration were also prevalent in parts of the North, where they were also directed against outsiders — immigrants, socialists, and opponents of the war.

The United States entered the Great War in 1917 to protect democracy abroad. But at home, civil liberties came under fierce attack — not for the first or last time in our history. The Espionage Act of 1917 punished those who obstructed the war effort or aided the enemy; the Trading with the Enemy Act of 1917 broadened censorship over foreign-language publications; the Sabotage Act of 1918 made sabotage of war materials a crime; and finally, the Sedition Act of 1918 outlawed any remarks opposing the American flag, government, uniform, or war effort.

The Abrams case reflected the tide of suppression of radicalism and dissent. The Supreme Court's decision upholding the criminalization of pamphleting in opposition to the war "destroyed old judicial barriers against assaults on the right of free expression." The Court's reasoning that the pamphlets presented a "clear and present danger" to national security allowed the government to define broadly that elastic limitation on speech. In addition, Wilson's attorney general, A. Mitchell Palmer, seized, arrested, and imprisoned thousands of suspected radicals without search warrants in flagrant violation of the law.[22] Though many of these people were later released, the notorious "Palmer Red Raids" demonstrated the government's disregard for the law during the emergency. In May 1920, a brochure titled *To the American People: Report Upon the Illegal Practices of the Department of Justice*, which was supported by twelve of the most distinguished attorneys in the country, brought the government's abuse of power to the public's attention.[23] It was a much-needed message from some leaders of the American legal profession that law and order were not to be demanded only from the people, but from the government as well.

Following the armistice in 1918, the insecurity of the American people led to significant social upheaval. Postwar inflation and labor troubles led to a wave of strikes. Race riots and violence plagued the period. Corruption in American life hit a new low when it touched America's national pastime during the Black Sox Scandal of 1919. The indictment of several baseball players, including Shoeless Joe Jackson, an American hero, in a scandal to fix the World Series of 1919 demonstrated "more than a betrayal"; it was "a symptom of American decay."[24] The famous response of an incredulous child to Joe Jackson — "say it ain't so, Joe" — can be seen as a larger reflection of Americans' disillusionment with corruption and the struggle to readjust to normalcy amid the upheavals of the postwar period.

So the first few decades of the twentieth century may not have been so "gilded" after all. Beneath the plating lay much of the dark and corroded cultural conflict that would become more obvious in the decades following the First World War: conflict between "old" and "new" Americans; issues of racism, prejudice, and xenophobia; and perhaps most of all, the problematic connections among wealth, influence, and power. And these great trials speak directly to these growing social rifts: Abrams and others were persecuted for their beliefs; Leo Frank was lynched for his religion; and the relatively poor and rural Joe Jackson was hung out to dry by the rich and powerful Charles Comiskey. These trials show how money, power, and prejudice can work their way into court, corrupting and corroding our laws and even our lives.

Paul Revere's inflammatory rendering of the Boston Massacre.
(© BETTMANN/CORBIS)

A crime scene photograph of
the body of Andrew Borden,
whose daughter Lizzie was
accused of killing him.
(COLLECTION OF FALL RIVER
HISTORICAL SOCIETY)

Ben Shahn's painting
The Passion of Sacco and Vanzetti.
(© ESTATE OF BEN SHAHN/LICENSED BY
VAGA, NEW YORK, NY)

This photo of the Leo Frank lynching was turned into a postcard and sent by citizens of Marietta, Georgia, to their friends and relatives.
(COURTESY OF THE ATLANTA HISTORY CENTER, KENNETH G. ROGERS COLLECTION)

Confrontation at the 1925 Scopes Trial: defense attorney Clarence Darrow stands with arms folded, center, while opposing counsel William Jennings Bryan is seated at left, holding a fan. Everyone present is in shirtsleeves because of the summer heat.
(© BETTMANN/CORBIS)

Nathan Leopold (left foreground) and Richard Loeb (right) sit beside their attorney, Clarence Darrow, whose eloquent closing statement saved them from execution. (© BETTMANN/CORBIS)

One of the so-called Scottsboro Boys giving testimony at his trial for raping a white woman. (© BETTMANN/CORBI)

Nazis accused of war crimes at the Nuremberg trials (Hermann Göring, leaning forward, is seated next to Rudolph Hess).
(© BETTMANN/CORBIS)

U.S. Senator Richard M. Nixon of California (right) inspects microfilm related to the Alger Hiss case.
(© BETTMANN/CORBIS)

Julius and Ethel Rosenberg embrace before their trial for treason. (© BETTMANN/CORBIS)

U.S. Senator Joseph McCarthy of Wisconsin (center, with pointer) during the Army-McCarthy hearings. (© BETTMANN/CORBIS)

U.S. Army Lieutenant William Calley, Jr., salutes as he is escorted by military police from the courthouse where he was sentenced to life imprisonment at hard labor for his responsibility in the My Lai massacre. His sentence was later commuted. (© Bettmann/Corbis)

O.J. Simpson and his attorneys (from left to right, Alan Dershowitz, Johnnie Cochran, and Robert Schapiro). (©Reuters Newmedia Inc/Corbis)

WANTED

INFORMATION AS TO THE
WHEREABOUTS OF

CHAS. A. LINDBERGH, Jr.
OF HOPEWELL, N. J.

SON OF COL. CHAS. A. LINDBERGH
World-Famous Aviator

This child was kidnaped from his home in Hopewell, N. J., between 8 and 10 p. m. on Tuesday, March 1, 1932.

DESCRIPTION:

Age, 20 months Hair, blond, curly
Weight, 27 to 30 lbs. Eyes, dark blue
Height, 29 inches Complexion, light
Deep dimple in center of chin
Dressed in one-piece coverall night suit

ADDRESS ALL COMMUNICATIONS TO
COL. H. N. SCHWARZKOPF, TRENTON, N. J., or
COL. CHAS. A. LINDBERGH, HOPEWELL, N. J.

ALL COMMUNICATIONS WILL BE TREATED IN CONFIDENCE

COL. H. NORMAN SCHWARZKOPF
Supt. New Jersey State Police, Trenton, N. J.

March 11, 1932

This poster of the missing Lindbergh baby was sent to police chiefs of more than 1,400 American cities in March 1932.
(©BETTMANN/CORBIS)

The Trial of Stanford White's Killer

Date: 1907, 1908
Location: New York City, New York
Defendant: Henry Thaw
Charge: Murder
Verdict: Not guilty by reason of insanity

If all politics are local, then all crime is temporal. Each age has its paradigmatic crimes, excuses, and defenses. The trial of Harry K. Thaw for the murder of architect Stanford White — the man who designed the original Madison Square Garden — represents an early-twentieth-century variant on the contemporary abuse excuse. It is a period piece about sexual mores, gender roles, and the hypocritical underside of American manners among New York's glitterati.

Stanford White was the most prominent architect at the end of the nineteenth century and beginning of the twentieth — an artist whose work was to be compared with that of Frank Lloyd Wright and Henry Richardson. Publicly, White was the epitome of grace, charm, and good manners, but privately, he was a rogue who took advantage of young women. In the parlance of the day, he "ruined" a particularly beautiful sixteen-year-old waif named Evelyn Nesbit. Nesbit's impoverished family utilized her striking face and figure as their primary source of income; by 1902, she had advanced from working as an artist's and photographer's model to a job as a vaudeville chorus girl, where she first caught the eye of Stanford White.[25] White, a married man, "thought a great deal" of Nesbit, and "aided her greatly in becoming a stage favorite. He was often seen in her company."[26] He set up Nesbit, her mother, and her brother in a comfortable love nest — a suite with a private bath — and also paid for Nesbit to attend acting school.[27] Shortly thereafter, however, Nesbit met and married Harry Thaw, a millionaire playboy with bizarre tastes who subjected his new wife to numerous acts of sadistic brutality (including one instance in which he purchased a dog whip while shopping with Evelyn in New York and proceeded to use it on her at home).[28] Nesbit did not end her affair with Stanford White, even after her marriage to Thaw.

One night in June 1906, Thaw murdered White in cold blood while he was eating dinner at his Madison Square Garden open-air rooftop restaurant. At Thaw's trial, one witness reported on a statement made by Thaw in an elevator shortly after the shooting. At one point, Thaw had turned to the witness, as if to utter a simple explanation: "I did it," said Thaw, "because he ruined my wife."[29]

Based on such an explanation, Thaw's counsel invoked the informal law under which, to quote his defense attorney's closing argument, "whoever violates the sanctity of his home, or the purity of his wife or daughter, he has forfeited the protection of the laws of this state or any other state." Thaw claimed that the murder had been provoked by White's mistreatment of Thaw's future wife, even though Evelyn Nesbit had not yet met Thaw at the time of her alleged "ruination" — and even though her ruination was presumably "repaired" by her marriage to Thaw. The defense's opening statement promised to "show to you that . . . this defendant had provocation and that he did what any one of you would have done under similar conditions."[30]

Yet while the defense claimed that provocation made the murder "an act justifiable in itself," Thaw's counsel added that the act was furthermore "performed by a man who had no control over himself or his acts at the time. . . ."[31] Over Thaw's objection, his lawyer raised a Lorena Bobbitt–type temporary insanity defense:[32] "He need not claim that he was sane or insane before he committed the crime, that he was insane the moment he committed the crime and then, a moment after, sane again. No, he must make the simple claim that at the time he killed Stanford White, he was insane."

Although Harry Thaw was the nominal defendant at the trial, the real defendant was the victim, Stanford White. Much of the testimony was devoted to an attack on the character of the victim. The case was tried both in the court of law and in the court of public opinion, with primitive public opinion polls showing that a majority of the citizens supported Thaw's execution of White.[33] As one of the typical letters to the editor stated, "The killing of White by Thaw was a great public service which all mothers and fathers should be thankful for. . . . Murder is terrible, but it falls into insignificance when one considers that this man White belonged to a set of cowards whose objects were so unspeakable."[34]

One of Thaw's most vocal supporters was, not surprisingly, Anthony Comstock — the self-appointed guardian of American morality. In addition to trying to ban birth control, abortion, and sex outside marriage, Comstock believed that the appropriate punishment for licentious behavior was vigilante murder. Comstock, the unofficial protector of American womanhood, issued a statement attesting to White's bad reputation as a "horrid monster," who "made a business of ruining young girls" and who therefore placed himself beyond the law's protection.[35]

The theory of the defense was as simple as it was blatant. The defendant admitted murdering White, but he said that he did it because his wife told him that she had been ruined by the victim. At the trial, Evelyn Nesbit Thaw testified emotionally on behalf of her husband. Outside court, she told the press, "My

husband was justified in killing Stanford White . . . I am his true
wife and will be with him in his fight. . . ."[36]

It was learned after the trial, however, that the Thaw family
had paid Evelyn Nesbit a large sum of money to lie about both
White and Thaw.[37] The truth appears to be that Nesbit was an
upwardly mobile seductress, and that both White and Thaw
were exploitative perverts with violent sexual tastes. Such was
the portrayal of the trio in the 1955 film *The Girl in the Red
Velvet Swing*, on which Nesbit herself worked as an adviser.
The film, which starred Joan Collins as Nesbit, depicted White
as a lascivious old man who lusted after the young showgirl,
taking her to his Manhattan apartment where he pushed her
back and forth — in the nude — on a large swing made of red
velvet.

The defense strategy of putting the victim on trial succeeded,
producing a hung jury at the first trial and a temporary insanity
acquittal at the second. Nesbit then turned against her husband,
seeking to extort a million dollars from his family and claiming
that she feared he might kill her.

For those who think the recent spate of high-profile trials —
such as the Menendez brothers, Lorena Bobbitt, O. J. Simpson,
Scott Peterson, Michael Jackson, and Kobe Bryant — are unique
to our age, the trial of Harry Thaw a century ago shows that every
age has its legal extravaganzas. In this case, American mores —
public and private — were on trial just as much as Thaw, White,
and Nesbit were in the dock. The end result was a finding of
moral guilt against *all* the defendants, especially the American
mores of the time. The Thaw-White-Nesbit scandal helped
bring sex out of the closet and put Comstock in the cellar.

There are no redeeming characters in this drama — only mutually exploitative hypocrites. Even the law does not come off
unscathed, because the inference is clear that money bought injustice here — not in the sense that O. J. Simpson's wealth may
have helped him secure extraordinary investigative resources,

but in the sense of corrupt payoffs and underhanded deals. For those who look back with nostalgia on America's golden age of law, the story of this trial helps the modern-day reader appreciate the improved, but still imperfect, nature of our current legal system.

The Haywood, McNamara, and Darrow Trials (The Great Labor Union Trials)

HAYWOOD
Date: 1907
Location: Boise, Idaho
Defendant: William Haywood
Charge: Conspiracy to commit murder
Verdict: Not guilty

MCNAMARA
Date: 1911
Location: Los Angeles, California
Defendants: James B. McNamara, John J. McNamara
Charges: Murder for James B. McNamara; dynamiting for
            J. J. McNamara
Verdict: Guilty: life imprisonment for J. B. McNamara;
            fifteen years in prison for J. J. McNamara

DARROW
Date: 1912
Location: Los Angeles, California
Defendant: Clarence Darrow
Charge: Attempted bribery
Verdict: Not guilty of Lockwood bribery; hung jury in
            Bain bribery

The common threads that tie these three cases together are organized labor and the great labor lawyer of the day, Clarence Darrow. The era of great legal orators such as Darrow, William E. Borah, and William Jennings Bryan is often regarded as the golden age of American law. A fair assessment of the historical reality reveals, however, that this gold, too, was tarnished. The juristic talents of past legal giants are commonly exaggerated, and their ethical standards are shocking to us today.

The 1907 conspiracy trial of union leader William "Big Bill" Haywood in Boise, Idaho — which pitted Darrow against Borah — illustrates how criminal law was practiced during its so-called golden age. The case was one of several during that period of labor–management conflict in which prominent labor leaders were charged with conspiring with hired killers to dynamite management property, personnel, and supporters. In this instance, the professional hit man Harry Orchard had blown up former governor of Idaho Frank Steunenberg in his home. Shortly after he was caught, Orchard admitted to an additional eighteen contract murders, several of which, he claimed, were arranged by the "inner circle" of the Western Federation of Miners, including Secretary-Treasurer Haywood.[38]

The stage was set, therefore, for a prosecution against not only Haywood himself, but also the entire labor movement and especially its alleged violence. Such a case was tailor-made for Darrow, who, although not yet a household name, had achieved renown within the labor movement and its more radical elements. It was also suited to Borah, who, having just been elected to the Senate, postponed taking his seat until he completed his role as co-prosecutor.

The lawyers in this case were not mere advocates; they believed heart and soul in the causes they represented. The prosecutors were not above vouching for the truth of their witnesses, as demonstrated by the state's remarkable closing argument:

Gentlemen, I wish that I could look over this evidence and find some way of satisfying myself that this man here upon trial was innocent and that these other men associated with him in this indictment were also innocent of this offense. I have no desire, gentlemen, to have the scalp of any innocent man hanging at my girdle. I don't, gentlemen of the jury, desire that any man shall be convicted through my efforts, or through any effort of mine in whole or in part, that is innocent of any offense. But I have arrived at a time of life, gentlemen, that I believe would, I think, preclude one from desiring through over-enthusiasm in a case that he is advocating to have a man punished for a serious offense who is guiltless of it. A young man may become inspired by his case, may reason that the only evidence worthy of belief is that which goes in upon his side, and may be so actuated by a desire to win that he may overlook those matters which should have been considered by him and which would show the innocence of the party accused. But I think after we have been in this business for nearly two score of years as I have been, we get beyond that stage and I hope that I have got beyond that stage, because I tell you frankly, gentlemen of the jury, if I did not believe in my heart that this man was guilty I would so state. I wish I could find some way by which I could conclude from this evidence that I was satisfied of his innocence, because I would a thousand times rather have a man vindicated than to have him dragged through the mire and dirt of a conviction. But we can come to but one conclusion, and that is that he is not only responsible for this atrocious murder but that for more than a score of other murders that have been proven here he is equally responsible.[39]

The defense responded in kind, as seen in the following excerpt from Darrow's closing argument:

[The prosecutor] said to you, gentlemen of the jury, that he would not prosecute this case unless he believed this defendant guilty. Now, why? Is he prosecuting it because he believes him guilty, is that it? Or is he prosecuting it because he may want to put another "ell" on his house and wants some more deficiency warrants with which to do it? Which is it? Has any man a right to make a statement like that? I hope there is not anybody here who cares a fig about what [the prosecutor] thinks about this case. He may be bug-house, and he is if all of his statements are true. Or he is worse. Let me show you what he said and then judge for yourself. . . . We will try him on an inquest of lunacy. He said to these twelve men, men of fair intelligence and fair learning, that you would be warranted in convicting Bill Haywood if you took Harry Orchard's [the hit-man-turned-prosecution-witness] evidence out of this case. And still he says he is honest. Maybe he is, but if he is honest, he is bughouse, and he can have his choice.[40]

Darrow frequently employed ad hominem attacks against his opposing lawyers and grand rhetoric about the evils of capitalism rather than carefully worked out factual and legal arguments. One historian notes that Darrow's colleagues easily recognized his weakness when it came to mastery of the law: "His Boise associate, John Nugent, called him 'Old necessity,' and when asked why he said 'because necessity knows no law.' But he was certainly a man to be reckoned with in criminal prosecutions susceptible of emotional defense before a jury."[41]

Historians have long speculated as to the reasons for the unexpected acquittal in the Haywood case. There was little compelling evidence beyond the questionable testimony of the government's bought witness, hit man Harry Orchard, who was a notorious mass-murderer-turned-state-witness.[42] But his testimony was apparently delivered in a credible manner. Orchard testified that he had been hired by Haywood to kill Steunenberg as an act of revenge for the former governor's harsh treatment of miners.[43] Orchard calmly and carefully recounted the details of

Steunenberg's murder, and his remarkable nonchalance when reciting the long list of his heinous criminal acts convinced many observers that he was sincere and telling the truth.[44] As one journalist explained:

> There was nothing theatrical about the appearance on the stand of this witness, upon whose testimony the whole case against Haywood, Moyer, and the other leaders of the Western Federation of Miners is based. Only once or twice was there a dramatic touch. It was a horrible, revolting, sickening story, but he told it as simply as the plainest narration of the most ordinary incident of the most humdrum existence. . . .
>
> It was just a plain recital of personal experience, and as it went on, hour after hour, with multitudinous detail, clear and vivid here, half forgotten and obscure there, gradually it forced home to the listener the conviction that it was the unmixed truth. Lies are not made as complicated and involved as that story. Fiction so full of incident, so mixed of purpose and cross-purpose, so permeated with the play of human passion, does not spring offhand from the most marvelous fertile invention.[45]

Thus Orchard masterfully covered the holes in his story through his manner of telling it, and the consensus was that the evidence demonstrated guilt.

It is impossible, then, to provide a definitive answer as to why the jury acquitted. That is, of course, not surprising, since jury verdicts are rarely amenable to scientific evaluation. It is entirely possible that the case was fixed — that the votes of the jurors and the silence of witnesses were bought. Such corruption was widespread in those days, especially in union–capital conflicts. Many of his contemporaries regarded Darrow as an "unethical lawyer,"[46] and as we shall see, there was a strong factual basis for this assessment.

The name of Clarence Darrow will always be associated in the public mind with great advocacy on behalf of the downtrodden, the unpopular, and the controversial. This indeed was an important part of the public life of America's most celebrated twentieth-century lawyer. But it was not the only part. Darrow also represented the powerful, the privileged, and the popular. He was a lawyer for many, if not all, seasons and a man who fully lived the passions of his time.

It is said that in England, great criminal defense lawyers are knighted, while in the United States they are indicted. Clarence Darrow was indicted twice, on two charges of tampering with the jury in the infamous trial of the McNamara brothers (which took place four years after the Haywood case). The McNamara case grew out of the deliberate bombing of the *Los Angeles Times* building on October 1, 1910, in which twenty people were killed. Two labor organizers, the brothers Jim and J. J. McNamara, were arrested for the crime; organized labor retained Darrow to defend the McNamaras in this "crime of the century" (the first of several "crimes of the century" that Darrow would argue before the 1930s).

Organized labor put its credibility on the line by declaring that big business had framed the innocent McNamaras. The problem with this claim was that not only were the McNamaras guilty, but the evidence of their guilt was overwhelming as well. For example, the prosecution called to the stand no less than twenty-eight separate witnesses to identify Jim McNamara, ranging from the drivers who had taken him around Los Angeles, to women he had known, to the bartender who sold him a drink just a few minutes before he planted the bomb behind the *Times* building, to the mail clerk who had handed him his mail under his alias, J. B. Brice.[47] Meanwhile, the government assembled a strong case against J. J., based on files seized from the secret vault of the ironworkers' union in Indianapolis. Such evidence would not directly connect J. J. to the *Times* bombing, but it contained clear evidence of J. J.'s involvement — and leadership — in other bombing incidents across the country. According to one community leader, this evidence would simply "bury J.J.M."[48]

Beyond the specific details of the case, Darrow believed that the defense faced a much larger problem: The system of justice seemed stacked against his labor clients. There is little doubt, as a historical matter, that corrupt practices — some subtle, others overt — were far more rampant in the early twentieth century than they are today. Judges were bribed, cases were fixed, and evidence was manufactured and destroyed with far greater regularity than occurs today. This was certainly true in Darrow's time. According to the prosecution, Darrow tried to level the playing field by bribing prospective jurors and witnesses in the McNamara case.

Though Darrow was acquitted on the first charge and had a hung jury on the second, there is now persuasive evidence that he may, in fact, have been involved in the bribery. In a recent account of the Darrow jury bribery case, the author Geoffrey Cowan — who is generally an admirer of Darrow — puts the issue in its contemporary context:

> With considerable justification, and a bit of paranoia, Darrow felt that the judicial system was rigged against his clients. The prosecutors controlled the police and the grand jury, and they were backed by Burns' detectives, by the Erector's Association's money and by a generally hostile press led by a *Times* that was bent on revenge. His clients had been illegally kidnapped, dragged across state lines and forced to face criminal charges. Their friends were harassed, their witnesses intimidated. The Judge was a member of the most elite club in the city, and no one would be allowed on the jury who did not own property and who was not acceptable to the prosecution. The jurors all knew that they would be rewarded for voting to convict the McNamaras and punished if they voted for acquittal. . . . The forces of capital bribed jurors too, but the approach was a bit more subtle.[49]

Cowan concludes that in light of these realities — and of Darrow's strong belief in the cause of labor — "Darrow may actually have believed that, under some circumstances, bribery was the right course, the moral course of action."[50] Understandably, but unfortunately, Darrow did not devote much of his autobiography to this painful episode in his life.

How then should history judge a renowned lawyer who — it now appears — was not above bribing jurors, paying hush money to witnesses, and employing other devices that, as Cowan delicately puts it, "students don't learn at Ivy League law schools"?[51] This is the question posed in Cowan's icon-shattering account of the bribery trial of Clarence Darrow that took place in Los Angeles in the spring and summer of 1912. For many American lawyers — this lawyer among them — Darrow was the epitome of success in the practice of criminal law. Not only was he a legend in the courtroom, but his life has been a model for generations of aspiring young lawyers as well. He went on to participate in some of the most notable cases of the century, including the Leopold and Loeb "thrill killing" trial in 1924 and the Scopes "monkey" trial in 1925. He devoted much of his life to the defense of the underprivileged and the worker. But if Cowan is to be believed — and the evidence appears convincing — then Darrow should be anything but a role model, because some of his methods for achieving justice were unethical, immoral, and just plain criminal.

Such accusations against Darrow are both general and particular. Cowan — a lawyer, teacher, and cofounder of the Clarence Darrow Foundation, which funds public interest law and gives awards to men and women whose work furthers Darrow's ideals — admits that he was himself surprised and disappointed to learn that the recurrent rumors of Darrow's corruption were supported by the evidence.

Cowan never really addresses the general allegations against Darrow, except to place them in the mouths of Darrow's friends and associates. For example: "Neither the press nor the court knew the extent to which Darrow's own circle of friends thought him capable of the crime — and, indeed, believed he had bribed juries before." Or the reference to his reputation in the profession at large: "As a legal tactician, he was, of course, a realist, and apparently had, from time to time, felt obliged to find a way to get rid of unwelcome witnesses and to make sure that the jury contained some members who were committed to vote for his client." Cowan is certainly correct in observing that this is not the kind of legal realism taught in Ivy League law schools today — except as negative examples in courses on legal ethics.

The specific accusation — that Darrow authorized the bribery of two jurors at the murder trial of labor organizer Jim McNamara — is proven, to the unhappy satisfaction of Cowan: "On the basis, then, of all the available evidence, it is fair to conclude that Darrow bribed both jurors." Without seeking to justify these criminal acts, Cowan tries hard to place them in an understandable historical and economic context. But two wrongs cannot make an uncorrupt right, and Cowan's attempt to "understand" Darrow's countercorruption is not persuasive: ". . . to understand Darrow's view, it is worth asking what measures would have been justified to help free the Scottsboro Boys, who were framed and railroaded . . . in the racist courts of Alabama in the 1930s; and what tactics would ethicists disallow for those seeking to free Jews facing punishment in Nazi Germany?"[52] For indeed, as Cowan himself quickly concedes, "[o]f course, Darrow's clients had not been framed; he knew that they were 'guilty as hell'; and America in 1911 was not Germany in 1940."[53]

History also reveals that Darrow was not always motivated by zealous support of labor. Indeed, in his bribery trial, he apparently "made a secret effort to win a lighter sentence for himself by offering to testify against Samuel Gompers," the leader of organized labor.[54] In the end, Darrow won his own case, thanks to his brilliant oratory, a friendly judge, and a sympathetic jury. It is one of the great vices of corruption that we cannot now ever be certain whether there were other — less savory — ingredients that contributed to his acquittal, as the prosecutors alleged.

Whatever Darrow's motives, the convincing evidence that he bribed jurors in the McNamara case forever disqualifies Darrow from being a role model for lawyers. There is simply no justification for corrupting the legal system, even if it is done to level the playing field. The reason we do not teach such "devices" at Ivy League law schools is that they are not lawyers' tools. They may indeed be the tools of revolutionaries and others who work outside the system, and they may perhaps even be justified by a revolutionary means–ends calculus. But a lawyer, who does lawyers' work, cannot employ such devices, regardless of the provocation. The lawyer may rail against the corruption of his opponent; the lawyer may expose or condemn — or perhaps even rightfully resign from the practice of law to become a revolutionary, if the cause is just and the provocation sufficient. But the lawyer may not become part of the corruption in order to fight for justice. If Darrow crossed that line, as it appears he did, then he does not deserve the mantle of honor he has proudly borne over most of the twentieth century.

Those of us who have long regarded Darrow as a hero will be disappointed to learn of his clay feet, but harsh claims of history must outweigh any inclination toward hagiography, even when the subject is one of the very few lawyers who have had plausible claims to legal sainthood.

The Trial of Leo Frank

Date: 1913–15
Location: Marietta, Georgia
Defendant: Leo Frank
Charge: Murder
Verdict: Guilty
Sentence: Hanging

The trial, conviction, death sentence and its commutation, and eventual lynching of Leo Frank during the second decade of the twentieth century constitute a major episode not only in American legal history, but also in the development of American political institutions. The Knights of Mary Phagan, formed to avenge the murder of the young factory worker for which Frank was convicted, became an important component of the twentieth-century resurrection of the Ku Klux Klan.[55] The Anti-Defamation League of B'nai B'rith was founded in reaction to the anti-Semitism generated — or at least disclosed — by the Frank case.

Sometimes characterized as the "American Dreyfus case" (a reference to the frame-up of a French Jew that fanned the flames of nineteenth-century European anti-Semitism), the trial and appeals of Leo Frank in Atlanta, Georgia, were conducted in a carnival atmosphere. Crowds — mobs, really — sang "The Ballad of Mary Phagan," which included the following lyrics:

Little Mary Phagan
She left her home one day;
She went to the pencil-factory
to see the big parade.

She left her home at eleven,
She kissed her mother good-by;
Not one time did the poor child think
that she was a-going to die.

Leo Frank he met her
With a brutish heart, we know;
He smiled, and said, "Little Mary,
You won't go home no more."

Sneaked along behind her
Till she reached the metal-room;
He laughed, and said, "Little Mary,
You have met your fatal doom."

Down upon her knees
To Leo Frank she plead;
He taken a stick from the trash-pile
And struck her across the head.[56]

Crowds inside the courtroom shouted anti-Jewish epithets and demanded Frank's death. The smell of the lynch mob was in the air.

The state's star witness was James Conley, a black maintenance worker at the factory which Frank managed and at which Mary Phagan worked. Conley testified that Frank killed the young girl, ordered him to dispose of the body, and then dictated notes that placed the blame on a "Negro." When the jury convicted Frank, it was the first time in memory that a white man had been convicted of murder on the basis of the uncorroborated testimony of a black witness. This apparent advance in racial justice was explained away by a local observer who said: "That wasn't a white man convicted by that N__'s testimony. It was a Jew." "It has even been written that [prosecutor Hugh] Dorsey deliberately chose to prosecute a 'Yankee Jew' rather than a 'N__' for purposes of sensationalism, regardless of Frank's innocence."[57] Frank was portrayed as a pervert and "sodomite" whose sexual abnormality had been caused by the Jewish ritual of circumcision; the prosecution withheld forensic evidence of his innocence and appealed to the widespread bigotry of the times.

Predictably, Frank was convicted, sentenced to death, and denied relief on appeal to the Supreme Court, despite some critical dissenting words from Justice Oliver Wendell Holmes. Unpredictably, the lame-duck governor of Georgia decided to commute Frank's death sentence and leave him to serve out a term of life imprisonment. Governor Slaton wrote a ten-thousand-word order commuting the sentence of Leo Frank. This order concerned itself with the facts of the case and evidence that raised doubts about Frank's guilt. The commutation order was not political and did not discuss Leo Frank's religion. It was almost a week later, at a luncheon honoring his successor, that Governor Slaton used the example of Pontius Pilate to explain his actions.[58] He was quoted as saying: "Two thousand years ago another governor washed his hands of a case and turned over a Jew to a mob. For two thousand years that Governor's name has been accursed. If today another Jew were lying in his grave because I had failed to do my duty I would all through life find his blood on my hands and would consider myself an assassin through cowardice."[59]

That appeared to be a great victory for Frank and his many supporters around the country, since the evidentiary foundation underlying Frank's conviction was beginning to crumble as a result of the discovery of new evidence strongly suggesting that it was the government's star witness — and not Frank — who had killed the victim. It seemed only a matter of time before Frank would be freed from his imprisonment.

In order to prevent Frank's freedom, several of the "best" citizens of Georgia — including a minister, a former governor, two former Georgia Supreme Court justices, the son of a former senator, an ex-sheriff, and a sitting judge — decided to take the law into their own hands. (They were encouraged by populist agitator Tom Watson, whose newspaper, *The Jeffersonian*, advocated and then applauded the lynching.) They constituted themselves as a vigilante committee and let it be known that they intended to kidnap Frank from prison and lynch him. Despite some perfunctory efforts by prison authorities to protect their controversial prisoner, the lynch mob had little difficulty entering the prison and kidnapping Frank without firing a shot. It was obvious that at least some of the prison authorities were in on the plan. Frank was taken to Marietta, where he was lynched and his body desecrated. Everyone in Marietta knew exactly who was involved in the lynching — indeed, some members of the lynch mob boasted about their participation and gave interviews to the press. Photographs of the lynching and souvenir pieces of the rope were sold throughout Georgia. Nonetheless, the grand jury investigating the murder of Leo Frank — which included at least "seven members of the Lynch Party"[60] — concluded that it was unable to identify any of the perpetrators. This was typical of lynchings in the South during that era. The only difference is that this victim was not black.

By any amoral criteria, the lynching of Leo Frank was a great success for those who incited it and for those who actually participated in it. Its chief inciter, Thomas Watson, rode the lynching all the way to the United States Senate. (The U.S. attorney general considered prosecuting Watson — "on the grounds that his articles calling for the lynching constituted obscenity"[61] — but this effort was aborted by prominent Georgians and only enhanced Watson's popularity.) Several lynch mob members also exploited their role in the murder in subsequent elections. A number of others "spent the 1930s and 40s working in patronage jobs."[62]

The lynching also succeeded in frightening an already timid Jewish community into silence. Jewish-owned stores were attacked and Jewish merchants threatened. One of Atlanta's leading rabbis, David Marx, urged his congregation to remain silent and to assimilate as much as possible. He "did all that he could to make his flock less conspicuous, so much so that he often cast aspersions on the ritual-heavy practices of Atlanta's growing Orthodox Jewish population." Rabbi Marx blamed "the anti-Semitism that led to the lynching on the Orthodox Jewish community, rather than on the anti-Semites."[63] The lynching also had its intended impact on Jews outside of Georgia: It apparently persuaded New York Times publisher Adolph Ochs to stop writing about the incident. Finally, it even had a negative impact on efforts to reopen the case. In the 1920s a young Dutch reporter working for the Atlanta Constitution came upon some photographs and X-rays which seemed to prove that "the murdered girl had been bitten on the left shoulder and neck before being strangled," and that "photos of the teeth marks on her body did not correspond with Leo Frank's set of teeth."[64] Leaders of the Atlanta Jewish community put enormous pressure on the journalist not to revisit the case, and he did not publish his findings until decades later.

There is a fascinating and largely unknown ethical story behind the public legal story of the Frank case. I use it as a teaching vehicle in my course on legal ethics. It turns out that while Leo Frank was on death row, one of Atlanta's most prominent lawyers, Arthur Gray Powell, learned that Frank was innocent and that another man — presumably the government's star witness — was the killer. Powell described the case in his memoir:

I am one of the few people who know that Leo Frank was innocent of the crime for which he was convicted and lynched. Subsequent to the trial, and after his conviction had been affirmed by the Supreme Court, I learned who killed Mary Phagan, but the information came to me in such a way that, though I wish I could do so, I can never reveal it so long as certain persons are alive. We lawyers, when we are admitted to the bar, take an oath never to reveal the communications made to us by our clients; and this includes facts revealed in an attempt to employ the lawyer though he refuses the employment. . . . The Law on this subject may or may not be a wise law — there are some who think that it is not — but naturally since it is the law, we lawyers and the judges cannot honorably disobey it.[65]

It is uncertain whether the real killer actually confessed to his lawyer or whether the lawyer found other evidence of his guilt in the course of representing his client. It seems certain, however, that the actual killer was James Conley and that his own lawyer knew that to be the case. That lawyer probably sought legal representation from Powell, who turned down the case but only after learning the truth in a confidential communication. We do know that William Manning Smith, who did represent Conley, decided that his own client, and not Frank, was guilty and went public with that conclusion. Smith's public statements, however, were limited to his own assessment of the evidence and did not include any confession or admission by his client.[66]

An eminent lawyer was thus forced into the most excruciating legal, ethical, and moral dilemma a professional can possibly confront. The ethical rules of the profession were, at the time, fairly clear. There was no available exception to the rule mandating confidentiality of privileged communications about past crimes. It is not a future crime for the guilty person to remain silent while an innocent man goes to his death for the murder committed by a silent, guilty client. The issue is a bit more com-

plicated if the confessing client was, in fact, the witness who testified against Frank, for the client would then be confessing to
perjury. Some courts and commentators have suggested that allowing perjured testimony to remain unrecanted, while the victim of the perjury remains under a death or prison sentence, may
constitute a continuing fraud on the court, and thus an exception to the lawyer–client privilege. However, that line of authority was hazy at best, and the eminent lawyer did not apparently
consider it. He saw the legal and professional ethics issue as simple and straightforward. That still left the moral and personal
issue of whether any human being — regardless of his or her profession — can and should allow a preventable miscarriage of justice to be carried out, especially in a capital case. My students in
legal ethics generally split down the middle over whether they
would violate the rules of the profession — and engage in an act
of civil disobedience against their own client — in order to save
an innocent nonclient.

In a typically lawyerlike way, the eminent lawyer in the real
case apparently saw to it that the governor learned the information known to him, but without his own "fingerprints" being on
the communication. This is how he put it: "Without ever having
discussed with Governor Slaton the facts which were revealed to
me, I have reason to believe, from a thing contained in the statement he made in connection with the grant of the commutation,
that, in some way, these facts came to him and influenced his action."

However, the eminent lawyer's compromise did not work. Although the governor did commute Leo Frank's sentence, he was
not able to persuade a vengeful public of Frank's innocence. I
doubt that Frank would have been lynched had the eminent
lawyer come forward and disclosed all of the information that led
him to "know that Leo Frank was innocent." Instead, his own
client might well have been lynched. The complexity of ethical
and moral issues in the law can rarely be resolved by simple com-

promise solutions of the kind attempted by the lawyer in the Frank case. Indeed, some such issues have no entirely satisfactory solutions.

After coming across this intriguing story, I tried to obtain access to Powell's file on the case, since the "certain persons" referred to by Powell were by then almost certainly dead. Only recently did I learn that following Powell's death his Jewish partner, Max Goldstein, "destroyed" Powell's file — the file that might well have proved Frank's innocence and his own client's guilt — "believing that it would only inflame the feelings of those in disagreement."[67]

Nearly seventy years after Leo Frank's murder, additional new evidence of his innocence emerged. An eighty-two-year-old man, who had been a youthful eyewitness to events surrounding the killing of Mary Phagan, came forward and told what he had seen back in 1913. His evidence contradicted the state's star witness and strongly suggested that the murder was committed by that same witness, the black maintenance man.[68] The murderer threatened the young witness with death if he ever mentioned what he had observed, and he did not come forward for all those years. Now he has told his story, and it seems to have persuaded most objective people that Leo Frank was lynched for a crime committed by someone else.

Finally, in 1986, the State of Georgia issued the following official apology: "The lynching aborted the legal process, thus foreclosing further effort to prove Frank's innocence. It resulted from the State of Georgia's failure to protect Frank. Compounding the injustice, the State then failed to prosecute any of the lynchers." Remarkably, many Georgians — including descendants of Frank's murderers — continue to resist even this apology.

The Leo Frank case manifested some of the worst features of American justice — really, injustice — all rolled into one. It had racism, anti-Semitism, sensationalism, and, most importantly, the extralegal, lynch mob finale that tarnished so much of Southern law and order — really, lawlessness and disorder — in the early twentieth century. The worst part of the lynching is that it succeeded: Most of those who took part lived happy, guilt-free, and rewarding lives; many of those who supported Frank's innocence or who condemned the lynching suffered financial and career setbacks. Lynching was thereby encouraged, and the practice persisted for decades. In that sense, the 1986 apology is at least a positive acknowledgment of our past and of how far we have come. But no apology can ever erase the horrible legacy of lynch mob justice that prevailed in so many parts of our nation.

The reason no great film or play was ever based on this case is that there are no real heroes, no uplifting message, and no positive lessons. It was a pure, unmitigated tragedy, one in which evil was rewarded, virtue was punished, and bigotry emerged triumphant. The Leo Frank case was an American *Dreyfus* in that it revealed a pervasive hatred of Jews in some parts of our nation — a hatred that infected the legal system. It was *not* an American *Dreyfus* in the sense that France, because it had no tradition of lynching, was able to rectify its judicial error during Dreyfus's lifetime.

The Abrams Case

Date: 1919
Location: New York City, New York
Defendants: Jacob Abrams and other authors of a Bolshevik
             pamphlet
Charge: Violation of the Sedition Act
Verdict: Guilty
Sentence: Twenty years in prison for the male defendants;
             fifteen years in prison for the woman

The free speech protections of the First Amendment, though enacted in 1793, remained essentially dead letters until the second decade of the twentieth century, when Justices Oliver Wendell Holmes and Louis Brandeis breathed life into the words "Congress shall make no law abridging the freedom of speech."

In our age of nearly total freedom of speech, it is difficult to imagine how close we came to a regime of censorship. The same Oliver Wendell Holmes — who in his *Abrams* dissent waxed eloquent about "the best test of truth [being] the power of the thought to get itself accepted in the competition of the market" — had written, just four years earlier, the majority opinion in *Fox v. Washington*, one of the silliest and most repressive decisions ever penned in this or any other country.[69] In that case, an editor was sentenced to jail for writing an editorial titled "The Nude and the Prudes" in a community newspaper. In this dangerous and seditious revolutionary piece, the editor criticized "opponents of nude swimming."[70] He was convicted under a Washington State law making it a crime "to encourage or advocate disrespect for law."[71] With an absolutely straight face, the great Holmes concluded that the "article encourages and incites" — albeit "by indirection but unmistakably" — a persistence in what "we must assume would be a breach of the state laws against indecent exposure."[72] As such, it is not protected by the Constitution. When criticized for his cavalier attitude toward freedom of speech, Holmes told Judge Learned Hand that a state should be as free to protect itself against dangerous opinions as against the spread of smallpox: "Free speech stands no differently than freedom from vaccination."[73]

It was this cramped view of speech that led Holmes to formulate the most famous legal phrase since the Bible: that freedom of speech does not protect "falsely shouting fire in a theatre," a phrase that has been characterized as "the most brilliantly persuasive expression that ever came from Holmes's pen."[74] I respectfully dissent. I regard it as one of the most dishonest, inapt, misleading, confusing, and misused phrases in legal history. As I have written:

> The example of shouting "Fire!" obviously bore little relationship to the facts of the Schenck case. The Schenck pamphlet contained a substantive political message. [Schenck, an antiwar activist, had been convicted of violating federal law on the basis of a pamphlet he had written urging people to become conscientious objectors.] It urged the draftee readers to think about the message and then — if they so chose — to act on it in a lawful and non-violent way. The man who shouts "Fire!" in a crowded theater is neither sending a political message nor inviting his listener to think about what he has said and decide what to do in a rational, calculated manner. On the contrary, the message is designed to force an action without contemplation. The message "Fire!" is directed not to the mind and the

conscience of the listener but, rather, to his adrenaline and his feet. It is a stimulus to immediate action, not to thoughtful reflection.

Indeed, in that respect the shout of "Fire!" is not even speech, in any meaningful sense of that term. It is a clang sound, the equivalent of setting off a nonverbal alarm. Had Justice Holmes been more honest about his example, he would have said that freedom of speech does not protect a kid who pulls a fire alarm in the absence of a fire. But that obviously would have been irrelevant to the case. . . . The analogy is thus not only inapt but also insulting. Most Americans do not respond to political rhetoric with the same kind of automatic acceptance expected of schoolchildren responding to a fire drill.[75]

Another important reason why the analogy is inapt is that Holmes emphasizes the factual falsity of the shout of "Fire!" The Schenck pamphlet, however, was not factually false. It contained political opinions and ideas about the causes of the war and about appropriate and lawful responses to the draft. As the Supreme Court recently reaffirmed (in *Hustler v. Falwell*), "The First Amendment recognizes no such thing as a 'false' idea." Nor, of course, does it recognize false opinions about the causes or cures for war.[76]

Holmes's contemporaries were equally contemptuous of the justice's analogy. As Professor Zechariah Chafee of Harvard put it: "How about the man who gets up in a theater between the acts and informs the audience honestly but perhaps mistakenly that the fire exits are too few or locked. He is a much closer parallel to Schenck. . . ." What was required, Chafee concluded, was not "the multiplication of obvious examples" but rather "the development of a rational principle."[77]

Holmes cared deeply about how his intellectual peers regarded him, and when the Abrams case came to the court, he did a dramatic about-face on the importance of freedom of speech. But first a few words about the colorful defendants whose Yiddish leaflet generated the important case of *Abrams v. United States.* The defendants were a motley array of Communists, anarchists, socialists, and labor reformers who shared a common antipathy toward President Wilson's decision to send in troops against the Bolshevik revolution. Prosecutors regarded them all as of the same ilk, despite their political differences. I am reminded of the story of the New York cops who were beating up City College kids during a Communist demonstration in the 1930s. One of the kids shouted, "Stop beating me, I'm an anti-Communist," to which the cop replied, "I don't care what kind of Communist you are," as he continued the beating.

The leaflet at issue was mild by today's standards, railing against the "chutzpahdik" administration that was employing all manner of pretense to stifle the Bolshevik revolution. It was pablum in comparison with the common fare at the time of our Revolution and in the years thereafter, when pamphlet writers were prosecuted under the alien and sedition laws. But it was enough to warrant prosecution under the newly enacted Sedition Act, which broadly criminalized all antiwar advocacy as well as any language that brings the country, the flag, the armed forces, or the Constitution into "contempt, scorn, contumely, or disrepute."[78]

The defendants were beaten (one to death) by the police, who then lied about the beatings under oath. The trial judge, Henry Clayton, was a bigot who refused to permit one of the foreign-born Jewish defendants to refer to the forefathers of the American Revolution as "my forefathers," and who asked, at trial, why Abrams and his kind would not just "go back to Russia."[79] (This was tame stuff compared to Supreme Court Justice James McReynolds, who wrote to Justice Holmes concerning Justice Brandeis that "for four thousand years the Lord tried to make something of the Hebrews, then gave it up as impossible and turned them out to prey on mankind in general — like fleas."[80] McReynolds reportedly would leave the conference room when his Jewish colleague began to speak.)

The defendants were all convicted and sentenced to twenty years in prison (the one woman was chivalrously given only fifteen years) for the seditious leaflet, and the Supreme Court agreed to review the case. The majority decision is eminently forgettable, but Holmes's dissent includes one of the most powerful paragraphs ever written in defense of freedom of speech:

> Persecution for the expression of opinions seems to me perfectly logical. If you have no doubt of your premises or your power and want a certain result with all your heart you naturally express your wishes in law and sweep away all opposition. . . . But when men have realized that time has upset many fighting faiths, they may come to believe even more than they believe the very foundations of their own conduct that the ultimate good desired is better reached by free trade in ideas — that the best test of truth is the power of the thought to get itself accepted in the competition of the market, and that truth is the only ground upon which their wishes safely can be carried out. That at any rate is the theory of our Constitution. It is an experiment, as all life is an experiment. . . . While experiment is part of our system I think that we should be eternally vigilant against attempts to check the expression of opinions that we loathe and believe to be fraught with death, unless they so imminently threaten immediate interference with the lawful and pressing purposes of the law that an immediate check is required to save the country. . . . Only the emergency that makes it immediately dangerous to leave the correction of evil counsels to time warrants making any exception to the sweeping command, "Congress shall make no law abridging the freedom of speech."[81]

It is difficult to reconcile these ringing words with the drivel that came from the same pen just four years earlier in the nude swimming case. But during those four formative years, Holmes was persuaded, not by the briefs or arguments of the lawyers who appeared before him, but rather by conversations with and letters from friends and colleagues such as Professors Chafee and Harold Laski, as well as Judges Hand and Brandeis. Indeed, despite the eloquence and influence of the Holmesean view of freedom of speech reflected in his *Abrams* dissent, it does not contain a single original idea. Every thought was lifted directly from the writings of Chafee and others. The Chafee view of freedom of speech eventually came to be identified with Holmes and Brandeis and to prevail on the Supreme Court until it was surpassed by an even more speech-protective formulation in the 1969 Brandenburg case.[82]

Professor Chafee's victory was not, however, without its costs. Chafee was accused by some Harvard Law School alumni of being unfit to be "entrusted with the training of youth." (Little has changed in three-quarters of a century. I am accused of such unfitness by reactionary alumni about once a month.) A "trial" was conducted and Chafee cleared, but not without considerable aggravation. He nonetheless continued to be entrusted with the training of youth for many years.

The defendants in the *Abrams* case were not so fortunate. Like most "troublemakers," they had difficulty fitting in anywhere. Eventually they were deported to the Soviet Union, where they opposed Lenin and were deported from the "workers' paradise." One of them ended up in Minsk, where he became a victim of Hitler's Holocaust. Another returned to the Soviet Union, where he was murdered by Stalin. A third moved to Mexico City, where he lived uneventfully until his death. Their pamphlet may not have changed the world in the way they wanted, but their case made an important contribution to the history and development of the right to free speech.

The Shoeless Joe Jackson Case

Date:	*1921*
Location:	*Chicago, Illinois*
Defendant:	*Joseph Jefferson Jackson*
Charge:	*Conspiracy to defraud the public, to commit a confidence game, to injure the business of Charles Comiskey*
Verdict:	*Not guilty*
Sentence:	*Banishment from professional baseball*

To Americans, baseball is more than a game. It is a pastime of memory and legend. At its apex stands the World Series. When I was growing up in Brooklyn, everything stopped during our secular "holy week." Our hometown favorites, the Dodgers, were always playing and almost always losing to the New York Yankees. Fifty years later, I remember nearly every inning. I can only imagine how it felt to be a Chicago White Sox fan in 1919—to learn that their hometown favorites, led by their living legend Joe Jackson, had thrown the World Series.

Shoeless Joe Jackson was the greatest natural hitter the game of baseball has ever seen. As legend has it, he was discovered playing mill-town ball in his stocking feet. In the second decade of the twentieth century, swinging Black Betsy, his famous homemade bat, he electrified the major leagues with his clutch slugging, bulletlike throws, and come-from-nowhere fielding.

But then, at the height of his career, he was disgraced and

thrown out of organized baseball for his alleged role in fixing the 1919 World Series. The "Black Sox Scandal," as it has come to be called, involved eight members of the Chicago White Sox who were indicted for throwing the Series to the Cincinnati Reds.

The rise and fall of this great natural ballplayer — followed by his gutsy comeback as an aging star of semipro "outlaw" ball — has inspired numerous American writers ranging from Nelson Algren to William Kinsella. His life and legend infuse Joe Hardy ("Shoeless Joe from Hannibal, Mo.") in *Damn Yankees*, as well as Roy Hobbs, the hero of Bernard Malamud's *The Natural*, the character portrayed on screen by Robert Redford. And he made another appearance in the movie *Field of Dreams*, which was based on Kinsella's novel *Shoeless Joe*. The gambler who orchestrated the fix, Arnold Rothstein, was the model for a character in *The Great Gatsby*, by F. Scott Fitzgerald. Whatever one thinks of Jackson's moral character, there is no doubt that he has become a unique figure in popular American mythology.

The most famous phrase to emerge from the Black Sox Scandal, and perhaps from all of baseball, was the tearful plea allegedly put to Shoeless Joe by a young fan: "Say it ain't so, Joe!" But Joe did not say that it wasn't so. An illiterate country boy, he gave contradictory answers about his involvement in a gambling scheme. Although he denied that he threw any games, his major-league career was over, and he entered history as a personification of corruption.

That was more than eighty years ago. Since then we have learned much about Jackson's real role in the Black Sox Scandal. This new information strongly suggests that it wasn't so, or at the very least was not as bad as the powers of organized baseball have led us to believe.

The White Sox cover-up was intended to protect club owner and president Charles Comiskey, much as contemporary political cover-ups are intended to protect presidents and other politicians. The big difference is that the White Sox cover-up worked. And therein lies an interesting story about how much our legal system has changed for the better over the intervening half century.

The facts, as they now have emerged, seem to be as follows: Jackson was approached by a teammate, who offered him ten thousand dollars to "frame up something" by throwing the World Series. He declined. A short time later the offer was renewed, this time for twenty thousand. Jackson refused again. This information comes from Jackson's own testimony before the Cook County Grand Jury, the very testimony that has, in garbled, twisted press accounts, been used as proof of Jackson's complicity.[83] (The transcript of Jackson's grand jury testimony suspiciously disappeared for sixty-five years after his 1924 civil trial against Comiskey.[84]) Furthermore, there is strong evidence that Jackson told one or more officials of the club well ahead of the first game that a fix was in the making. There were rumors, even before the Series began, that a fix was on, because large sums of money were being bet on the underdog Reds. Jackson even asked to be benched for the Series to avoid any suspicion that he was involved, but his request was refused. "Tell the newspapers you just suspended me for being drunk, or anything," Joe apparently said, "but leave me out of the series and then there can be no question."[85]

Some people believe that Jackson did originally agree to throw the Series in exchange for twenty thousand dollars, but then changed his mind after receiving "only part of the $20,000 he was promised." Almost no one believes he actually tried to lose even a single game. My own review of the available evidence leads me to believe that he never agreed to throw the World Series — that "it ain't so."[86] Several of Jackson's teammates did conspire to throw the Series, and the White Sox lost to the Cincinnati Reds, five games to three. (The Series was extended to "best-of-nine" games for the sake of public entertainment in the wake of World War I.) Jackson, however, playing under the watchful eyes of club officials, was the star of the Series: He hit the only home run, fielded flawlessly, and batted .375 to lead all players; his twelve hits set a World Series record that stood for decades. Yet the players who had joined the conspiracy persistently tried to involve Jackson in the scandal, and even told the gamblers that Jackson had consented to participate in the scheme.

Like most of the known facts about the Jackson case, the event that is usually cited to prove his guilt has also been misrepresented. On the evening after the last game of the Series, one of Jackson's teammates came to his hotel room and offered him an envelope containing cash. Jackson refused to accept it, an argument ensued, and Jackson stormed out of his own room. His teammate, pitcher Lefty Williams, threw the envelope down and left. This version of the crucial event in Jackson's case was attested to, under oath, by the only two men who were there: Jackson and Williams. Their accounts agree. Jackson did not take the money; it was dumped on him. According to Jackson's later testimony about the incident, he knew nothing about the frame-up until this point and was completely unaware that "his name had been used" by the other players in negotiating with the gamblers. Jackson allegedly told Williams that "they had a lot of nerve. I don't know just the word I used, but 'Big bums' or something, to be out pulling that kind of stuff on me, knowing that it was the only way I had of making a livelihood."[87]

Returning to his room, Jackson found the envelope and saw that it contained five thousand dollars in cash. He put it in his pocket. The next morning he went to Comiskey's office at the ballpark, planning to "tell him all about it," but he was told "Comiskey was busy" and would not see him.[88] Jackson waited for an hour, and then he left.

Comiskey, who at that very moment was in a secret meeting with two of the fixed players hearing the story of the scheme, chose a hypocritical course of action. While publicly proclaiming his commitment to "clean baseball," he privately spent the winter and almost all of the 1920 season denying the rumors that stubbornly clung to the 1919 Series and perpetrating a cover-up, in part to protect his valuable property — namely, the guilty players. But in September 1920, for reasons that had more to do with political infighting and greed than with "clean baseball," a grand jury was impaneled and the fix was exposed.

Now Comiskey's priority was to protect his own reputation, which was not very good to begin with. He was known as "the cheap stingy tyrant" for the low salaries he paid players. His star pitcher, Ed Cicotte, was promised a bonus, in addition to his five-thousand-dollar salary, if he won thirty games. When he reached twenty-nine, Comiskey had him benched, so that he couldn't earn the bonus. Not surprisingly, Cicotte was one of the players who took money from the gamblers.

Comiskey's best option was to feed the suspected players to the grand jury, but only after they had been counseled by Comiskey's own lawyer, Alfred Austrian. The point of this exercise seems to have been damage control — Comiskey would have looked bad if the public learned what he knew and when he knew it. Of the players fed to the grand jury, Jackson was the most problematic. He had been the only one to warn Comiskey before the Series began. If he told everything, Comiskey's self-proclaimed integrity would be impugned and he would be revealed as a hypocrite and perhaps worse.

Jackson was working under two misconceptions when he met with Austrian: He believed the truth would protect him, and he believed Austrian was his lawyer. Neither belief was true. Jackson began by protesting his innocence, but in a session that lasted for several hours, Austrian finally convinced Jackson that the truth would not be believed by the grand jury. We do not know exactly what Austrian suggested to Jackson (while Austrian admitted under oath that he had kept notes on his pre-testimony meetings with the other players, he claimed he kept no notes during his session with Jackson), but we can make some logical deductions by analyzing the grand jury testimony Jackson subsequently gave. A careful reading of that testimony reveals that Jackson told two diametrically opposed stories, one confessing his guilt and the other protesting his innocence. Logic leads us to believe the first story was probably Austrian's; the second, Jackson's.

Jackson was eventually indicted, tried in criminal court, and found not guilty. The trial itself was something of an anticlimax, but the events — and the impact they had on our national pastime — warrant inclusion in any catalog of great cases. Notwithstanding Jackson's acquittal, he was banished from organized baseball. That is when his love of the game led him to his second career in semipro "outlaw" ball.

In 1924, during a civil trial in which Jackson sued Comiskey for back wages on a three-year contract, the likely truth of how and why Jackson's name had been falsely implicated in the Black Sox scheme finally came to light. Sleepy Bill Burns, the fixer who put the players and the gamblers in touch with each other, testified under oath that he had never talked to Jackson about the fix. Instead, he took the word of Lefty Williams, who claimed he was empowered to speak for Jackson. And Williams himself, also under oath, swore he never received Jackson's permission to use his name with the fixers. This is perhaps the most compelling evidence we have, because it provides both motivation and means. The gamblers wanted a sure thing, and since Jackson was capable of going on a hitting streak that could carry the White Sox to victory despite the fix, they wanted Jackson in. So the fixed players, in the person of Williams, said he was. The means were equally simple: Williams and Burns both wanted the scheme to work, so one lied and the other took him at his word with no effort to substantiate his claim.

The outcome of the civil suit was ambiguous. The jury found in Jackson's favor, but the judge overruled the verdict. Nevertheless, it was the second jury to hear Jackson's story and find him innocent of culpable involvement in the Black Sox Scandal. Still, the powers that be in organized baseball ignored the jury verdicts and refused to lift his lifetime banishment.

Jackson received shoddy treatment, but this probably would not happen today. A modern-day Jackson would have his own lawyer from the very beginning, as Pete Rose did. Nor would the bar today tolerate the shenanigans employed by Comiskey's lawyer. Most important, an honest prosecutor today generally seeks to follow the criminal trail to the top of the mountain. Convicting the Watergate burglars was not enough. The special prosecutor followed the trail to the attorney general and eventually to the president.

But in post–World War I Chicago, corruption tainted more than the White Sox. The entire city — judiciary and all — reeked with influence peddling and power brokering, and among the most influential brokers was Charles Comiskey. Therefore, it is no surprise that Comiskey now holds an honored place in the Baseball Hall of Fame, while Shoeless Joe Jackson remains a scapegoat. Though both are now long dead, the true story deserves to be known. In the last years of his life, former baseball commissioner A. B. "Happy" Chandler got behind the efforts to clear Jackson's name. "I never in my life believed him to be guilty of a single thing," said the man who was privy to the secret files of the major leagues.

If one thing is certain in the Black Sox Scandal, it is that the real villain was Charles Comiskey. It was he who abused the game for money — not using his best pitcher to prevent him from getting his bonus, and practically inciting his players to throw the Series with his low salaries and cost-saving mistreatments. He lined his pockets, acting for his own sake and not for baseball, and remarkably, it is *he* who finds himself enshrined in Cooperstown in the Baseball Hall of Fame. He may not have bet on the game, as Pete Rose did more than half a century later, but

Charles Comiskey certainly gave less to baseball, and took much much more from it, than Shoeless Joe and Pete Rose ever did. Pete Rose and Shoeless Joe gave all of themselves to the game and accomplished great things, and though Rose wagered on games he managed, he never tried to hurt his team for personal financial gain. The same cannot be said of Comiskey, who put the profit motive above playing his best pitcher, paying his best players, and winning the most games. Baseball should thus strongly consider putting up a plaque for Shoeless Joe and taking down the one for Comiskey.

Baseball is a game of legends. Memories play as important a role as current events. If it "ain't so" — or even if it wasn't as bad as legend has it — big-league baseball should be big enough to admit it made a mistake about Shoeless Joe. Like any other institution, baseball can only be honest in the present if it is honest with its own past. And since baseball is still viewed by many as a metaphor for America itself, such an act of corrective justice would have meaning beyond baseball as a mere game.

1. J. Leonard Bates, *The United States 1898–1928: Progressivism and a Society in Transition* (New York: McGraw-Hill, 1976), pp. 35–36.

2. *Ibid.*, p. 35.

3. Michael MacDonald Mooney, *Evelyn Nesbit and Stanford White: Love and Death in the Gilded Age* (New York: William Morrow and Co., 1976), p. 239.

4. *Ibid.*, p. 299.

5. Richard M. Abrams, *The Burdens of Progress: 1900–1929* (Glenview, IL: Scott, Foresman and Co., 1978), p. 85.

6. Fon W. Boardman, *America and the Progressive Era: 1910–1917* (New York: Henry Z. Walck, 1970), p. 13.

7. *Ibid.*, p. 34.

8. Joseph R. Conlin, *Big Bill Haywood and the Radical Union Movement* (New York: Syracuse University Press, 1969), p. 58.

9. *Ibid.*, pp. 59, 73.

10. *Ibid.*, p. 59.

11. Selig Perlman and Philip Taft, *History of Labor in the United States, 1896–1932*, vol. 4 (New York: Augustus M. Kelley, 1966), p. 212.

12. *Ibid.*, p. 323.

13. *Ibid.*, p. 322.

14. *Ibid.*, pp. 323–24.

15. Albert S. Lindemann, *The Jew Accused: Three Anti-Semitic Affairs: Dreyfus, Beilis, Frank, 1894–1915* (Cambridge: Cambridge University Press, 1991), p. 223.

16. Leonard Dinnerstein, "Atlanta in the Progressive Era: A Dreyfus Affair in Georgia," in *Jews in the South,* ed. Leonard Dinnerstein and Mary Dale Palsson (Baton Rouge: Louisiana State University Press, 1973), p. 194.

17. *Ibid.*, p. 183.

18. Jeffrey Melnick, *Black–Jewish Relations on Trial: Leo Frank and Jim Conley in the New South* (Jackson: University Press of Mississippi, 2000), p. 46.

19. *Ibid.*, p. 63.

20. Dinnerstein, "Atlanta," pp. 189–90.

21. Lindemann, p. 240.

22. Bates, p. 234.

23. *Ibid.*

24. Eliot Asinof, *1919: America's Loss of Innocence* (New York: Donald I. Fine, 1990), p. 342.

25. Gerald Langford, *The Murder of Stanford White* (New York: The Notable Trials Library, 1996), pp. 115–16.

26. *Ibid.*, p. 28.

27. *Ibid.*, p. 116.

28. *Ibid.*, pp. 47–48.

29. Cited in *ibid.*, p. 71.

30. Cited in *ibid.*, p. 73.

31. *Ibid.*

32. For a discussion of the Bobbitt case, in which the defendant cut off her husband's penis, see Alan Dershowitz, *The Abuse Excuse* (Boston: Little, Brown and Co., 1994).

33. Langford, p. 49.

34. *Ibid.*

35. *Ibid.*, p. 34.

36. *Ibid.*, p. 206.

37. *Ibid.*, p. 240.

38. David H. Grover, *Debaters and Dynamiters: The Story of the Haywood Trial* (New York: The Notable Trials Library, 1994), pp. 118–26.

39. *Ibid.*, p. 186.

40. *Ibid.*, p. 213.

41. *Ibid.*, p. 211.

42. Douglas Linder, *Famous American Trials: Bill Haywood Trial, 1907* (1998), www.law.umkc.edu/faculty/projects/ftrials/haywood/haywood.htm.

43. Douglas Linder, "Biography of Harry Orchard," *Famous American Trials: Bill Haywood Trial, 1907* (1998), www.law.umkc.edu/faculty/projects/ftrials/haywood/HAY_BORC.HTM.

44. Grover, p. 123.

45. Oscar King Davis, "Orchard Tells About Murders," *New York Times*, June 6, 1907, available at www.law.umkc.edu/faculty/projects/ftrials/haywood/HAY_N66.HTM.

46. See, generally, Geoffrey Cowan, *The People v. Clarence Darrow* (New York: The Notable Trials Library, 1995), pp. 279–94.

47. *Ibid.*, pp. 191–92.

48. *Ibid.*, p. 197.

49. *Ibid.*, p. 439.

50. *Ibid.*, p. 438.

51. *Ibid.*, p. 437.

52. *Ibid.*, pp. 439–40.

53. *Ibid.*, p. 440.

54. *Ibid.*

55. Leonard Dinnerstein, *The Leo Frank Case* (Birmingham: The Notable Trials Library, 1991), pp. 149–50.

56. *Ibid.*, p. 166. Although the actual ballad was composed by "Fiddlin'" John Carson only after the trial, its sentiments were expressed loudly and clearly during the trial and subsequent legal proceedings.

57. Edward W. Knappman, *Great American Trials* (Detroit: Visible Ink Press, 1994), pp. 269–70.

58. Dinnerstein, *Leo Frank*, p. 129.

59. *Ibid.*

60. Steve Oney, *And the Dead Shall Rise* (New York: Pantheon, 2003), pp. 588–89.

61. *Ibid.*, p. 603.

62. *Ibid.*, p. 620.

63. *Ibid.*, p. 608.
64. *Ibid.*, p. 617.
65. Arthur Gray Powell, *I Can Go Home Again* (Chapel Hill: University of North Carolina Press, 1943), p. 291.
66. Oney, pp. 427–54.
67. *Ibid.*, p. 618.
68. See "Statement of Alonzo Mann" in Dinnerstein, *Leo Frank.*
69. *Fox v. Washington*, 35 S. Ct. 383 (1915).
70. Jay Fox, ed., "The Nude and the Prudes," *The Agitator*, July 1, 1911.
71. *State v. Fox*, 127 P. 1111, 1112 (Wash. 1912).
72. *Fox v. Washington*, p. 277.
73. Richard Polenberg, *Fighting Faiths: The Abrams Case, the Supreme Court and Free Speech* (New York: The Notable Trials Library, 1996), p. 211.
74. *Ibid.*, p. 213.
75. Alan Dershowitz, *Shouting Fire: Civil Liberties in a Turbulent Age* (Boston: Little, Brown and Co., 2002), pp. 143–44.
76. *Ibid.*, p. 145.
77. Polenberg, pp. 222–23.
78. U.S. Sedition Act, *Statutes at Large*, Washington, DC, 1918, vol. XL, p. 553.
79. Polenberg, pp. 118, 119.
80. *Ibid.*, p. 205.
81. *Abrams v. United States*, 40 S. Ct. 617, 627 (1919).
82. *Brandenburg v. Ohio*, 89 S. Ct. 1827 (1969).
83. Donald Gropman, *Say It Ain't So, Joe! The True Story of Shoeless Joe Jackson* (New York: Citadel Press, 1992), p. 269.
84. *Ibid.*, p. 275.
85. Cited in *ibid.*, p. 169.
86. Paul Weiler, *Leveling the Playing Field: How the Law Can Make Sports Better for Fans* (Cambridge, MA: Harvard University Press, 2000), p. 51.
87. Gropman, p. 294.
88. Cited in *ibid.*, pp. 294–95.

PART VIII

The Roaring Twenties and the Depression Thirties

THE PERIOD BETWEEN THE WORLD WARS was marked by a struggle between Christian religious fundamentalism and an emerging religious and cultural pluralism and skepticism. One manifestation of this conflict was the effort to ban the teaching of evolution led by William Jennings Bryan. The Scopes trial, in which a teacher in a Tennessee public school challenged an antievolution law by teaching Darwin in his classroom, led to the birth of several organizations, including the Supreme Kingdom, lobbying for the adoption of an antievolution amendment.[1] The movement enjoyed success in 1928 with the adoption of an antievolution bill in Arkansas. The Scopes trial was significant because it exposed the great "cultural schism" in America regarding the proper role of religion and modern scientific theory in public schools and the larger debate between fundamentalism and enlightenment.[2] Fundamentalists, who were predominantly Southerners, viewed the trial as a fight "to preserve the best features of the American heritage — a belief in spirituality of the universe and in the God-like character of man."[3] Rationalists, in Clarence Darrow's words, "were fighting 'to prevent bigots and ignoramuses from controlling the educational system of the United States.'"[4]

Movements for preservation of "tradition" and accompanying manifestations of intolerance were not limited to the antievolution crusade; the era between the world wars was marked by intensive nativism, religious persecution, and racial prejudice. From immigration restriction laws that effectively curtailed immigration from anywhere but northwestern Europe, to discrimination against Roman Catholics, many Americans were bold and outspoken in their intolerance for "outsiders."[5] Nowhere was such intolerance more pronounced than in the trial of Sacco and Vanzetti, the Italian immigrants convicted of murder during a robbery in Massachusetts in 1920.

The trial of Sacco and Vanzetti and their subsequent execution "reflected once again the breakdown of the rule of law under anti-alien and anti-radical pressure and the willingness of the legal profession to acquiesce in the process."[6] Essentially, the radical movement, rather than the two particular defendants, was put on trial; this led to nearly uniform support for Sacco and Vanzetti from the American immigrant left, which drafted petitions and organized mass meetings and rallies all over the world.[7] The trial was significant in American history because "in the eyes of the world the United States was cast in the role of oppressor."[8] Ultimately, the Sacco and Vanzetti trial was symptomatic of the larger problem of the era: the inability of "outsiders" to overcome prejudice and achieve justice.[9]

While new immigrants struggled to achieve justice in the courts or through the legislature, African Americans faced formidable struggles under threats of violence and terror from racist organizations such as the Ku Klux Klan. The Scottsboro trial, in which nine African American young men were convicted of, and sentenced to death for, raping two white women on a freight train in Alabama, reflected societal repulsion at the thought of a black man having sex with a white woman. The trial affected American history by stimulating a broad coalition of people to seek justice for African Americans. "More even than the Sacco-Vanzetti case, 'the Scottsboro boys' became a cause célèbre in the United States and all over the world."[10] Eventually they, unlike Sacco and Vanzetti, escaped execution and were freed, after serving considerable time in the shadow of death.

Two other famous trials in which the death penalty was challenged were the Leopold and Loeb case in 1924 and the Lindbergh kidnapping trial in 1935. In the Leopold and Loeb trial, the defendants' guilt for the murder of young Bobby Franks was evident, as was their cold, calculating premeditation of the murder; yet Leopold and Loeb avoided the death penalty. In contrast, Bruno Richard Hauptmann, whose guilt for kidnapping and killing the baby of American hero Charles A. Lindbergh was anything but certain, was sentenced to death and executed. Clarence Darrow was able to use the Leopold and Loeb trial as "a national platform from which to argue against the death penalty."[11] In contrast, in 1932, Congress was able to use the kidnapping and murder of the Lindbergh baby to enact the death penalty for kidnapping across state lines.[12]

While Americans struggled to cope with developments at home brought about by immigration and other social changes in the years between world wars, the government was also faced with constructing a viable foreign policy in the postwar period. During the 1920s, the United States maintained a policy advocating peace while purposely avoiding any affirmative obligations to uphold the peace in times of crisis.[13] During the 1920s, the Harding administration refused to join the League of Nations.[14] In effect, the United States allowed "new aggressors . . . to make a hollow mockery of [its] vain efforts in the following decade."[15] American resistance to addressing the changing state of foreign affairs was exemplified by the trial of Colonel Billy Mitchell. Mitchell appreciated the volatility of the world climate, the high probability of another world war, and the United States' lack of preparation in the event that war came. American disregard for Mitchell's fateful prophecies and calls for change reflected the larger problem of American isolationism and unwillingness to respond during these tumultuous years between world wars.

The American legal system reached a certain level of maturity between the world wars. Lawyers — with some striking exceptions — became more than mere orators. Legal and factual research was taken more seriously. The press began to understand the drama of the trial, and gavel-to-gavel coverage became the order of the day. Several trials of the 1920s and 1930s became the subjects of books, plays, and films. Some are still remembered today.

The Trial of Sacco and Vanzetti

Date: 1921–27
Location: Dedham and Boston, Massachusetts
Defendants: Nicola Sacco and Bartolomeo Vanzetti
Charge: Murder
Verdict: Guilty
Sentence: Electrocution

The case of Sacco and Vanzetti is a murder mystery — with political and ethnic overtones — that has never been completely solved. In 1920, a band of five armed robbers made off with the payroll of a South Braintree, Massachusetts, shoe company. In the course of this bold daylight robbery, the paymaster and a guard were shot and killed. Two left-wing radicals of Italian origin were arrested after attempting — with two other people — to retrieve a car believed to have been used in the robbery. At the time of their arrest, they were carrying pistols and anarchist literature.

The two accused extremists, Nicola Sacco and Bartolomeo Vanzetti, were charged with the felony murder and brought to trial. The evidence against them, primarily ballistic and eyewitness, was disputed from the very beginning. The jury, which consisted entirely of "native" Americans — to use the quaint, if inaccurate, language of the day — was instructed on the evidence by a Brahmin bigot, Judge Webster Thayer, who could barely conceal his contempt for the Italian troublemakers.

The trial was unjust, in the sense that the evidentiary rulings and instructions were one-sidedly favorable to the prosecution.[16] Following the conviction and a worldwide outcry against Massachusetts's justice, Governor Alvan Fuller appointed an independent commission to advise him concerning the fairness of the trial.

The problem was that the commission's chairman and moving force was also an anti-Italian bigot and an avowed racist — Abbott Lawrence Lowell, the president of Harvard University. President Lowell — who introduced racial and religious quotas to Harvard — was anything but objective on a matter pitting the fairness of Brahmin justice against the claims of Italian radicals. His report, which was forcefully criticized by Professor Felix Frankfurter of Harvard Law School and others, was a whitewash of Judge Thayer and the prosecutor.[17] Despite the availability of new evidence, which cast considerable doubt on the ballistic and eyewitness testimony at the trial, Governor Fuller refused to commute the sentence.[18]

On August 22, 1927, more than seven years after the murders at South Braintree, Sacco and Vanzetti were executed. Their death certificates designate their cause of death as "judicial homicide." It was not intended to be ironic, but many people believe it to be an apt description. The controversy did not die with them. The question of their guilt or innocence is still debated today. Indeed, in recent years, two purportedly definitive books were published.[19] Each reconsidered the old evidence, provided new information, and reviewed the trial transcript. Each claimed to resolve the question with finality and, in the words of one reviewer, to "bring to a close six decades of controversy."[20] The only problem is that the two definitive books arrived at diametrically opposing conclusions! One said that Sacco and Vanzetti were "irrefutably guilty."[21] The other was equally certain of their innocence.[22]

That should not be surprising in a highly politicized case with no "smoking gun." Evidence does not generally become clearer with the passage of time. It only appears more certain to those with a stake in a particular conclusion. A case such as Sacco-Vanzetti, which grew out of a highly politicized climate, can never become depoliticized, even with a diminution in the political passions that nurtured the original controversy. Too many people still have too much at stake in a particular version of the truth.

A reading of the transcript by the contemporary eye will convince most readers of the unfairness of the trial, but it will not resolve the question of guilt or innocence. For example, doctors removed six bullets from the bodies of the two murdered men, Alessandro Berardelli and Frederick Parmenter. At trial, relying on expert testimony, the prosecution claimed that one of the bullets removed from Berardelli had passed through Sacco's Colt automatic pistol.[23] This argument was not especially convincing — the most that the state police captain could say, based on his examination of the pistol and the bullet, was that the bullet was "consistent with being fired by [Sacco's] pistol."[24] The testimony of the prosecution's two ballistics experts was similarly inconclusive, particularly since their measurements of the bullets varied widely from those recorded by the defendants' ballistics expert, and from measurements made after the trial using a higher-power microscope.[25] In contrast, the defense expert testified that based on "the 11 bullets that I examined that were fired from the Sacco gun," the bullet found in Berardelli "doesn't compare at all."[26] Neither set of expert opinions could be correlated with the testimony of the eyewitnesses, who claimed that one of the suspects had fired five shots, and that the other had fired twice.[27] Yet in the end, it seems, such technical disputes mattered little to the jury. Judge Thayer, writing his opinion in 1924, reasoned that the verdict against Sacco and Vanzetti did not rest on the expert or eyewitness testimony, but rather on evidence of the defendants' "consciousness of guilt" — that is, actions that reflect the defendants' belief in their own culpability, such as flight or cover-up.[28] This is a vague and subjective concept and one amenable to misapplication by a jury from one culture evaluating the emotions of defendants from a very different one.

There seems to be a reasonable doubt both of the defendants' guilt and of their innocence. Too much depends on matters outside the trial record. Much of the controversy relates to new evidence — much of it forensic and technical, such as the new measurements of the bullets — presented after the trial, and indeed, after the execution. If there was reasonable doubt, then the verdict of the Massachusetts court was wrong. However, it does not mean that the verdict of history — which generally regards Sacco and Vanzetti as the innocent victims of a racist miscarriage of justice — is necessarily right. Indeed, there may have been a legal miscarriage of justice even if it were to turn out that Sacco and Vanzetti were factually guilty. It is possible for substantively guilty defendants to be convicted following an unfair trial. It is also possible for innocent defendants to be wrongly convicted after a trial that is procedurally fair. Indeed, it is even possible — as some scholars have suggested — that Sacco was guilty and Vanzetti innocent. An excellent film directed by Giuliano Montaldo, *Sacco and Vanzetti* (UMC Pictures, 1971), portrays Sacco and Vanzetti as the innocent victims of anti-immigrant bigotry. It also paints a vivid picture of the plight of Boston's Italian American community in the post–World War I period.

Different standards of proof govern courtroom verdicts and historical conclusions. And that is as it should be, since courtroom verdicts — especially in capital cases — cannot be revised over time. The judgments of history, on the other hand, are continually subjected to reconsideration and revision, as evidenced by the continuing controversy over the Sacco-Vanzetti case.

In 1977 Governor Michael Dukakis of Massachusetts asked me to assist him in reviewing the Sacco and Vanzetti case for purposes of deciding whether he would issue some sort of a posthumous pardon. I did considerable research and sent it to the governor. On July 19, 1977, Dukakis issued an official proclamation declaring that the "atmosphere of their trial and appeal was permeated by prejudice against foreigners and hostility towards unorthodox political views." It also declared that the "conduct of many of the officials involved in the case shed serious doubt on their willingness and ability to conduct the prosecution and trial of Sacco and Vanzetti fairly and impartially." Finally, the governor declared that "any stigma and disgrace should forever be removed from the names of Nicola Sacco and Bartolomeo Vanzetti." But "stigma" and "disgrace" are neither legal nor political concepts that can be eradicated by gubernatorial pronouncements. They can be removed only by public acceptance of the possibility that a real injustice has been perpetrated.

The Trial of Leopold and Loeb

Date: 1924
Location: Chicago, Illinois
Defendants: Nathan Leopold Jr. and Richard Loeb
Charges: Kidnapping, murder
Verdict: Guilty plea
Sentence: Life plus ninety-nine years

It was called "the murder of the century." The defense attorney was "the lawyer of the century." And this would be "the trial of the century"—the second or third in Clarence Darrow's distinguished career. The crime was the stuff of films and novels. Indeed, two movies—one called *Rope* by Alfred Hitchcock, the other *Compulsion* starring Orson Welles—were based on the infamous Leopold-Loeb case. Numerous books were written about it, in part because it features one of the most remarkable legal arguments in the history of advocacy—Clarence Darrow's successful plea for the lives of his teenage clients, Nathan Leopold Jr. and Richard Loeb. No lawyer, indeed no civilized person, should go through life without reading—if only there were a tape recording!—Darrow's eloquent defense of young human life.

The crime itself was indefensible. The brilliant, spoiled, and bored sons of two of Chicago's wealthiest families planned to commit the perfect crime both for the thrill of it and to prove their perverse misunderstanding of Friedrich Nietzsche's philosophy of the "superman," who was above all law so long as he made no mistake. Their plan, worked out over several months, was to kidnap and immediately kill one of their younger neighbors and hide his body. They would then demand and collect a ransom. The body would never be discovered, the crime would never be solved, and only they would know that they had prevailed over ordinary human beings and their simple-minded legal system.

But far from being the "perfect crime," the murder of fourteen-year-old Bobby Franks turned out to be amateurishly botched. Before any ransom could be paid, the boy's body was discovered in a culvert near where Nathan Leopold often went bird-watching. A pair of telltale glasses was found adjacent to the body. They were easily traced to Leopold, who first came up with a paper-thin alibi and soon thereafter confessed to the crime. His fellow murderer likewise confessed. Each of the "superboys" placed the blame for the actual killing on the other.[29]

The already famous Clarence Darrow — who generally, but not always, defended working-class people — was called into this rich-boy case. There was no hope for a factual defense, since hard evidence corroborated virtually every detail of the confessions. Nor was an insanity defense a realistic prospect, since the boys did not meet the rigorous "right–wrong" test then applicable in Illinois. Their crime had been carefully planned, and the young criminals were fully cognizant that what they were planning was wrong, as a matter of conventional morality and legality. The fact that they regarded themselves as above such bourgeois constraints would not make for a compelling insanity defense.

But it was clear to Darrow that whether or not they qualified for an insanity defense, these kids were emotionally disturbed. He determined, therefore, to present a plea for enlightened compassion based on their youth, their emotional makeup, and the irrationality of the crime itself. He waived a jury trial, pleaded his clients guilty, and presented his case for mitigation to a judge. In support of his argument, Darrow offered the testimony of three of the nation's leading psychiatrists. Based on their comprehensive examinations of the two defendants, these psychiatrists offer a wide range of information about Leopold and Loeb. The subjects of the reports range from a description of the circumstances surrounding the defendants' decision to murder Bobby Franks, to an exploration of their childhood "phantasies" and "delinquencies," to a recounting of their experiences with friendship, love, and sex.[30] These reports are quite informative, but not altogether convincing.

Citing Loeb's behavior in jail, for example, the psychiatrists' report comments that "the patient appears to be quite unconcerned and indifferent, he does not show the normal amount of emotional reaction to the situation in which he finds himself."[31] Indeed, the psychiatrists conclude, Loeb's "total lack of appropriate emotional response to situations is one of the most striking features of his present condition."[32] Leopold, according to the psychiatrists, displayed a similar reaction: "He got no pleasure from the crime. He got no sexual reaction from the crime. With him it was purely an intellectual affair, devoid of any emotion."[33] Furthermore, the psychiatrists suggest that Leopold simply lacked any normal sense of morality, because he "has substituted for the conception of morals which the ordinary man has and which is regarded as normal, a bizarre philosophy which he has evolved, based on selfishness, superiority, atheism, denial of the existence of right and wrong, intellectuality, and scraps of metaphysics which he has picked up here and there."[34] While these reports portray the defendants as more emotionally disturbed than the average teenager, they fall short of suggesting that Leopold and Loeb were troubled enough to be acquitted for murder by reason of insanity.

What was convincing, apparently, was Darrow's eloquence.

His reasoning is as relevant today as it was in 1924. We are still debating whether to execute teenagers, and Darrow's combination of philosophy, psychology, and compassion in his presentation of this case remains among the most compelling arguments on the side of life.

Darrow's brilliance lies in the obviousness of his arguments. He makes it easy for the listener to agree with him. He never asks for long logical or moral leaps. He appeals to common sense, to everyday experience, and to moral consensus. As you read his words, you begin to nod your head in agreement with his premises. Consider, for example, the following excerpt:

> I say again, whatever madness and hate and frenzy may do to the human mind, there is not a single person who reasons who can believe that one of these acts was the act of men, of brains that were not diseased. There is no other explanation for it. And had it not been for the wealth and the weirdness and the notoriety, they would have been sent to the psychopathic hospital for examination, and been taken care of, instead of the state demanding that this court take the last pound of flesh and the last drop of blood from two irresponsible lads.[35]
>
> They pull the dead boy into the back seat, and wrap him in a blanket, and this funeral car starts on its route.
>
> If ever any death car went over the same route or the same kind of route driven by sane people, I have never heard of it, and I fancy no one else has ever heard of it.
>
> This car is driven for twenty miles. First down through thickly populated streets, where everyone knew the boys and their families, and had known them for years. . . . They go down The Midway, through the park, meeting hundreds of machines, in sight of thousands of eyes, with this dead boy.
>
> For what? For nothing! The mad act of the fool in *King Lear* is the only thing I know of that compares with it. And yet doctors will swear that it is a sane act. They know better.[36]

Before long, Darrow easily has you agreeing with his conclusion. By the time you finish reading his argument, you wonder whether any fair-minded judge could impose the death penalty on these two confused boys.

Darrow thought that if he could save these two young killers, he would help put an end to what he considered the barbarity of executing children:

> I am not pleading so much for these boys as I am for the infinite number of others to follow, those who perhaps cannot be as well defended as these have been, those who may go down in the storm, and the tempest, without aid. It is of them I am thinking, and for them I am begging of this court not to turn backward toward the barbarous and cruel past.[37]

Later, he added:

> I know your Honor stands between the future and the past. I know the future is with me, and what I stand for here; not merely for the lives of these two unfortunate lads, but for all boys and all girls; for all of the young, and as far as possible, for all of the old. I am pleading for life, understanding, charity, kindness, and the infinite mercy that considers all. I am pleading that we overcome cruelty with kindness and hatred with love. I know the future is on my side.[38]

Darrow succeeded in saving "these two unfortunate lads." But his impact on the "future" remains to be seen. I wonder if we would still be executing "boys and girls" if we had a Clarence Darrow today who could appeal with his eloquence to the evolving historical conscience of our Constitution, and not just to its dry words.

One disturbingly lingering question remains about the judge's decision not to impose the death penalty on these two cold-blooded, calculating, overprivileged teenagers. This was, after all, Chicago — which had one of the most corrupt judiciaries in the nation. The defendants were rich. Their lawyer had almost certainly employed bribery in his career. There was no accounting for a portion of his large legal fee in this case.[39] Despite Darrow's brilliant and compelling advocacy, the distinct possibility remains that he enhanced its receptivity to this Chicago judge through bribery. This sort of suspicion becomes inevitable when a lawyer has employed improper tactics in the past. The taint of bribery is difficult to remove. There is, of course, no possibility that bribery was involved in Darrow's next great case — which he lost in court but won in history. But there are serious questions about the quality of Darrow's advocacy in the Scopes trial.

The Scopes Trial

Date: 1925
Location: Dayton, Tennessee
Defendant: John Thomas Scopes
Charge: Violation of Tennessee antievolution statute
Verdict: Guilty
Sentence: Small fine, later rescinded by the Supreme Court
             of Tennessee

Some trials are about people; others are about events; and still others are about issues. The Scopes trial of 1925, the so-called monkey trial, was about the clash between religion and science in public education. Though the trial itself took only a few days, the great issues that separated William Jennings Bryan from Clarence Darrow still divide our nation today. Neither a jury verdict nor a Supreme Court decision will make them go away. They are concerns as old as humankind and as new as genetic engineering.

As has become all too common with regard to famous and infamous trials, the popular perception of what transpired in the courtroom comes not from the transcript of the court proceeding itself, but rather from the motion picture and/or stage play that was based — often loosely — on the trial. *Inherit the Wind* was both a prizewinning play and movie. On the stage, it starred Paul Muni, one of the greatest actors of his time. (It was the first Broadway play I ever saw, and it had some influence on my career decision.) The movie version, now available on video, starred Fredric March and Spencer Tracy. These fictionalized accounts presented the conflict as stark and simple: the forces of fundamentalist darkness versus those of progressive light. The William Jennings Bryan character, Scopes's prosecutor, was a burlesque of know-nothing religious literalism. The Clarence Darrow character, Scopes's defender, was the champion of tolerance, understanding, and pluralism.

In the most dramatic scene, the Darrow character calls the Bryan character as an expert witness on the Bible. The attack is scathing and merciless, as the man of science destroys the man of religion before our very eyes. The questions are devastating: How could the early days be measured before the creation of the sun? Were they really twenty-four-hour days? How could Joshua order the sun to stop, when we all know that the earth moves around a fixed sun?

The fictional answers are true to the caricature of know-nothing literalism manufactured by the authors of Inherit the Wind: God knows how to measure time without a sun. Of course they were twenty-four-hour days, if God wanted them to be. God can make the sun move and stop.

As usual, the real story, as told in the trial transcript and in contemporaneous accounts, was more complex and far more interesting. The actual William Jennings Bryan was no simple-minded literalist, and he certainly was no bigot. He was a great populist who cared deeply about equality and about the downtrodden.

Indeed, one of his reasons for becoming so deeply involved in the campaign against evolution was that Darwin's theories were being used — misused, it turns out — by racists, militarists, and nationalists to further some pretty horrible programs. The eugenics movement, which advocated sterilization of "unfit" and "inferior" stock, was at its zenith, and it took its impetus from Darwin's theory of natural selection. German militarism, which had just led to the disastrous world war, drew inspiration from Darwin's ideas on survival of the fittest. The anti-immigration movement, which had succeeded in closing American ports of entry to "inferior racial stock," was grounded in a mistaken belief that certain ethnic groups had evolved more fully than others. The Jim Crow laws, which maintained racial segregation, were rationalized on grounds of the racial inferiority of blacks.

Indeed, the very book — Hunter's *Civic Biology* — from which John T. Scopes taught Darwin's theory of evolution to high school students in Dayton, Tennessee, contained dangerous mis-applications of that theory.[40] It explicitly accepted the naturalis-tic fallacy (that moral conclusions can be drawn from descriptions of nature) and repeatedly drew moral instruction from nature. Indeed, its very title, *Civic Biology*, made it clear that biology had direct political implications for civic society. In discussing the "five races" of man, the text assured the all-white, legally segregated high school students taught by Scopes that "the highest type of all, the Caucasians, [are] represented by the civilized white inhabitants of Europe and America." The book, the avowed goal of which was the improvement of the future human race, then proposed certain eugenic remedies. After a discussion of the inheritability of crime and immorality, the au-thor proposed an analogy: ". . . Just as certain animals or plants become parasitic on other plants or animals, these families have become parasitic on society. They not only do harm to others by corrupting, stealing, or spreading disease, but they are actually protected and cared for by the state out of public money. Largely for them the poorhouse and the asylum exist. They take from so-ciety, but they give nothing in return. They are true parasites."

From the analogy flowed "the remedy": "If such people were lower animals, we would probably kill them off to prevent them from spreading. Humanity will not allow this, but we do have the remedy of separating the sexes in asylums or other places and in various ways preventing intermarriage and the possibilities of perpetuating such a low and degenerate race. Remedies of this sort have been tried successfully in Europe and are now meeting with success in this country." These "remedies" included involuntary sterilizations, and eventually laid the foundation for involuntary "euthanasia" of the kind practiced in Nazi Germany.

Nor were these misapplications of Darwinian theory limited to high school textbooks. Eugenic views held sway at institutions of higher learning such as Harvard University, under racist president Abbott Lawrence Lowell. Even so distinguished a Supreme Court justice as Oliver Wendell Holmes upheld a mandatory sterilization law on the basis of a pseudoscientific assumption about heritability and genetics. His widely quoted rationale — that "three generations of imbeciles are enough"— was later cited by Nazi apologists for mass sterilization.[41] Ironically, the journalist character in the play and movie was based on the real-life reporter H. L. Mencken, whose newspaper paid some of the legal expenses for the defense. The real-life Mencken was himself a rabid racist as well as an antireligious bigot.

It should not be surprising, therefore, that William Jennings Bryan, who was a populist and an egalitarian, would be outraged — both morally and religiously — at what he believed was a direct attack on the morality and religion that had formed the basis of his entire political career.

Nor was Bryan the know-nothing biblical literalist of *Inherit the Wind*. For the most part, he actually seems to have gotten the better of Clarence Darrow in the argument over the Bible (though not in the argument over banning the teaching of evolution). To Darrow's question, "Do you think the earth was made in six days?" Bryan's actual answer was: "[N]ot six days of twenty-four hours."[42] He then proceeded to suggest that these "days" were really "periods," and that the creation may have taken "6,000,000 years or . . . 600,000,000 years."[43]

When Darrow questioned Bryan about the biblical story of Joshua ordering the sun to stand still, he obviously expected

Bryan to claim that the sun orbited around the earth, as the Bible implies. But Bryan disappointed him by testifying that he believed that "the earth goes around the sun."[44] He then proceeded to explain why the divinely inspired author of the Joshua story "may have used language that could be understood at that time."[45] All in all, a reading of the transcript shows Bryan doing quite well defending himself, while it is Darrow who comes off quite poorly — in fact, as something of an antireligious cynic.

Bryan, of course, won the case at trial, although the judgment of history — and eventually the Supreme Court — would eventually be in Darrow's favor. Still, a close reading of the transcript in this case discloses more complex lessons than the easy ones available in the stylized version of events in *Inherit the Wind*. The textbook Scopes wanted to teach was a science text rather than a religious tract, but it was also a *bad* science text, filled with misapplied Darwinism and racist rubbish. Still, religious censorship of the kind dictated by the Tennessee antievolution law was not the proper response to the dangers of teaching high school students the kind of nonsense contained in the textbook used by Scopes. Religion may indeed have its proper role in constraining the misapplications of science, but not in the classrooms of public schools. The danger is simply too great that, as Jefferson warned, religiously motivated teachers and school boards may try to proselytize — rather than to educate — their highly impressionable young and captive audiences.

It is interesting to speculate how a current-day Scopes trial would be decided by a jury in Tennessee or, for that matter, in other areas of our nation. According to a recent article in the *New York Times*, "Americans are three times as likely to believe in the Virgin birth of Jesus (83 percent) as in evolution (28 percent)."[46] This is apparently true despite the reality that most Christian churches accept the scientific validity of evolution and regard the Virgin birth the way prominent Catholic theologian Hans Küng does: as a "collection of largely uncertain, mutually contradictory, strongly legendary" narratives, "an echo of virgin birth myths that were widespread in many parts of the ancient world."[47]

We live in an age of increasing fundamentalism among all faiths. It affects our politics, our schools, our laws and — almost certainly — our juries. The Scopes trial may not be an anachronism. It may be a portent.

The Court-Martial of Billy Mitchell

Date: 1925
Location: District of Columbia
Defendant: Colonel William Mitchell
Charge: Insubordination
Verdict: Guilty
Sentence: Suspension

Throughout history, prophets have been placed on trial. Generally, their proscribed prophecies have been of a religious nature and hence unconfirmable by real-world events. Colonel Billy Mitchell was a secular prophet whose predictions were in fact confirmed by events that transpired, though not until after his death. The Billy Mitchell case — among the most prominent and controversial courts-martial of the twentieth century — teaches important lessons about how time often proves that people accused of "poor judgment" by their contemporaries turn out to be right after all.

Colonel Mitchell, a hero of World War I, came back from that deadly ground and sea war convinced that future wars would be fought primarily from the sky. Among his predictions was that Japan would attack Pearl Harbor from the air and destroy our Pacific Naval Fleet.[48] He even predicted the precise time of day and direction of the attack. He also predicted that Germany would quickly rearm and use its air force to wage a renewed war against Europe. He predicted that in any future war, bombs would be dropped on cities and civilians would be targeted. He predicted air-to-air missiles, smart bombs, and airborne chemical weapons.

Mitchell, who was second in command of the fledgling U.S. Air Service, railed against the nation's lack of preparation for the coming air war. He demanded the creation of a unified Department of Defense, capable of coordinating the army, the navy, and the air force.[49] He called for the development of a system of air routes and landing fields, as well as regular weather reports. He pressured the navy to rely on aircraft carriers and submarines, rather than heavily armed battleships. He called for a civil defense system against air attacks.

The army and navy bureaucracy resisted Mitchell's calls for change. The brass was convinced that the next war would again be fought with battleships and ground troops. Franklin Delano Roosevelt, then assistant secretary of the navy, dismissed Mitchell's views as "pernicious."[50] Roosevelt, too, offered a prediction: "It is highly unlikely that an airplane or a fleet of them could ever successfully attack a fleet of navy vessels under battle conditions."[51]

Mitchell set out to prove that he was right and Roosevelt and the army and navy brass were wrong. With great difficulty, he arranged for a number of experiments in which primitive one-engine airplanes dropped bombs on captured and out-of-commission battleships. He proved that the ships could be sunk from the air and that anti-aircraft machine guns were virtually useless against flying bombers. When the navy concocted a film distorting these results, Mitchell railed against his superiors. When the inaction of his superiors resulted in the deaths of several of his flying colleagues in training accidents, he expressed his opinion that "these accidents are the result of the incompetency, the criminal negligence, and the almost treasonable negligence of our national defense by the Navy and War Departments."[52]

Mitchell also charged his superiors with improperly using propaganda to undercut his arguments.[53] This was all too much for the higher-ups, and they convened a court-martial.

Mitchell was formally charged with insubordination and related offenses, but the real charge was poor judgment about the future of warfare. As Colonel Sherman Moreland, the prosecutor, put it, "the statement of the accused consisted of nothing more than prediction and prophecy, and is not the subject of confirmation. . . ." But predictions and prophecies, at least with regard to military events, are often subject to confirmation, though not necessarily at the time they are made. In this case, the verdict of the court-martial and the verdict of history reached diametrically opposite conclusions. The court-martial convicted Mitchell, and shortly thereafter he resigned his commission and returned to private life. He would not live to see his vindication by the verdict of history, but it formally arrived in 1957 when the secretary of the air force, James H. Douglas, issued the following statement: "The history of recent years has shown that Colonel Mitchell's vision concerning the future of air power was amazingly accurate. He saw clearly the shape of things to come in the field of military aviation, and he forecast with precision the role of air power as it developed in World War II, and as we see it today. Our nation is deeply in his debt. . . . Colonel Mitchell's views have been vindicated."[54]

One of the most misused and misunderstood concepts in the vocabulary we employ to evaluate people is *judgment*. How often we hear people praised for their "sound judgment" or condemned for their "poor judgment"! Yet what is meant by these terms? Often they are implicitly predictive: We believe that those with sound judgment will turn out to be correct about their predictions and that those with poor judgment will turn out to be wrong. But how often do we bother to check whether sound judgments turn out to be right and poor judgments wrong? Weather forecasters and short-term stock pickers are judged every day, but longer-term prognosticators are rarely evaluated. And we pay the price for not realizing that appraisals of judgment are often verifiable, if we have the patience.

I recall a fellow senior professor whom everyone said had excellent judgment about the appointment of junior faculty. He always spoke in balanced and modulated terms, and so his colleagues *believed* he had good judgment. But his predictions about who would succeed and fail as professors turned out to be almost universally wrong. He did not *have* good judgment; he only *appeared* to have good judgment.

The mirror image was true of Billy Mitchell. He only *appeared* to have bad judgment; he actually *had* superb judgment, as time eventually proved. The essential lesson of the Mitchell case is that "prediction and prophecy" are sometimes indeed "subject" to "confirmation." And when they are, they should be tested empirically, the way we test predictions about the weather. Only by testing the judgment of those on whose predictions we rely can we learn from our mistakes before it is too late.

The world paid a heavy price for ignoring Mitchell's predictions. His court-martial qualifies as a great trial because the terrible consequences that flowed from the wrongheaded verdict caused so much harm, not only to Mitchell, but also to the people and armed forces of the United States and its allies at so crucial a time in world history.

The Lindbergh Kidnapping Trial

Date: 1935
Location: Flemington, New Jersey
Defendant: Bruno Richard Hauptmann
Charge: Murder
Verdict: Guilty
Sentence: Electrocution

In real life, unlike on television, there are rarely videotapes of murders (except if the killing takes place in the course of a bank robbery). The investigation and trial, therefore, are fallible human efforts at reconstructing the past. Unless the proof is overwhelming or the culprit confesses, it is difficult to know for certain precisely what occurred. It should come as no surprise that despite unanimous jury verdicts of guilt, appellate affirmances, and executions, there are still plausible claims of innocence on behalf of some convicted murderers. Indeed, one of the most powerful arguments offered by opponents of the death penalty is the assertion that innocent defendants — some say a few, others claim many — have been executed for crimes committed by others.

The execution of Bruno Richard Hauptmann on April 3, 1936, is frequently cited as an instance of the capital punishment of an innocent defendant.[55] Hauptmann was convicted in 1935 of the kidnap-murder of Charles A. Lindbergh Jr. — the twenty-month-old son of America's most beloved couple of the day — in the spring of 1932. The murdered baby's father was Colonel Charles A. Lindbergh, who had captured the imagination of the world by flying solo across the Atlantic. His marriage to Anne Morrow, daughter of a popular politician, approximated a royal wedding. The birth of their child a year later was a joyous occasion celebrated by Americans of all backgrounds. His kidnapping, the ransom payment, and the subsequent discovery of his dead body enraged the nation and stimulated one of the most frustrating manhunts in American history.

For two and a half years — amid charges and recriminations among law enforcement agencies — the horrible crime remained unsolved. Then in September 1934, Richard Hauptmann was arrested after depositing one of the ransom bills in a New York bank. Another ransom bill was found on his person at the time of the arrest. Shortly thereafter, a search of his garage uncovered an additional $14,600 of ransom money hidden in a hollowed-out wooden block. Hauptmann claimed that the money had been left in his car by a friend and business associate who had since died.[56]

Hauptmann was the perfect suspect. In addition to the considerable evidence of his complicity, Hauptmann was precisely the kind of man Americans wanted to be guilty of this crime against "America's First Family." Hauptmann was a recent immigrant from Germany. He had fought against America in the world war and had entered this country under "irregular" circumstances after having been denied immigration status.

The trial itself — in New Jersey, where the kidnapping, but perhaps not the killing, took place — was conducted in the atmosphere of "a circus maximus," according to Hauptmann's defense attorney.[57] The trial judge's summation — which is supposed to be objective — reads like the closing argument of a prosecutor entirely convinced of the defendant's guilt. Some excerpts:

It is argued that Doctor Condon's testimony is inherently improbable and should be in part rejected by you, but you will observe that his testimony is corroborated in large part by several witnesses whose credibility has not been attacked in any manner whatsoever.

. . . upon the whole, is there any doubt in your mind as to the reliability of Doctor Condon's testimony?

Was not the defendant the man who left the ransom note on the windowsill of the nursery, and who took the child from its crib, after opening the closed window?

It is argued by defendant's counsel that the kidnapping and murder . . . was done by a gang, with the help or connivance of some one or more servants of the Lindbergh or Morrow households. Now do you believe that? Is there any evidence in this case whatsoever to support any such conclusion?

The defendant says that these ransom bills, moneys, were left with him by one Fisch, a man now dead. Do you believe that?

. . . you should consider the testimony of Mr. Hochmuth along with that of other witnesses. . . . He testified that on the forenoon of that day, March 1, 1932, he saw the defendant. . . . This testimony, if true, is highly significant. Do you think that there is any reason, on the whole, to doubt the truth of the old man's testimony? May he not well and easily have remembered the circumstance, in view of the fact that that very night the child was carried away?[58]

Not surprisingly the jury convicted, the appellate courts affirmed, and the court of pardons denied clemency, over the governor's dissent. Despite persistent claims of innocence — indeed, frame-up — Hauptmann was electrocuted on April 3, 1936. But his death did not end the controversy.

An important article in the Stanford Law Review by Hugo Adam Bedau and Michael L. Radelet, titled "Miscarriages of Justice in Potentially Capital Cases," characterizes the Hauptmann case as "the most famous" example of the genre of cases in which the weight of the available evidence points to a miscarriage of justice.[59] The authors cite all the recent sources in support of their conclusion that: "There is no doubt that the conviction rested in part on corrupt prosecutorial practices, suppression of evidence, intimidation of witnesses, perjured testimony, and Hauptmann's prior record."[60]

Few today deny that the trial was unfair — not only by current standards, but even by the far less rigorous standards of the 1930s. But many who acknowledge the trial's unfairness insist that Hauptmann was plainly guilty. Others disagree, pointing to inconsistencies in the state's case, new evidence, and the old frame-up theory. Yet others argue — quite plausibly — that in light of the procedural unfairness at the trial, it is impossible to arrive at a reasoned judgment concerning Hauptmann's guilt or innocence at this late date.

The Hauptmann verdict joins a significant category of cases about which reasonable people disagree and about which only unreasonable zealots are absolutely certain.

The Scottsboro Trials

Date: 1931–37
Location: Scottsboro and Decatur, Alabama
Defendants: Nine African American males between the ages
             of twelve and twenty
Charge: Rape
Verdict: Guilty (as to most defendants)
Sentence: Electrocution (not carried out)

At a time when the death penalty is under active reconsideration, the case of the so-called Scottsboro Boys can teach us something important. In 1931, nine young African American males — ranging in age from twelve to twenty — were accused of raping two white women on a train. They received a perfunctory trial, represented by a lawyer with little experience and even less talent, and after the predictable conviction were sentenced to death. The fact that they were not immediately lynched demonstrated some degree of progress in Alabama.

From that point on, the case assumed a political dimension that would continue for many years. The American Communist Party, then at its zenith, tried to use the case to further its political agenda. The NAACP sought to take it away from the Communists, but failed. The lawyer at the center of the case was a New York Jew named Samuel Leibowitz, then regarded as a worthy successor to Clarence Darrow as the nation's leading criminal lawyer. At first he worked with the Communists, but he soon distanced himself from them, especially after they tried to bribe one of the complainants to change her story. Leibowitz was a master of cross-examination and careful investigation whose reputation was well deserved. But in the courts of Alabama, he was just a "Jew lawyer" sent down to slander the good people of Alabama with "New York Jew money." This, despite the fact that Leibowitz took the case without fee and spent thousands of dollars of his own money on expenses.

Leibowitz managed to secure a new trial from the U.S. Supreme Court and then, at the retrial, showed how much difference a good lawyer could make. At the first trial, the two rape victims were presented as virtuous women — "flowers of Southern womanhood" — who had been brutally raped beyond any doubt. After Leibowitz's investigation, a very different picture emerged. The two women were both prostitutes who had engaged in voluntary sex with men just before boarding the train. The small amount of semen found in their vaginas was old and all the sperm were dead, thus suggesting that it was more likely the residue of the earlier consensual sex than of a rape just hours before the tests were conducted. Leibowitz's defense provided much more than a reasonable doubt of the defendants' guilt: It strongly suggested the alleged victims were never raped. But in an Alabama rape case involving black men and white women, strong evidence of innocence was not nearly enough.

The trial judge, a decent man, became convinced of the defendants' innocence and tried his best to instruct the jury in a manner that would assure their acquittal or, at least, a sentence other than death. He failed, however, and the all-white jury again returned a verdict of guilty and sentences of death. The judge eventually wrote an opinion ordering a new trial on grounds of probable innocence, but another judge — less sympathetic — was assigned to retry the cases, and the defendants were again convicted and all but one sentenced to death.

The case was never resolved definitively. Eventually, after several retrials and convictions, a deal was struck whereby four of the defendants had the cases against them dropped, one of them had his death sentenced commuted to life imprisonment, and the rest pleaded guilty to lesser crimes. To this day, there are some who believe that the Scottsboro Boys — or at least, some of them — may have raped the two prostitutes, though they can point to no evidence beyond the discredited words of the alleged victims. But almost no one believes that the case against them was proved beyond a reasonable doubt, or that the trials even approached the standards of fairness and due process demanded by the Constitution.

The Scottsboro case demonstrates the dangers of questioning the death penalty by relying exclusively on claims of factual innocence capable of being proved scientifically. Innocence can rarely be proved beyond a reasonable doubt. Nor should it ever have to be proved by so high a standard. DNA evidence, which can prove innocence to a near certainty in some cases, is available in only a small proportion of capital crimes. Most cases are based on eyewitness testimony and circumstantial inferences. In many cases, we will never know for sure whether the defendants are factually guilty. My friend and colleague Barry Scheck, a brilliant and effective opponent of the death penalty, likes to say that whenever an innocent man is executed, a guilty man remains free to commit new crimes.[61] The Scottsboro case demonstrates that this conclusion is not always correct. If the Scottsboro Boys were innocent, then there was no rape and therefore no guilty criminals free to commit other crimes. Indeed, even if the Scottsboro Boys were innocent, they may well have been dangerous. In fact, one of them was subsequently accused of another rape (of which he was acquitted). Another killed a man and then took his own life. A third escaped from prison.

The only conclusions one could reach with absolute certainty is that the *process* by which the Scottsboro Boys were convicted and sentenced to death was inherently flawed by institutional racism and the political agendas of the prosecutors and judges involved in the case, and that they were *probably* all innocent.

It is understandable that the popular media focuses on those cases involving factually innocent defendants. The public does not like gray-area cases. They want to know the simple truth: Did the defendant do it, or did someone else do it? But the truth is rarely that simple. The Perry Mason approach — proving the innocence of his client, while at the same time proving the guilt of the government's star witness — is largely fiction, and fiction demands heroes and villains. *To Kill a Mockingbird* would not have been nearly as successful as a book, or as popular as a movie, if the defendant in that case had, in fact, committed the rape. Atticus Finch would not have become a cultural icon if he successfully defended a *guilty* black man who would otherwise have been unjustly executed on the basis of an unfair trial — for a crime he *actually committed*. Issues of guilt or innocence are often gray. They are rarely black and white. But the system of justice in Alabama in the 1930s *was* black and white. One system for whites; another for blacks; and yet a third for black men accused of raping white women. Much has changed over the past three-quarters of a century, but a residue of racial discrimination still survives. Reading the Scottsboro case reminds us of our past and cautions us about our future.

1. Arthur S. Link and William B. Catton, *American Epoch: A History of the United States Since 1900*, vol. 1 (New York: Alfred A. Knopf, 1955), p. 281.

2. Richard M. Abrams, *The Burdens of Progress: 1900–1929* (Glenview, IL: Scott, Foresman and Co., 1978), p. 163.

3. Link and Catton, p. 281.

4. Abrams, p. 163.

5. Link and Catton, p. 282.

6. Paul L. Murphy, *World War I and the Origin of Civil Liberties in the United States* (New York: W. W. Norton and Co., 1979), p. 272.

7. Michael Miller Topp, "The Italian-American Left: Transnationalism and the Quest for Unity," in *The Immigrant Left in the United States*, ed. Paul Buhle and Dan Georgakas (Albany: SUNY Press, 1996), pp. 141–42.

8. Abrams, p. 161.

9. *Ibid.*

10. Patrick Renshaw, *America in the Era of the Two World Wars, 1910–1945* (London: Longman Group Ltd., 1996), p. 108.

11. Richard J. Jensen, *Clarence Darrow: The Creation of an American Myth* (New York: Greenwood Press, 1992), p. 61.

12. Laurence Urdang, ed., *The Timetables of American History* (New York: Simon and Schuster, 1996), p. 323.

13. Link and Catton, p. 324.

14. *Ibid.*

15. *Ibid.*

16. Osmond Fraenkel, *The Sacco-Vanzetti Case* (Birmingham: The Notable Trials Library, 1990), pp. 535–50.

17. *Ibid.*, pp. 21–22.

18. *Ibid.*

19. Francis Russell, *Sacco and Vanzetti: The Case Resolved* (New York: Harper and Row, 1986); William Young and David E. Kaiser, *Postmortem: New Evidence in the Case of Sacco and Vanzetti* (Amherst: University of Massachusetts Press, 1985).

20. William Shannon, *Book World*, Jan. 26, 1986.

21. See, generally, Russell.

22. See, generally, Young and Kaiser.

23. Fraenkel, pp. 331–32.

24. Cited in *ibid.*, p. 342.

25. *Ibid.*, p. 370.

26. Cited in *ibid.*, p. 361.

27. Cited in *ibid.*, pp. 337–42.

28. Cited in *ibid.*, p. 406.

29. Maureen McKernan, *The Amazing Crime and Trial of Leopold and Loeb* (Birmingham: The Notable Trials Library, 1989), pp. 49–51.

30. Medical report by Drs. Hulbert and Bowman, cited in *ibid.*, pp. 83–166.

31. *Ibid.*, p. 101.
32. *Ibid.*, p. 107.
33. *Ibid.*, p. 133.
34. *Ibid.*, p. 140.
35. *Ibid.*
36. Cited in *ibid.*, pp. 237–38.
37. Cited in *ibid.*, p. 251.
38. Cited in *ibid.*, p. 304.
39. Geoffrey Cowan, *The People v. Clarence Darrow* (New York: The Notable Trials Library, 1995), p. 444.
40. George W. Hunter, *A Civic Biology: Presented in Problems* (New York: American Book Co., 1914).
41. *Buck v. Bell*, 47 S. Ct. 584, 585 (1927).
42. National Book Company of Cincinnati, *The Scopes Trial* (New York: The Notable Trials Library, 1990), p. 299.
43. *Ibid.*, p. 302.
44. *Ibid.*, p. 286.
45. *Ibid.*
46. Nicholas Kristof, "Believe it or not," *New York Times*, August 15, 2003.
47. *Ibid.*
48. Edward W. Knappman, *Great American Trials* (Detroit: Visible Ink Press, 1994), pp. 319–22.
49. *Ibid.*
50. National Defense Miscellaneous (1924–25) (unpublished material on file with the Library of Congress, Manuscripts Division, Box 45, William Mitchell Papers).
51. *Ibid.*
52. Knappman, p. 320.
53. *Ibid.*
54. Lloyd J. Matthews, "The Speech Rights of Air Professionals," *Airpower Journal*, Oct. 1, 1998.
55. See, e.g., Robert R. Bryan, "The Execution of the Innocent: The Tragedy of the Hauptmann-Lindbergh and Bigelow Cases," *New York University Review of Law and Social Change* 18 (1991–92), pp. 831, 832, n. 3.
56. *Ibid.*, p. 835.
57. Hugo Adam Bedau and Michael L. Radelet, "Miscarriages of Justice in Potentially Capital Cases," *Stanford Law Review* 40 (21) (1987), pp. 124–25.
58. Sidney B. Whipple, *The Trial of Bruno Richard Hauptmann* (Birmingham: The Notable Trials Library, 1989), pp. 561–63.
59. Bedau and Radelet, p. 21.
60. *Ibid.*
61. See, generally, www.innocenceproject.org/.

PART IX

World War II

G OVERNMENTAL EFFORTS to silence political opposition in times of war have produced some of the most troubling restrictions on basic freedoms. The Civil War saw the suspension of the writ of habeas corpus. World War I brought with it the sweeping prosecution of draft opponents and political radicals. But nothing that came before it compared to the U.S. government's suppression of individual liberties during World War II. The Japanese attack on Pearl Harbor, followed by the landing of German saboteurs on American soil, brought about two dangerous legal precedents, though neither of them were the result of a great trial.

The first was the forced relocation of more than 110,000 Americans of Japanese descent in a process initiated by the president, ratified by a unanimous Congress, and upheld by the Supreme Court.[1] In February 1942, just two months after the surprise Japanese attack on Pearl Harbor that brought the United States into World War II, President Franklin D. Roosevelt issued an executive order authorizing military officials to relocate residents of "military areas," soon defined as all of California, Oregon, and Washington.[2] By the end of the year, virtually all of the West Coast's Japanese Americans were held behind barbed wire in ten inland detention camps.[3] Although small groups of detainees were quietly released beginning in 1942, some Japanese Americans remained incarcerated until the last camp was closed in March 1946.[4]

Over this period of Japanese internment, the U.S. Supreme Court was accorded not one, but three opportunities to rule on the constitutionality of the government's policies. In the spring of 1942, Minoru Yasui refused to observe the curfew imposed on individuals of Japanese ancestry, Fred Korematsu failed to report for relocation to the detention camps, and Gordon Hirabayashi violated both the curfew and the relocation order.[5] All three were arrested and convicted, and, with the backing of the American Civil Liberties Union, all three saw their appeals reach the Supreme Court.[6]

The actual trials of these cases were not particularly eventful or dramatic. It was the High Court's decisions in these highly problematic mass detentions that will be remembered — and regretted.

In 1943 and 1944, the Supreme Court upheld both the curfew and the relocation orders, stressing that the government's policies had been implemented in a time of war. Vigorously dissenting in the Korematsu case, Justice Robert Jackson warned that the principle of racial discrimination and relocation of citizens validated by the Court "lies about like a loaded weapon ready for the hand of any authority that can bring forward a plausible claim of an urgent need. . . . A military commander may overstep the bounds of constitutionality, and it is an incident. But if we review and approve, that passing incident becomes the doctrine of the Constitution."[7] In only one case during World War II did the Court call into question the government's treatment of Japanese Americans, issuing a writ of habeas corpus to free a Sacramento woman, Mitsuye Endo, whom military officials had detained even after finding her to be a loyal citizen.[8]

In 1981, a presidential commission concluded that the incarceration of Japanese Americans "was not justified by military necessity," but was motivated by "race prejudice, war hysteria, and a failure of political leadership."[9] In 1988, Congress authorized restitution payments of twenty thousand dollars for each survivor of the government's program of mass internment. The Supreme Court's decisions sanctioning severe restrictions on the liberties of Japanese Americans have never been overturned. Ironically, the principle that racial classifications are not always unconstitutional has been cited in support of race-based affirmative action programs.

The Supreme Court was just as deferential in considering the military commission hastily appointed to try eight suspected German saboteurs. On June 12, 1942, a German submarine secretly landed Richard Quirin and three other men at Amagansett Beach, Long Island; five nights later, four more Germans landed at Ponte Vedra Beach, Florida. The eight men were armed with explosive and incendiary devices, and had previously lived in the United States before returning to Berlin to study the art of sabotage. After one man turned himself in to the FBI, federal authorities were able to arrest all eight by the end of June.

The government initially planned to try the eight defendants in the civil courts, but soon realized that a conviction would only carry a prison sentence of two years, for conspiracy to commit sabotage. Moreover, a public trial could cast doubt upon the effectiveness of the United States' defenses. Instead, President Roosevelt appointed a military commission empowered to seek the death penalty in its trial of the eight Germans as spies. The lawyers for the eight defendants, also appointed by President Roosevelt, applied to the Supreme Court for writs of habeas corpus, challenging the legal authority of the commission. A resolute President Roosevelt told his attorney general, Francis Biddle, "I won't give them up. . . . I won't hand them over to any United States marshal armed with a writ of habeas corpus. Understand?"[10]

Once again the secret trials of the alleged saboteurs were not notable, since the evidence clearly established their guilt. The important issue — decided by the High Court — was whether these defendants, at least one of whom had a plausible claim to American citizenship, could be deprived of their right to trial by jury in an ordinary court.

The Supreme Court heard two days of argument in a special

session, and in *Ex parte Quirin* the Court upheld the president's power to appoint such a commission under the Articles of War.

On August 3, 1942, the commission convicted all eight men and sentenced them to death by electrocution. President Roosevelt commuted the sentences of two defendants to hard labor in prison. The remaining six were executed on August 8 — less than two months after they landed on the U.S. coast.[11] There were no further landings by German saboteurs following these highly publicized executions.

The government's eagerness to stamp out political opposition during the war also led to the decision to prosecute the American poet Ezra Pound. Beginning in 1941, the prominent, if eccentric, poet made numerous anti-American speeches on Italian radio — broadcasts that were monitored by the Federal Communications Commission and, later, the FBI.[12] In May 1945, with the war in Europe already over, Pound was arrested by American troops in Italy and charged with treason.[13] What ultimately made Pound's case famous, however, was his lawyers' ability to convince the jury that he was incompetent to stand trial — not the government's questionable use of the treason law to criminalize the expression of opinions.

Finally, no trial has captured the world's attention like the international military tribunal held at Nuremberg, Germany, from 1945 to 1946. "The greatest trial in history," according to one of the presiding judges,[14] was the prosecution of twenty-two Nazi officials for war crimes, including plotting and waging aggressive war, using slave labor, looting occupied countries, and abusing and murdering civilians and prisoners of war.[15] The prosecutors from the United States, Soviet Union, United Kingdom, and France secured the convictions of nineteen of the twenty-two defendants; in the end, ten Nazi officials were sent to their deaths. The first Nuremberg trial set the stage for twelve subsequent trials, organized by the United States and targeting the doctors, judges, and functionaries of Nazi Germany.

Whether these trials were "for show" or not, they make an important point. In a time where so much wrong was done in the name of expediency — the internment of the Japanese and the military trials of the suspected German spies included — the cumbersome and somewhat unwieldy Nuremberg trials were an attempt to show that imperfect justice was preferable to no justice at all. The impact of the trials, on both International and American law, thus cannot be underestimated. They continue to influence current debates regarding the state and nature of international justice. This chapter, therefore, focuses on the two postwar trials, Nuremberg and Ezra Pound, that sought justice for evil actions taken and evil words spoken during World War II.

The Nuremberg Trial

Date: 1945–46
Location: Nuremberg, Germany
Defendants: Twenty-two Nazi leaders
Charges: Conspiracy, crimes against peace, war crimes,
             and crimes against humanity
Verdict: Nineteen convicted; three acquitted
Sentence: Twelve sentenced to death; seven sent to prison

Was the 1946 Nuremberg trial of Nazi leaders a cynical example of "victor's justice," as Hermann Göring characterized it?[16] Or was it the foundation of a new legal order that would create enforceable legal rules against aggressive war and crimes against humanity, as Justice Robert Jackson — who took a temporary leave from the Supreme Court to serve as chief American prosecutor — hoped and expected?[17] More than half a century after the conviction and execution of two handfuls of Nazi criminals, it is still difficult to assess the impact of the Nuremberg tribunal (and the subsequent trials of Nazi judges, doctors, and functionaries) on the state and progress of international law.

Whether the captured Nazi leaders — those who did not commit suicide or escape — should have been placed on trial, rather than summarily shot, was the subject of much controversy. Even before the end of the war, Secretary of the Treasury Henry Morgenthau had proposed that a list of major war criminals be drawn up, and as soon as they were captured and identified, they would be shot.[18] President Roosevelt was initially sympathetic to such rough justice, but eventually both he and President Harry Truman were persuaded by Secretary of War Henry Stimson that summary execution was inconsistent with the American commitment to due process and the rule of law.

It was decided, therefore, to convene an international tribunal to sit in judgment over the Nazi leaders. But this proposal was not without considerable difficulties. Justice must be seen to be done, but it must also be done in reality. A show trial, with predictable verdicts and sentences, would be little better than no trial at all. Indeed, Justice Jackson, who prosecuted the case for the United States, went so far as to suggest, early on, that it would be preferable to shoot Nazi criminals out of hand than to discredit our judicial process by conducting farcical trials.[19]

The challenge of the Nuremberg tribunal, therefore, was to do real justice in the context of a trial by the victors against the vanquished — and specifically those leaders of the vanquished who had been instrumental in the most barbaric genocide and mass slaughter of civilians in history. Moreover, the blood of Hitler's millions of victims was still fresh at the time of the trials. Indeed the magnitude of Nazi crimes was being learned by many for the first time during the trial itself. Was a fair trial possible against this emotional backdrop?

Even putting aside the formidable jurisprudential hurdles — the retroactive nature of the newly announced laws and the jurisdictional problems posed by a multinational court — there was a fundamental question of justice posed. Contemporary commentators wondered whether judges appointed by the victorious governments — and politically accountable to those governments — could be expected to listen with an open mind to the prosecution evidence offered by the Allies and to the defense claims submitted on behalf of erstwhile enemies. The answer, of course, still remains unclear.

A review of the trial nearly sixty years after the fact leads to the conclusion that the judges did a commendable job of trying to be fair. They did, after all, acquit three of the twenty-two defendants, and they sentenced another seven to prison terms rather than hanging. But results, of course, are not the only or even the best criteria for evaluating the fairness of a trial. Furthermore, it is impossible to determine with hindsight whether the core leaders, such as Göring, von Ribbentrop, and Rosenberg, ever had a chance, or whether the acquittals and lesser sentences for some of the others was a ploy to make it appear that proportional justice was being done.

Reading the fascinating transcript of the trial has the effect of demythologizing both the heroes and the villains. For example, Justice Robert Jackson, the American chief prosecutor and hero of Nuremberg, is shown as a bungling cross-examiner who loses virtually every verbal battle with Göring. Jackson was unprepared and sloppy, while Göring was ready for every question with a precise Germanic recollection. At one point Jackson produced a document hoping to show that in 1935 Göring was planning "the liberation of the Rhineland."[20] But the poorly translated document, in fact, concerned the "cleaning of the Rhine" — removing physical obstacles in the Rhine River, such as sunken boats, that might hinder navigation.[21] Following his disastrous cross-examination of Göring, Jackson became angry and sullen, frequently exploding in open court and then hiding out alone in his quarters.

But Jackson was vindicated by his opening and closing speeches to the court, which were masterful in their marshaling of the documentary evidence. Listen to the final words of his eloquent closing argument to the tribunal:

We have presented to this Tribunal an affirmative case based on incriminating documents which are sufficient, if unexplained, to require a finding of guilt on Count One against each defendant. In the final analysis, the only question is whether the defendant's own testimony is to be credited as against the documents and other evidence of their guilt. What, then, is their testimony worth? The fact is that the Nazi habit of economizing in the use of truth pulls the foundations out from under their own defenses. Lying has always been a highly approved Nazi technique. . . .

. . . Even Schacht showed that he, too, had adopted the Nazi attitude that truth is any story which succeeds. Confronted on cross-examination with a long record of broken vows and false words, he declared in justification and I quote from the record: "I think you can score many more successes when you want to lead someone if you don't tell them the truth than if you tell them the truth."

This was the philosophy of the National Socialists. When for years they have deceived the world, and masked falsehood with plausibilities, can anyone be surprised that they continue their habits of a lifetime in this dock? Credibility is one of the main issues of this Trial. Only those who have failed to learn the bitter lessons of the last decade can doubt that men who have always played on the unsuspecting credulity of generous opponents would not hesitate to do the same, now.

It is against such a background that these defendants now ask this Tribunal to say that they are not guilty of planning, executing, or conspiring to commit this long list of crimes and wrongs. They stand before the record of this Trial as bloodstained Gloucester stood by the body of his slain king. He begged of the widow, as they beg of you: "Say I slew them not." And the Queen replied, "Then say they were not slain. But dead they are . . ." If you were to say of these men that they are not guilty, it would be as true to say that there has been no war, there are no slain, there has been no crime.[22]

In the end it was the documentary evidence, the Germans' own detailed record of their aggression and genocide, that provided the smoking guns. Document after document proved beyond any doubt that the Nazis had conducted two wars: One was their aggressive war against Europe (and eventually America) for military, political, geographic, and economic domination. The other was their genocidal war to destroy "inferior" races, primarily the Jews and Gypsies. Its war aim was eventually crushed by the combined might of the Americans and the Russians. Their genocidal aims came very close to succeeding. Nearly the entire Jewish and Gypsy populations within the control of the Third Reich were systematically murdered while the rest of the world — including those nations sitting in judgment — turned a blind eye.

The Nuremberg tribunal and those that followed it administered justice to a tiny fraction of those guilty of the worst barbarism ever inflicted on humankind. The vast majority of German killers were eventually "denazified" and allowed to live normal and often productive lives.

Among those Nazis convicted, and sentenced to death, was one who never killed or ordered the killing of a single human being. His case was, perhaps, the most difficult one, because without his poison pen and filthy mouth there might have been no genocide. I am referring to Julius Streicher, the editor of *Der Stürmer*, the notorious anti-Semitic propaganda rag that became the bible of Hitler's racism. Streicher was a raving bigot who insisted on being represented by an anti-Semitic lawyer, because the Nuremberg tribunal was a "Jewish" court.[23] He claimed that Jackson was a Jew whose real name was "Jacobson" and that Roosevelt ("Rosenfeld") and Eisenhower were also Jewish.

Streicher's editorials and speeches contributed substantially to a racist atmosphere that encouraged the eventual genocidal acts against European Jewry. But his weapon was the word, not the sword, though his words incited resort to the sword, and indeed to the gas chamber. His prosecution presented the classic — if extreme — challenge to the limits of free speech. Of course there was no free speech for those who disagreed with Streicher. There was no marketplace of ideas in Hitler's Germany, only a monopoly of bigotry.

In the end, the Nuremberg judges convicted Streicher and sentenced him to death "without much difficulty."[24] Although American judge Francis Biddle at first protested that it would be "preposterous" to call Streicher a conspirator just because he was a "little Jew-baiter," eventually he was persuaded to regard Streicher as an "accessory" to murder.[25] He was compared to the cheerleader who "by his continual goading of the crowd to frenzied excitement . . . is a key personality in his team's success."[26]

The analogy is flawed, however, especially in the Anglo-American tradition, which distinguishes between speech — even racist propaganda — and actions. Perhaps the court was relying on the classic, though controversial, limitation of free speech that is an invitation to violent actions. But it seems clear that the Nuremberg judges "failed to debate [the] fundamental question of whether Streicher's words could be linked directly with others' deeds."[27] Critics have long worried that Streicher was sentenced to death not "strictly on the law but on the physical and moral revulsion he evoked."[28] Other critics have pointed to the thousands of Nazi murderers who escaped punishment because they did not "look" or "act" like the butchers they had been during Hitler's wars. (In 2003 an international court with jurisdiction over the Rwandan genocide found media inciters guilty.)

Nearly sixty years after Nuremberg, it is necessary to ask whether, on balance, the Nuremberg trials did more good than harm. By convicting and executing a tiny number of the most flagrant criminals, the Nuremberg court permitted the world to get on with business as usual. The German economy was quickly rebuilt, unification between East and West Germany became a reality — and anti-Semitism is once again rife throughout Europe. Perhaps Henry Morgenthau was asking for too much when he demanded that German industry and military capacity be destroyed "forever," and that Germany must be "reduced to a nation of farmers."[29] But perhaps the Nuremberg tribunal asked for too little when it implicitly expiated the guilt of thousands of hands-on murderers by focusing culpability on a small number of leaders who could never have carried out their wholesale slaughter without the enthusiastic assistance of an army, both military and civilian, of wholesale butchers.

The Nuremberg trial was an example of both "victor's justice" and of the possible beginning of a "new legal order" of accountability. Trying the culprits was plainly preferable to simply killing them. But trying so few of them sent out a powerful message that the "new legal order" would be lenient with those who were "just following orders."

The reality that, following Nuremberg, the world was to experience genocide again and again — in Cambodia, the former Yugoslavia, and Rwanda — demonstrates that trials alone cannot put an end to human barbarity. But the fact that tribunals were established to judge at least some of these crimes against humanity also demonstrates a willingness to attempt, at least, to prevent and punish evil by the rule of law.

The International Criminal Court, based in The Hague, recently came into existence without the support or participation of the United States. Its mandate is to prevent, deter, and punish the kinds of crimes against humanity prosecuted at Nuremberg. Only time will tell whether the Nuremberg trials were the beginning of a new regime of enforceable international criminal law or merely an important incident in history.

In the meantime, Saddam Hussein faces trial before a tribunal that must do justice and be seen to do justice. It will be a daunting task.

The Ezra Pound Case

Date: 1946
Location: District of Columbia
Defendant: The poet Ezra Pound
Charge: Treason
Verdict: Incompetent to stand trial
Sentence: Commitment to a mental hospital

The so-called trial of Ezra Pound, the eccentric American poet, was one of the great travesties of American justice. In fact, there was no trial. Instead, there was an ersatz proceeding at which Pound was found incompetent to stand trial. The entire matter demonstrated how psychiatry could be abused in a well-intentioned but misguided effort to circumvent the strictures of the law. And it illustrates how the celebrity of a criminal defendant can distort the criminal process.

Ezra Pound was a great poet with perverse and bizarre opinions about world politics. Like many others in the 1930s and 1940s, Pound attributed the ills of the universe to a worldwide "Jewish conspiracy." According to Pound, the "Morgenthau-Lehman gang" controlled "99 percent" of the media and ran the "Jew-governed" radio, as well as the national government.[30] The "Jews and their Roosevelt" were responsible for the Second World War, and only their elimination would end the killing. (Pound was not the only great writer to expound racist views of this kind. Dostoyevsky expressed similar views in his essay on the "Jewish Question.")

During the war, Pound lived in Mussolini's Italy and broadcast anti-American and pro-fascist commentaries throughout Italy and Europe. At war's end, Pound was arrested by American troops and indicted for treason. A trial on treason charges growing out of Pound's Italian broadcasts would have raised profound First Amendment issues because Pound's choice of words was carefully calculated to avoid the rather technical definition of treason. Even the announcer who introduced Pound's commentary seems to have been briefed by an American constitutional lawyer. This is what he said at the opening of each broadcast: "The Italian radio acting in accordance with the Fascist policy of intellectual freedom and free expression of opinion by those who are qualified to hold it, following the tradition of Italian hospitality, has offered Dr. Ezra Pound the use of the microphone twice a week. It is understood that he will not be asked to say anything whatsoever that goes against his conscience, or anything *incompatible with his duties as a citizen of the United States of America* [italics added]."[31]

But the First Amendment–treason conflict was never to be resolved — or even confronted — in the Pound case. Instead, a conspiracy of well-meaning lawyers, psychiatrists, and literati arranged for Pound to be declared incompetent to stand trial. I use the words *conspiracy* and *arranged* because it is obvious from the historical record that nobody really believed Pound was seriously mentally ill. He was clearly eccentric, he had bizarre ideas, and he was a disagreeable person. But he was not psychotic. He was not out of touch with reality. And he was certainly able to understand the legal situation into which he had gotten himself. Had he been an ordinary person charged with an ordinary crime rather than a literary celebrity accused of a speech crime, his competency to stand trial would not even have raised a close question. For example, Tokyo Rose, a Japanese American woman who broadcast anti-American propaganda speeches over Radio Tokyo, was prosecuted on treason charges and sentenced to ten years in a U.S. federal prison.[32] Many convicted defendants are now imprisoned — indeed some are even executed — with far more severe mental impairments than that suffered by Pound. But these inmates did not have psychiatrists — especially government psychiatrists — who were willing to fudge the facts in their favor in order to spare them the ordeal of trial and possible imprisonment.

Pound, on the other hand, had Dr. Winfred Overholser in his pocket. Dr. Overholser, the dean of institutional psychiatry in the United States and the superintendent of Saint Elizabeths Hospital in Washington, DC, the federal hospital for the criminally insane, was the government's star witness in many psychiatric cases. He could generally be counted on to take the prosecution's side in contested cases. But not this time. He was a fan of Ezra Pound's and a friend of several of his literary supporters. Dr. Overholser's testimony was a sham. It showed how easy it was for psychiatrists to disguise their personal opinions about the desired outcome of a case in the scientific-sounding jargon of their profession. Here is some of what Dr. Overholser told the District of Columbia jury that had been convened to decide whether Pound was competent to stand trial:

Q. Will you tell us the reasons which lead you to the conclusion that he is unable to participate in the trial of this indictment intelligently?

A. In the first place, it is quite obvious that the man has always been unusually eccentric through the years. He has undoubtedly a high regard of his own opinion, and has been extremely vituperative of those who disagree with him.

He has a very high degree of intelligence, there is no question on that score, and his relations with the world and other people during practically all his life have been those of a person who was very skeptical to say the least. He is extremely free in his conversation; he has not been reticent by any stretch of the imagination, but his production had been unusually hard to follow. He speaks in bunches of ideas. . . .

He lays a great deal of his difficulty at the door of British Secret Service, and other groups, which have opposed him. He assures me, too, that he served a very useful purpose to the United States by remaining at the Italian prison camp to complete his translation of Confucius, which he regards as the greatest contribution to literature.

He is sure that he should not have been brought to this country in the capacity of a prisoner, but in the capacity of someone who was to be of great benefit to the United States in its post-war activities.

I might state that this constitutes a grandiosity of ideas and beliefs that goes far beyond the normal, even in a person who is as distraught in his mind as he is.

From a practical view of his advising with his attorney, there would be the fact that you cannot keep him on a straight line of conversation; he rambles around, and has such a naive grasp of the situation in which he finds himself, it would not be fair to him or his attorney to put him on trial.[33]

Other psychiatrists testified similarly, and the judge virtually directed the jury to find Pound incompetent:

. . . you have heard the testimony of all these physicians on the subject, and there is no testimony to the contrary and, of course, these are men who have given a large part of their professional careers to the study of matters of this sort, who have been brought here for your guidance.

. . . in a case of this type where the Government and the defense representatives have united in a clear and unequivocal view with regard to the situation, I presume you will have no difficulty in making up your mind.[34]

After three minutes of "deliberation," the jury returned a verdict of unsound mind. Pound was committed to Saint Elizabeths until his competency was restored. There was the rub. Since his incompetency was based on vague, nonspecific personality traits — his lifelong eccentricity, for example — it was unlikely that he would "recover." Suddenly, his lawyer, the psychiatrists, and his friends were playing down his mental problems. ("In [Dr. Overholser's] opinion [Pound] does not require hospitalization . . . his mental condition is of a mild nature."[35]) Efforts were made to have him released on a writ of habeas corpus, but the trial court declined to issue the writ and Mrs. Pound, who had been appointed as her husband's guardian, refused to authorize an appeal.

For twelve years Pound remained in Saint Elizabeths, writing poetry, meeting with other literary figures, and harassing other patients and staff. (As Dr. Overholser wrote: "He has supreme contempt for the patients on the ward regardless of the ward he might be on since he is inclined to be rather supercilious in his views of practically everyone with whom he comes in contact."[36])

Finally, in 1958, the Justice Department agreed to drop all charges against Pound and allow him to return to Italy. Dr. Overholser once again prostituted his profession by swearing under oath that Pound's Italian broadcasts were probably the "result of insanity," despite the fact that Pound had harbored similar anti-Semitic and pro-fascist views for virtually the whole of his life. The trial judge once again parroted Dr. Overholser's results-oriented opinions and ordered Pound freed.

The Pound case represents the absolute nadir in the relationship between law and psychiatry. The psychiatrists misused their professional skills, their jargon, and their prestige to pull the wool over the eyes of a legal system already confused by Pound's bizarre behavior and ambivalent about the desired outcome of his case. In the decade following Pound's release, the legal system became more skeptical of psychiatrists such as Winfred

Overholser and less willing to abdicate responsibilities to experts, especially when they offer opinions well beyond their areas of expertise. In the decades and cases that followed, the role of psychiatrists in the legal process would diminish considerably, and psychiatric testimony would come to be viewed more skeptically by jurors and judges alike.

1. Roger Daniels, "Asian Americans," in *Encyclopedia of American Social History*, vol. 2, ed. Mary Kupiec Cayton, Elliott J. Gorn, and Peter W. Williams (New York: Charles Scribner's Sons, 1993), p. 882.

2. I. C. B. Dear, ed., *The Oxford Companion to the Second World War* (Oxford: Oxford University Press, 1995), p. 633.

3. Roger Daniels, *Prisoners Without Trial: Japanese Americans in World War II* (New York: Hill and Wang, 1993), p. 72; Mitchell T. Maki, Harry H. L. Kitano, and S. Megan Berthold, *Achieving the Impossible Dream: How Japanese Americans Obtained Redress* (Urbana: University of Illinois Press, 1999), p. 33.

4. Daniels, *Prisoners*, p. 72.

5. Maki et al., pp. 35–36.

6. *Ibid.*, p. 36.

7. *Korematsu v. United States*, 323 U.S. 214, 256 (1944) (Jackson, J., dissenting).

8. Daniels, *Prisoners*, p. 63.

9. *Ibid.*, p. 3.

10. Francis Biddle, *In Brief Authority* (Garden City, NY: Doubleday, 1962), p. 331.

11. See Supreme Court Historical Society, "History of the Court: The Stone Court, 1941–1946," www.supremecourthistory.org/02_history/subs_history/02_c12.html; and remarks by Chief Justice Rehnquist at the DC Circuit Judicial Conference, June 14, 2002, titled "The Use of Military Tribunals," www.supremecourtus.gov/publicinfo/speeches/sp_06-14-02.html.

12. Noel Stock, *The Life of Ezra Pound* (San Francisco: North Point Press, 1982), p. 396.

13. *Ibid.*, p. 407.

14. Michael R. Marrus, "The Nuremberg Trial: Fifty Years After," *American Scholar* 66(4) (autumn 1997), p. 563.

15. Eric Foner and John A. Garraty, eds., *The Reader's Companion to American History* (Boston: Houghton Mifflin, 1991), p. 802.

16. Ann Tusa and John Tusa, *The Nuremberg Trial* (New York: Atheneum, 1986), p. 13.

17. *Ibid.*, p. 69.

18. *Ibid.*, p. 51.

19. *Ibid.*, p. 77.

20. *Ibid.*, p. 281.

21. *Ibid.*

22. Justice Robert Jackson, "Summation for the Prosecution," July 26, 1946.

23. Tusa and Tusa, p. 121.

24. *Ibid.*, p. 457.

25. *Ibid.*

26. *Ibid.*

27. *Ibid.*
28. *Ibid.*
29. *Ibid.*, p. 51.
30. Julien Cornell, *The Trial of Ezra Pound* (New York: The Notable Trials Library, 1992), pp. 139–40.
31. *Ibid.*, p. 1.
32. Federal Bureau of Investigation, "Tokyo Rose," in *Famous Cases*, www.fbi.gov/libref/historic/famcases/rose/rose.htm.
33. Cornell, pp. 188–89.
34. *Ibid.*, pp. 214–15.
35. *Ibid.*, p. 63.
36. *Ibid.*, p. 111.

PART X

The Cold War and McCarthyism

THE DEVELOPMENT OF THE ATOMIC BOMB by scientists on behalf of the United States helped to end the Second World War. The development — or theft — of nuclear weaponry by the Soviet Union helped begin the "Cold War" and McCarthyism, a national hunt for Communist spies and sympathizers in America. The movement was named for Joe McCarthy, the junior senator from Wisconsin who publicly spearheaded the nation's "Red-hunting" campaign.

But McCarthyism was not the only movement of note that followed World War II. The civil rights movement gained momentum in the mid-1950s with the Supreme Court's decision to order desegregation of schools, closely followed by Martin Luther King Jr.'s nonviolent protest movement. Some women also began to express dissatisfaction with the wife and homemaker roles assigned to them by tradition, and beyond that, sexuality itself also came under scrutiny. The birth control pill was tested through the 1950s and became available as a contraceptive device in May 1960.[1] Moreover, the science of sexuality was already the subject of popular interest owing to the publication of Alfred Kinsey's best-selling studies of American sexual habits. But despite the emergence of race and gender as issues of concern to many Americans, the dominating issue of the immediate postwar period was Communism.

In the immediate afterglow of victory over Germany and Japan, America emerged as a superpower. Its development of the atomic bomb, and its successful deployment of that awesome weapon to end the war in the Pacific, made us seem invincible. But in 1949, the Soviet Union tested its own bomb. Historian Margot Henriksen describes the American reaction: "the government shrouded the Soviet attainment in suspicion, somewhat arrogantly assuming that the Soviets had achieved their atomic explosion only as a result of the information provided by spies who had infiltrated America's centers of defense and science."[2]

Militarily, the United States continued to develop its hydrogen bomb, successfully testing it in 1954 at Bikini Island in the Pacific. The term *Cold War* accurately describes the "years of limbo between war and peace" when the two nuclear powers faced off across the global stage, each rapidly building its atomic arsenal.[3] Anxiety about the possibility of atomic war became part of American life, as buildings added fallout shelters and schoolchildren performed "duck and cover" drills in anticipation of atomic war.

The Soviet attainment of atomic capability — and the suspicion that spies and traitors made it possible — lent itself to a growing paranoia that was quickly exploited by opportunistic politicians. The House Un-American Activities Committee (HUAC), almost defunct in 1944, secured a new purpose by seizing on the issue of domestic Communism. When Whittaker Chambers, managing editor of *Time* magazine, accused Alger Hiss, a former government official under Roosevelt, of being a member of a Communist group in government in the 1930s, HUAC held hearings.[4] Chambers claimed that he, too, had been an active Communist in that era, and recognized Hiss as a fellow active party member; Hiss denied any Communist party affiliation and prior association with Chambers.[5] The committee, stirred by its active young "Red-hunting" member Richard Nixon, determined that someone was lying.[6] After Hiss admitted that he "may" have known Chambers under a different name, he was tried for perjury and ultimately convicted. As Eric Goldman points out, "As 1949 went on, Whittaker Chambers receded into the background; the specific testimony was less and less discussed. Even the figure of Alger Hiss, the individual, blurred. Everything was turning into Alger Hiss, the symbol."[7]

The Hiss case polarized the country; to supporters of both sides, it represented a sort of referendum on New Deal liberalism because Hiss had worked in the Roosevelt administration.[8] Interestingly, some commentators note that the popular imaginations on both sides in the Hiss case tended to inflate Hiss's influence in the Roosevelt administration: "In fact, Hiss had hardly been a key player in the State Department. . . . He was a high-level clerk,"[9] though some blame him for what they considered the "giveaway" to Stalin at Yalta in Roosevelt's final days as president. The truth, as usual, lay somewhere in between.

Though very much a Cold War anti-Communist, President Truman was vulnerable to charges of being "soft on Communism," a factor that may have dissuaded him from more forcefully challenging the often questionable methods of investigators.[10] As historian Ellen Schrecker has pointed out, "Hiss's conviction also legitimized HUAC by showing how useful a congressional investigation could be in exposing Communist subversion."[11]

Nationwide concern about Communist spies active in government intensified in early 1950 when Senator Joe McCarthy gave a speech in Wheeling, West Virginia, in which he suggested that he was privy to damning information about spy infiltration: "While I cannot take the time to name all the men in the State Department who have been named as active members of the Communist Party and members of a spy ring, I have here in my hand a list of 205 — a list of names that were made known to the Secretary of State as being members of the Communist Party and who nevertheless are still working and shaping policy in the state department."[12]

McCarthy did not in fact have such a list. The number "205" was derived from a three-year-old memo related to general screening of federal employees transferred to the State Department; the memo did not include a list of names, nor did it refer to Communism.[13] The purported list generated enormous publicity for McCarthy, even as it led some to criticize his "Red-baiting" tactic.

Undeterred by the fact that this first supposed list did not actually exist, McCarthy began to refer to other lists. There were "57 card-carrying communists in the State Department."[14] Never mind that the Communist party had long since recalled its cards, and that the memo where McCarthy found the number "57" did not mention Communists.[15] Over the next few months, McCarthy, aided by his assistant, Roy Cohn, did produce some names, and several individuals were hauled in to testify in congressional committees. The public was transfixed: McCarthy had hit a nerve with many Americans.

Suddenly, suspected Communists were everywhere. As with many movements of mass hysteria, the charges contained a kernel of truth. It was true that individuals who had harbored Communist sympathies were in government and other positions of power. In the 1930s, a considerable number of left-leaning intellectuals were often sympathetic to the Communist cause, and the dividing lines among liberals, leftists, socialists, and Communists were vague and amorphous. Furthermore, recent scholarship — based largely on newly opened Soviet KGB files — has confirmed that some charges of spying for the Soviets were also true, though many were not.[16]

At the same time, many moderate anti-Communists became concerned with McCarthy's tactics, which appeared to involve vague charges about associations bolstered by questionable evidence obtained through threats, intimidation, and coercive actions. Aided by information provided by J. Edgar Hoover's FBI, investigators would threaten former Communist sympathizers with public exposure unless they named others as Communists.[17] "'Are you now or have you ever been a member of the Communist party' was the culminating question of a congressional hearing, and being forced to answer it could be devastating: those that invoked their Fifth Amendment right against self-incrimination were often 'blacklisted' from their jobs."[18]

One prominent, and tragic, case was that of William Remington, an anti-Communist who had flirted with Communism in college and then denied that fact to investigators. In a trial rife with prosecutorial misconduct, Remington was convicted to serve a three-year sentence for perjury. He was murdered in prison by "Commie"-hating inmates.

The HUAC also went after the liberal entertainment industry. The "Hollywood Ten," a group of screenwriters and directors who were former Communists, were subject to a blacklist and unable to work in Hollywood for years, except occasionally under pseudonyms.[19]

The 1951 Rosenberg spy trial was the case that most embodied all the complexities of the McCarthy era. The case originated when British physicist Klaus Fuchs, who had worked on America's Manhattan Project, admitted passing documents related to the development of the bomb to Soviet agents.[20] The search for his American contact eventually led to accusations that Julius Rosenberg, aided by his wife, Ethel, had passed along plans delivered to him from Los Alamos National Laboratory to Soviet agents. The Rosenbergs were accused of wartime espionage. Their trial — based in part on evidence fabricated by the FBI — ultimately led to their conviction and execution.[21] The debate about their guilt — especially Ethel Rosenberg's — continues to this day. As a young man growing up in Brooklyn during the case, I vividly recall my parents warning me not to sign any petitions on their behalf, lest it go on my "permanent record." McCarthyism resulted in several of my teachers being fired. It hit very close to home despite my own family's strong religious opposition to Communism. In my house, we hated Stalin and McCarthy with similar passion.

By the mid-1950s, McCarthyism was beginning to lose its hold on America. President Eisenhower personally despised McCarthy. During a meeting discussing a new type of life insurance, Eisenhower reportedly noted, "I know one fellow I'd like to take that policy out for," referencing McCarthy.[22] Publicly, however, he refused to confront him; "I will not get in the gutter with that guy," he would say.[23] Legendary newscaster Edward R. Murrow presented a television program criticizing McCarthy in the winter of 1954.[24] The tide was beginning to turn.

McCarthy's final downfall was precipitated by a Senate subcommittee investigation of his efforts to pressure the army to win special treatment for a member of his staff.[25] The army–McCarthy hearings were televised, demonstrating the political power of the new medium. Illustrative of McCarthy's missteps during the hearings was a famous smear against a young lawyer representing the army. Though it had no relation to the content of the hearing, McCarthy mentioned that, as a law school student, this lawyer had belonged to the left-wing National Lawyers Guild, implying a Communist association.[26] At this point, the army chief counsel, a Boston lawyer named Joseph Welch, stirringly replied, "Have you no sense of decency, sir?"[27] The hearing ended in a Senate censure of McCarthy for lack of respect, and he faded from public view thereafter. He died in 1957 at the age of forty-eight, a victim of alcoholism and cirrhosis of the liver.[28] "If nothing else," comments David Halberstam, "he had illustrated the timidity of his fellow man."[29] Now Senator McCarthy is making something of a posthumous comeback, as revisionist writers of the extreme right — such as Ann Coulter — claim that he was a prophet rather than a pariah.[30]

The Alger Hiss Case

Date: 1949–50
Location: New York City, New York
Defendant: Alger Hiss
Charge: Perjury
Verdict: Guilty
Sentence: Imprisonment for five years

Few cases have divided the nation, and defined an age, more sharply than the Whittaker Chambers–Alger Hiss imbroglio in the post–World War II decade. Even more than the Rosenberg case, the Hiss case mirrored the Cold War. The Rosenbergs were, after all, obscure children of immigrants. Alger Hiss — a Harvard Law School graduate who clerked for Justice Oliver Wendell Holmes — was the personification of the Roosevelt revolution: He served trusted roles in the New Deal, the preparation for and fighting of World War II, the Yalta Conference near war's end, and the establishment of the United Nations to prevent future wars. He was one of the Roosevelt administration's fair-haired boys, among its best, brightest, and most presentable embodiments, though the extent of his actual influences on policy making has been questioned.

It is difficult to imagine, more than half a century later, what it must have been like when a senior editor of *Time* magazine, Whittaker Chambers — himself an admitted former Communist undercover agent — accused Alger Hiss of having served as a So-

viet agent while employed by the government. Not since Bene-
dict Arnold and Aaron Burr had an individual with so high a position in government been accused of so serious a breach of
loyalty. Hiss denied the charges under oath before a House subcommittee headed by an obscure young congressman named
Richard Nixon.

The testimony of the two men diverged so sharply that it soon
became clear that one of them would be charged with perjury.
That one was Alger Hiss. His prosecution became a cause
célèbre, dividing Americans as few other cases have done. This
division did not fall along class or even party lines, as is the case
with most such controversies. Hiss was an upper-crust elitist
whose supporters included Supreme Court justices, former sec-
retaries of state, and other prominent politicians and statesmen
from both parties.

Even following his eventual conviction — after a deadlocked
jury at the first trial — Americans remained divided over whether
a terrible miscarriage of justice had occurred.

More than a quarter century later, in 1972, a young Cold War
historian named Allen Weinstein set out to prove Hiss's innocence. With the help of the American Civil Liberties Union, he
filed a lawsuit under the Freedom of Information Act to obtain
secret files on the case. Weinstein interviewed hundreds of witnesses, including Alger Hiss himself, and those closest to him.
Then, suddenly, the young historian experienced an epiphany:
He realized that Hiss was, in fact, guilty. Historical objectivity
required Weinstein to change his expected conclusion and reveal the truth, painful as that would be.

This, at least, is the version Allen Weinstein would have us believe. It may well be true, but this sort of transformation is becoming too common not to raise some suspicion. In 1986, I
commented on this phenomenon in a book review I wrote for
the *Washington Post* about the Sacco and Vanzetti case:

Francis Russell's writings on the notorious Sacco and Vanzetti case are part of what appears to be a growing genre of "personal revisionism" about controversial criminal cases. The formula goes something like this. A liberal believer in the dogma of the defendant's innocence starts to write a book that will conclusively establish what all right-thinking people believe — that the defendant was the innocent victim of a terrible miscarriage of justice. While writing the book, the author solicits and/or accepts assistance from the defendant or his strongest supporters, who are under the impression that he is on their side. But, lo and behold, after reviewing the files of the case, a sudden insight strikes: the defendant is really guilty. Commitment to principles of truth and justice requires the born-again disbeliever to disclose the sad reality. The book is then marketed with an emphasis on the enhanced credibility of the author, because he wanted so badly to believe in innocence, but had no choice other than to follow the facts. Other books that seem to fit this formula — albeit with variations — include: *The Rosenberg File* by Ronald Radosh and Joyce Milton, *Fatal Vision* by Joe McGinniss, and *Perjury: The Hiss-Chambers Case* by Allen Weinstein.[31]

Once converted, Weinstein became a fierce advocate for his new position. His one-sided advocacy comes through clearly in such self-protective lines as these: "Final judgment on whether or not the prosecution violated Hiss's procedural rights at his two trials — *an issue which does not touch upon the merits of his conviction itself* — will be determined by the courts after a thorough review of the evidence [emphasis added]."[32] Only a zealot would discount the possibility that prosecutorial violation of a defendant's procedural rights might not "touch on the merits of the conviction itself." Many procedural rights, particularly the ones at issue here, are designed to ferret out the truth. It is precisely because the case against Hiss was so flawed procedurally that no one can have confidence in the jury verdict. The verdict of history is equally flawed by the polemical nature of the debate.

The evidence presented at the Hiss–Chambers trial was high on drama, but low on substance. At the center of the case lay the so-called Pumpkin Papers, a series of State Department documents and materials that Chambers turned over to HUAC investigators in November and December 1948, several months after Hiss's first hearing. The first part of this series, which Chambers removed from a dumbwaiter shaft in his nephew's home, consisted of sixty-five pages of retyped State Department documents dated between January and April 1938 (on subjects that ranged from U.S. policy toward the Soviet Union to the Spanish Civil War) and four handwritten copies of State Department cables.[33] A few weeks later, in a dramatic incident, Chambers drove two HUAC investigators to his Maryland farm and pulled several rolls of thirty-five-millimeter film from a hollowed-out pumpkin: three developed rolls, which contained State Department documents from the same period as the typed and handwritten material, and two undeveloped rolls holding Navy Department documents, which also dated from early 1938.[34]

At trial, Hiss agreed that the four handwritten copies were his own handwriting, but the two sides fiercely disputed the identity of the sixty-five typed pages. Based on FBI laboratory tests of the pages (the results of which were subsequently confirmed by Hiss's own experts), the government argued that the documents had been typed on the Hisses' Woodstock typewriter, serial number N230099.[35] In his defense, Hiss labeled the documents a "forgery by typewriter"[36] — he insisted that neither he nor his wife could have typed any of the documents, since they had given the typewriter to relatives at the end of 1937. Yet as Weinstein notes in his review of the case, there was "no solid evidence supporting the Hisses' belated assertion that Woodstock N230099 changed hands earlier than April 1938."[37] In his closing argument, prosecutor Thomas Murphy glossed over such questions about the Pumpkin Papers by placing them within the broader context of the Cold War:

> Each of these documents, the typewritten documents, and the handwritten documents, each has the same message. . . . And what is this message? "Alger Hiss, you were the traitor. Alger Hiss, your feathers are but borrowed and you can't change those documents." . . . Why? Why did he do it? Because he was in love with their philosophy, not ours. We were not at war then. He was concerned with their philosophy. . . . Take them with you to the jury room, those photographs; take the machine, the instruments. What do they prove? Ladies and gentlemen, it proves treason, and that is the traitor.[38]

Murphy's argument proved extremely persuasive: After less than twenty-four hours of deliberation, all twelve jurors convicted Hiss of perjury.[39]

Hiss quickly mobilized a new group of lawyers to appeal his conviction.[40] In the decades that followed, Hiss and his supporters suggested more than a dozen full-fledged conspiracy theories, alleging that Chambers acted on behalf of Russian agents, that the documents were forged by the Kremlin or that the typewriter was faked by the FBI, and even that Chambers framed Hiss because of his frustrated and unrequited homosexual passion for his adversary.[41] Lending some support to arguments that the government was highly motivated to convict Hiss, subsequent White House tapes reveal that Hiss's old nemesis, President Richard Nixon, was consumed by the case during the Watergate cover-up.[42]

Weinstein, whose historical research converted his skepticism about Hiss's guilt into skepticism about his innocence, discounts this "pursuit of conspiracy."[43] One final observation about Weinstein's conversion: In his introduction to the paperback edition,

Weinstein tantalizes the reader with an incident that is not re-counted in the 1978 first edition:

> I had no occasion to describe my own last meeting with Alger
> Hiss, in which, amidst great tension on both sides, I tried to ex-
> plain why my research had forced a change of judgment about
> his innocence. This and other personal encounters during the
> course of my research showed in unmistakable ways the sheer
> "messiness" which attends the study of such incidents in con-
> temporary history, when the clarification of vital evidence
> often emerges in part from observing the raw emotions of par-
> ticipants, again a more normal situation for the historical nov-
> elist than for the historian.

That is one conversation at which I would have wished to be a fly on the wall.

Hiss's petition to overturn his conviction was rejected in 1982. Yet Hiss and his supporters were able to celebrate a few minor victories in their campaign to prove his innocence, particularly in the wake of the Watergate scandal. In 1975, for example, the Massachusetts Supreme Judicial Court unanimously approved Hiss's readmission to the state bar. The court reasoned that Hiss "has the moral qualifications, competency and learning in law required," and that his readmission "will not be detrimental to the integrity and standing of the bar, the administration of justice or to the public interest."[44] Alger Hiss died in 1996, at the age of ninety-two, still asserting his innocence.

The Trial of the Rosenbergs

Date: 1951
Location: New York City, New York
Defendants: Julius and Ethel Rosenberg
Charge: Wartime espionage
Verdict: Guilty
Sentence: Electrocution

Among candidates for the dubious honor of the "Trial of the Twentieth Century," the Rosenberg spy case garners many votes, since it represented one of the darkest periods of American history and some of the worst abuses of our legal system. It claimed McCarthyism's first and second fatalities, and the controversy surrounding it has hardly abated, though the nature of the debate has changed.

Were Julius and Ethel Rosenberg guilty of transmitting American atomic secrets to the Soviet Union in the 1940s? Or were they scapegoats of the Cold War whose execution was a grave miscarriage of justice? That both statements may be correct is the intriguing possibility that several historians have persuasively argued, and I believe is probably true (at least as to Julius).[45]

The basic story of the Rosenberg case is familiar. Following the arrest for espionage of the British atomic scientist Klaus Fuchs in England in February 1950, the Federal Bureau of Investigation found his courier, Harry Gold, in Philadelphia.

Gold, in turn, led the FBI to David Greenglass, a soldier who had worked at the atomic bomb facility in Los Alamos, New Mexico. Greenglass was pressured to incriminate others. He testified at the trial of the Rosenbergs that he had given notes and sketches of the atomic bomb to his brother-in-law, Julius Rosenberg, who had them typed by his wife, Ethel, and then turned them over to the Russians. The Rosenbergs were convicted of conspiracy to commit espionage, and — after massive international protests and several stays of execution — they were put to death in the electric chair at Sing Sing on June 19, 1953. Half a century later, advocates and opponents of the Rosenbergs are still debating whether "the crime of the century" was the Rosenbergs' theft of American atomic secrets or the government's execution of two young idealists.

From recent studies of extensive government files opened under the Freedom of Information Act, and from hundreds of interviews, two scholars — Ronald Radosh, a historian at the Graduate Center of the City University of New York, and Joyce Milton, a freelance writer and critic — reached the following conclusions:

- Julius Rosenberg played a central role in the Soviet espionage ring and transmitted material that he believed contained important atomic secrets.

- Klaus Fuchs had already given those secrets to the Russians, but David Greenglass's amateurish sketches provided some confirmation of his information.

- Ethel Rosenberg was not deeply involved in her husband's espionage activities, but she knew about them and may have typed the notes he passed on.

- The FBI was aware of Mrs. Rosenberg's limited role but deliberately exaggerated it and insisted that federal prosecutors demand the death penalty for her in order to increase the bureau's leverage on her husband to cooperate in its investigations.

- Some of the evidence against the Rosenbergs was highly questionable and probably false.

- Nearly all those involved — from the Soviet intelligence agency KGB to the FBI to some of the Rosenbergs' own "defenders" — were willing to see the Rosenbergs die so their case could be used to serve partisan interests.

The complex truths uncovered by this thorough assessment of the evidence and others pleased neither side in the rancorous controversy. For three decades, the battle lines had been neatly drawn: One side had argued that the Rosenbergs were guilty and the process was fair, while the other side had argued that the Rosenbergs were innocent and the process was unfair. The truth apparently comes closer to the uncomfortable conclusion that although Julius Rosenberg was guilty, "the government's zeal (in prosecuting both he and his wife) led to questionable tactics and eventually to a grave miscarriage of justice."[46]

It is widely recognized among criminal lawyers that some of the most egregious governmental misconduct occurs in cases involving guilty and despised criminals. Miscarriages of justice can be perpetrated against the guilty as well as the innocent. For example, in prosecutions for organized crime, the government, with the implicit cooperation of some courts, has been known to bend the law and twist the facts in order to assure the conviction of a guilty mob leader whom it fears might otherwise get off because members of organized crime families observe a code of silence.

The framers of the Constitution deliberately designed the Bill of Rights to protect the guilty as well as the innocent from injustice. That ideal is often difficult to realize, especially during times of political hysteria such as the 1950s. It is important, therefore, to look back at historical events such as the execution of the Rosenbergs from a distant perspective. Supreme Court justice Felix Frankfurter wrote in a dissenting opinion published after the deaths of the Rosenbergs: "To be writing an opinion in a case affecting two lives after the curtain has been rung down upon them has the appearance of pathetic futility. But history also has its claims."[47] When he wrote these prescient words, Frankfurter had no idea that history would eventually tell so complex a tale of pervasive wrongdoing by so many — including several Supreme Court justices.

The evidence that Julius Rosenberg played a central role in a Soviet spy ring emerges from so many independent — indeed, mutually antagonistic — sources that it is impossible to discount. Those who persist in claiming that he was innocent and framed must postulate a conspiracy so global as to include the FBI, the KGB, some officials of the American Communist Party, and dozens of individual Americans from different points on the political spectrum. The value of the Radosh-Milton research is that it almost never relies on one type of source. It corroborates FBI files by interviews with people who were active in the American Communist Party in the 1940s and 1950s such as John Gates, who was editor in chief of *The Daily Worker*; Junius Scales, who was chairman of the Communist Party of North Carolina; and James Weinstein, a former member of the party who is now editor in chief of *In These Times*.

Though the official line of the Communist party was that the Rosenbergs were framed, individual members of the party now seem willing to acknowledge the reality. A "venerable and well-established Communist Party lawyer" has admitted:

Of course they were guilty. But you can't quote me. My public position is that the Rosenbergs were innocent. . . . What's wrong with what they did? If I were in their place, I would have done the same things. What was so bad about helping Stalin get the A-bomb? It was the responsibility of a good Communist to do whatever he could do to help the Red Army gain victory. . . . Don't think I'm so dumb that I don't believe the Rosenbergs weren't engaged in espionage.[48]

Of course, informed speculation by unnamed sources does not prove the guilt of Julius Rosenberg. But the combined evidence — facts corroborated independently in a number of different ways — leaves few lingering doubts about his factual guilt. For example, an informer who had been in jail with him told the FBI a detailed story about an espionage trip Julius Rosenberg took to Ithaca, New York. One of the alleged witnesses to these events was subpoenaed by the federal grand jury but refused to talk. Thirty years later, "in the belief that the time had now come to set the record straight," the witness told Radosh and Milton the facts he had refused to reveal in 1951.[49] Through many checks on those facts, they confirmed the details of the informer's story and Julius Rosenberg's role.

After the Soviet Union fell, many files of Soviet intelligence agencies were made public. These files confirmed the guilt of Julius Rosenberg beyond any reasonable doubt. Roy Cohn, who helped prosecute the Rosenbergs, proudly told me shortly before his death that the government had "manufactured" evidence against the Rosenbergs, because they knew Julius was the head of a spy ring. They had learned this from bugging a foreign embassy, but they could not disclose any information learned from the bug, so they made up some evidence in order to prove what they already knew. In the process, they also made up evidence against Ethel Rosenberg.

The evidence about Ethel Rosenberg's involvement is seriously flawed. Given that Ethel Rosenberg was charged with participating in a conspiracy to commit espionage, her legal guilt could be established merely by her knowledge of the conspiracy, her intent to join it, and any minimal involvement in it. However, she was executed on the assumption that, in President Eisenhower's words, she was "the apparent leader of the two."[50] Radosh and Milton conclude that "Ethel Rosenberg probably knew of and supported her husband's endeavors."[51] They also say she may have typed the notes Greenglass gave her husband, though that critical charge was based largely on a questionable last-minute change of testimony by Greenglass.[52] There is absolutely no hard information to support the conclusion that she was a leader of, or even actively involved in, a spy ring. Subsequently disclosed Soviet intelligence files corroborate the conclusion that Ethel Rosenberg was, at worst, a loyal wife and was not regarded by the Soviets as a spy.

The only real evidence of her participation was the court testimonies of David Greenglass and his wife that Mr. Greenglass gave Julius Rosenberg handwritten notes and sketches in the Rosenberg living room, and that Rosenberg then gave his wife the notes to type. However, government files reveal that Mr. Greenglass's original version of this event was completely inconsistent with his testimony during the trial. Shortly after his arrest, Mr. Greenglass said that he had given the notes to Julius Rosenberg "on the street" and that Ethel Rosenberg was not present; he did not mention any typing.[53] It is possible that Mr. Greenglass was originally trying to protect his sister, but the shifting sands of his accounts provide an uncomfortable foundation for a conclusion that she was actually involved in the work of the spy ring.

It now seems clear that the FBI was fully aware of the fact that Ethel knew little or nothing about the Soviety spy ring. Just prior to their execution, the FBI prepared a list of questions for Julius Rosenberg (but none for his wife), just in case Julius had an eleventh-hour change of heart and decided to barter his cooperation for their lives. Only one question proposed for Julius concerned Ethel: "Was your wife cognizant of your activities?"[54] Thus, "the U.S. government seemed willing to let her die when the FBI was not even sure she was aware of Julius' espionage activities."[55] It is fair to characterize the execution of Ethel Rosenberg as a case of judicial homicide far more criminal than anything she may have done.

Why, then, did the government persist in executing a mother of two children who, at most, was marginally involved in her husband's espionage? The FBI files provide a plausible, if bone-chilling, explanation: "Ethel was undoubtedly being used as a pawn to push Julius into confessing."[56] The files establish that the reason Ethel Rosenberg was investigated in the first place was so that, in J. Edgar Hoover's words, she "might serve as a lever" to make her husband talk.[57] This deadly game was played out until the very end. When the Rosenbergs refused to confess and cooperate, the Justice Department felt that it had to follow through on its threat. Ethel Rosenberg was executed minutes after her husband, despite the FBI's uncertainty about her involvement. (One of my relatives was the prison rabbi who provided them religious counseling before their execution.)

And why did President Eisenhower say she was apparently the leader of the spy group? As part of the strategy, the Justice Department had sent the president information suggesting just that. Fearing that Eisenhower's basic decency and sympathy for a young mother might induce him to grant her clemency, the department wanted him to believe that she was no mere typist-wife. The story of how this piece of malicious fiction found its way into the FBI files is perhaps the most shocking episode in the case.

The late Morris Ernst, who was co-counsel to the American Civil Liberties Union for many years and a senior partner in a prestigious New York law firm, was asked by Julius Rosenberg's brother and sister to become involved in the case on behalf of the defendants. Ernst immediately reported this request to the

FBI and proposed that he go to work for the Rosenberg defense team in order to serve the interests of the FBI. His goal was to get the Rosenbergs to confess, because — according to an FBI report of his conversation — "this would be a terrific story, and probably would be most helpful to the Bureau."[58] It was a classic conflict of interest hidden from the clients. If true, it warranted disbarment and perpetual disgrace. It is just about the worst thing a lawyer can do.

Ernst, who died in 1976, cannot respond to these serious charges of perfidy, the legal analogue of espionage and treason. It is, of course, possible that the FBI memoranda do not accurately reflect his motivations or his precise words; possibly he was using unorthodox measures in a desperate effort to save the Rosenbergs' lives. Perhaps some rebuttal or explanation will be forthcoming from his legion of friends and admirers. If not, this revelation will require reassessment of Ernst's important place in the history of American civil liberties.

In the end, the FBI refused to become involved, but an agent's report says that Ernst communicated to the bureau the results of a "psychological study" he conducted and in which he concluded that "Julius is the slave and his wife, Ethel, the master."[59] This amateur conclusion, though without any factual basis, was "eagerly seized upon" by the FBI "because it gave some semblance of justification for going ahead with the execution of Ethel."[60] Echoes of Ernst's conclusion eventually appear in President Eisenhower's correspondence justifying his refusal to spare her life. Radosh and Milton conclude that the FBI file "paints a shocking picture of a lawyer offering to represent prospective clients only with the FBI's permission and then, in effect, only to act as the Bureau's servant."[61]

Ernst is not the only Rosenberg "defender" whose reputation could be sullied by recent disclosures. The files raise questions about several other "heroes" of the Rosenberg ordeal. Emanuel Bloch, the chief defense lawyer, appeared more eager to cover up his own blunders than to allow other lawyers to get credit for possibly saving the Rosenbergs' lives. Justice William O. Douglas, whose last-minute stay of execution was reversed by the Supreme Court, is said to have voted against the Rosenbergs during deliberations on the case by the court on several prior occasions.[62] Chief Justice Fred Vinson and Justice Robert Jackson engaged in improper ex parte communications with the Justice Department while the case was pending. The ACLU and the American Jewish Committee, fearful that the broad brush of Communism might taint them, appear to have gone out of their way to announce that there were no civil liberties or constitutional problems with the trial or sentence. The American Communist Party, while publicly working to save the Rosenbergs, apparently welcomed their deaths as serving several important functions: Death would silence the Rosenbergs forever and create international martyrs. The Rosenbergs' death also would deflect world attention from the trial and execution in Prague of Rudolf Slansky and ten other former leaders of the Czechoslovakian Communist Party, a trial in which the prosecuting Stalinists were blatantly anti-Semitic and that threatened a split in the international Communist movement.

The Rosenbergs "were indeed hapless scapegoats of a propaganda war — a war in which their deaths would be counted as a victory for both sides."[63] It should come as no surprise, then, that many who debated about the Rosenberg trial at the time — and their successors — perpetuated their doctrinaire charges and countercharges for so many years, regardless of what actually happened.

Many important questions still remain, especially about the actions of the government. But false claims of innocence play directly into the hands of those who perpetrate injustice against the guilty. Once they persuade the public, or the courts, that the shrill claims of innocence are false, they need not apologize for their unjust conduct. Julius Rosenberg's guilt has now been convincingly proved. We must now turn to the important task of ensuring that legal injustices, whether directed against the innocent or the guilty, are not tolerated even in times of political hysteria.

The Remington Case

Date: 1950–51
Location: New York City, New York
Defendant: William Remington
Charge: Perjury
Verdict: Guilty
Sentence: Three years' imprisonment

No nation has been spared witch hunts, show trials, scapegoating, political prosecutions, and the like. In the United States, we have had more than our share of such travesties of justice, when the public has been whipped up into a mood of hysteria by opportunistic politicians. Usually, the hysteria has been based on a germ of reality, as it was in the Rosenberg case; otherwise the public would not be as responsive to the opportunists. However, that germ is often grossly exaggerated, and the fears of the public are often played upon for political or personal gain.

Perhaps the worst manifestation of this phenomenon in twentieth-century America was the McCarthyism that followed on the heels of the Rosenberg case. The full story of this disgraceful episode has yet to be told. Some of the dramatis personae — perpetrators, victims, collaborators, heroes, and cowards — are still alive. The story — the real story — comes out piecemeal.

It is useful to recall that McCarthyism had three dominant elements, embodied in three questions. The first was political McCarthyism: Are you now or have you ever been a member of the Communist party? The second was sexual McCarthyism: Have you ever done anything in your private sex life that might subject you to extortion or blackmail? The third was legal McCarthyism: If you are a lawyer, have you ever represented a Communist, a fellow traveler, or anyone who has ever invoked the Fifth Amendment when asked about these issues?

The case of William Remington presented each of those issues. Remington was almost certainly a member or supporter of the Communist party, or one of its numerous fronts, in his youth. While a student at Dartmouth College, Remington believed in Soviet-style Communism and participated in party activities. Later he became staunchly anti-Communist, out of either ideological or pragmatic considerations. But instead of forthrightly acknowledging his youthful flirtation with Stalinism, he lied and thereby destroyed any chances of making a principled defense against McCarthyism. His lies did, however, secure for him the advantage of excellent lawyers, who first had to convince themselves that he was not a Communist before they would agree to represent him. Finally, his active sex life, including — heaven forgive him — private nudity, made him easy prey for the witch hunters.

It is somewhat difficult for those who did not live through the McCarthy era to appreciate the atmosphere surrounding "Commie trials." One vignette may help set the stage. When Remington was ultimately indicted — for perjuriously denying that he had ever been a member of the Communist party — no bank or bail company was willing to allow him to borrow the bail money or purchase a bond. This was not because he was a flight risk, but rather because no one wanted to be perceived as helping an accused Communist. One bail bond company acknowledged that it would willingly write a bond "for a man charged with . . . armed robbery," but not for a Communist.[64] Remington's mother had to cash in her life's savings to post cash bond.

Proving that Remington had committed perjury when he denied membership in the Communist party would not be an easy task, even for an FBI determined to make an example of Remington. In the mid-1930s at places like Dartmouth, "there was no clear dividing line separating radicals and liberals from Communists."[65] Nearly all decent people favored the Communists over the fascists in the Spanish Civil War and supported other principles and policies espoused by the Communist party — such as equal rights for racial and religious minorities and the right of workers to organize. The issues that would ultimately divide liberals from Communists — Stalin's temporary alliance with Hitler and his anti-Semitic purges of Jewish party leaders and intellectuals — were still in the future, and even the repressive tactics employed by Stalin against ordinary Russians did not have the notoriety they would later receive.

But none of this mattered to the opportunistic Red haters in the FBI, the Justice Department, Congress, the courts, or the media. A Communist was a Communist, even if he was never a formal member of the party. Nor did it matter that Remington had become a strident anti-Communist, unless he was willing to work for the McCarthyites against his former friends.

The atmosphere extended to judges as well, several of whom engaged in overt misconduct — including cheating and lying — in order to help put Communists in prison. This is what the writer Gary May, who gained access to the grand jury testimony, says about Judge Gregory Noonan, who presided at the first Remington trial:

Just as disturbing is Judge Noonan's conduct regarding [Ann Remington's] grand jury testimony. He had promised that if he found contradictions, he would give her transcripts to Chanler [who was Remington's lawyer] and permit her to be re-examined. But when the trial resumed in January, Noonan told the lawyers he had found no evidence of inconsistency between her grand jury and trial testimonies, so their request to inspect her minutes and those of the other thirteen witnesses was denied. It is impossible to understand Noonan's ruling; Ann Remington's trial testimony is riddled with contradictions, and one is forced to conclude that the judge did not read the transcripts or received a fraudulent copy from [Irving] Saypol [the prosecutor] or did read the minutes and, given his pro-government sympathies ("Chanler's lost his case and he's desperately trying anything he can think of," Noonan was heard to remark to a reporter), ignored the inconsistencies. Whatever is the truth, Noonan apparently violated his oath to see that the law was fairly administered.[66]

The chief prosecutor, too, was engaged in misconduct, even bigotry. Though he himself was a Jew who had changed his name from Ike Sapolsky to Irving Saypol, he asked a defense witness named Redmont why he had changed his name from Rothenberg:

> . . . I remember . . . saying that I was going into a career of journalism, and I felt that . . . Anglicizing the name . . . would [mean] an effective and shorter byline. . . . His advice was that it was a good idea and he thought it should be done by court order, which we did . . . I [also] remember discussing with him other questions which I will go into if your Honor thinks it is fitting, which are because of religious matters.
> "What do you mean by that?" asked Saypol.
> "Well," Redmont said, "there is a certain amount of anti-Semitism in the world, unfortunately."
> Redmont had given Saypol the opportunity to make his point. "And you were going to hide under a phony name. Is that your idea?"
> Chanler jumped up. "I object to that, your Honor . . . Mr. Saypol has tried to bring religious prejudice into this case."
> "Sustained," said Noonan, but Saypol continued to pursue that line anyway. "I take it you are of the Hebrew heritage?"

"That is correct."

"So you wanted to conceal that by taking this other name. Is that the idea?"

"It was not a question of concealment," Redmont insisted.

"That is your concept of good Americanism?" Saypol sneered. "As a matter of fact, it is the Communists who take the false names, isn't it?"

"It is not a false name, Sir," Redmont protested. "If it were . . . , I am sure the court would not have ordered it."

"I am sorry if I offended your sensibilities."[67]

The combination of a biased judge and an unethical prosecutor produced a conviction, but the court of appeals reversed. The panel consisted of judges Learned Hand, Augustus Hand, and Thomas Swan, all three highly regarded jurists with the courage to stand up to McCarthyism. The main ground for reversal was the trial judge's vague charge on what the prosecution had to prove about the defendant's alleged association with Communism: actual membership, active association, mere support? The court also criticized the prosecutor for badgering Redmont on his name change:

> In case of a retrial there should be no repetition of the cross-examination attack upon defense witness Redmont. . . . Redmont testified that he had changed his name for professional reasons and that he had done so pursuant to Court order. On cross-examination the prosecutor continued his inquiry of this matter long after it became clear that the change of name had no relevancy to any issue at the trial, and could only serve to arouse possible racial prejudice on the part of the jury.[68]

Undaunted, the prosecutor pressed forward with a retrial. Again the jury convicted (on three counts, unable to agree on two others). This time, however, the court of appeals affirmed,

over a dissent by Learned Hand, who was outraged by the prosecutorial misconduct that permeated this case from the outset.

Remington's lawyers sought review by the U.S. Supreme
Court, which requires that at least four justices agree to hear the
case. Only three did, and so the Supreme Court declined review.
Remington would have to serve his three-year sentence. But
McCarthyism did not end at the prison gate. Remington was
murdered in prison by thugs looking to knock some sense into a
Commie. Remington's persecutors tried to cover up the motive
of the thugs, alleging that gays, gangs, and robbers attacked Remington, but the evidence of anti-Communist frenzy was overwhelming. Journalist Murray Kempton summarized the tragedy
well when he said that Remington was the "least fortunate of
men . . . the small sinner who paid capital penalties."[69] He was
also a tragic victim of his times.

The real tragedy, however, is that so many of those who
cheated, lied, and broke the law to assure that he and others like
him would be destroyed went on to the rewards of judgeships
and places of honor in judicial history. McCarthyism was a low
point — one of several — in the history of free speech, free
thought, and our constitutional commitment to a free marketplace of ideas. It dragged through the mud not only the good
names of decent people but our entire legal system as well. It
remains to be seen how the legal system will respond to the next
wave of repression we are certain to experience over time.

1. David Halberstam, *The Fifties* (New York: Fawcett Books, 1993), p. 605.

2. Margot A. Henriksen, *Dr. Strangelove's America: Society and Culture in the Atomic Age* (Berkeley: University of California Press, 1977), p. 46.

3. *Ibid.*, p. 18.

4. Halberstam, p. 12.

5. *Ibid.*

6. *Ibid.*, p. 14.

7. Eric Goldman, *The Crucial Decade: America 1945–1955* (New York: Knopf, 1956), p. 104.

8. Halberstam, p. 15.

9. *Ibid.*

10. See, e.g., Ellen Schrecker, *The Age of McCarthyism* (Boston: Bedford Books, 1994), p. 31.

11. *Ibid.*

12. Thomas C. Reeves, *The Life and Times of Joe McCarthy* (New York: Madison Books, 1997), p. 224.

13. *Ibid.*

14. *Ibid.*, p. 228.

15. *Ibid.*, p. 229.

16. See, e.g., Ronald Radosh and Joyce Milton, *The Rosenberg File* (Delran, NJ: The Notable Trials Library, 1999).

17. See, e.g., Halberstam, p. 12.

18. Schrecker, pp. 56, 59–60.

19. *Ibid.*, pp. 33–34.

20. *Ibid.*, p. 33.

21. *Ibid.*, p. 34.

22. Halberstam, p. 252.

23. *Ibid.*

24. Schrecker, p. 65.

25. *Ibid.*

26. *Ibid.*

27. *Ibid.*

28. Halberstam, p. 253.

29. *Ibid.*

30. See Ann Coulter, *Treason* (New York: Crown Forum, 2003); see also *Time*, July 14, 2003, p. 8.

31. Alan Dershowitz, "Sacco and Vanzetti: The Debate Goes On," *Washington Post*, Mar. 23, 1986.

32. Allen Weinstein, *Perjury: The Hiss-Chambers Case* (New York: The Notable Trials Library, 1995).

33. Douglas Linder, "The Pumpkin Papers: Key Evidence in the Alger Hiss Trials," in *Famous Trials: The Alger Hiss Trials, 1949–1950* (2003), www.law.umkc.edu/faculty/projects/ftrials/hiss/pumpkinp.html.

34. Weinstein, pp. 184–85.

35. *Ibid.*, pp. 255–56.
36. *Ibid.*, p. 569.
37. *Ibid.*, p. 263.
38. Cited in *ibid.*, p. 497.
39. *Ibid.*
40. *Ibid.*, p. 498.
41. *Ibid.*, pp. 575–77.
42. *Ibid.*, pp. 553–57.
43. *Ibid.*, pp. 570–89.
44. Cited in *ibid.*, p. 563.
45. See, e.g., Radosh and Milton.
46. *Ibid.*, p. 451.
47. *Rosenberg v. United States*, 346 U.S. 273, 310 (1953).
48. Radosh and Milton, p. xiii.
49. *Ibid.*, p. 312.
50. *Ibid.*, p. 378.
51. *Ibid.*, p. 450.
52. *Ibid.*, pp. 163–65.
53. *Ibid.*, p. 164.
54. *Ibid.*, p. 417.
55. *Ibid.*
56. *Ibid.*, p. 102.
57. *Ibid.*, p. 99.
58. *Ibid.*, p. 357.
59. *Ibid.*, p. 358.
60. *Ibid.*
61. *Ibid.*
62. *Ibid.*, p. 398.
63. *Ibid.*, p. 452.
64. Gary May, *Un-American Activities: The Trials of William Remington* (New York: The Notable Trials Library, 1999), p. 182.
65. *Ibid.*, p. 196.
66. *Ibid.*, p. 217.
67. *Ibid.*, pp. 238–39.
68. *Ibid.*, p. 272.
69. *Ibid.*, p. 321.

PART XI
The Civil Rights Movement

THE SECOND WORLD WAR portended the end of segregation — at least in law if not in fact. The gradual integration of our victorious armed forces coupled with the racist nature of the enemy we defeated made it inevitable that America's unique form of apartheid — based on Jim Crow laws and widely accepted practices throughout the South and other areas of our nation — would not withstand legal, political, and social challenges. By 1947, Jackie Robinson had joined the Brooklyn Dodgers as the major leagues' first black baseball player. I remember his first at-bat as if it were yesterday. For the children and grandchildren of immigrants — whether Jewish, Italian, Irish, or Chinese — it was a signal that anything was possible in this great country. At the same time, most of the American South remained deeply segregated, a practice legally justified by the Supreme Court's 1896 decision in *Plessy v. Ferguson*, which declared that "separate but equal"— and no separate institution for blacks was ever really equal — did not violate the Constitution's equal protection clause.

In this context, overturning *Plessy*, the legal basis for segregation, was a chief concern of proponents of racial equality. The movement against segregation was led by the National Association for the Advancement of Colored People (NAACP), which had been founded in 1910 to promote black welfare by a group of black and white liberals that included scholar W. E. B. DuBois. In the late 1940s and early 1950s, stewarded by special counsel Thurgood Marshall, and often supported by Truman's Justice Department, the NAACP had mounted legal attacks on segregated law schools, primary elections, and other facilities and institutions. In those cases, the Supreme Court had ruled with the NAACP on the specific facts of a situation — agreeing that a certain facility was not in practice equal for blacks and was therefore unconstitutional under *Plessy*—but it had not yet taken the additional step of directly overruling *Plessy*, which had been a bedrock of constitutional jurisprudence for more than half a century.[1]

The Court's approach changed, however, with Eisenhower's 1954 appointment of former California governor Earl Warren as the Court's newest member and chief justice, replacing Chief Justice Vinson, who had expressed doubts about reversing *Plessy*.[2] Eisenhower appointed Warren, a fellow Republican, based on a belief in his moderate politics and stature as "one of the finest public servants this country has ever produced."[3] Warren, however, did not conform to expectations. In addition to the civil rights ruling in *Brown v. Board of Education*, the Warren Court pursued an activist agenda of not only expanding personal rights, but also assuring that practical remedies were available to enforce these rights. In *New York Times v. Sullivan* (1964), the Court curtailed libel law to encourage freedom of the press, and in *Griswold v. Connecticut* (1965) it articulated a fundamental right to privacy. The Court imposed constitutional limits on police and prosecutorial tactics in decisions such as *Mapp v. Ohio* (1961), *Gideon v. Wainwright* (1963), and *Miranda v. Arizona* (1966). The Gideon case ruled that all indigent criminal defendants must have access to counsel in serious criminal cases. Appraising the Warren Court's activism, particularly in the civil rights arena, Eisenhower reportedly later called his decision to elevate Warren to the Supreme Court "the biggest damnfool mistake" he ever made.[4]

In studying the segregation issue, Warren, newly appointed in 1954, concluded that *Plessy* punished black children by allowing them to be educated in segregated schools that were almost always inferior.[5] In *Brown v. Board of Education*, which presented the issue in the form of a legal challenge to the segregated public schools of several communities, Warren was able to lead the court to a decisive stand on this issue by convincing wavering judges that *Plessy* had proved unfair and that a unanimous court would add legitimacy to its ruling.[6] Months of backroom conversations proved successful for Warren: *Brown*, which overruled *Plessy* by finding that "separate but equal" was "inherently unequal" and therefore unconstitutional, was a 9–0 decision. Relying on controversial social science research more than on legal precedent, the Court's opinion was divisive not only among politicians but also among academics. But it was the law of the land, at least in theory.

The *Brown* ruling established a crucial legal precedent for civil rights advocates by removing the legal basis for state-sponsored segregation, but it also activated latent opposition to civil rights "by threatening white supremacy so forthrightly."[7] The result was that schools in many Southern districts flatly refused to desegregate despite the ruling. In addition, President Eisenhower, a believer in states' rights, maintained "neutrality" in the years following *Brown* and did not use his office vigorously to pressure Southerners into desegregation.[8] Moreover, implementation and effective enforcement mechanisms for desegregation did not exist at the time, and even a Supreme Court addendum to the *Brown* ruling itself suggested that the implementation process might take some time.[9] As a result, enforcement of *Brown* was sporadic, with many schools remaining segregated. In addition, Jim Crow segregation extended to many public accommodations in the South — including drinking fountains, public swimming pools, and restaurants. *Brown* did not explicitly cover such institutions, and local law enforcement officials enforced these restrictions with a vengeance.

On December 1, 1955, an unlikely hero of racial equality emerged on the national scene challenging Jim Crow practices in the street rather than in the court. On that day, in Montgomery, Alabama, Rosa Parks's feet were tired, and she sat herself down in the (whites-only) front part of the public bus she was riding. When the conductor asked her to move, she refused. "I felt it was just something I had to do," Parks later explained. The conductor summoned police, who arrested Parks for disturbing the peace. The news of the arrest of the forty-two-year-old seamstress enraged blacks throughout the South. In Montgomery, black residents organized against the bus company, orchestrating the Montgomery Bus Boycott.[10] For almost a year, black residents walked, organized car pools, and even rode mules and horse-drawn buggies rather than patronize city buses.[11] It was the beginning of more widespread collective protest against segregation.

Rosa Parks's refusal to move to the back of the bus helped stimulate actions by other civil rights activists. Foremost among them was Martin Luther King Jr., a leading minister in Montgomery with a Gandhi-influenced philosophy of mass nonviolent direct action and a powerful and moving oratorical ability. King rose to national prominence after he was drafted by leading Montgomery blacks to lead the bus boycott. King and other black ministers organized the Southern Christian Leadership Conference (SCLC) to make the moral and religious case for civil rights, using tactics from the nonviolent protest model.

In September 1962, James Meredith, a twenty-eight-year-old black student, applied to transfer from a black college to "Ole Miss," the University of Mississippi at Oxford. On Meredith's first attempt to register, Governor Ross Barnett personally blocked his path. He would give President Kennedy — who was elected in 1960 — no assurances for Meredith's safety as he attempted to register a second time.[12] Kennedy sent five hundred federal marshals and servicemen to the campus to protect Meredith. The forces, under strict orders to use tear gas and clubs — no rifles — faced a mob of thousands, including lethally armed militants who had swarmed the campus.[13] Twenty-eight marshals were shot and 160 people were wounded, and the president ordered five thousand army troops to the campus.[14] They were able to restore order due to superior numbers. Historian Robert Weisbrot argues that the events at Ole Miss changed Kennedy's attitude toward the urgency of civil rights action, suggesting that as a result of the confrontation the president began to look "with greater skepticism at the notion that moral suasion alone could effect major changes in race relations in the South."[15]

Nonetheless, King and other civil rights leaders felt that Kennedy, while clearly sympathetic to their cause, might not respond with decisive action unless circumstances made action necessary.[16] Searching for a cause that would mobilize the president and reach the sympathies of the nation, King began a campaign to desegregate Birmingham, Alabama, one of the most Jim Crow cities of the South. Despite the strides the sit-in movement had made in other Southern cities, Birmingham public facilities remained segregated. King and other civil rights leaders developed a strategy for Birmingham that focused on protest marches and a boycott of downtown businesses. Eight days into the campaign, Martin Luther King was served a state court injunction that prohibited further demonstrations.[17] Though he had obeyed a similar federal order in Albany, Georgia, in order to avoid tension with his supporters in the federal government, he felt that the state injunction was a "pseudo" law, used to perpetuate "raw tyranny under the guise of maintaining law and order."[18] King told reporters, "Here in Birmingham, we have reached the point of no return."[19] He violated the order and was imprisoned in solitary confinement on Good Friday.[20] President Kennedy quietly intervened after a few days to secure his release on bail.[21] Over the course of those solitary days, King wrote his famous "Letter from a Birmingham Jail." The "Letter" was intended as a moral response to a group of eight ministers and rabbis who had previously condemned King's civil disobedience tactics,[22] but it also touched broadly on the moral issues at stake, arguing, essentially, that an unjust law was no law at all. The "Letter" was circulated as a pamphlet and reprinted in national newspapers. Weisbrot notes, "The letter came at a time when demonstrations held wide attention but had to struggle against the public reflex to side with the forces of 'law and order.' "[23] The protests continued, and Police Commissioner "Bull" Connor, while initially civil in the face of marches, soon ordered the police to use nightsticks, attack dogs, and water jets against the protesters because his jails had filled up.[24] When captured on film, these actions produced some of the civil rights movement's most enduring images of brutality. The brutality, in turn, inspired some rioting in Birmingham's poorest black neighborhoods.[25] Birmingham's downtown businessmen, fearing further chaos, brokered a settlement with King and the civil rights protesters, in which they agreed to desegregate stores and hire blacks for "white" positions.[26]

It was the beginning of the end for widespread, officially sanctioned segregation, but a long road still lay ahead for advocates of equality. Many murders — Medgar Evers, Michael Schwerner, Andrew Goodman, James Chaney, Martin Luther King, Malcolm X, and both Kennedy brothers — bloodied that road, but eventually, under the presidency of Lyndon Johnson, significant civil rights legislation was enacted. This legislation included provisions mandating equal access to public facilities, equal employment opportunity, and a heightened federal enforcement power.[27] Johnson announced his intention to implement Kennedy's vision for America by telling a joint session of Congress, "No words are strong enough to express our determination to continue the forward thrust of America that he began." Privately, Johnson acknowledged that passing a strong civil rights bill would be important for his own political future because he already faced criticism from the liberal side of the Democratic party. "If I didn't get out in front on this issue . . . [the liberals would] throw up my background against me, they'd use it to prove that I was incapable of bringing unity to the land I loved so much. . . . I had to produce a civil rights bill that was even stronger than the one they'd have gotten if Kennedy had lived."[28] The enactment of the Johnson civil rights legislation succeeded in dismantling the legal structure of segregation, but laws alone could not end the legacy of discrimination, which would persist for generations.

Two other notable trials are representative of this era, and although they do not pertain directly to civil rights and the struggle for racial equality, they are nonetheless related. The first was *Gideon v. Wainwright*, which established the right to counsel for all persons charged with serious crimes. While civil rights cases such as *Brown* mandated equal protection for blacks and whites, *Gideon* dealt with equal protection, in court, for rich and poor alike. As for the second case, we will probably never know whether it related to the civil rights movement, to organized crime, or simply to the rage of one individual. Speculation abounds as to why Jack Ruby shot Lee Harvey Oswald, but we know the shooting precluded what might have become the trial of the century, especially if it revealed the actual motive underlying the Kennedy assassination. Still, John F. Kennedy was an important pillar of the civil rights movement, and the trial of the man who shot his assassin serves as a useful way to close the chapter on the great trials of the civil rights era.

The Brown Case

Date: 1954
Location: Topeka, Kansas, and other cities; District of
             Columbia
Plaintiffs: Parents of African American students
Defendants: Topeka Board of Education and others
Claim: Segregated public schools violate equal protection
Decision: In favor of plaintiffs

Whenever the role and power of the Supreme Court are debated, as they have been since the Federalist Papers, questions
arise concerning the mission of an appointed high national court
in a federal democracy. Many theories have been proposed. To
me, the most persuasive has always been the simplest: In a constitutional democracy, minorities have constitutional rights that
cannot always be enforced effectively through the popular
branches of government, because these branches are necessarily
responsive to the majorities that elect them. Accordingly, it is the
central role of the courts — especially the Supreme Court — to
enforce constitutional rights that would not otherwise be enforced by legislative or executive action.

This was surely the situation faced by African Americans in regard to equal public education, especially in the South, in the
period between the enactment of the post–Civil War amendments and *Brown v. Board of Education*. African Americans did
not constitute a majority of voters in any state. Malapportioned

state legislatures and disenfranchisement by subterfuge diluted the meager power of African American voters even in areas where they constituted a majority or a plurality.

Lacking political and economic power, African Americans simply had no way to use the ballot box or the power of the purse to correct the horrible reality of separate and unequal schools. Only the courts carried any realistic hope of vindicating the "equal protection of the laws" as it related to public education.

The constitutional mandate of equal protection was far from clear, however. The history of the post–Civil War amendments was one of segregation, including segregated schools. Equal protection at the time of post–Civil War amendments meant separate (in theory and practice) but equal (in theory only) in virtually every aspect of life, from the most intimate (miscegenation laws) to the most public (transportation, restaurants, drinking fountains).

It was evident that separate had never been equal for blacks. Indeed, when separation is legally enforced on a theory of racial superiority and inferiority, as Jim Crow segregation plainly was, then separate must necessarily mean unequal, even if the physical facilities were somehow comparable, as, of course, they never were. The challenge was to get the Supreme Court to do what no president, no Congress, no Southern governor or state legislature would do: to declare that as a matter of federal constitutional law, enforced segregation of schools was necessarily a denial of equal protection, as guaranteed by the Fourteenth Amendment, without regard to the physical facilities.

To end educational apartheid in the United States, the Supreme Court had to interpret the equal protection clause not in accordance with its narrow historical meaning but rather as a living doctrine, capable of adapting to the realities of an evolving history. By 1954, it had become clear, as perhaps it had not been to the framers of the Fourteenth Amendment, that equal protection of the laws was not compatible with legally enforced educational segregation. It was the proper role of the Supreme Court to recognize this changing reality and to enforce the broad meaning of equal protection for a disenfranchised minority that had endured the indignity of slavery, segregation, and discrimination.

The story behind *Brown v. Board of Education* is an intriguing drama of legal tactics and tacticians, of principle and passion, of huge personalities and small children, and of the triumph of justice over legal barriers, complete with heroes and villains, good lawyers and not-so-good lawyers, brave politicians and cowards. We see in it the best and worst of the United States at the midpoint of the twentieth century.

The hagiography of the civil rights movement attributes legal sainthood to Thurgood Marshall, who was the NAACP's lead counsel before the Supreme Court. But according to legal historian Richard Kluger, Marshall "seemed to come unhinged" by the barrage of questions thrown at him by the justices during the crucial argument in *Brown:*[29]

It was one of his least credible performances before the court. Marshall had come prepared to review the court's prior rulings on racial classification laws, on cases interpreting the reach of the Fourteenth Amendment, and on the so-called *Plessy* line of decisions. The Court was not in the mood to hear it all hashed over anew. After Marshall had made his intentions known but before he had launched into the cases, Justice Jackson intruded. "I do not believe the court was troubled about its own cases," he said. "It has done a good deal of reading of those cases." What Jackson wanted to know was Marshall's view of the propriety of the court's exercising its judicial power to overturn the segregation laws under challenge. It was the very question Marshall had burlesqued back at his New York office by insisting the white folks had the power to do anything they wanted. That did not seem the ideal answer at this moment of confrontation with the well-honed mind of Robert

Jackson. The question hung in the air: In the absence of congressional action on the subject, was it right for the Court to
overrule segregation after the passage of so many years? Instead
of noting, as the NAACP's brief did, that "the court has repeatedly declared invalid state statutes which conflicted with
section 1 of the fourteenth amendment, even though congress
had not acted," Marshall groped. He sailed off into some in-
coherent remarks about other cases, which he said interpreted
the same amendment broadly — a thought that was disconnected from Jackson's question. Then he made matters worse
by invoking an 1871 federal statute that said anyone acting
under color of state law or custom to deprive a citizen of his
rights and immunities was liable in a lawsuit; the law declared
itself to be aimed specifically at enforcing the Fourteenth
Amendment. But this was really very little help to the NAACP
position and merely begged the question. For the NAACP's
basic argument was that the amendment was a flat and total
prohibition on discriminatory action by the states — a self-
executing edict that was of course to be invoked by the federal
courts whenever necessary. Frankfurter riddled Marshall: "I do
not know what the act [of 1871] has to do with this, our problem. If your claim prevails, it must prevail by virtue of what
flows out of the Fourteenth Amendment, as such."[30]

The "villain" of the case was John W. Davis, the eighty-year-
old former presidential candidate and dean of the bar, who argued in favor of preserving the status quo:

At the age of eighty, Davis was making the last of his 140 ap-
pearances before the Court. He came in his cutaway, a throw-
back to a more formal era, and he was reduced by age to
consulting his notes more often than he ever had, but there
was nothing antique about the working of his mind or tongue.
No one else in the cases came near matching him for bite,
eloquence, or wit. Early in his remarks, he summed up the

Court's dilemma in trying to evaluate the answers it had received to the five questions it had put to the parties:

> Now your honors then are presented with this: we say there is no warrant for the assertion that the Fourteenth Amendment dealt with the school question. The appellants say that from the debates in Congress it is perfectly evident that the Congress wanted to deal with the school question, and the Attorney General, as a friend of the court, says he does not know which is correct. So your honors are afforded a reasonable field for selection.

That brought laughter from the Court. Little of it lingered, though, as he paraded the evidence that, in his hands, seemed to destroy the NAACP's interpretation of the congressional history. From its first act in this area, the Freedmen's Bureau Bill, Congress had countenanced racially separate schools, and the same Thirty-ninth Congress that had passed the Fourteenth Amendment had legislated to donate lots and distribute funds to the schools for Negroes which had previously been established in the District of Columbia. It had been suggested by "the learned Attorney General" said Davis, alluding to the government's brief, that those acts of Congress affecting the District of Columbia schools:

> . . . were mere routine performances, that they came very late in the congressional session, that they were not even honored by having any debate.
> Apparently, to have a law which is really to be recognized as a congressional deliverance, it must come early in the session, it must be debated, and the mere fact that it is passed by unanimous consent and without objection more or less disparages its importance as an historical incident. I have never, that I can recall, heard a similar yardstick applied to congressional action.

He was no less devastating in dismissing the NAACP's claim that the states understood that the amendment had outlawed school segregation. Nor could Congress have gained the power to outlaw the practice under Section 5 of the amendment, since all that Congress had been empowered to enforce were the rights embraced by the first section of the amendment — and the right to attend unsegregated schools was not among them. The Court moreover, had ruled not once but seven times over the years in favor of the separate-but-equal doctrine, and "somewhere, some time, to every principle there comes a moment of response when it has been so often announced, so confidently relied upon, so long continued, that it passes the limits of judicial discretion and disturbance." But even if legal precedent were not deemed governing, Davis went on, could it genuinely be contended that the state of South Carolina had acted unreasonably in classifying the schoolchildren of Clarendon County along racial lines? He then graphically warned the Court of the problem it would confront at once if it ordered the schools desegregated in a heavily Negro district such as the one in Clarendon, where there were 2,800 black pupils and 300 white ones:

Who is going to disturb that situation? If they be reassorted or commingled, who knows how that would best be done?

If it is done on the mathematical basis, with 30 children as a maximum . . . you would have 27 Negro children and 3 whites in one schoolroom. Would that make the children any happier? Would they learn more quickly? Would their lives be more serene?

Children of that age are not the most considerate animals in the world, as we all know. Would the terrible psychological disaster being wrought, according to some of these witnesses, to the colored child be removed if he had three white children sitting somewhere in the same schoolroom?

Would white children be prevented from getting a distorted idea of racial relations if they sat with 27 Negro children? I have posed that question because it is the very one that cannot be denied.

You say that is racism. Well it is not racism. Recognize that for sixty centuries and more, humanity has been discussing questions of race and race tension, not racism. . . . [T]wenty-nine states have miscegenation statutes now in force which they believe are of beneficial protection to both races. Disraeli said, "No man," said he, "will treat with indifference the principle of race. It is the key of history."

As he neared the end of his argument, the drain on him became apparent to chief Justice Warren, who looked down on the great old advocate from a distance of just a few feet. "Mr. Davis was quite emotional," Warren recalled later. "In fact, he seemed to me to break down a few times during the hearing." With deep conviction, Davis wound up pleading for the integrity of states' rights and the good intentions of his client. "Your honors do not sit, and cannot sit, as a glorified board of education for the state of South Carolina or any other state," he declared. "South Carolina has not come before the court as Thad Stevens would have wished — in sack cloth and ashes. . . . It is confident of its good faith and intention to produce equality for all of its schoolchildren of whatever race or color," as it had done in equalizing the schools of Clarendon County. "So much had been gained in race relations," he said, adding,

I am reminded — and I hope it won't be treated as a reflection on anybody — of Aesop's fable of the dog and the meat: The dog, with a fine piece of meat in his mouth, crossed a bridge and saw [his] shadow in the stream and plunged in for it and lost both substance and shadow.

Here is equal education, not promised, not prophesied, but present. Shall it be thrown away on some fancied question of racial prestige?

Thurgood Marshall remembered seeing tears on the cheeks of John W. Davis as he turned away from the court for the final time in his life.[31]

Thurgood Marshall had the last word, and he apparently redeemed himself somewhat by playing to his own strength, which was less in the arena of legal analysis and more in the world of common sense and experience:

Then Marshall seemed to stand back from the fray for a moment, check the battlefield, and launch his last salvo; his words were as informal and loosely grammatical as John Davis's were polished and precise, but they were hardly less effective for it:

. . . I got the feeling on hearing the discussion yesterday that when you put a white child in a school with a whale lot of colored children, the child would fall apart or something. Everybody knows that is not true.

Those same kids in Virginia and South Carolina — and I have seen them do it — they play in the streets together, they play on their farms together, they go down the road together, they separate to go to school, they come out of school and play ball together. They have to be separated in school.

There is some magic to it. You can have them voting together, you can have them not restricted because of law in the houses they live in. You can have them going to the same state university and the same college, but if they go to elementary and high school, the world will fall apart. . . .[32]

The case was now in the hands of the justices. The real arguments were just beginning. Earl Warren knew what the decision should be. As he recalled twenty years later:

> I don't remember having any great doubts about which way it should go. It seemed to me a comparatively simple case. Just look at the various decisions that had been eroding *Plessy* for so many years. They kept chipping away at it rather than ever really facing it head-on. If you looked back — to *Gaines,* to *Sweatt,* to some of the interstate-commerce cases — you saw that the doctrine of separate-but-equal had been so eroded that only the *fact* of segregation itself remained unconsidered. On the merits, the natural, the logical and practically the only way the case could be decided was clear. The question was *how* the decision was to be reached.[33]

Warren's goal was to produce a unanimous decision and a single opinion — no simple task considering how different the nine justices were from each other. That he succeeded is a testament to the political skills he brought to the court from a lifetime of politics. The opinion itself was elegant in its simplicity. Warren posed the essential question: "Does segregation of children in public schools solely on the basis of race . . . deprive the children of the minority group of equal educational opportunities?"[34]

The answer was "we believe that it does": "To separate [grade school children] from others of similar age and qualifications solely because of their race generates a feeling of inferiority as to their status in the community that may affect their hearts and minds in a way unlikely ever to be undone."[35]

In retrospect, it is remarkable how controversial *Brown* was at the time it was rendered. Today, virtually no lawyer, regardless of judicial philosophy, tries to justify the constitutionality of legally segregated schools. *Brown v. Board of Education* has become a fixed star in virtually every theory of constitutional law; any theory that cannot justify the result in *Brown* is immediately regarded as suspect. It is fascinating to watch the strictest adherents of the "original intent," "original understanding," or "literal interpretation" theories, such as Robert Bork, Antonin Scalia, and others, struggle to stretch their theories to fit the conclusion reached in *Brown*, regardless of how uncomfortable the fit may be. Very few Supreme Court decisions carry this status. The famous aphorisms of Oliver Wendell Holmes Jr. that the life of the law has been "experience" rather than logic is certainly confirmed by the approach the Supreme Court took to *Brown*. Experiences proved that separate but equal, even if somehow "logical," had been shown to produce pervasive inequality by experience and thus could not be squared with the constitutional guarantee of equal protection under the law.

The Prosecution of Martin Luther King Jr.

Date: Original trial 1963; Supreme Court decision 1967
Location: Birmingham, Alabama
Defendant: The Reverend Martin Luther King Jr.
Charge: Criminal contempt of court
Verdict: Guilty
Sentence: Five-day sentence

Those who expect to learn historical truths from judicial opinions will generally be disappointed, if not misled. Court cases deal with only one genre of truth — that established by the rules of evidence, the rulings of judges, and the selective editing of appellate courts. In order to understand what really happened in a case, the historian must independently investigate the political, economic, religious, racial, and other forces that gave rise to the case and controversy.

The story of *Walker v. Birmingham* is the story of the civil rights movement of the 1960s. The dramatis personae include the entire cast of familiar characters who participated in the monumental struggle between apartheid and desegregation in the American South. Martin Luther King Jr. confronted Bull Connor, against the backdrop of the Kennedy and then the Johnson administrations' efforts to walk a fine line between destroying the Southern base of the Democratic party and accepting the segregationist ways of the old South. Immediately at stake was the enactment of a broad-based civil rights law. Ultimately at stake was the soul of a nation, committed in theory to equal rights for all, but, in practice, reserving many of the most important rights for whites only. At the center of the day-to-day conflict was the judiciary, both state and federal. Without the intervention of the judiciary, Jim Crow could not have been dismantled. Yet it was also the judiciary that enforced legal segregation.

In the *Walker* case, Martin Luther King Jr. and his associates defied the judiciary by deliberately violating the order of a court to refrain from conducting a demonstration. The court's order was almost certainly unconstitutional. But the courts — ever protective of their own powers — have held that disobeying a court order, even an unconstitutional court order, is contempt of court, and the unconstitutionality of the order is not a defense to a criminal contempt charge. This contrasts sharply with the attitude of courts toward disobedience of a legislative enactment. If it turns out that the disobeyed statute is unconstitutional, *that* is a defense to criminal charges. But court orders *must* be obeyed, even if they turn out to be unconstitutional. The only remedy against an unconstitutional court order is to appeal, but appeals take time and time can destroy the effectiveness of a protest, as King had learned from previous experiences.

Martin Luther King Jr. could not wait for the appellate courts to vindicate his right to protest. A reading of the court decisions does not do justice to the dynamics of the situation faced by King. Other, more radical African Americans were vying for the leadership of the civil rights movement and were critical of King's previous willingness to accept guidance from the Kennedy Justice Department, which had urged him to comply with the directives of the courts. Their logic was compelling: It was the segregationists who defied court orders, and if King were to claim the right to place conscience before compliance with a court order, he would be lending support to the defiance tactics of his enemies. King understood this argument and respected those who made it, but circumstances were quickly getting beyond his control. Ultimately, and with some reluctance, he decided to defy the court order and march. He knew he was risking imprisonment, and he indeed ended up in a Birmingham jail cell, after a perfunctory trial in which the judge, at the outset and in keeping with the rule followed by most courts, made clear that regardless of the constitutionality of the injunction, anyone who had knowingly violated it was guilty of contempt. Thereafter, the prosecution quickly proved that the defendants knew of the injunction and then violated it, while the defendants, looking ahead to the appellate courts, futilely tried to get evidence on the record demonstrating the injunction's unconstitutionality.[36] It was from this jail cell that King wrote the famous "Letter from a Birmingham Jail" in which he explained his actions and placed them in the larger context of the struggle against all oppression:

> We can never forget that everything Hitler did in Germany was "legal" and everything the Hungarian freedom fighters did in Hungary was "illegal." It was "illegal" to aid and comfort a Jew in Hitler's Germany. But I am sure that, if I had lived in Germany during that time, I would have aided and comforted my Jewish brothers even though it was illegal. If I lived in a communist country today where certain principles dear in the Christian faith are suppressed, I believe I would openly advocate disobeying these anti-religious laws.[37]

The letter became the most enduring legacy of the case. Eventually the Supreme Court decided the case against King in a 5–4 decision written by Justice Potter Stewart. Stewart asked whether "the Constitution compelled Alabama to allow the petitioners to violate this injunction, to organize and engage in these mass street parades and demonstrations, without any previous effort on their part to have the injunction dissolved or modified, or any attempt to secure a parade permit in accordance with its terms."[38] After emphasizing the failure to address the injunction through the courts, Stewart concluded that "[t]he rule of law that Alabama followed in this case reflects a belief that in the fair administration of justice no man can be judge in his own case, however exalted his station, however righteous his motives, and irrespective of his race, color, politics, or religion. This Court cannot hold that the petitioners were constitutionally free to ignore all the procedures of the law and carry their battle to the streets. One may sympathize with the petitioners' impatient commitment to their cause. But respect for judicial process is a small price to pay for the civilizing hand of the law, which alone can give abiding meaning to constitutional freedom."[39]

Justice William Brennan blisteringly dissented: "Under cover of exhortation that the Negro exercise 'respect for judicial process,' the Court empties the Supremacy Clause of its primacy by elevating a state rule of judicial administration above the right of free expression guaranteed by the Federal Constitution. And the Court does so by letting loose a devastatingly destructive weapon for suppression of cherished freedoms heretofore believed indispensable to maintenance of our free society."[40] Brennan criticized the Court for failing to distinguish the case from one in which an individual who violated an unconstitutional law could raise the unconstitutionality as a defense at trial. He claimed that, according to the majority's reasoning, "by some inscrutable legerdemain, [the constitutionally secured right to challenge a facially unconstitutional law[41] at trial] was lost if the State takes the precaution to have some judge append his signature to an *ex parte* order which recites the words of the invalid statute."[42] Stewart's opinion, not Brennan's, may have carried the majority's verdict in the Court, but the verdict of history has been in King's favor. And it was, after all, in order to get the case "removed" to the court of history and of public opinion that King was willing to go to jail in the first place. In this respect, he won his case.

The Case of Clarence Earl Gideon

Date: 1961–63
Location: Panama City, Florida; District of Columbia
Defendant: Clarence Earl Gideon
Charge: Breaking and entering
Verdict: Guilty (without a lawyer); not guilty (with a lawyer)
Sentence: Imprisonment for five years (first trial)

Although Clarence Earl Gideon was never part of the civil rights movement, his case was at the center of the revolution relating to criminal defendants — an important, if highly controversial, aspect of the struggle for equality beyond race alone. The Gideon decision itself was among its least controversial battles. Indeed, any objective review of the legal history of the Warren period makes it evident that the unanimous ruling in *Gideon v. Wainwright* — that the Sixth Amendment requires the appointment of counsel in every felony or potentially lengthy imprisonment case — was inevitable: It would have been issued even if Clarence Earl Gideon, Abe Fortas (the attorney who argued Gideon's case before the Supreme Court), and even Earl Warren had never been born. It was a ruling whose time had simply come. Even the most conservative elements within the legal profession — the American Bar Association, state and federal attorneys general, and the right wing of the bench — had come to understand that criminal defendants needed the guiding hand of counsel at trial. The old rule, under which many defendants charged with serious felonies had to represent themselves, had put the legal profession in a terrible light: It made it seem that the assistance of professional legal representation was not all that important; that it was a luxury for the rich rather than a necessity for all facing the power of the prosecution. More than a century earlier, attorney Abraham Lincoln had quipped that the lawyer who represented himself "had a fool for a client." Yet indigent nonlawyers who did not want to be fools were being denied legal counsel by a few backward states. It was this kind of inequality that cut across racial lines. As one wag observed, "old Clarence Gideon could have been anyone's black-sheep uncle."

By the time the Gideon case came before the High Court, most of the states had already changed the old rule and were providing counsel to indigent criminal defendants. The Gideon case, in practical terms, was a constitutional mop-up operation. It broke no new ground, either conceptually or practically. Any first-year law student would have "won" Gideon's case in the Supreme Court.

Nor was Clarence Earl Gideon any kind of a unique constitutional hero. The Supreme Court deliberately selected his case from among the many petitions that raised the issue of right to counsel precisely because he was a run-of-the-mill, nonviolent, white defendant. One of the most important decisions the justices make is the public relations ploy of selecting cases whose facts and personalities best suit the result they are planning to announce. Thus, in deciding to review a case for the purpose of announcing a rule requiring counsel in all criminal cases, the justices would not pick a brutal murderer or rapist whose court-appointed lawyer might free him on what would be perceived as a technicality. They would pick a somewhat sympathetic and nonthreatening "victim" of injustice like Clarence Earl Gideon. When the ruling is subsequently announced, the media will be sure to learn all they can about the characters involved in the legal drama. If the central character is everybody's eccentric Uncle Clarence, who is always getting into trouble but never really hurting anyone, the new rule will go down a lot easier with the public than if he were a serial killer. Experienced politicians like Earl Warren, former governor of California, understand these dynamics, even if some of the less politically savvy justices do not.

I recall vividly when the Escobedo case — the case that moved the right to counsel back to the arrest stage — came into Justice Arthur Goldberg's chambers. I was Justice Goldberg's law clerk during the 1963–64 term of the Supreme Court, when that case was assigned to him for decision. The first research task the justice gave me was to find out about Danny Escobedo's background: "How will the Chicago newspapers play a story freeing that character?" he wanted to know. When I told Justice Goldberg that Escobedo was a Mexican American with no prior record whose crime was an interfamily one, he was relieved. "As long as he's not some kind of sadistic murderer, the reaction won't be all that terrible." He was right.

The opposite side of that coin is now in evidence, as the current Supreme Court reverses or narrows many of the Warren Court criminal justice decisions. For example, when the Burger Court decided to chip away at the exclusionary rule (the judge-made law that prevents a prosecutor from using certain illegally obtained evidence) by establishing the "inevitable discovery" exception (which permits the illegal evidence to be used if it would eventually have been found legally), the justices quite deliberately selected the case of Robert Anthony Williams. Williams was as unsympathetic as Gideon had been sympathetic. He had murdered a ten-year-old girl at the local YMCA, carried out her body in an army blanket, and left it to rot in a shallow grave. Though the doctrine the Court announced was highly questionable, the press reports shifted the focus of public reaction away from the doctrine and onto the heinousness of Williams's crime.

This public relations component of the High Court's discretionary decision whether or not to take a case for review has long been a fact of life neglected by Court observers. It was plainly at work, however, in the Court's decision to select Clarence Earl Gideon as the vehicle for expanding the right to counsel.

None of this is to undercut the importance of the Gideon case in American legal history or of the excellent lawyering job done by Gideon's Supreme Court lawyer, Abe Fortas. But in law, as in Olympic diving, points are given for the degree of difficulty of the task at hand. No lawyer could have lost Gideon's case once the Supreme Court decided to review it. And Fortas played no role in the Court's decision to select Gideon's case for review. The result of the case was foreordained by history. Abe Fortas made the Court's job easier by providing precedents, data, and analysis to buttress its conclusion. But he had no influence — nor did Clarence Earl Gideon himself — on the outcome of the case or the establishment of the rule requiring the appointment of counsel in all serious criminal cases.

The Gideon case takes its place in the pantheon of great cases for two reasons. First, its impact on indigent criminal defendants was considerable; second, Anthony Lewis used this case to bring the workings of the High Court to the attention of the general public. Reading Gideon's Trumpet, or viewing the film based on it, is an elevating — even ennobling — experience. It makes the reader glow with pride about an American institution that works. There is, to be sure, a healthy dose of legal realism in Lewis's portrayal of the High Court at work. But the realism is tinged with romanticism. The characters are all great men (this is an all-male story) with conflicting visions of the High Court's true calling. Thus, despite the jurisprudential differences between Justices Black and Frankfurter, Lewis writes: "Justice Frankfurter was just as dedicated to fair criminal procedure as Justice Black. It was Justice Frankfurter who wrote, in a Federal criminal case, 'This history of liberty is largely the history of the observance of procedural safeguards.' His deep belief in federalism made him draw back from imposing identical requirements on the states, but even there his difference with Justice Black — for all the talk — may often have come down to a question of timing. In 1942, Justice Frankfurter might have said, the country was not ready for a universal requirement of counsel in serious criminal cases; the bar was not prepared for such a burden; the states would have resisted, and the decision would have been widely ignored. But that would not have ended the matter for Justice Frankfurter. 'It is of the very nature of a free society to advance in its standards of what is deemed reasonable and right,' he once wrote. 'Representing as it does a living principle, due process is not confined within a permanent catalogue of what may at a given time be deemed the limits or essentials of fundamental rights.'"[43]

Contrasting Lewis's affectionate presentation of the justices with Woodward and Armstrong's cynical expose in The Brethren (published in 1979) is instructive. Lewis sees statesmanship where Woodward and Armstrong sense manipulation. Lewis resolves doubts in favor of the justices where Woodward and Armstrong resolve doubts against them in The Brethren. Lewis clearly does not enjoy making the few criticisms he must make of the Supreme Court, where Woodward and Armstrong relish every jab they can take at the justices, even the most liberal ones. For example, in Moore v. Illinois, the petitioner faced life in prison, despite several claimed errors at trial. The original vote was 7–2 to uphold the conviction, with Justice Blackmun writing for the majority and Justice Marshall for the dissent. However, after an incensed Marshall prepared a detailed analysis of the evidence critiquing Blackmun's position, both Justices Powell and Stewart switched their votes. At that point, only the liberal Justice Brennan was necessary to void Moore's conviction. Amazingly, however, Brennan refused to switch votes since he knew that

Blackmun, who had worked hard on the case, would view it as an insult. As Woodward and Armstrong portray it:

> If Brennan switched, Blackmun would be personally offended. That would be unfortunate, because Blackmun had lately seemed more assertive, more independent of the Chief [Justice Burger]. Brennan felt that if he voted against Blackmun now, it might make it more difficult to reach him in the abortion cases or even the obscenity cases.
>
> Sure, "Slick Moore" deserved a new trial. But more likely than not, it would result in his being convicted again. After all, Moore had a long record. He was not exactly an angel. Anyway, the Court could not concern itself with correcting every injustice. They should never have taken such a case, Brennan said. He felt he had to consider the big picture. . . . The clerks were shocked that such considerations would keep a man in prison . . . [but] Brennan had his priorities. His priority in this case was Harry Blackmun. There would be no new trial for "Slick Moore."[44]

There is some virtue in both approaches. They reflect different eras in American reporting, the pre-Watergate trusting age of Camelot versus the post-Watergate cynical age of seeing corruption everywhere.

I was a law clerk in the Supreme Court during the so-called Camelot era. Yet what I saw did not drive me toward Lewis's romantic vision of the justices. Nor did it leave me with Woodward and Armstrong's surrealistic caricature. What I saw was nine men of varying degrees of intelligence, integrity, and prejudice. They had enormous power not only to decide cases, but also to determine — within limits — the direction our nation would take on important issues. They decided cases and issues largely on their own instincts, instincts they brought with them to the High Court from their earlier careers and backgrounds. They were occasionally influenced by the arguments of the lawyers, more often in the least important and least controversial cases. They cared deeply about what the public and the legal profession thought of them and their work product. Not surprisingly, they liked — and continue to like — *Gideon's Trumpet* and its author. I am told that most of them did not like *The Brethren* and subsequent critiques of that genre.

Neither of Clarence Gideon's trials can be called "great" or "notable." What is significant is the *difference* between the two trials. In the first, Gideon was on his own; unrepresented by counsel, he didn't stand a chance. For example, he went out of his way to have witnesses testify that he was not drunk when they saw him; however, under Florida law, intoxication was in fact a defense to the crime with which he was charged, so the opposite testimony might have benefited him.[45] At his second trial, Gideon was represented by a court-appointed lawyer, and it made all the difference in the world. His lawyer convincingly impeached the star prosecution witness, Cook, by implying that the only reason he was even at the scene was that he was involved in the robbery himself. In fact, Gideon's counsel took trips to the town where Cook claimed to have been earlier that night and spent an afternoon picking pears with his mother, all in order to learn more about him. And his work paid off — he found a surprise witness who testified that not only had Cook himself been questioned by the police, but his initial identification of Gideon was much less positive than his subsequent testimony.[46] Gideon was acquitted at the second trial. That doesn't necessarily mean he didn't do it, but it does show the difference a decent lawyer can make. In some states — such as Texas — certain trial judges do everything in their power to assure that appointed lawyers are not particularly good, so that guilty defendants are not acquitted because of the advocacy of their lawyers.

Lawyers, in general, undoubtedly help their clients receive justice — though I have seen lawyers who would serve their clients better if they slept though the trial instead of bungling their way through it.[47] The legacy of *Gideon* is that every American facing a serious criminal charge is constitutionally entitled not only to the assistance of counsel, but also to the *effective* assistance of counsel. And yet, because some public defender offices remain woefully underfunded and understaffed, that legacy has yet to be achieved in practice.

The Trial of Jack Ruby

Date: 1963–64
Location: Dallas, Texas
Defendant: Jack Ruby
Charge: Murder
Verdict: Guilty
Sentence: Death penalty (later reversed)

Every presidential assassination seems to produce a notable trial, at least in the sense that great public attention is focused on the terrible act, the motive behind it, and the person or persons who carried it out. The "trial" of Lee Harvey Oswald for killing John F. Kennedy might well have been the trial of the twentieth century, especially if it turned out that there was more to it than a lone assassin motivated by individual concerns. But there was to be no trial of Lee Harvey Oswald, and many still suspect that the reason there was no trial was that those behind the assassination feared that a public trial would disclose some uncomfortable and disturbing truths. To prevent any such disclosures, Oswald was murdered by Jack Ruby. It was thus Ruby who was put on trial, and although his trial lacked the drama that would have accompanied the trial of Oswald, it still qualifies as a notable legal event in the history of presidential assassinations.

Can all criminal defendants — even those whose factual guilt is self-evident — receive a fair trial in the United States? This is among the questions I am most frequently asked by students, lawyers, and laypeople. The question always brings to mind the trial of Jack Ruby for the shooting of Lee Harvey Oswald. The killing was viewed live on television by millions of Americans awaiting their first glimpse of the man who just two days earlier had murdered President John F. Kennedy. By his act, Jack Ruby had become, in the apt words of John Kaplan and Jon R. Waltz, the authors of a superb account of the case: "history's most public assassin."[48]

Could an assassin whose crime was not only witnessed by millions but also videotaped for posterity hope to receive a fair trial?

Ruby's trial was, in many ways, the surrogate legal proceeding for the murder of President Kennedy. Since Lee Harvey Oswald could never be brought to trial — though he was "tried" by the Warren Commission and is still being retried by its critics — his killer's trial would become the judicial focal point of the Dallas tragedy.

Ruby's chief counsel, Melvin Belli, tried to capitalize on the fact that nearly every American adult had seen the shooting of Oswald at least once. He challenged each potential juror who had watched the videotaped scene, claiming that they were all "witnesses" to the crime and thus disqualified for jury service.[49] Although this ploy failed, it brought home to the court and to the legal profession the difficulty of receiving a fair jury trial in so highly visible a case.

The issue before the jury was not, of course, whether Ruby had shot Oswald. That was conceded by the defense. It was whether Ruby was sane or insane at the moment he fired that shot seen "round the world." But even as to that issue, the facts surrounding the shooting were critical: the look on Ruby's face, the way he fired the gun, what he said immediately thereafter. Each such fact was relevant to Ruby's state of mind and was bitterly contested.

The defense was insanity, based on an epilepsy-like organic brain disease. A battle of experts ensued, with psychologists, psychiatrists, and specialists from various fields disagreeing on the implications of ambiguous test results and other data. For the defense, Dr. Manfred Guttmacher claimed that Ruby suffered from episodic dyscontrol and that his "very abnormal personality structure" affected his ability to distinguish right from wrong when he killed Oswald. "He has, to use the technical language, a very weak ego structure . . . and when he came upon this perpetrator of the assassination . . . it was a disruption of his ego; . . . all his defenses crumbled, and the deep, heavy, hostile, aggressive part of his makeup, which is very strong, became focused on this one individual, and the homicide was the result of it."[50] Another expert, Dr. Martin Towler, claimed that, based on EEG recordings, Ruby suffered from psychomotor epilepsy that left him "behaving as an automaton."[51] However, Dr. Sheff Olinger, testifying for the prosecution, disputed the finding of epilepsy based solely on EEGs; he replied that upon "consideration of all the available data — the neurological examination results, the laboratory reports, the Towler and Bromberg reports and the EEGs," he would not diagnose Ruby with psychomotor epilepsy.[52] In the end, the jury rejected the defense and sentenced Ruby to death — not an uncommon verdict in the execution capital of our nation.

Eventually the judgment was reversed on the ground that the trial judge should have granted a motion for a change of venue and that he improperly admitted certain testimony. Ruby died of cancer before he could be retried.

Part of the conclusion reached by Kaplan and Waltz is worth quoting.

When we say that even the obviously guilty are entitled to a fair trial we are saying that the trial must do more than reach the right answer. Fair trial is a complicated concept, which involves, at least to some, a sporting theory that even where the defendant's guilt can easily be demonstrated, he is entitled to a chance of acquittal. At minimum, however, fair trial implies two notions — that of equality (has the accused been given the same protection and chance of acquittal as others similarly situated?) and that of rational procedure (has there been an adherence to procedures rationally adapted to determine the guilt or innocence of the accused?). In this sense of the term it is difficult to isolate blatant sources of unfairness in the trial of Jack Ruby.[53]

Every trial is different, depending on the players, the location, the time, and public opinion. Fairness is a continuum on which the Ruby trial can be found toward the unfairness end. As highly publicized trials go, however, Ruby's was fairer than many, probably because it was so public and so widely covered by the international media. It demonstrated that a relatively impartial legal process — trial and appeal — is possible in the United States even for "history's most public assassin."

1. These cases included *Shelley v. Kraemer, Henderson v. United States, McLaurin v. Oklahoma State Regents for Higher Education,* and *Sweatt v. Painter.*

2. David Halberstam, *The Fifties* (New York: Fawcett Books, 1993), p. 416.

3. Tom Wicker, *Dwight D. Eisenhower* (New York: Times Books, 2002), p. 48.

4. Robert Weisbrot, *Freedom Bound: A History of America's Civil Rights Movement* (New York: Plume, 1991), p. 12.

5. Halberstam, p. 420.

6. Wicker, p. 52.

7. Weisbrot, p. 11.

8. Wicker, pp. 52–54.

9. Weisbrot, p. 12.

10. *Ibid.,* pp. 14–15.

11. *Ibid.,* p. 17.

12. *Ibid.,* p. 66.

13. *Ibid.,* p. 67.

14. *Ibid.*

15. *Ibid.*

16. *Ibid.,* p. 68.

17. *Ibid.,* p. 69.

18. *Ibid.*

19. *Ibid.*

20. *Ibid.*

21. *Ibid.*

22. *Ibid.*

23. *Ibid.,* p. 70.

24. *Ibid.*

25. *Ibid.,* p. 71.

26. *Ibid.,* pp. 71–72.

27. *Ibid.,* p. 87.

28. *Ibid.,* p. 88.

29. Richard Kluger, *Simple Justice: The History of Brown v. Board of Education* (New York: Knopf, 1976), p. 669.

30. *Ibid.,* pp. 669–70.

31. *Ibid.,* pp. 671–73.

32. *Ibid.,* p. 674.

33. *Ibid.,* p. 678.

34. *Ibid.,* p. 704.

35. *Ibid.,* p. 705.

36. Alan Westin and Barry Mahoney, *The Trial of Martin Luther King* (New York: The Notable Trials Library, 1997), p. 97.

37. *Ibid.,* p. 135.

38. *Ibid.*, p. 245.

39. *Ibid.*, p. 247.

40. *Ibid.*, p. 251.

41. "Facially unconstitutional" refers to a statute that, on its face, violates the Constitution, without regard to its particular application to a set of facts.

42. Westin and Mahoney, p. 252.

43. Anthony Lewis, *Gideon's Trumpet* (Birmingham: The Notable Trials Library), p. 221.

44. See Bob Woodward and Scott Armstrong, *The Brethren: Inside the Supreme Court* (New York: Simon and Schuster, 1979).

45. Lewis, p. 60.

46. *Ibid.*, p. 234.

47. See, e.g., Alan Dershowitz, *The Best Defense* (New York: Vintage Books, 1983), pp. 413–14.

48. John Kaplan and Jon Waltz, *The Trial of Jack Ruby* (New York: The Notable Trials Library, 1992), p. 3.

49. *Ibid.*, pp. 96–97.

50. *Ibid.*, p. 226.

51. *Ibid.*, pp. 214–15.

52. *Ibid.*, p. 249.

53. *Ibid.*, pp. 370–71.

PART XII

The Vietnam War Era and Its Aftermath

THE VIETNAM WAR divided Americans and left its mark on many corners of the American consciousness. The conflict tested each branch of the government.

What developed into the nation's most divisive issue of the late 1960s and early 1970s began quietly soon after the end of World War II, when American policy makers began viewing Vietnam (then called French Indochina) as a central battleground of the Cold War with the Soviet Union. According to the domino theory espoused by some within the U.S. government, if the pro-Western Catholic government in South Vietnam, established in 1955, fell under Communist control, the rest of Southeast Asia would follow. The result was a steadily increasing flow of aid to France, and then South Vietnam, that sought to contain Communism.

Direct U.S. military involvement began in the summer of 1964. With the South Vietnamese government's survival in jeopardy and a presidential election approaching, President Johnson used an alleged torpedo attack on U.S. warships in the Gulf of Tonkin to secure from Congress the authority to use military forces in Vietnam.[1] Johnson immediately authorized retaliatory bombing raids of North Vietnam, ushering in a decade of U.S. military participation in Vietnam. Two hundred thousand American troops were shipped to Vietnam in 1965, joined by another two hundred thousand in 1966.[2] At the height of the conflict in 1968, half a million American troops were stationed in Vietnam.[3]

Even as it waged a costly war overseas, the U.S. government found itself fighting a second front within its borders: the battle for public opinion. By the late 1960s, as U.S. leaders continued to paint an optimistic picture of the war, daily television reports were bringing the horrors of Vietnam into America's living rooms. As the casualties mounted — 40,000 Americans dead and 250,000 wounded by early 1968 — the United States appeared no closer to victory.[4] Moreover, Americans began learning of wartime atrocities committed by both sides in the conflict; the most haunting would become known as the My Lai massacre of March 1968, during which American soldiers massacred an entire village of Vietnamese civilians.

What began on college campuses as peaceful teach-ins against the war (I taught the first non-credit law school course about the Vietnam conflict in 1968) soon turned to violent clashes with the police and the National Guard.[5] A nationwide series of demonstrations in October 1967 — the protests that gave rise to the conspiracy trial of Dr. Benjamin Spock — involved not just acts of civil disobedience but violent confrontation.[6] The following August saw thousands of protesters riot outside the Democratic National Convention in Chicago, leading to the Justice Department's prosecution of the Chicago Seven for conspiring to incite violence.

Many protesters — building on the experience with the civil rights movement — deliberately violated the law by burning their draft cards or refusing induction, then tried to use their trials to question both the morality and legality of American military policy.[7] An older generation of radical lawyers, some who had been relatively quiet during the McCarthy era, returned to prominence, joined by an influx of young attorneys who went to law school at the height of the civil rights movement.

The Vietnam War cases also brought into focus the conflict between First Amendment free speech rights and the demands of national security during times of military conflict.[8] The most famous First Amendment battle of the Vietnam War era centered on President Nixon's efforts to prevent the publication of the Pentagon Papers, seven thousand pages of government documents recounting the history of U.S. involvement in Vietnam. Although the Nixon administration initially secured an injunction against the *New York Times* and several other newspapers, the Supreme Court ultimately ruled that the papers could not constitutionally be subjected to prior restraint.

The release of the Pentagon Papers in 1971 sparked controversy over whether the government had deliberately misled its citizens about the war, and increased the public's distrust of the government.[9] Secretary of State Henry Kissinger finally negotiated a treaty in 1973 that brought about American withdrawal from Vietnam.

On another front, although women in the 1960s had made gains in the workplace and academia, the law still lagged behind until two major developments in the early 1970s. The first was short-lived: the Equal Rights Amendment, passed by Congress in 1972 and ratified within a year by thirty states, failed to gain the approval of the required thirty-eight states. The second, however, had a more enduring impact. In 1973, the Supreme Court decided *Roe v. Wade*, constitutionalizing the right of a woman to obtain an abortion under most circumstances. The repercussions of the Supreme Court's decision were dramatic. On one hand, the ruling struck down forty-six state laws restricting a woman's right to choose to terminate a pregnancy, granting to women control over their reproductive lives. But the decision also pacified a pro-choice movement that had realized substantial victories in state legislatures and in public opinion over the previous decade.[10] Even more significantly, *Roe v. Wade* triggered a conservative backlash that moved the Republican party farther to the right and created, in the right-to-life movement, one of the most powerful political forces in the nation.[11]

Native Americans in the 1970s continued to pursue their own campaign for equal rights. The 1950s had seen the U.S. government institute a "termination" policy calling for the gradual elimination of reservations and the assimilation of Native Americans into mainstream American life.[12] But many Native Americans remained in poverty upon moving to the cities, receiving little or no aid from the federal government.

When peaceful means of empowerment — from pride movements and lobbying, to lawsuits charging violations of treaty
rights — seemed to move too slowly, some Native Americans
confronted authority more directly, even violently.[13] Supported
by the militant American Indian Movement, Native Americans
seized Alcatraz Island in 1969, occupied the Bureau of Indian
Affairs in Washington, DC, in 1972, and took over the village of
Wounded Knee, South Dakota, in 1973.[14] The subsequent trial
of two leaders of the Wounded Knee occupation, tarnished by
prosecutorial misconduct, represented yet another incidence of
governmental abuse at the expense of Native Americans. In this
particular case, however, the court served its function as a check
on governmental abuse, dismissing the case based on the conduct of the prosecutors. The same cannot be said about the trial
of Leonard Peltier for the cold-blooded murder of two FBI agents
during a violent confrontation. A controversy rages still over
whether justice was done in that case.

In 1978, the Supreme Court delivered its landmark opinion in
University of California Regents v. Bakke. In *Bakke*, the Court
upheld the constitutionality of affirmative action programs in
higher education, although it ruled that fixed numerical racial
quotas violate the principle of equal protection. This precedent
was to govern university admissions until June 2003, when the
High Court upheld the University of Michigan Law School's affirmative action policy, which took race into account, while striking down the same university's college admission program,
which assigned a specific numerical score to an applicant's race.

Affirmative action in higher education helped make the college campuses of the 1970s the most diverse that the United
States had ever seen. Out of this meeting and mingling of cul-
tures came not just educational and economic benefits but also
tragedy. In 1977, national headlines reported the murder of Bonnie Garland, a white woman from a prominent Westchester family, by Richard Herrin, a Mexican American raised in poverty in

Los Angeles. These two students from starkly different back-grounds had met and dated at Yale University. Herrin's trial served in some ways as a metaphor for the clashes — racial, gen-der, class, political — of the 1970s as a whole.

The final trial of this era involved a highly publicized murder case — a classic whodunit that has still not been resolved to the satisfaction of many observers. A Green Beret doctor named Jef-frey MacDonald was convicted of murdering his wife and two daughters in 1970. His claim that a gang of drug-crazed hippies did it was rejected by the courts, and Captain MacDonald re-mains in prison despite compelling proof, including a confession corroborated by forensic evidence, that the murder was commit-ted by others. Two books written about this case have arrived at dramatically opposing conclusions.[15] Indeed, it is fair to say that the many books written about the 1970s have arrived at very dif-ferent assessments of not only particular cases but of this con-tentious and divisive era in American life as well.

The Trial of Dr. Spock

Date: 1968
Location: Boston, Massachusetts
Defendants: Dr. Benjamin Spock and four other antiwar activists
Charge: Conspiracy to violate the Selective Service Act
Verdict: Guilty; convictions reversed on appeal

The conspiracy prosecution of Dr. Benjamin Spock, author and pediatrician, was the first major antiwar prosecution of the Vietnam era. It is now widely regarded as a national disgrace. Its genesis, its intended impact, and the manner in which it was conducted were unworthy of the American system of justice.

What prompted the government to prosecute the "Boston Five"—Dr. Spock, the Reverend William Sloane Coffin Jr., Mitchell Goodman, Marcus Raskin, and Michael Ferber? Who were these respectable, even famous, opponents of the Vietnam War? In October 1967, about ten weeks before the indictment was handed down, General Lewis Hershey issued his notorious letter to every local draft board recommending that "misguided registrants" who participated in demonstrations or other acts that, in the opinion of the board, were illegal should be declared delinquent, reclassified 1-A, and subjected to immediate induction. There was a loud public outcry against what President Kingman Brewster Jr. of Yale called an "absolutely outrageous usurpation of power."[16] Great pressure was put on the Justice Department — then under the leadership of a liberal attorney general, Ramsey Clark — to repudiate Hershey's lawless policy on the ground that it is for the courts and not for local draft boards to prosecute those who engage in illegal demonstrations.

About four weeks prior to the indictment, the government issued a face-saving joint statement, over the signatures of the attorney general and General Hershey, that modified the general's earlier letter. At the same time, the statement announced the formation of a special unit of the Justice Department to investigate violations of the Selective Service Act and related statutes. Two days later, that unit went to work on the Spock case.

The unit's chief, John Van de Kamp, has explained why the prosecution was brought: "The prosecution came about as a result of our flap with Hershey and his October 26 letter to the draft boards. The prosecution of these five was thought to be a good way out — it was done to provide a graceful way out for General Hershey."[17] It was thus a clear case of a politically motivated prosecution.

After having decided to bring a prosecution, why did the government choose to charge a conspiracy among virtual strangers? Even after the indictment, when the five defendants met for the first time to plan their legal strategy, Leonard Boudin, Spock's brilliant and courageous lawyer, felt it necessary to introduce the "conspirators" to each other. (I was at that meeting.)

One reason prosecutors often prefer to bring conspiracy charges even in the absence of an actual conspiracy is that many safeguards — such as the rule against hearsay, the statute of limitations, and the venue requirement — are relaxed in conspiracy cases. But this does not explain why the government chose to charge conspiracy in this particular case.

The prosecutorial advantages brought about by the relaxation of these safeguards were simply not needed here. There was no dispute about the underlying facts: The prosecutor did not need hearsay evidence; he did not require an expanded statute of limitations; and he would have had substantial flexibility in selecting the place of the trial (or trials) even if there had been no charge of conspiracy.

Not only did the government not strengthen its case by charging a conspiracy, but it actually weakened its chances of obtaining a final judgment of conviction — because by relying on a conspiracy theory, the government significantly increased the likelihood of reversal on appeal. This conclusion is not based solely on the hindsight derived from the court of appeals' reversal of Spock's conviction. Any knowledgeable lawyer would have advised the government that, on the facts of the Spock case, its chances of ultimately prevailing would be significantly higher if it charged a substantive or accessory crime rather than a tenuous conspiracy among strangers.

It has even been suggested that some of the defendants might have pleaded guilty had they not been charged with a conspiracy of which they believed themselves innocent. Yet the government, which at that time had the benefit of excellent legal talent, decided to pursue the conspiracy approach, even though it carried with it the highest likelihood of an eventual appellate reversal.

Why should the prosecutors have deliberately jeopardized so important a case when they probably could have brought other, more tenable, accusations? Perhaps they simply acted in an automatic, knee-jerk manner. Prosecutors almost always charge conspiracy when they can; this prosecutor, without weighing the advantages and disadvantages of a conspiracy charge in this case, may have reacted instinctively.

Another hypothesis is more plausible and far more sinister. It seems entirely possible that the government made a deliberate decision to increase the risks of ultimate reversal in order to charge the kind of crime — a loosely knit, widespread, and uncircumscribed conspiracy — that would have the greatest impact on discouraging organized opposition to the Vietnam War.

By bringing a conspiracy charge, the government could cast a wide net and threaten an even wider one. The Spock indictment says that the five defendants did "combine, conspire, confederate and agree together and with each other, and with diverse other persons, some known and others unknown." Just who these "diverse other persons" were was the object of a guessing game throughout the trial, replete with tantalizing hints. When the defense asked to have these "other persons" identified, the prosecutor, Assistant U.S. Attorney John Wall, replied that the faces of the co-conspirators had already been seen in TV films of various mass meetings, church services, and press conferences. These films took three hours to show and contained thousands of faces.

After Mr. Wall made this provocative and irresponsible remark, a journalist asked him to elaborate:

Did he mean that anybody who happened into the range of the camera at those large gatherings is automatically considered to be a co-conspirator? He answered that the law is clear: that anybody who gives encouragement, who aids and abets the conspiracy, can be so considered. [The law governing encouragement is about as "clear" as the Mississippi River.] So, I asked, the man who claps and cheers like mad after Dr. Spock has spoken is a co-conspirator, but the man who sits glum, whose face betrays disapproval, is not? That is substantially correct, answered Mr. Wall.[18]

Lest anyone suspect that this was just prosecutorial puffing to impress a reporter, the prosecutor actually pursued this applause theory of complicity with one of the defendants. "Was your applause merely perfunctory politeness to Mr. Coffin or did you applaud in agreement with the position and in advocacy of the same position?"[19] Nor did the judge stop this perverse line of questioning. When Leonard Boudin, who by nature is quiet and decorous, objected, saying "I didn't know applause was a crime" and that this "is intolerable," the trial judge, instead of sustaining this entirely proper objection, threatened Boudin with contempt.[20] Another hint, this time not so subtle, about the scope of the conspiracy was dropped by the prosecutor when he described Noam Chomsky, a professor of modern languages and linguistics at MIT who was among the many signers of "A Call to Resist Illegitimate Authority," as a person "'not sitting at the bar as a defendant' (impressive pause) 'today.'"[21]

The same journalist probed more deeply into the reach of the net by asking Van de Kamp whether Dell, the publishers of *Dr. Spock on Vietnam*, could be prosecuted as part of the conspiracy. "'It's a question . . . I imagine Dell, technically, could be liable, conceivably they could be prosecuted.' 'And the booksellers?' 'Yes, and the booksellers.'"[22] The prosecutor did, however, reassure the press that there was "no intention" of indicting the journalists who reported antiwar activities, even though such reporting could contribute to the aims of the conspiracy.[23]

Thus, the fact that five men who barely knew each other were indicted for a contrived conspiracy, the nature of the indictment, and the various comments of the prosecutor, both at trial and to the press, all lend credence to the theory that an intended effect of the conspiracy charge was to stifle organized public opposition to the war. The Spock prosecution represented a deliberate effort to frighten away scores of opponents of the war who might consider signing statements such as the "Call," attending demonstrations like the one at the Pentagon, or organizing efforts to help young people who had decided not to serve.

In order to accomplish its purpose of frightening away large numbers of respectable future "conspirators," it was not essential that the government prevail ultimately in the litigation. It was enough that there was an indictment, a prosecution, and a conviction, even if the conviction would be reversed a year later.

In other words, the government's decision to charge a conspiracy was not, it seems, motivated by the usual desire to deprive the defendants of their constitutionally guaranteed safeguards (ethically questionable as that would be); it was even more outrageous than that. The government was willing to jeopardize its chances of winning the case in order to secure an impermissible *interrorem* effect that would necessarily extend to entirely proper, and constitutionally protected, organized political activities.

This is a serious accusation against the government. It is difficult to believe that an attorney general such as Ramsey Clark could have been party to such a performance. But the evidence appears to support the conclusion that the government, in prosecuting the "Boston Five" for conspiracy, sought to undercut the First Amendment by frightening citizens away from exercising their rights.

The trial was held in a courtroom on the twelfth floor of the Boston Post Office Building. It was described by the *London Times* as "vaguely lavatorial." Judge Francis J. W. Ford, who presided, was an eighty-five-year-old former prosecutor. The prosecutor — who had directed the FBI to run a "check" on each prospective juror — had cleansed the jury such that all women, blacks, and intelligent-looking people (such as a young man carrying a book) were excused.

After the prosecutor made an especially nasty and improper remark, "the judge was heard whispering urgently to his clerk, 'Tell that son of a bitch to cut it out! He'll blow the case if he keeps this up, and get us all in trouble.'"[24] The judge's apparent bias for the prosecutor's case, which subsequent interviews showed was not lost on the jury, manifested itself in at least one other, particularly shocking, incident.

After the close of evidence, the trial judge announced that he had decided to ask the jury for special findings in the form of a series of questions — a novel procedure that was disapproved of by the court of appeals. One of the defense lawyers noticed that these very questions (slightly varied in form) had been in the government's possession the day before. The judge's response was, "They had prescience."[25] This incident suggests, though it does not establish, that there may have been ex parte communication between the judge and prosecutor during the trial (as there had been in the Rosenberg case). Such communication is absolutely improper and in violation of the canons of judicial ethics, though practicing criminal lawyers say it occurs not infrequently.

Jack MacKenzie, a perceptive and courageous reporter for the *Washington Post*, summed it up in the following way:

> The trial of Dr. Spock was a disaster for all concerned . . . a deep embarrassment for the American system of justice. Sixteen volumes of transcript tell part of the story, but they can never tell it all. They do not convey the manner in which [the judge] showed his disbelief in the defense case and his tolerance for the government's. . . . The judge's display of bias may not be enough in itself to overturn the convictions. But it demeaned the Federal bench and deprived the nation of a trial that was fundamentally fair.[26]

It is thus no surprise that four of the "Boston Five" were convicted at trial. On July 11, 1969, however, the convictions of Dr. Spock and the other defendants were reversed.

The court freed Dr. Spock and Michael Ferber from further prosecution, but ruled that the cases against Mitchell Goodman and William Sloane Coffin Jr. should be returned to the district court for retrial. Judge Frank M. Coffin (no relation to defendant Coffin) wrote in a dissenting opinion that all the defendants should have been acquitted. There were never any retrials.

The government lost its case, but unfortunately for all Americans it seemed to accomplish its sinister purpose. The majority opinion of the court of appeals left the way open for more prosecutions, on equally tenuous theories and with increasingly wide dragnets.

Not everybody will be frightened away from organized opposition to governmental policies. Certainly the more radical will not. But a great many people of goodwill who might have joined hands in entirely legitimate ways will be frightened away by the specter of a political trial that no defendant can ever win — even a defendant who secures a reversal. The decision to prosecute Dr. Spock for conspiracy, and the manner in which it was done, was a national disgrace. And although there have been no similar prosecutions against dissenters from our current wars against terrorism and alleged weapons of mass destruction, the seed for such prosecutions were sown during the Vietnam era (and earlier), and we must always remain vigilant against those who regard dissent as treason.

The Trial of the Chicago Seven

Date:	1969
Location:	Chicago, Illinois
Defendants:	Seven antiwar activists (eight including Seale): David Dellinger, Rennard Davis, Thomas Hayden, Abbott Hoffman, Jerry Rubin, Lee Weiner, John Froines, and Bobby Seale (eventually severed from the case)
Charges:	Conspiracy, incitement
Verdict:	Some guilty, some not guilty, one mistrial, contempt
Sentence:	Imprisonment; all convictions reversed on appeal

When a political prosecution is met by a political defense, the resulting trial is likely to be confrontational. When the participants in the trial are colorful defendants such as Abbie Hoffman, Jerry Rubin, and Bobby Seale; lawyers like William Kunstler and Leonard Weinglass; witnesses such as Allen Ginsberg and Mayor Richard Daley; and a judge like Julius J. Hoffman, the resulting trial is certain to be great theater. (This contrasts sharply with the Spock trial, which was far more intellectual and legalistic.)

The trial of the Chicago Eight — which became the Chicago Seven after Bobby Seale, a leader of the Black Panther movement, was first bound and gagged in the courtroom and then severed from the trial — was a transforming event in American political and legal history. The prosecution grew out of demonstrations at the 1968 Democratic National Convention in Chicago, which included some violent confrontations between Chicago police and demonstrators. For the first time in a major federal trial, defendants and their lawyer responded to a political prosecution by being disrespectful and contemptuous. They refused to comply with the orders of the court. They shouted obscenities at the judge. They challenged the court's very authority. For example, after the court refused to adjourn on October 15 so that the defendants could participate in a national observance to protest the war, the defendants entered the court with black armbands and spread a large Vietnamese flag over counsel's table. After Abbie Hoffman and a marshal engaged in a tugging match over the flag, David Dellinger proceeded to rise and attempt to read aloud the names of both the American and Vietnamese dead as well as to make a motion for a moment of silence after the jury had been seated.[27] Likewise, their lawyer, William Kunstler, encouraged a witness, the Beat poet Allen Ginsberg, to chant in the middle of testimony: "Hare Krishna, Hare Krishna, Krishna, Krishna, Hare, Hare, Hare Rama, Hare Rama, Rama, Rama Hare, Hare"; Ginsberg also played a harmonium, provided by co-counsel Leonard Weinglass, replying to the judge's admonition with the statement: "It adds spirituality to the case."[28] The defendant Abbie Hoffman referred to himself as Judge Julius Hoffman's "illegitimate child," though they were not related, and the defendants brought a birthday cake to the court on the judge's birthday. The surprise is that in the end, the defendants won both legally and politically. They won legally because their substantive convictions were eventually reversed on appeal, after the jury acquitted all the defendants of conspiracy but convicted most of them on various charges such as crossing state lines with the intention of inciting a riot. The court of appeals also reversed the contempt citations and prison sentences imposed by the judge on the defendants and their lawyers. They won politically because they were able to use the trial to present to the public their skewed image of the American political and legal system.

Although I was one of the lawyers who drafted the appellate briefs in the case, I can claim little credit for the legal victory. The reason the defendants and their lawyers won can be summarized in three words: Judge Julius Hoffman.

The judge selected to preside at this high-profile trial could not have better suited the interest of the defendants. Ironically, Judge Hoffman, according to inside sources, was handpicked to try the case by the chief judge. What a mistake. Judge Hoffman was an arrogant and pompous martinet who played right into the hands of the defendants and their antics. His legal rulings were one-sidedly in favor of the government. He hauled lawyers halfway across the country and threw them in jail, thus provoking demonstrations by hundreds of other lawyers. He showed poor judgment in not allowing Bobby Seale to be represented by counsel of his choice, who needed a few weeks to recover from surgery. He showed even worse judgment by gagging and chaining the Black Panther leader, thus giving rise to cries of racism. He prattled on about how he was the best friend the Negroes ever had. He excluded defense witnesses, such as former attorney general Ramsey Clark and civil rights leader Ralph Abernathy. He demonstrated, better than any lawyer's arguments, his own obvious bias against the defendants and their lawyers. He was Exhibit A in the court of law as well as the court of public opinion. He became the laughingstock of the judiciary, the target of the defendants' venom during trial and their mockery during sentencing. During the trial, Bobby Seale (before he was gagged) called the judge "a pig and a fascist and a racist,"[29] while Abbie Hoffman called him a "disgrace to the Jews" who "would have served Hitler better."[30] At sentencing, Dellinger told the judge that "he was a man who had too much power over too many people for too many years," but that he admired his "spunk"; Rennie Davis informed him that he would move next door to the prosecutor's children after he got out of prison and bring them "into the revolution"; Jerry Rubin offered him a copy of his new book with the inscription: "Julius, you radicalized more young people than we ever could. You're the country's top Yippie"; and Abbie Hoffman recommended the judge try LSD: "I know a good dealer in Florida — I could fix you up."[31]

I have often wondered how differently the case would have come out had the trial judge been a dignified, fair, and self-confident jurist. I suspect that the defendants and their trial lawyers would have come off looking like fools had the judge given them a fair trial. But he did not give them a fair trial, and by his obvious unfairness he made the defendants look good, at least in comparison to him. Getting the convictions — especially the contempt citations — reversed on appeal was made far easier by the judge's provocative misconduct. Judge Hoffman was the best weapon the appellate lawyers had in their successful efforts to reverse the convictions, and we used that weapon to our maximum advantage.

Beyond the larger-than-life personalities, the case raised profound issues concerning the scope of conspiracy law in the context of confrontational political demonstrations. "We couldn't even agree on lunch," as one of the alleged conspirators put it. The means and ends of the very different conspirators were diverse. Yet they were charged with a single agreement and conspiracy, as in the Spock case. But unlike the Spock jury, this jury could not agree that these defendants had agreed on anything. The case also raised difficult issues of federal jurisdiction over local riots, as well as controversial issues regarding the appropriate police response to potentially violent street demonstrations. As Abbie Hoffman put it on the eve of the trial:

The Chicago Eight are probably the most nonconspiring conspiracy ever hatched and yet we are going down. It's a question of intent, the judge will say, and the jury will look over at us nasty eight and come down hard, for the jury will have a difficult time drawing a line between intent to overthrow the government, intent to incite riot, intent to be black, intent to help the Vietnamese keep their land, intent to give LSD to everyone who wants and intends to live in a family of man. At times I think I'll just scream out something like "Guilty Due to Sanity."[32]

In the end, the personalities overpowered the issues, and the case will be remembered more for the shouting matches between Abbie Hoffman and Julius Hoffman than for the important legal precedents it set. The fundamental lesson to be learned from this case is that the dignity of the law and the courts must be earned by judges, who are supposed to administer justice even to the most obnoxious of defendants and the most confrontational of lawyers. Judge Hoffman failed this test, but the legal system eventually vindicated itself despite his failure. The question remains whether the trial is a period piece reflecting the peculiarities of the early 1970s or whether it will remain an enduring part of our legal history. We have certainly not seen its like in recent years. Perhaps we never will.

The Court-Martial of Lieutenant William L. Calley Jr.

Date: 1970–71
Location: Fort Benning, Georgia
Defendant: Lieutenant William Calley
Charge: Mass murder
Verdict: Guilty
Sentence: Life imprisonment, later reduced to ten years, paroled after three years

Many Americans, certainly those who were adults during the Vietnam War, have heard of the My Lai massacre, but very few know precisely how brutal the killings of innocent noncombatants were, nor do many realize how extensive a cover-up was attempted and how close it came to succeeding. Because the name most closely associated with My Lai is that of Lieutenant William L. Calley Jr., and because Calley's sentence was repeatedly reduced — eventually to parole — many people diminish the seriousness of what took place on March 16, 1968, in My Lai-4 — an area in and around Thuan Yen. It was an unjustified massacre that, although on a smaller scale, ranks in its barbarity with the war crimes committed by our enemies in some past wars.

After reviewing the evidence, General William R. Peers — who was part of the army's official investigation team — concludes that this is what U.S. Army soldiers did at My Lai:

As they moved into Mi Lai-4 they shot numerous fleeing Vietnamese and bayoneted others; they also threw hand grenades
into houses and bunkers, destroyed livestock and crops, and
committed other atrocities. As they proceeded further they
began rounding up groups of civilians (women, children, and
old men). . . .

Shortly after Calley's arrival, at about 9:15, the Vietnamese
who had been herded into the ditch were shot down by members of the 1st Platoon. Estimates of various witnesses as to the
number killed varied from 75 to 150. Some witnesses told of
huge holes being blown into bodies, limbs being shot off, and
heads exploding. . . . None of the Vietnamese was armed. . . .

In some instances grenades were thrown into family shelters. In others, the occupants were called out and then shot
down as they emerged. It was also reported that in at least three
instances groups of five to ten persons were rounded up and
shot on the spot. No detainees were kept. Because of the in-
termingling of units it is difficult to assess the number of civilians killed in Mi Lai-4 by the 2nd Platoon, but it was probably
between fifty and a hundred. . . . With this kind of action going
on it seems incredible, but at least two rapes were committed
by the 2nd Platoon, and in one case the rapist is reported to
have then shoved the muzzle of his M-16 rifle into the vagina
of the victim and pulled the trigger. . . .

In one instance, ten to twenty women and children were
rounded up and forced to squat in a circular formation. Then
one of the men in the platoon fired several rounds from his
M-79 grenade launcher into their midst. Those who were not
killed by the grenade blasts were finished off by rifle fire from
other members of the platoon. Other cases of rape and sodomy
were reported — one girl was raped by three men in succes-
sion, and another was the victim of a three-on-one gang rape.
Again, it was a gruesome picture.

. . . A large number of Vietnamese civilians — estimates
ranged from three to five hundred — were fleeing southwest
along Highway 521 to Quang Ngai City. As the 3rd squad

moved south toward the highway they fired upon those Vietnamese on the road immediately ahead of them, reportedly killing from three to fifteen people. Upon crossing the road, a woman hiding in a ditch was shot and killed.

They also reportedly killed five or six wounded Vietnamese to "put them out of their misery." In one instance, they herded together seven to twelve women and children and then shot them down.

Of the ninety VC reportedly killed, only the three killed by [the soldiers] could legitimately be termed enemy killed in action. . . .

From the testimony of the many witnesses from Charlie Company and others who participated in the operation, the Inquiry arrived at what must be characterized as a very conservative figure of 175 to 200 women, children, and old men, all noncombatants, killed by Charlie Company during the morning of March 16.[33]

It is difficult enough to read these kinds of accounts when the perpetrators are Hitler's Nazis, Stalin's Communists, or Tojo's Imperial army. But when these cold-blooded murderers of babies, women, and old men are our neighbors and friends — all-American boys — it becomes incomprehensible to the decent reader. No amount of provocation, no desire for revenge, no dehumanization of the enemy can explain, not to say justify, the kinds of actions described in General Peers's summary. Yet there is little doubt that a massacre of these dimensions, give or take a few lives in the inevitably imprecise body count, was carried out under the supervision and direction of officers ranking from lieutenants to generals.

General Peers asks how such a massacre could have occurred, how it could have been covered up for so long, and how its repetition can be prevented. As to the causes, General Peers offers several, including lack of proper training, negative attitudes toward the Vietnamese people, and lack of leadership. As to the cover-up, General Peers is left with a sense of incredulity: "To this day the matter that most greatly concerns me is that so many people in command positions — perhaps as many as fifty — had information that something most unusual had occurred during the Mi Lai operation and yet did nothing about it. To my mind this has had the most damaging effect upon the image of the U.S. Army as a professional institution and has cast doubt upon the integrity of all its officers and men."[34]

As to the future, Peers shows far too much confidence that a massacre of this dimension is unlikely to recur. In light of the fact that every one of the perpetrators, except Calley, was either acquitted — some on the ground of "superior orders" — or received administrative slaps on the wrist, the likelihood of recurrence, if our soldiers were ever to find themselves in a frustrating and deadly situation comparable to Vietnam, is very high. We neither taught nor learned a lesson from the disaster of My Lai, and those who do not understand the lessons of the past are destined to repeat them.

Perhaps General Peers overstates the analogy somewhat when he observes: "The American people showed little sympathy to those of our World War II enemies who committed war crimes, yet our system of military justice was more than lenient to those responsible for the Mi Lai incident even though our country, as a signatory to the Geneva Convention, was obligated to punish those guilty of war crimes."[35] But he is surely correct when he concludes: "In effect two standards were created — one for the enemy and one for ourselves."[36] This kind of double standard cannot be justified by a nation that rightly proclaims itself to be the leader of the free world.

The trial itself began with the prosecution calling witnesses who testified to the horror of My Lai without ever directly implicating Calley; however, the prosecution's case only concluded after the testimony of Paul Meadlo, who testified under a grant of immunity as to Calley's participation in the massacre. Calley's defense was two-pronged: first, that considering the stress of war, the charge of premeditated murder was excessive; and second, that Calley was only following orders from his superiors.[37] Calley was found guilty of premeditated murder on all specifications and sentenced to life imprisonment at hard labor. The verdict and the sentence were followed by vociferous public disapproval based on the perception that Calley was a scapegoat, and President Nixon immediately ordered Calley released to house arrest pending appeal. Two years later, the secretary of the army reduced his sentence to ten years, and just a year after that, in 1974, Calley was paroled.[38]

The message of the case seemed to be that while we disapprove of the massacre of innocent civilians, we understand how a war like the one we fought in Vietnam could drive a soldier to do such things. It also sent an unmistakable message about the perceived comparative value of American and Vietnamese life.

The specter of My Lai thus hovers over the current debate concerning American participation in the newly constituted International Criminal Court in The Hague. Opponents of the ICC worry that American soldiers like Lieutenant Calley might be selectively charged with genocide and subjected to "Third World" politicized justice — which Israel has experienced while facing United Nations' tribunals. Proponents point to a provision in the court's charter denying it jurisdiction over people whose own nation has subjected them to fair trials and adequate punishment. Whether the Calley prosecution and punishment meet this test is, of course, still subject to debate.

Recently there have been new revelations of American war crimes in Vietnam by retired soldiers — now old men — who perpetrated or witnessed them and cannot live silently with their guilt. For them, the widespread cover-up worked — at least as a legal matter — as it has throughout history for most victors in most wars.

The Pentagon Papers Case

Date: 1971
Location: District of Columbia
Defendant: New York Times
Charge: Publishing classified material
Verdict: No prior restraint

History, including legal history, is a seamless web of unpredictable contingencies. An action taken at one time in order to achieve a goal may lead inexorably to other — often unforeseeable — consequences. Those who subscribe to conspiracy theories of history — those who partake in what has been characterized as the paranoid streak in American history — underestimate the impact of coincidence, contingency, and dumb luck. The poet correctly described much of history when he wrote, "Oh what a tangled web we weave when first we practice to deceive."

The Nixon administration's efforts to prevent the publication of the Pentagon Papers, and to punish those who made their publication possible, sowed the seeds of self-destruction planted by that administration — seeds that ultimately grew into a tangled briar patch of corruption that caused the forced resignation of President Richard Nixon.

The White House plumbers, whose actions were at the center of Watergate, were originally tasked by the Nixon administration to plug the Pentagon Papers leaks and to prevent similar leaks.

They bungled that job, just as they bungled the third-rate burglary that precipitated the Nixon resignation. But at least they weren't caught breaking into the offices of Daniel Ellsberg's psychiatrist in their futile effort to get some dirt on the man who made the Pentagon Papers public. Perhaps if they had been caught, the Watergate burglary would not have been attempted and history would be quite different.

The story itself is familiar, especially to those who lived through it.[39] And it teaches a familiar, if often forgotten, lesson. That lesson is distrust of — or at least skepticism about — governmental claims for secrecy based on national security. In the Pentagon Papers case, the government solemnly predicted — warned — that if the papers were allowed to be published, that decision would affect lives. It would affect the process of the termination of the war. It would affect the process of recovering prisoners of war. The clear implication of this somber warning was that publication would *negatively* impact on these important interests.

For the government, Solicitor General Erwin Griswold — the former dean of Harvard Law School — argued a moderate position, despite his strong statements that publication would affect lives and the conclusion of the war. As opposed to the government's position in the lower courts, Griswold asked only for a "much narrower injunction" as to a very limited number of items in the study.[40] Griswold also stressed that a prior restraint was necessary in order to protect the government's ability to win a criminal prosecution in connection with the initial dissemination of the papers: "I find it exceedingly difficult to think that any jury would convict or that an appellate court would affirm a conviction of a criminal offense for the publication of materials which this Court has said could be published."[41] In rebuttal, he emphasized that the phrase *no law* in the First Amendment "does not mean no law at all, under any circumstances, but must be interpreted under contemporary conditions and exigencies."[42]

Arguing for the *New York Times*, Alexander Bickel also advo-cated a moderate position, recognizing he would need the swing vote of either Potter Stewart or Byron White. He noted that there was a strong presumption against prior restraint with exceptions solely to redress private, rather than public, wrongs. Bickel em-phasized that Congress had never passed legislation authorizing prior restraints to deal with security risks; for the president to seek such a restraint under his inherent powers required at least that "the probability of a disastrous event be high and the chain of causality be direct" as opposed to the government's instant case, where the chain's "links are surmise and speculation, all going toward some distant event."[43] Bickel's moderate stance was evi-dent in a colloquy with Justice Stewart. Stewart asked: "Let us as-sume that when the members of the Court go back and open up this sealed record, we find something there that absolutely con-vinces us that its disclosure would result in the sentencing to death of a hundred young men whose only offense had been that they were nineteen years old and had low draft numbers. What should we do?" After trying to avoid the question on the grounds that those were not the facts of this case, Bickel conceded: "I am afraid that my inclinations to humanity overcome the somewhat more abstract devotion to the First Amendment in a case of that sort."[44]

The Supreme Court ruled in favor of the newspapers by a vote of 6–3, although there were nine separate opinions written. Jus-tices Black and Douglas advocated an absolutist position, noting that the First Amendment was adopted against the widespread use of seditious libel to punish the dissemination of material that embarrassed the government. Justice Brennan also strongly con-demned every temporary restraining order issued in the case, though he left the door open for future interim restraining orders that dealt with publication that would "inevitably, directly, and immediately cause the occurrence of an event kindred to imper-iling the safety of a transport already at sea."[45] Justice Marshall also ruled completely in favor of the newspapers; however, his opinion rested on the lack of congressional support for a prior restraint and did not even mention the First Amendment.

Justices Stewart and White, as predicted, took a more moderate position. Stewart recognized the important balance between a free press that informed the people, and the executive branch's need to preserve internal security. He emphasized that in the absence of congressional action, the Court was asked "to perform a function that the Constitution gave to the executive, not the Judiciary."[46] Although convinced that the executive was correct about the danger of some of the documents, he did not find publication of any of them would "surely result in direct, immediate, and irreparable damage."[47] Although largely agreeing with Justice Stewart, Justice White did note that while injunctions were not the proper remedy, he saw no bar to potential criminal prosecutions under several statutes that he thought applicable.

Justices Harlan and Burger both dissented largely on the procedural grounds that the case had been rushed to the Supreme Court in less than two weeks and that the record was inadequate for appropriate review. Nevertheless, both also felt that the newspapers were not granted a free license by the First Amendment. In particular, Justice Burger mocked the *Times* for asserting "a sole trusteeship" over the public's right to know and chastised the paper for failing in the duty of every good citizen with respect "to the discovery or possession of stolen property or government documents."[48] Of all the justices, only Justice Blackmun found that publication would lead to harm, concluding: "I hope that damage already has not been done. If, however, damage has been done . . . then the nation's people will know where the responsibility for these sad consequences rests."[49]

In the end, of course, the Pentagon Papers, including large parts of them deemed by the government or the dissenting justices to be dangerous, were published. I am aware of no negative effects that resulted from their publication, and certainly none of the dire consequences predicted by the government came to pass. Indeed, it is arguable that publication led to some positive consequences.

As with most attempts to secure government secrecy, the actual concern was more about political embarrassment than national security. There are, of course, valid claims to secrecy in matters such as troop movements, weapons, spies, negotiating positions, and the like. But when it comes to the kinds of broad issues of policy and history involved in the Pentagon Papers case, there are rarely compelling arguments for the broad censorship sought by the government.

Freedom of the press today is in grave danger. The excesses and irresponsibility — the hubris — of the press itself has contributed to this danger. Having won the Pentagon Papers case, and most other important court cases, much of the media today regards itself as not only above the law, but also above public accountability. It has failed to self-regulate and to recognize the public trust it holds under the First Amendment. Unless the media begins to control itself, I fear that the pressures for governmental regulation may become irresistible. The victory in the Pentagon Papers case may ring hollow if the public distrust of the media continues to grow.

Freedom of the press is a fragile reed, as the Pentagon Papers case shows. It must be nurtured not only by the First Amendment but also by the responsibility of those who are entrusted with democracy's most powerful private tool.

Roe v. Wade

Date: 1973
Location: District of Columbia
Plaintiff: Norma McCorvey, alias Jane Roe
Defendant: District Attorney Henry Wade
Claim: Absolute prohibition on abortion is unconstitu-
             tional
Decision: First-trimester abortions and some second-
             trimester abortions are protected by the Consti-
             tution

Great American cases often take on a mythical dimension. Clarence Earl Gideon, the man whose case gave rise to the universal right to counsel, is widely believed to have been innocent of the crime for which he was convicted in the absence of counsel and acquitted after counsel was appointed. Although the evidence points fairly convincingly to guilt, it is important to the mythology of the case that Gideon be an innocent man whose initial conviction was solely the result of his having to represent himself.

Similarly, the case of *Roe v. Wade* originally took on a mythical dimension, generated largely by the deliberate deception of the case's heroine, Norma McCorvey, who used the pseudonym Jane Roe to protect her privacy. The fabrication was that Ms. McCorvey had been gang raped at a local Texas carnival by an African American man, a Hispanic man, and a Caucasian man, and thus that her unwanted pregnancy was caused by circumstances completely beyond her control. That scenario was thought to make the most sympathetic case for choosing abortion. Although her lawyers apparently did not believe her false cry of rape and did not allege it in official court papers, Jane Roe garnered sympathy for her plight by describing herself to receptive reporters as the victim of a crime. Only years after the case was over did she confess that she made up the entire story because she was "so frustrated and bitter at being denied an abortion." So another legal myth crumbled, while the case that generated it continues to divide a nation.

Perhaps the most persistent mythology surrounding great cases, especially great Supreme Court cases, is that the lawyers — especially the lawyers for the winning side — played pivotal roles in the victory. That myth is certainly prevalent with regard to the lawyers who argued *Roe v. Wade*, the case that first established a woman's constitutional right to choose abortion. The reality is that broad-agenda cases involving large and controversial issues of constitutional policy are almost never influenced by the advocacy of the lawyers. The justices have made up their minds on how they are going to vote before the briefs are written or the cases argued. Despite the lame claims of judicial nominees, most recently Justice Clarence Thomas, that they have open minds on such issues as abortion, the truth is that they have made up their minds, and the nominating president generally knows which way they will vote. The eloquence or lack thereof of lawyers is unlikely to change any minds in "hot-button" cases. To be sure, a bad lawyer can snatch defeat from the jaws of victory by making a tactical blunder in the preparation or presentation of a case, and a truly great lawyer can help posture a litigation so as to maximize the chances of pressuring a vacillating justice toward his or her client's desired result. But in general, advocacy before the High Court is largely ceremonial in broad-agenda cases such as *Roe v. Wade*.

The lawyers in this transforming case seem to have understood the limited impact their advocacy was expected to have. There was considerable infighting among the lawyers over who would get the honor of delivering the argument before the justices, with little regard for the ability of the contending advocates.[50]

The main brief itself, in the words of a writer who chronicled the case, "was a serviceable if not brilliant brief."[51] That is a euphemism for "mediocre." The appraisal is not surprising; the two leading lawyers were rookies who had never written Supreme Court briefs before. Several of the amicus curiae briefs were of a higher professional caliber, having been written by excellent and experienced lawyers who should have been recruited to draft the main brief. But petty and proprietary jealousies prevailed as to both the brief writing and the oral argument. That a totally inexperienced lawyer should have insisted on arguing this or any other case in the Supreme Court either borders on malpractice or recognizes the relative unimportance of oral argument. The neophyte nevertheless won the battle for the honor of arguing the case and proceeded to do so, making several significant mistakes in the process. Fortunately for the appellants, the lawyer for the other side was even worse.

Marian Faux, who chronicled the case in *Roe v. Wade: The Untold Story*, described the arguments in critical terms. Sarah Weddington argued for "Jane Roe." Justice Potter Stewart asked her the most obvious question: Where in the Constitution was there a right to abortion? Weddington "faltered," flailing from right to right. She cited the Ninth Amendment, the common law, a previous case concerning birth control, the Fourteenth Amendment, and "a variety of others." Justice White added sarcastically, "and anything else that might be appropriate."[52] Her strategy "seemed to be backfiring." She was not handling the Court's entirely predictable questions "deftly enough." She was presenting the justices with a potpourri of the rights and no real arguments to support any of them.

But Weddington looked like a superstar in comparison with the clown who argued for the state of Texas. Assistant Attorney General Jay Floyd started his argument with an attempt at humor:

"Mr. Chief Justice, and may it please the Court, it's an old joke, but when a man argues against two beautiful ladies like these, they're going to have the last word."

Expecting laughter, no doubt, he was greeted instead with pained silence from the spectators and the justices. Chief Justice Burger's face reddened, he looked as if he were about to say something, and then he nodded to Floyd to get on with his arguments.

Floyd then argued that the appeal had become "moot" because Roe, "whom he carefully characterized as a married woman, was no longer pregnant."

It was too much even for Stewart, who only half-jokingly responded that [since this was a class-action lawsuit] surely the Court could take judicial notice of the facts that there were at any given time, unmarried pregnant females in the state of Texas, again provoking laughter in the courtroom. . . .

When a justice asked how a woman in Texas could sue for the right to abortion, Floyd replied that he did not think it could be done at all, that "no remedy is provided." Sensing that he had finally seized the Court's attention, he continued, "There are situations in which of course, as the Court knows, no remedy is provided. Now, I think she makes her choice prior to the time she becomes pregnant. That is the time of the choice. . . . Once a child is born, a woman no longer has a choice; and I think pregnancy makes her make that choice as well."

A voice from the bench replied: "Maybe she makes her choice when she decides to live in Texas."

Again, the courtroom erupted in laughter.

Slightly miffed, Floyd asked, "May I proceed?" Then, in a feeble attempt to banter back, he added, "There's no restriction on moving, you know."

Although some of those present felt that the Court had mocked the counsel for Texas, something more important had happened. Floyd had approached the justices with an age-old assumption, namely that he and they belonged to the same old-boy network, one that excluded and even occasionally belittled women. And while there were undoubtedly men sitting on that bench who held some traditional values with regard to women, while they sat on the highest court in the nation, they were charged to treat all people equally. They succeeded in doing so to a greater or lesser degree depending upon the issues presented to them, but that day in court, in large part thanks to some presumptions of a male lawyer from Texas, they could not help but be reminded of their obligation.[53]

Justice Thurgood Marshall pressed Floyd about when, under Texas law, "life began."

"At any time, Mr. Justice, we make no distinction."

"You make no distinction from the moment of impregnation."

"Well, we begin, Mr. Justice, in our brief, with the development of the human embryo, carrying it through to the development of the fetus, from about seven to nine days after conception."

"Well, what about six days?" Marshall asked.

"We don't know."

"But this statute," Marshall asked, now obviously enjoying himself, "goes all the way back to one hour."

Frustrated at being pinned down in such a manner, Floyd could only say, "I don't — Mr. Justice, there are unanswerable questions in this field, I —"

The spectators could no longer contain their laughter, and

even Justice Marshall chortled: "I appreciate it, I appreciate
it."

An obviously embarrassed Floyd said, "This is an artless
statement on our part."

To which Justice Marshall politely replied: "I withdraw the
question." There was more laughter.

"Thank you," responded a grateful Floyd, and then, still
fumbling, he added, "That's really when the soul comes into
the unborn, if a person believes in a soul, I don't know."[54]

Finally Floyd was asked about the fact that

... Texas abortion law made no exception in cases of rape, a
situation in which a woman might find herself pregnant without having made the choice to be. Floyd could only answer
that off the record, as he understood the state's policy, it was
acceptable to "estop whatever has occurred immediately by
the proper procedure in the hospital." In other words, a hospital could — without fear of reprisal — abort a woman who had
been raped.

His time was up. Having just admitted that the state of Texas
made exceptions to its own abortion law, Floyd's argument had
hardly ended on a strong note.[55]

The justices decided the case exactly as they would have had
both lawyers stayed home. Despite the widespread recognition of
this reality, the lawyers are still treated as larger-than-life heroes.
The law presumably needs its myths. But it also needs its de-
bunkers.

The remaining question surrounding *Roe v. Wade* is whether,
on balance and over the long run, the pro-choice movement was
helped or hurt by the constitutionalization of the right to choose
abortion. The answer to this complex question is not self-evident.

In the short term, *Roe* produced at least three undeniable results. The first and most important is that it afforded thousands

of pregnant women the right to choose an abortion under most circumstances. The second is that it galvanized the "right-to-life" movement and made it a potent force in local and national politics. The third is that it put the "right-to-choose" movement into a political coma. Advocates of choice came to rely on the courts rather than on the political branches to vindicate their point of view.

Some observers even credit the political victories of Presidents Reagan and Bush to *Roe v. Wade*. Because of that decision, right-wing Republicans could pander to the powerful right-to-life voters without really endangering a woman's right to choose, which was protected by the courts. Only when the votes in the High Court became close did pro-choice voters begin to flex their political muscle. Had the Supreme Court not constitutionalized choice, the argument goes, perhaps the pro-choice movement would have organized politically far sooner and far more effectively.

Unlike *Brown v. Board of Education*, which has become something of a fixed star in the constellation of our constitutional law, *Roe v. Wade* remains a highly contentious precedent even today. The issue splits the public, the political parties, and even the current Supreme Court almost down the middle. Among the landmark decisions of the Supreme Court, *Roe* is thus especially unsteady. Whether it will someday become another *Brown* or, as Justice Scalia hopes, another *Dred Scott* still remains to be seen.

The American Indian Movement Trials

Date: 1974–78
Location: Pierre, South Dakota
Defendants: Russell Means, Dennis Banks, Leonard Peltier
Charges: Burglary, larceny, assault, possession of firearms,
             theft, conspiracy to commit criminal acts, and
             murder
Verdict: Case dismissed against Means and Banks;
             Peltier convicted
Sentence: Two consecutive life sentences

Great injustices often produce protests, violence, and then trials.
The trials, when conducted by those who perpetrated the injustice, are often "show trials" designed to demonstrate that there
was no injustice and/or that the protests and violence were disproportionate to any perceived injustice. Among the greatest injustices in modern world history was the manner by which those
who "discovered" and "settled" the American continents displaced and murdered their Native populations. The European
American genocide against Native Americans is a moral infection that still festers, because so little has been done to remedy
its awful consequences. Like so many other great injustices, the
destruction of Native Americans was done in the name of higher
virtues: conversion of the "heathens" to Christianity, the mani-

fest destiny of America, the need to civilize the "barbarians," and the settling of a continent needed for Europeans who had been oppressed in their own birthplaces.

Since most of us have been educated about our country's original population by cowboy-and-Indian movies and by commercials that show a stoic brave shedding a tear over our pollution of his land, it is perhaps unremarkable how ignorant most of us are about American Indians. When we visit Mount Rushmore and gaze patriotically at the sculptures of Washington, Jefferson, Lincoln, and Teddy Roosevelt, how many of us realize that these American faces were chiseled out of a sacred mountainside? How many of us understand that our "national monument" constitutes a continuing affront to many Indians?

The late John Fire Lame Deer, chief of the Lakotas, explained the significance of Mount Rushmore to Native Americans: "It means that these big white faces are telling us, 'First we gave you Indians a treaty that you could keep these Black Hills forever, as long as the sun would shine, in exchange for all of the Dakotas, Wyoming and Montana. Then we found the gold and took this last piece of land, because we were stronger. . . . And because we like the tourist dollars, too, we have made your sacred Black Hills into one vast Disneyland. And after we did all this we carved up this mountain, the dwelling place of your spirits, and put our four gleaming white faces here. We are the conquerors.'"[56]

Knowing these realities makes it impossible for any sensitive visitor ever again to enjoy Mount Rushmore guiltlessly or to forget the dark side of the saga of the American West. It is, moreover, a continuing tragedy. We cannot simply feel a distant guilt about past massacres, land expropriations, and cultural annihilations. We are part of the persisting assault on the dignity, property, and life of our original Native population.

We are General Custer. Though we no longer dress in the uniform of the cavalry or carry Gatling guns, we continue to employ the weapons of law and power to deny American Indians what rightfully should be theirs. Our giant corporations ravage their land in search of minerals; our confused government policy on the status of reservations deprives Indians of both real and genuine participation in American political life; our continuing racial discrimination against Native Americans — both on and off the reservation — denies them the most basic tools for survival. Advocates for Native Americans probably overstate it when they claim that Pine Ridge Indians "commonly lived for a hundred years or more" and now die at an average age of forty-four.[57] But they are surely correct that we bear some responsibility for the intolerable physical and economic conditions that many Indians face today.

We can do something now to prevent our children and grandchildren from having to live with our guilt tomorrow. And more importantly, we can do something now to assure that the present generation of American Indians will indeed have children and grandchildren who will carry forward the culture of a great people.

Now, barely a century after the genocide ended, European Americans are finally beginning to understand the evil we perpetrated on the innocent and often helpless Native populations of this bountiful land. We study their plight, we sympathize with their current conditions, and we go on benefiting from the way this nation was founded and expanded. As former secretary of the interior Rogers Morton put it: "There is no way I or any other Secretary can undo the events of the past. If it was wrong for the European to move on to this continent and settle it by pioneerism and combat, it was wrong. But it happened and here we are."[58]

It should not be surprising, therefore, that some Native Americans have organized in an effort to reclaim their past, improve their present, and assure their children's future. Among these, some have resorted to violence, and the events at Wounded Knee, with the resulting trial, were the culmination of these efforts.[59] In 1973, several hundred members of the American Indian Movement occupied the South Dakota village of Wounded Knee, where U.S. soldiers had killed more than two hundred Sioux in an 1890 massacre. The occupation lasted seventy-one days, involved a series of shootouts with the FBI, and ended in a negotiated peace and the arrest of 120 occupiers. The defendants were charged with numerous crimes ranging from burglary to assault. As with other political trials, the defendants in the Wounded Knee trials tried to use the courtroom to make broad political points, while the prosecutors sought to focus on the narrower issues of criminal conduct. The prosecutors asked "whether," while the defendants asked "why."

Fortunately for the defense, the trial judge who presided over the major Wounded Knee trial was a fair-minded man who did not defer to the government, as many judges do. After a lengthy trial, one juror became ill during deliberations, and the government — fearing an acquittal — refused the judge's request to proceed with eleven jurors. The judge, citing government misconduct throughout the case, then dismissed the remaining counts (some had been dismissed earlier), saying, "this has been a bad year for justice." The government's effort to demonstrate that it was applying the rule of law and fundamental fairness to unlawful conduct by Native American rabble-rousers backfired. Though it did secure some convictions in related cases — most notably the murder conviction of Leonard Peltier — the take-home message from Wounded Knee, for most Native Americans and for many of the rest of us, was that the descendants of those who treated our original population so unjustly on the plains were continuing to treat their descendants unjustly in the courts. The other take-home message was that judges could help restore justice — at least in some cases.

Few judges today would rule as Judge Fred Nichol did in September 1974.[60] Prosecutorial misconduct, which persists, rarely results in dismissals or other sanctions these days. "Harmless error" trumps prosecutorial misconduct whenever the courts believe the defendant is probably guilty — which is in the vast majority of cases. The Wounded Knee trials remind us of a time when courts served as an effective check and balance on the excesses and inadequacies of the other branches of government, especially in political trials.

Leonard Peltier was not as fortunate. His trial — which still generates much criticism and condemnation — resulted in his conviction and imprisonment for the murder of two FBI agents. Despite repeated efforts to secure relief, he remains in federal prison.

Peltier's case grew out of the more violent confrontation between AIM and the FBI at Ogala, South Dakota, on June 26, 1975.

The background facts are not in dispute: After years of virtual warfare between AIM militants and FBI agents, a lethal "firefight," started by armed Indians and involving several FBI agents, took place. A rifle shot from a distance left an Indian named Joe Killsright Stuntz dead. Two FBI agents, Jack Coler and Ronald Williams, were killed at close range after being seriously wounded from a distance.

The issues of Peltier's guilt and innocence — both in their technical legal sense and in their broader moral sense — are still vigorously disputed. The two executed FBI agents were gunned down at close range. They were disarmed, helpless, and probably begging for their lives. There were no eyewitnesses, or at least none who would testify, to who murdered them. But considerable circumstantial evidence pointed toward Leonard Peltier, one of the most militant AIM leaders. There can be little doubt that the FBI was out to get Mr. Peltier. Nor can there be any doubt that the FBI desperately wanted to bring to justice the murderers of its agents. The real question is whether the FBI framed Mr. Peltier for killings he may not have committed, as many still believe, or whether Peltier murdered the hated agents.

One of the AIM lawyers has said that Peltier's chief lawyer, the late William Kunstler, thought that Peltier had killed the agents, though "he believes that they were innocent whether they did it or not."[61] But a history of discrimination and abuse, while perhaps explaining murder, can never justify it, especially against innocent agents of the law.

There is considerable validity to many of AIM's complaints against the FBI. Some — such as infiltration of the movement for purposes of engendering internal distrust and dissension — carry indications of credibility. These tactics, indefensible though they are, have been commonly used by the FBI against radical groups of all political persuasions. But other allegations, such as systematic beatings and "contracts" on the lives of AIM leaders, do not seem as credible.

The trials of the AIM leaders — regardless of the specific guilt or innocence of individual defendants — highlight the imperfections of the American legal system, especially when it is mustered against a political group as potentially violent as the American Indian Movement. They also remind us of the self-destructive quality of many of the self-appointed leaders of that movement. Drawn from among the most vocal, the most violent, and the most radical Native Americans, many of these leaders exploited their newly discovered heritage for their own personal ends. Some have ended where they belong — in jail. Others have simply drifted away. What remains are thousands of poverty-stricken Indians, first driven by years of neglect to accept false prophets of violence and then shorn even of that ineffective leadership.

None of these trials of AIM leaders, standing alone, qualifies as "great" or "notable" with regard to the legal issues involved. But they represent an important part of American history — our pervasive mistreatment of the original population of our country, not ending with Custer in the nineteenth century, but continuing in the courts into the twentieth and twenty-first centuries. Because these trials are so important to Native Americans and because of their representative character, they warrant inclusion in any catalog of important American trials.

On February 3, 2004, the *New York Times* reported that on the twenty-eighth anniversary of Leonard Peltier's imprisonment, federal prosecutors brought murder charges against two American Indian activists accused of killing a young woman — herself an active member of AIM — back in 1975. The alleged motive for the murder of Anna Mae Piltou Aquash was to protect Peltier, who had, according to the editor of a Native American periodical called *News from Indian Country*, bragged to Aquash "about shooting both FBI agents, and even reenacted the crime." Peltier, according to former AIM leader Russell Means, was afraid that Aquash would become "a federal informer, and AIM leaders ordered her killing." The editor, Paul DeMain, started out believing that Peltier did not kill the FBI agents or Aquash, "but after years of interviews, he became convinced [that Peltier] was a murderer." "What I found was not a case where the government framed an innocent man, but where the government may have framed a guilty man." Peltier has sued DeMain for libel.

On February 13, 2004, a federal jury convicted Arlo Looking Cloud, one of the accused activists, of murdering Aquash; the other accused activist is in Canada, fighting extradition to the United States.

The Bakke Case

Date: 1978
Location: District of Columbia
Claimant: Alan Bakke
Claim: UC–Davis Medical School's policy of race-based affirmative action was unconstitutional
Decision: Fixed racial quotas were unconstitutional, but affirmative action in university admissions was upheld

Race-based affirmative action in university admissions is one of the most divisive issues of our age. When the admission is to medical school and the program under challenge sets aside a specific number and percentage of slots for minority applicants who will be judged by considerably less demanding criteria, the issue becomes even more contentious. The specters of reverse discrimination, quotas, and "unqualified" doctors loom large in the minds of many, especially those who remember when quotas (really ceilings) were used to limit the number of Jews, Catholics, and other "undesirables" admitted to medical schools, law schools, and undergraduate colleges.

The Bakke case, brought by a white man denied admission to the University of California's medical school at Davis, went up to the Supreme Court. There the justices struck down the Davis program but made it clear that other race-based programs that re-

lied more on discretion and less on fixed formulae would be upheld.

The *Bakke* decision remained the only Supreme Court precedent guiding university affirmative action programs until 2003,
when the High Court essentially reaffirmed it in two cases from
the University of Michigan.

We now have access to internal memoranda of the justices in
the Bakke case. These memos tell the fascinating story of how
the *Bakke* compromise developed out of this litigation.

The early drafts of internal memoranda show that without the
personal politicking of Justice William Brennan — who emerges
as not only as a great theoretician but also a first-rate tactician —
the *Bakke* decision would have been a total defeat for all race-
based affirmative action programs. But Justice Brennan
persuaded Justice Powell, who was the swing vote, that race
should be *one* of several permissible criteria an admissions committee may employ in order to achieve a diverse student body.
Justice Brennan realized that there was no practical distinction
between racial quotas (really floors) of the kind adopted by Davis
and a discretionary system in which race is one factor. As he put
it in an early internal memorandum: ". . . we were just deluding
ourselves if we think that there is a meaningful, judicially enforceable distinction between setting aside a reasonable number
of places for *qualified minorities* and a process that accomplishes
the same end by taking race into account as one of several admissions factors. . . ."[62] Justice Powell understood this as well, but
he preferred an admissions program that did not look as overt as
the Davis program.[63] Accordingly, he cast his swing vote against
the constitutionality of explicit racial quotas such as the one employed by Davis but in favor of the constitutionality of considering race — among other factors — in a fully competitive
admissions program.

This cosmetic compromise seemed to satisfy nearly everyone.
Alan Bakke was admitted to Davis Medical School because his

exclusion had been based on a racial quota, and most universities fixed up their systems to look better — no quotas, only goals. And approximately the same number of minority students continued to be admitted under the pretext that quotas had been replaced by a system in which race was simply one of many variables.[64]

Ultimately, a five-man majority held — with a morass of rhetoric, citations, footnotes, and dicta, and for a variety of irreconcilable reasons — that the type of admissions program used by Davis Medical School does not pass constitutional and/or statutory muster, while the type used by Harvard College does. Justice Powell, whose opinion contained the judgment of the Court, expressly singled out Harvard College for approval. He quoted extensively from the description of the Harvard program contained in the amicus curiae brief submitted by Harvard, Columbia, and Stanford and Pennsylvania universities. Powell apparently found it easier to point to an existing system than to define the factors that would satisfy the constitutional and statutory standard. (Justice Potter Stewart once similarly said he could not define the factors that make for a pornographic movie, but he knew one when he saw one.)

It is unfortunate that Powell chose Harvard College. Harvard is the wealthiest school in the world, with an international applicant pool that is like an ocean compared to the fish tanks from which many other schools must select their students. Moreover, Powell's use of an undergraduate liberal arts college as a model for medical school admissions reflects a degree of educational inexperience that demonstrates the wisdom of keeping judges as uninvolved as possible in university admissions programs. Colleges want a diverse student body because they are educating in the broadest sense of the term: They want athletes, musicians, foreigners, legacies, and so on. Medical schools, on the other hand, want to produce the best possible doctors, without regard to their athletic or musical skills.

But Justice Powell had a good reason for pointing to the Harvard undergraduate admissions program: It is so vague and discretionary as to defy description. It reposes all decision making with a group of Platonic guardians whose task is to shape an entering class so as to maximize its diversity in certain unspecified ways. Harvard admissions officers may be unable to define the factors that make a good candidate for admission, but they are supposed to know a Harvard man (or, more recently, woman) when they see one.

The *Bakke* decision was a triumph of ambiguity and discretion over clarity and candor. Powell condemns Davis Medical School for reserving a discrete number of places in such-and-such class for disadvantaged members of specified minority groups, while he applauds Harvard College for employing a process that eschews target-quotas for the number of blacks but allows "the race of an applicant [to] tip the balance in his favor just as geographic origin or a life spent on a farm tip the balance in other candidates' cases."

At bottom, Powell's opinion really says nothing at all about affirmative action as such. It simply delegates universities the discretionary power to decide on the degree and definition of the diversity — including or excluding racial factors — that they feel enhances the educational experiences of their students.

The Harvard College description, as quoted in the Powell opinion, tells far from the whole story of Harvard's quest for diversity. It fails to disclose the enormous efforts that Harvard College undertakes simultaneously to assure a certain kind of uniformity in its student body over time. Harvard (like many other Ivy League colleges) always has given great weight to genealogy — whether the applicant's parents or other family members attended or taught at Harvard. Since Harvard's past student and faculty bodies were anything but diverse, this grandfather policy guarantees a good deal of homogeneity over the genera-

THE BAKKE CASE   423

tions of Harvard College classes, as well as homogeneity in a large part of any given class.

Justice Blackmun doubted whether there was much difference between the Davis and Harvard programs, commenting that the cynical may say that under a program such as Harvard's one may accomplish covertly what Davis openly concedes that it does. Justice Powell nowhere disputes this. His answer seems to be that even if both programs produce the same result, the Davis program — because of its explicit acknowledgment of racial quotas — will be viewed as inherently unfair by the public generally as well as by applicants for admission, whereas the Harvard program — with its vague consideration of many unquantified factors — will not be as grating to the public or to its unsuccessful applicants.

But there is one way in which the Harvard system is ultimately less fair than the Davis one. In order to receive special consideration under the discredited Davis program, an applicant had to be both individually disadvantaged and a member of a specified racial minority. Under the approved Harvard program, an applicant's race alone may tip the balance in his favor even if he is the scion of a wealthy and powerful family who attended the best schools and personally experienced almost none of the trauma of racial discrimination. (Indeed, I was told about a case where one student sought a double preference: as a disadvantaged black and as an advantaged offspring of a Harvard alumnus.) Harvard's program has the effect of preferring the wealthy and advantaged black applicant, for example, to a poor and disadvantaged black or white applicant. In practice, Harvard probably makes more turn on race alone than did Davis. But it does it with typical Harvard class: low-key, muted, and without displaying too much exposed skin. Moreover, the history of Harvard's use of geographic distribution as a subterfuge for religious quotas leaves lingering doubts about the bona fides of its alleged quest for diversity — at least in the past. It also leaves doubts about how other schools have implemented the *Bakke* decision.

Let us assume that Blank University seeks diversity by trying to include musicians, farm boys, and Oklahomans among its entering class, but that it does not instruct its admissions officers to aim for a specified minimum number of farm boys, musicians, or Oklahomans in each entering class. May Blank University direct its admissions officers — either implicitly or explicitly — to make certain that the number of blacks or other minority groups should not go beneath a certain approximate percentage in the class? Would that put race on a different footing than the other elements of diversity?

The answer to that question may well turn on whether one looks for legal guidance to the description of the Harvard program as quoted in Mr. Justice Powell's opinion, or to the real-world operation of the Harvard program as it probably works in practice. The following description of the policy in place at the time of the Bakke case certainly implies that race is not treated differently from other elements of diversity:

> In Harvard College admissions the Committee has not set target-quotas for the number of blacks, or of musicians, football players, physicists or Californians to be admitted in a given year. At the same time, the Committee is aware that if Harvard College is to provide a truly heterogeneous environment that reflects the rich diversity of the United States, it cannot be provided without some attention to numbers. It would not make sense, for example, to have 10 or 20 students out of 1,100 whose homes are west of the Mississippi. Comparably 10 to 20 black students could not begin to bring to their classmates and to each other, the variety of points of view, backgrounds and experiences of blacks in the United States. Their small numbers might also create a sense of isolation among the black students themselves and thus make it more difficult for them to develop and achieve their potential. Consequently, when mak-

ing its decisions, the Committee on Admissions is aware that there is some relationship between numbers and achieving the benefits to be derived from a diverse student body, and between numbers and providing a reasonable environment for those students admitted. But that awareness does not mean that the Committee sets a minimum number of blacks or of people from west of the Mississippi who are to be admitted. It means only that in choosing among thousands of applicants who are not only admissible academically but have other strong qualities, the Committee, with a number of criteria in mind, pays some attention to distribution among many types and categories of students.[65]

A closer look at the admissions program in practice might well reveal that the Harvard admissions officers, though interested in assuring geographic, occupational, and musical diversity, really pay little or no attention to numbers: It would be no great crisis if one particular entering class at Harvard College had few or even no violinists, Oklahomans, or farm boys. (Football quarterbacks might be another thing altogether.) But these very same admissions officers may well be under instructions — explicit or implicit — to pay close attention to the number of blacks so as to assure that the proportion does not fall below a certain approximate floor. If a judge were thus to look to Powell's model, she might very well rule that Blank University's program was illegal. On the other hand, if she were to look to the Harvard program in practice, she might well conclude that Blank's program was really no different from Harvard's.

Mr. Justice Powell also is unclear about whether a university's initial process for screening out applicants must be color-blind. Many universities, particularly professional schools, have a procedure under which nonminority applicants whose combined grade scores do not reach a specified total are placed into an automatic or presumptive reject category, while minority candidates are not placed into such categories unless their combined grade scores are considerably lower. There is a serious question whether such a double-track screening procedure, or any of its subtle variants, complies with Mr. Justice Powell's requirement that all institutions must adhere to a policy of individual comparison. The Harvard description says: "When the Committee on Admissions reviews the large middle group of applicants who are admissible and deemed capable of doing good work in their courses, the race of an applicant may tip the balance in his favor just as geographic origin or a life spent on a farm may tip the balance in other candidates' cases."[66] This certainly implies that race is not considered in the initial screening decision. But a closer look at the program in practice may disclose that there is no initial color-blind screening for admissibility and that even initial criteria for qualification may depend — at least to some degree — on an applicant's race. If Blank University adopted an admissions procedure that initially screened applicants differently on the basis of race, a court might again have to decide whether to look to the Harvard model or to the Harvard reality.

It would be the crowning irony if a *Bakke*-type lawsuit were brought against Harvard College itself, and if the Court were to evaluate the Harvard admissions program *as practiced* against the model Harvard program *as described in the Powell opinion*. Harvard College might well flunk its own test. But Harvard would probably not flunk the slightly different test enunciated by the Supreme Court, on June 23, 2003, in the Michigan cases *Grutter v. Bollinger* and *Gratz v. Bollinger*. In these cases, the Court essentially reaffirmed *Bakke* and once again seemingly concerned itself far more with the description of the program than its actual application. The Court began by clearing up a central ambiguity of *Bakke*, with at least five justices clearly holding that diversity could serve as a compelling state interest for affirmative action programs. The Court also, however, reaffirmed that quotas were illegitimate and found that the undergraduate program, which mechanically awarded minorities a fixed twenty points, was therefore impermissible because it was too similar to a quota. However, it upheld the law school's program, which purportedly treated race as merely a vague "plus" and aimed for a "critical mass" of minorities rather than a fixed quota. But Justice O'Connor's majority opinion barely responded to the criticisms of the dissent that the so-called plus ended up being statistically dispositive and that the critical mass was in fact, historically, a disguised quota, largely taking the government's word that the process was individualized. Since even Justice Brennan in *Bakke* realized, as noted above, that most discretionary systems will end up functioning as quotas, O'Connor and the rest of the Court once again followed Powell's preference in *Bakke* for a disguised quota rather than an overt one. Thus, any future challenge to Harvard's program, as *applied* rather than as *described* by Powell, would seem unlikely to succeed. (It would be difficult, in practice, for anyone to challenge Harvard's program, since it is a private university.)

The Court's 2003 amplification of the *Bakke* principle in the Michigan cases did little to clarify the underlying rationale for taking race into account as a means toward eventually achieving a "color-blind" society. Nor did it satisfy critics who believe that *diversity* is a euphemism for "quotas," or at least for "floors" for some groups (which, of course, become "ceilings" for others). The most that can be said for these decisions is that they offer a pragmatic solution to a difficult racial problem that may have no perfect theoretical solution.

The Trial of Richard Herrin

Date: 1978
Location: White Plains, New York
Defendant: Richard Herrin
Charge: Murder
Verdict: Convicted of manslaughter
Sentence: Eight and a third to twenty-five years' imprisonment

The trial of Richard Herrin for killing Bonnie Garland had been dubbed the "affirmative action murder trial," because the defendant — a Mexican American — was believed to have been admitted to Yale on the basis of affirmative action. It was at Yale that he met the victim, a wealthy student named Bonnie Garland.

Bonnie Garland was a brilliant, charming, and beautiful young woman. While a freshman at Yale College, the seventeen-year-old daughter of a wealthy international lawyer became involved with twenty-one-year-old Yale junior Richard Herrin. Herrin came from a very different background. Raised in Los Angeles by his impoverished Mexican American mother, Richard worked hard and became valedictorian of his high school class. At Yale, however, he was not as successful, courting academic failure and spending much of his time alone. Then he met, and fell madly in love with, Bonnie. At first the feelings were reciprocated, but soon Bonnie felt constrained by her relationship with Richard and started to date other Yalies. When Bonnie left for a European trip (accompanied, Richard correctly suspected, by another boyfriend), Richard became morose, angry, and confused. Upon her return, Richard traveled to the Garland family home in Scarsdale, New York, seeking a reconciliation. The young couple talked lovingly and decided to spend the night together in Bonnie's room. All seemed well as Bonnie drifted off to sleep. But then something seemed to snap within Richard's fragile psyche. Suddenly, while looking at her sleeping body, Richard decided that he had to kill her. Methodically, he looked around the house for a hammer, found one, wrapped it in a towel, and proceeded to bash in Bonnie's skull. He then got into the Garland family car, drove around for several hours contemplating suicide, and ended up at a Catholic church, where he confessed his crime to a priest. Eventually he was tried for murder, convicted of manslaughter, and sentenced to prison for a term of eight to fifteen years.

That, in a nutshell, is the tragic story of Bonnie and Richard. Had the crime occurred in the ghettos of New York City or the barrios of Los Angeles, we would never have learned so much about its dramatis personae. Since the killing was a crime of passion by a first offender with little risk of recidivism, a plea bargain would probably have been arranged. The defendant would have quietly pleaded guilty to manslaughter, received a sentence of a few years in prison, and that would have been the end of the matter — at least as far as the public was concerned.

But this case was different. The participants were from Yale. The victim was the daughter of a prominent family. The perpetrator struck a sympathetic chord within certain elements of the Yale religious community. The attorney selected to defend Richard Herrin — Jack Litman — is among the most brilliant, sensitive, and psychologically sophisticated in the country. Litman put Yale on trial, portraying Herrin as a victim of Yale's policy of admitting disadvantaged students, but then essentially ignoring them as they struggled to keep up with Yale's demanding standards — both academic and social.

Litman presented Herrin as a disturbed young man, struggling to learn why he did his terrible deed but failing to comprehend its complex dynamics. Adding to the complexity was the fact that Herrin was lionized by elements of the Yale Catholic community, which tried to "explain" and "forgive" his crime in their theological terms. His lawyer, however, explained his crime in legal terms. And Herrin was also interviewed by forensic psychiatrists, who explained his crime in psychiatric terms. After all this, Richard seemed farther from self-awareness than he was at the moment of the killing or during the tortured hours immediately following it.

This should not be surprising, because the "truths" of law, the "truths" of religion, and the "truths" of psychiatry are incomplete. They each work in the service of their particular master.

Herrin's lawyer did a masterful job explaining why the young man did what he did.

For I suggest to you, as the evidence shows, Richard Herrin literally went beyond the pale and crossed into a machinelike state of, essentially, unfeeling destruction. Why else did all his controls fail? Why was he unable to debate or reflect on the thought to kill Bonnie and kill himself? Why else could he not call upon his excellent and previously unimpeachable morality, as has been testified to by people who knew him well over the years? Why else was he unable to call upon his religious training, his intelligence, and his background? . . .

Were his actions on the morning of July 7th — not the result of a mind pressed beyond its endurance, literally broken down, as the doctors testified, attempting to resolve conflicting and uncontrollable, unconscious drives and emotions, in a way that is so bizarre and so inhuman and so unlike the Richard Herrin that you have come to know? Were his normal mechanisms working?

Richard Herrin, as you've heard, keeps things under control more than most of us. He never experienced in an overt way anger or rage, and you have that not from Richard Herrin — and, certainly, not just from a psychiatrist — but from the people who knew him. The person who raised him, the people who roomed with him at Yale and knew him at Yale, the people — the person who lived with him for two years at Texas Christian University.

How many of us can state that position, that we've never externalized our anger or even rarely done so? And yet, the first time he does anything which is suggestive of anger or rage, is to pick up a hammer and put it through the skull of another person and of the woman he loved, without any conscious motive, profit, self-protection, revenge. Nothing. Is that not a diseased mind? How else do you understand, ladies and gentlemen, the inability to juxtapose two thoughts? One to kill, and, two, not to cause pain? It may sound poetic from a distance, but it is inhuman and irrational to be able to consider these two things without appreciating, while you're considering them, the enormity and the horror of what you're doing.

In short, how can a highly moral, gentle, religious, sensitive young man perform an act which is so totally foreign to his character, to the way he has acted for the first twenty-three years of his life? . . . Mr. Frederick, as he told you in his opening statement, wants you to believe that this is a planned, cold, calculated killing, as if, somehow or other, Richard Herrin sat down and reflected about whether he would kill Bonnie or not, as if, like going on a robbery, he cased the bank, he figured out where the guards are, what the best escape route was, had to change license plates on a car, to get a car, choose a good weapon, loaded it, weighed the benefit to himself — that is, the money he could possibly get, against the risk, which is getting caught, getting tried, getting convicted and getting punished — and then making a decision to do it? Is that the type of thing you think happened here? Is that in accord with anyone's common-sense view of the evidence, as you have heard it?

A moment's reflection, ladies and gentlemen, will show that there would be no way for Richard Herrin to get away with this. Halfway across the country, from his home, from where he was at school, without $5 in his pocket, dressed only in a pair of pants — he had no thought, no desire to get away with it. But simply a desire to get on with his death.[67]

In the end, the jury may well have understood why Herrin killed. But to understand is not necessarily to forgive. Science requires that we try to understand, but traditional justice demands that we punish in proportion to the harm caused and, perhaps, to its intentionality.

What sentence is proportional to the bludgeoning of an innocent young woman? According to her parents, no punishment would be harsh enough. But according to the Catholic religious community at Yale, Richard had been punished sufficiently by his own suffering. The priests and nuns rallied to his support as if he were a martyr rather than a villain. After arranging for him to await trial in a monastery — rather than a jail — they raised a defense fund and hired one of the best criminal lawyers in the country to defend him.

All this enraged the victim's parents, who complained bitterly that their daughter's death was being diminished by the undue concern for her killer. They believed that their daughter's worth as a brilliant and productive human being should have been emphasized.

The temptation to focus on the "worth" of the murder victim is entirely understandable. It was her tragic death that invoked the legal process and triggered the demand for justice. It is she who is being mourned by her family and friends.

But to introduce her worth at the defendant's trial would distort the proper workings of our legal system. It would make the seriousness of murder — and, indeed, the guilt of the murderer — seem to depend on the worth of the victim. That might be true in some ultimate moral sense: The killer of a great musician is, perhaps, deserving of more condemnation than the killer of an unemployed wino. The legal system must, however, resist this temptation to recognize distinctions based on the worth of the victim.

Already there are considerable pressures in that direction. When a prominent person is murdered, those in power tend to identify more closely with the victim than when an "ordinary" person is killed. The attention of the media is enhanced. The public demand for justice is more insistent. This is all quite understandable, as a matter of human nature. But for the legal system to join in this cry and measure the defendant's guilt by the "worth" of the victim would be to take a giant step backward. From the law's perspective all victims must be deemed equal — regardless of how they were perceived by the public. To make the seriousness of the crime depend on the worth of the victim would be to hark back to the most primitive origins of our legal system — the wergild, under which the criminal could expiate the crime by paying an amount equivalent to the worth of the victim. Each person — or class of persons — had a definable worth that was explicitly recognized by the legal system. Remnants still survive under current law: enhanced punishment for killing certain public officials, police, and so forth. But in general we have come a long way toward regarding all deliberate killings of human beings as equally culpable.

After listening to all the evidence, the jury convicted Richard Herrin of manslaughter; he was sentenced to eight and one-third to twenty-five years in prison. He was released in 1995 and relocated to New Mexico.

The Trial of Jeffrey MacDonald

Date: 1979
Location: Raleigh, North Carolina
Defendant: Captain Jeffrey MacDonald
Charge: Murder of his wife and children
Verdict: Guilty
Sentence: Life imprisonment

Everyone who's read the book or seen the TV movie *Fatal Vision* is convinced Green Beret doctor Jeffrey MacDonald murdered his family.[68] But did he?

I followed the Jeffrey MacDonald case from its grisly inception on February 17, 1970, when the wounded Green Beret doctor told authorities that his pregnant wife, Colette, and his daughters, Kimberly, five, and Kristen, two, had been murdered by drug-crazed intruders. Like most Americans, I had my doubts about his story. I knew that the statistics showed that wives are more likely to be killed by husbands, other family members, or friends than by strangers. I wondered why there was no hard evidence — no fibers, hair, or fingerprints — left by the alleged intruders. My doubts were not allayed by reading Joe McGinniss's best seller *Fatal Vision*, which concluded that MacDonald was guilty, or by seeing the TV movie, which was even more persuasive of his guilt. Several times during the course of the lengthy legal proceedings, Jeffrey MacDonald wrote and called me, pleading with me to help him. Each time I declined. But then a few years ago I went to Terminal Island Federal Prison in California to visit an inmate, and as I left the room in which lawyers confer with prisoners, a graying man quietly introduced himself. He was Jeffrey MacDonald, and he asked if he could have five minutes of my time to show me some documents. I agreed. What I learned that day — and afterward — convinced me to try to help him.

In one of the most dramatic scenes in the TV movie *Fatal Vision*, investigators dig up the graves of Colette, Kimberly, and Kristen MacDonald. The government's chief lawyer (played by Andy Griffith) explains to the grieving Freddie Kassab (played by Karl Malden) why the bodies of his stepdaughter and grandchildren must be exhumed: "We've got to know if the hair found in Colette's hand was her own, Jeff's, the kids' . . . [Freddie Kassab interjects] . . . or someone with a floppy hat."

In the actual trial, as well as in the TV movie, the prosecution's case against Jeffrey MacDonald relied heavily on the source of this evidence: blond hair found in the murdered Colette MacDonald's hand. It had already been found not to match Jeffrey MacDonald's hair. Thus, if it did not match Colette's own hair or the hair of the children, that finding would lend support to MacDonald's claim that there had been intruders — including a woman with long blond hair who was wearing a floppy hat and boots — in his home on the night of the attack. It would also indicate that at least one of these intruders had come in contact with Colette.

By the time the victims' bodies were exhumed, a woman named Helena Stoeckley had told police and others that she and three friends had been in the MacDonald house on the night of the murders and that her friends had committed the crimes. Though Stoeckley's word alone may not have been worth very much — she was known to be a drug addict — she provided some details that tended to corroborate her story and the story Jeffrey MacDonald had told police.

For example, she described a broken rocking horse like one found in Kristen's bedroom. At the time of the crime, she had owned a floppy hat, black clothing, boots, and a long blond wig, all of which corresponded with MacDonald's description. And a woman fitting that description had been seen by a military policeman near the MacDonald home shortly after the crime.

But the single hair in Colette's hand turned out to have come from her own head. The government investigators had already reported that they had found no other physical evidence — no hairs, no fibers, no skin, no blood — that could not be traced to the inhabitants of the MacDonald house.

The prosecution could therefore argue to the jury that Jeffrey MacDonald was lying — because if there had been intruders, they surely would have left some evidence behind: The absence of such evidence was "not reconcilable" with MacDonald's story. Moreover, outside the jury's hearing, the prosecution had managed to exclude some of Stoeckley's testimony because of the lack of forensic corroboration, thus further decreasing the likelihood that MacDonald's story would be believed.[69]

Now, however, in a shocking turn of events, Jeffrey MacDonald's legal team has discovered that, before the trial, the government had in its possession handwritten lab notes indicating that investigators had actually discovered long blond wig hairs at the scene of the crime that did not match anything in the MacDonald household. This evidence was already in the government's secret files before the graves of the victims were disturbed.

Nor was this all the prosecution had in its secret files. The handwritten lab notes confirmed the presence of black wool fibers on the murder weapon used against Colette, and around her mouth. These fibers did not match any clothing belonging to Jeffrey MacDonald or to anyone else in the MacDonald household. (Helena Stoeckley, however, had said she often wore black clothing.)

In addition, in the bedclothes of each victim — Colette, Kimberly, and Kristen — the government experts found other unmatched human hairs, which did not belong to any of the victims, or to Jeffrey MacDonald. But — because the government never fully explored the possibility that MacDonald was telling the truth — these hairs were never tested against Stoeckley or any members of her group.

These lab notes were powerful evidence that an intruder wearing a long blond wig and black wool clothing was at the murder scene on the night of February 17, 1970. But Jeffrey MacDonald's trial lawyers were not aware of the notes' contents. Had they been, the entire trial would undoubtedly have unfolded differently.

For example, Helena Stoeckley testified to the jury that she could not remember where she had been on the night of the murders. MacDonald's attorneys tried to introduce the testimony of six witnesses — including a police officer — to whom she had previously admitted that she was in the MacDonald house with her friends that night. Since testimony about Stoeckley's prior admissions would technically constitute "hearsay" — that is, testimony by one witness about what another witness had said outside the courtroom — the judge ruled that the jury could hear about Stoeckley's hearsay admissions only if "corroborating evidence [showed] that they [were] 'trustworthy.'"

The judge — who was unaware of the handwritten lab notes — ruled that there was no "physical evidence" that corroborated Stoeckley's admissions; therefore, her admissions were not trustworthy.

Thus, the jury never learned that there was hard, scientific evidence of intruders in the house — or that a woman matching MacDonald's description of one of the intruders had actually ad-

mitted to six different people that her friends, not Jeffrey Mac-
Donald, were the killers.

These revelations have finally come to light because of Dr. Jeffrey MacDonald's search for evidence of his own innocence,
which he has protested for more than two decades. Over many
years, he and his lawyers filed requests under the Freedom of Information Act, seeking access to the government documents on
the case — the documents that contained the facts that were not
revealed during the trial. Slowly, they pieced together the amazing story.

But it is a story that raises some disturbing questions. These are
the two most important ones:

1. *Why would the government suppress such critical evidence?*

It is impossible to know the mind-set of the chief government
lawyer in the case, Brian Murtagh, whose responsibility it was to
see that the defense received any evidence in the government's
file that could help the defense. We do, however, know that he
was aware of the contents of the lab notes. He wrote a memo to
a legal assistant asking him whether "the detailed data of a lab
report, as distinguished from the conclusions of the report,
[must] be disclosed [to the defense]." This question is significant,
because the "detailed data" refers to the blond wig hair, the
black wool, and the human hairs, which were described in the
handwritten lab notes but somehow not mentioned in the lab's
final typed report.

Thus far, Murtagh has refused comment, except for a cryptic
statement that "if there were fibers useful to the defense, Mac-
Donald's original trial lawyers should have found them" among
the crates of raw evidence to which they had access. But a murder trial should not be a game of hide-and-seek, in which the
punishment for a lawyer's failure to find an exculpatory needle
in a haystack of raw evidence is the conviction of a possible innocent defendant.

THE TRIAL OF JEFFREY MACDONALD

How much more exculpatory evidence may be hidden in some government file — or may have been destroyed or lost — we will probably never know. For example, a fragment of human skin was found under a fingernail on Colette MacDonald's left hand. Yet, unbelievable as it sounds, the government claims that it lost this singularly important item of evidence. If that skin fragment were now available, it could prove conclusively — through DNA matching — whether or not Jeffrey MacDonald was the killer. Even without DNA testing (which was not available at the time of the original investigation), it could have cleared MacDonald.

2. *Will the new evidence finally get Jeffrey MacDonald the new trial he has been seeking since he was convicted in 1979?*

On this question, the law seems fairly clear. If the government suppressed the lab notes — and if the evidence contained in those notes was material to the issue of MacDonald's guilt or innocence — a new trial should be granted.

But one big problem remains: Most Americans who have read the book or seen the TV movie *Fatal Vision* already "know" that Jeffrey MacDonald is guilty. They know it because the Jeffrey MacDonald portrayed in those one-sided presentations was guilty. On TV, the actor, Gary Cole, *played* him guilty.

The evidence shown to the audience — like the evidence presented to the real-life jury — did not include the physical evidence that corroborates the Stoeckley confessions. So a second jury would have to be made up of people who did not see *Fatal Vision* — or can at least ignore its conclusions.

Whatever happens, I believe that Jeffrey MacDonald has not yet received a fair trial. I believe he deserves one — and the American people deserve to know the full story.

Sometimes a trial is noteworthy for what it failed to do, rather than for what it did. The trial of Jeffrey MacDonald reflects the worst of American justice. By suppressing evidence that might have proved the defendant's innocence, the prosecution denied MacDonald the due process of law. By refusing to reopen the case and give MacDonald a real trial, at which jurors could hear all the evidence, the appellate courts elevated "finality" and "closure" above the search for truth.

1. Eric Foner and John A. Garraty, eds., *The Reader's Companion to American History* (Boston: Houghton Mifflin, 1991), p. 1120.

2. Howard Zinn, *A People's History of the United States: 1492–Present* (New York: Harper Perennial, 1995), p. 467.

3. Foner and Garraty, p. 1120.

4. Zinn, p. 474.

5. Alan Dershowitz, *The Best Defense* (New York: Vintage Books, 1983), p. 207.

6. John F. Bannan and Rosemary S. Bannan, *Law, Morality and Vietnam: The Peace Militants and the Courts* (Bloomington: Indiana University Press, 1974), p. 88.

7. Bannan and Bannan, p. 3.

8. Dershowitz, p. 207.

9. David Rudenstine, *The Day the Presses Stopped: A History of the Pentagon Papers Case* (Berkeley: University of California Press, 1996), p. 5.

10. Alan M. Dershowitz, *Supreme Injustice: How the High Court Hijacked Election 2000* (New York: Oxford University Press, 2001), pp. 191–92.

11. *Ibid.*, p. 192.

12. Allan M. Winkler, "Modern America: The 1960s, 1970s, and 1980s," in *Encyclopedia of American Social History*, vol. 1, ed. Mary Kupiec Cayton, Elliot J. Gorn, and Peter W. Williams (New York: Charles Scribner's Sons, 1993), p. 228.

13. *Ibid.*

14. *Ibid.*, p. 229.

15. Joe McGinniss, *Fatal Vision* (New York: Putnam, 1983); Jerry Allen Potter and Fred Bost, *Fatal Justice: Reinventing the MacDonald Murders* (New York: W. W. Norton and Co., 1995).

16. Jessica Mitford, *The Trial of Dr. Spock* (New York: Alfred A. Knopf, 1969), p. 55.

17. *Ibid.*, p. 56.

18. *Ibid.*, p. 71.

19. *Ibid.*, p. 161.

20. *Ibid.*, pp. 160–61.

21. *Ibid.*, p. 104.

22. *Ibid.*, p. 70.

23. *Ibid.*, p. 71.

24. *Ibid.*, p. 162.

25. *Ibid.*, p. 198.

26. *Ibid.*, p. 236.

27. Jason Epstein, *The Great Conspiracy Trial* (New York: The Notable Trials Library, 1998), p. 213.

28. *Ibid.*, pp. 313–14.

29. *Ibid.*, p. 266.

30. *Ibid.*, p. 400.

31. Douglas Linder, "The Chicago Seven Conspiracy Trial," in *Famous American Trials: "The Chicago Seven" Trial, 1969–1970* (2003), www.law.umkc.edu/faculty/projects/ftrials/Chicago7/Account.html.

32. Epstein, p. 101.

33. Lieutenant General W. R. Peers, *The My Lai Inquiry* (New York: The Notable Trials Library, 1993), pp. 173–77, 180; George C. Herring, *America's Longest War*, 2nd ed. (New York: Knopf, 1986), p. 242.

34. Peers, p. 209.

35. *Ibid.*, p. 251.

36. *Ibid.*

37. Douglas Linder, "An Introduction to the My Lai Courts-Martial," in *Famous American Trials: The My Lai Courts-Martial, 1970* (2003), www.law.umkc.edu/faculty/projects/ftrials/mylai/Myl_intro.html.

38. Mark Gado, "The Verdict," in *Into the Dark: The My Lai Massacre* (2003), www.crimelibrary.com/notorious_murders/mass/lai/verdict_12.html?sect=8.

39. I was one of the lawyers for Senator Gravel in the complicated series of legal proceedings growing out of the publication of the "Gravel Edition" of the Pentagon Papers.

40. Sanford J. Ungar, *The Papers and the Papers* (New York: The Notable Trials Library, 1996), p. 229.

41. *Ibid.*, p. 235.

42. *Ibid.*, p. 238.

43. *Ibid.*, pp. 230, 236.

44. *Ibid.*, p. 236.

45. *Ibid.*, p. 245.

46. *Ibid.*, p. 243.

47. *Ibid.*

48. *Ibid.*, pp. 248–49.

49. *Ibid.*, p. 248.

50. Marian Faux, *Roe v. Wade: The Untold Story of the Landmark Supreme Court Decision That Made Abortion Legal* (New York: The Notable Trials Library, 1994), pp. 231–36.

51. *Ibid.*, p. 224.

52. *Ibid.*

53. *Ibid.*, p. 247.

54. *Ibid.*, p. 250.

55. *Ibid.*

56. Quoted in Peter Matthiessen, *In the Spirit of Crazy Horse* (New York: The Viking Press, 1991) p. xl.

57. *Ibid.*, p. 435.

58. John W. Sayer, *Ghost Dancing the Law: The Wounded Knee Trials* (Delanco, NJ: The Notable Trials Library, 2001), p. 34.

59. Zinn, pp. 524–25.

60. 383 F. Supp. 389.

61. Matthiesen, p. 524.

62. Bernard Schwartz, *Behind Bakke: Affirmative Action and the Supreme Court* (New York: The Notable Trials Library, 1995), p. 92.

63. *Ibid.*, p. 88.

64. *Ibid.*, p. 154.

65. *Bakke*, 438 U.S. 265, 316 (1978).

66. *Ibid.*, p. 316.

67. William Gaylin, *The Killing of Bonnie Garland* (New York: Penguin Books, 1983), pp. 211–12.

68. Of course those who read the rebuttal to *Fatal Vision*, Potter and Bost's *Fatal Justice*, may have a very different opinion.

69. Potter and Bost, p. 183.

Part XIII

The 1980s and 1990s

B Y THE 1980s AND 1990s, media coverage of trials had become "tabloid justice."[1] The decisions most influencing the hearts and minds of the nation were decided as much in the Court of Public Opinion as in the rightward-shifting Supreme Court. Much of this change was as the result of the impact of television on American society. As one commentator has noted: "Within less than a generation after its introduction in the late 1930's, television had woven itself completely into the fabric of all modern societies. By the 1990's, Americans spent about ¼ of their lives watching television, and on average, American households had at least one set tuned on for seven hours each day."[2]

Television soon became an isolating force in local communities, with a couch-potato lifestyle usurping individual contact with friends, print media, and radio. In 1970, 75 percent of Americans read a newspaper daily; by 1998 that number had dropped to 43 percent.[3] According to a report compiled by Professors Richard Fox and Robert Van Sickel, there were 343 news segments covering the 1993 murder trial of the young and rich Menendez brothers on the three major networks, as opposed to only 277 segments covering the Iran-Contra affair just three years earlier.[4] The O. J. Simpson trial garnered a staggering 2,237 segments from 1994 to 1997.[5] By the start of the last two decades of the twentieth century, television news had become America's primary source of information.

The most important consequence of the rise to primacy of television news in American life was that entertainment programmers were now setting the information agenda. As opposed to some other nations, the American television industry is primarily a private enterprise — ratings and advertiser dollars determine programming decisions. "It is not much of a secret anymore . . .

that the agenda formerly known as tabloid has picked up and moved — to the front page of the *New York Times*. After years of being disdained by the mainstream media, traditional supermarket-tabloid subjects have become everybody's subjects, whether it's JonBenet, Monica, O. J., Princess Di — or for that matter, diet and health tips."[6]

By the "last decade of the twentieth century television continued to be a defining characteristic of modern life."[7] Therefore, whatever drew the highest ratings drew the most coveted time slots, and for much of the 1980s and 1990s, courtroom drama — be it fictitious, such as *L.A. Law*, or real, such as the trials of the Menendez brothers — drew big audiences. And not just any crimes were in the spotlight, but the most shocking offenses with the most salacious or glamorous of settings.

Celebrity had been a fixture of American society since the advent of the motion picture. MGM's claim to fame in the 1930s and 1940s was not so much in the quality of its product, but in its having "more stars than there are in the heavens." Fan magazines and newsreels accompanying films chronicled the lives and loves of everyone from Bette Davis and Joan Crawford to the young Ronald Reagan and Jane Wyman.

What changed as the twentieth century drew to a close, however, was the dominance of celebrity on the information agenda. In a Pew Survey, significantly more Americans were able to identify JonBenet Ramsey than Dick Cheney; more were able to identify Judge Ito than Chief Justice Rehnquist; and more were able to identify William Kennedy Smith than Al Gore.[8] What do the results of this survey tell us about contemporary America? One commentator has put it as follows: "Without satisfactory opportunities to know people, Americans rely upon the media to supply important information about human frailties and strengths, as told through coverage of celebrities. The media's urge to tear down the celebrity, usually over drug, monetary or sexual misdeeds, even before he or she has achieved star status, enacts what Fowles calls Americans' 'latent destructive urge' to find 'gratification when an idol is rocked.'"[9]

The 1980s began with the trial of Jean Harris for murdering the famous Scarsdale diet doctor, Herman Tarnower. This sensational trial divided men and women in much the same way that the O. J. Simpson case would later divide whites and blacks.

The Scarsdale trial was followed a year later by the insanity trial of John Hinckley, who had shot, and nearly killed, President Reagan. The verdict — not guilty by reason of insanity — outraged most Americans and prompted changes in the laws governing the insanity defense.

The trials of Claus von Bülow were the first carried live on television from gavel to gavel. The prosecutor recognized the impact the trials would have on the public: "It [the von Bülow trial] has money, sex, drugs; it has Newport, New York and Europe; it has nobility; it has maids, butlers, a gardener. . . . Most people can't see inside. This case is where the little man has a chance to glimpse inside and see how the rich live."[10]

The reversal of von Bülow's conviction merited first-page coverage in the *New York Times*. Following the von Bülow trials, a series of star-studded trials left their mark on popular conceptions of the justice system in this country. From Lorena Bobbitt to the Clinton-Lewinsky scandal, television heralded a new era of gavel-to-gavel coverage by the mainstream print and television media of the sort of scandals that had once been the preserve of the tabloids.[11] A wealthy heiress, her dying husband, and a hotel empire; a member of America's royal family and a beachfront sexual encounter; a handsome, charismatic sports car entrepreneur and corruption; an all-American athlete, two murders, and the race card — each of these cases could have easily been lifted from an episode of *As the World Turns*: "These days, it's hard to tell when you're watching *Inside Politics* and when you're tuned to *Melrose Place*. Both feature unhealthy quantities of lust, lies, betrayal and adultery, though the latter has more believable scripts."[12]

With the advent of twenty-four-hour news channels, as well as the proliferation of "infotainment" programming such as *Inside Edition, Dateline,* and *Hard Copy,* the public was able to get reality and sensationalism in lurid detail. One commentator coined the phrase *court news as miniseries* to describe this new phenomenon.[13] No miniseries, not even *The Thorn Birds,* approached the drama of the O. J. Simpson trial. From the slow-speed chase to the civil trial verdict, the Simpson trial redefined the nation's understanding — for better or worse — of the legal process. The trial was covered around the world; the police prepared for riots following the criminal verdict; and the civil verdict preempted the State of the Union Address in March 1997 on CNN and MSNBC, and received a crawler on ABC.[14]

The relationship between race and crime became another important theme in the 1990s. Alleged prosecutorial and police misconduct in such racially divisive cases as the Central Park Jogger, Bernhard Goetz, Rodney King, and O. J. Simpson helped widen the gaps in an already divided society. "The media emphasis on sensational images clearly embraced the principle of entertainment over measured reporting . . . [thus] tap[ping] into divisive social fault lines in U.S. culture."[15]

The positive consequences of such pervasive trial coverage are obvious: Americans can learn more and more about the trial and appeal processes. But there may be negative consequences as well. According to Professor Barry Scheck: "the perennial tension that lies at the heart of the fair trial/free press controversy concerns the desire of people in the press to know privileged information that should not be disclosed if you're going to have a fair trial." The extensive in-court camera coverage of the O. J. Simpson criminal trial contributed to something of a backlash, with cameras being prohibited in the Simpson civil trial, the Menendez brothers' second trial, and other noteworthy trials. As the courts seek a balance between freedom of the press and the integrity of the judicial process, public confidence in our criminal justice system continues to erode: In another Fox and Van Sickel study, after the Simpson criminal verdict, 75 percent of those polled felt less confident in the criminal justice system, and 70 percent felt less confident in the system as a result of the failure to indict JonBenet Ramsey's killer.[16] But the long-term effects of these trends remain to be seen. As one commentator has noted: "When news oozes twenty-four hours a day it's not really news anymore. The TV becomes ambient noise. The newspaper becomes wallpaper. Finding the patterns of importance becomes hard. It's easier — and more profitable — just to make the consumer gape."[17]

The Clinton impeachment case represented the merger of sexual sensationalism and politics. It posed the important constitutional question of whether a president's effort to cover up sexual indiscretions rose to the level of an impeachable offense. The House of Representatives concluded that it did, but the Senate, by a tie vote — a two-thirds vote is needed to remove a president — acquitted Clinton. The millennium ended on this sour note, but it was only a prelude to the next millennium, which began with the most corrupt decision in the history of our Supreme Court.

The Trial of Jean Harris for the Scarsdale Diet Doctor Murder

Date: March 10, 1980
Location: Scarsdale, New York
Defendant: Jean Harris, headmistress of the Madeira girls' school
Charge: Murder in the second degree
Verdict: Guilty
Sentence: Fifteen years in prison

On March 10, 1980, Jean Harris, better known as headmistress "Integrity Jean" of the high-class Madeira girls' school, shot and killed her longtime lover, Herman Tarnower, author of the best-selling book *The Scarsdale Diet*. Harris admitted to the act of killing — the question was one of intent.

The days preceding the crime were not good ones for Jean Harris. She had been given a bad review by the board of governors of the Madeira girls' school, which was considering her dismissal. She ran out of the antidepressants that Tarnower had prescribed for her and was having difficulty having the prescription refilled. Then students (leaders of the student council, no less) were caught with marijuana paraphernalia and expelled. Rather than applauding the headmistress for taking the hard line with the students, the parents of the expelled girls began hurling insults, calling Harris's governance techniques "Gestapo-like" and hypocritical.[18] The so-called trigger event for Harris came when one of her favorite students wrote to express her disappointment in Harris's decision to expel the girls. According to Harris herself, "It sort of put a box on my life."[19] She began composing a will and unearthed the gun she had bought some time earlier with which she had planned to kill herself.

The infamous "Scarsdale letter," which Harris wrote Tarnower not long before the shooting, was presented by the defense as evidence of Harris's extreme emotional distress, possibly even paranoia and irrationality. To the prosecution it was proof positive of Harris's intent to kill her lover. The letter does catalog a series of infidelities, recriminations, and other wrongs allegedly done to Harris, which punctuated Harris and Tarnower's long and tumultuous relationship. Indeed, the shooting did not surprise some who were close to the couple; one friend commented: "Oh, my God, it's finally happened."[20]

What can be said of Harris's physical state is that she was experiencing the extreme stages of withdrawal from Desoxyn when she composed the "Scarsdale letter" and when she arrived at Tarnower's home the night of March 10. Harris stated that the weekend leading up to the Monday shooting was an indescribable blur, which led not only to mental disorientation but even total disassociation.[21]

The central question of the trial was intent: Did Jean Harris deliberately murder Herman Tarnower, or was his death, as defense attorney Joel Aurnou argued, a tragic accident during a struggle for the gun? According to Harris's testimony, when she arrived at the house in Scarsdale at 10:40 PM, Tarnower refused to speak to her; after she gathered a few of her items from the dressing room, she went into what she described as "her" bathroom, where she found numerous items belonging to Lynne Tryforos — Tarnower's younger and blonder current girlfriend. Harris began throwing Tryforos's things out of the bathroom, and it was, according to Harris, at this time that Tarnower first hit her.

The prosecution grilled Harris about her feelings concerning Tryforos and tried to paint a picture of someone consumed by jealousy:

PROSECUTOR:	"What did you think of Lynne Tryforos?"
HARRIS:	"I think she denigrated him, and she gave me a great deal of trouble with my own integrity."
PROSECUTOR:	"You felt she did not have the education you had?"
HARRIS:	"It wasn't a matter of education, Mr. Bolen. It was a question of —"
PROSECUTOR:	"Breeding?"
HARRIS:	"Perhaps just common sense and taste."
PROSECUTOR:	"Lynne Tryforos had no taste?"
HARRIS:	"I didn't say that. You did."
PROSECUTOR:	"Well, did Lynne Tryforos have taste?"
HARRIS:	"I think you have to judge people's taste by some of the things they do. I think writing to a man for eight years, when he is traveling with another woman, is rather tasteless."[22]

Harris testified that after this, she removed the gun from her purse and put it to her temple. As Tarnower tried to knock the gun away from her head, he was shot in the hand. After a struggle, Tarnower got control of the gun while Harris kneeled on the floor. There was then a second struggle, a seemingly violent one as evidenced by the amount of bruising Harris suffered. By the end of that struggle, Tarnower was dead.

At the trial, the prosecution's medical expert argued against Harris's account of the shooting, stating that Tarnower was shot while lying down. The defense medical expert contradicted this theory, asserting that "the same bullet that went through Tarnower's hand went into his chest" during a struggle.[23] Harris, testifying on her own behalf, swore that the shooting was accidental. The prosecutor grilled her on cross-examination, but she continued to maintain that her only purpose for having the gun was suicide: "I wasn't the slightest bit interested about the gun except filling up the gun with bullets to shoot myself, so I could simply shoot myself. I didn't know what he told me, and I didn't listen, and I didn't ask. The only thing I asked him was, how do you put a bullet in this gun?"[24]

The prosecutor pressed her on cross-examination:

PROSECUTOR:	"Mrs. Harris, isn't it a fact that Dr. Tarnower had told you he preferred Lynne Tryforos over you? . . . Isn't it a fact that during the morning telephone conversation you had, he told you that you had lied?"
HARRIS:	"No!"
PROSECUTOR:	". . . He told you that you had cheated?"
HARRIS:	"No!"
PROSECUTOR:	". . . He told you that you were going to inherit $240,000?"
HARRIS:	"No. He didn't."
PROSECUTOR:	"Isn't it a fact that he told you, and I quote, 'Goddammit, Jean, I want you to stop bothering me!'"
HARRIS:	"No, he didn't! How long can this go on — forever?"
PROSECUTOR:	"Isn't it a fact, Mrs. Harris, that on March 10, 1980, you intended to kill Dr. Tarnower, and then kill yourself, because if you couldn't have Dr. Tarnower, no one would? Yes or no, Mrs. Harris?"
HARRIS:	"No, Mr. Bolen."[25]

At the conclusion of the trial, Harris's defense lawyer requested that the judge not include the lesser charge of voluntary manslaughter in his final instructions to the jury. Instead, the jurors were left with the charge of murder in either the first (meaning premeditated) or second degree. According to Aurnou, "Usually it's the defense lawyer who asks to have lesser included offenses charged. In this instance, the DA will ask it, and I will insist that they not be. I want to force that jury to choose either murder or acquittal, no compromise."[26]

After eight days of deliberation, the jury returned a verdict of guilty of murder in the second degree. Harris was looking at fifteen years to life. When she finally rose and spoke to the judge prior to hearing her sentence, Harris challenged the jury to find evidence of premeditation on her part anywhere in the record:

> I want to say that I did not murder Dr. Herman Tarnower, that I loved him very much and I never wished him ill, and I am innocent as I stand here. For you or for Mr. Bolen to arrange my life so that I will be in a cage for the rest of it, and that every time I walk outside I will have iron around my wrists . . . [this] is not justice; it is a travesty of justice. The people in that jury were told Mr. Bolen will prove to you beyond a reasonable doubt that Mrs. Harris intended to kill Dr. Tarnower. In their many statements, and a number of them decided to become public figures now, and they have written for the newspaper and they have been on television shows and they have been on radio shows in every single statement they have said, in essence, Mrs. Harris took the stand and didn't prove to us she was innocent, and therefore we find her guilty. In the 10,000 pages of testimony that have been taken here, there isn't a page, there isn't a paragraph and there isn't a sentence in which anyone suggests, in which the prosecution suggests, how I was guilty of intentionally hurting Dr. Tarnower. And certainly for [Mr. Bolen] to suggest that he cannot adequately articulate how people feel the loss, that is really gratuitous, because he certainly doesn't have to explain it to me. No one in the world feels that loss more than I do. I am not guilty, your Honor.[27]

On March 20, 1981, Jean Harris was sentenced to fifteen years in prison. Each appeal was lost, but on December 29, 1992, after she had served twelve years of her sentence and suffered two heart attacks, New York governor Mario Cuomo commuted Harris's sentence. Not one to be idle, Harris had published three books while in prison and worked at the Bedford Prison's Children's Center giving parenting classes. Today she continues to speak about prison life for women and raise money for the education of children of inmates.

Jean Harris was unfortunate in the timing of her case. Had she been tried a decade later — when juries were more sensitized to the plight of abused and battered women — she might have been regarded by jurors as a woman suffering from "battered woman's syndrome." But her trial took place before the "abuse excuse" became a common defense tactic. Moreover, her lawyer's decision to go for broke denied the jury the power to reach a compromise decision. Hers was a notable case, because it focused public attention on abused women who kill and laid the foundation for many subsequent cases that reached different results.

The Attempted Assassination of President Reagan by John Hinckley Jr.

Date: *March 30, 1981*
Location: *District of Columbia*
Defendant: *John Hinckley Jr.*
Charge: *Attempted murder of President Ronald Reagan*
Verdict: *Not guilty by reason of insanity*
Sentence: *Confinement at Saint Elizabeths maximum-security mental ward*

On March 30, 1981, as he was entering the Washington Hilton Hotel for an AFL-CIO meeting, President Ronald Wilson Reagan was shot at by a young man named John Hinckley Jr. Four people were hit. (By coincidence, I was delivering a speech at that very moment at the Hilton.) A ricocheting bullet hit the president in the chest; he spent twelve days in the hospital.[28] While Secret Service agent Timothy McCarthy was only slightly wounded, the others injured in the attack were not so lucky: Press Secretary James Brady was paralyzed by a shot to the head from which he has still not fully recovered, while DC police officer Thomas Delahanty suffered permanent nerve damage in his neck and had to retire on full disability.[29]

Brady and his wife, Sarah, have since lobbied for stricter gun control legislation — including establishing the Brady Center to

Prevent Gun Violence — leading to passage of the Brady bill requiring background checks on purchasers and waiting periods before weapons could be bought.

Hinckley had a long history of mental illness and an obsession with the actress Jodie Foster whom, he said, he was trying to impress with his bold actions. He knew that he was shooting at the president and his entourage, but his lawyer claimed that he did not really appreciate or understand the nature of what he was doing.

The trial itself was a battle of the experts, with eminent psychiatrists opining with equal certainty that Hinckley was sane and insane. Dr. Park Elliott Dietz, expert for the government, testified that Hinckley had the substantial capacity to appreciate the wrongfulness of his conduct. He emphasized that Hinckley had "concealed successfully all of his stalking from his parents, from his brother, from his sister, from his brother-in-law, and from his doctor, including hiding his weapons, hiding his ammunition, and misleading them about his travels and his plans. This concealment indicates that he appreciated the wrongfulness of his plans."[30] Dr. Dietz also pointed to the fact that in his letter to Foster, Hinckley said that he could be killed by the Secret Service during his attempt, which was an indication that he appreciated the Secret Service might shoot him for his wrongdoing. On the other hand, Dr. William Carpenter Jr., the defense expert, testified that Hinckley lacked the substantial capacity to appreciate the wrongfulness of his actions. Dr. Carpenter claimed that although Hinckley intellectually knew what he was doing was illegal, "on the emotional side of appreciation" he was not concerned about the impact of his actions on the victims; thus his emotional drives concerning Foster "weighed far heavier in his emotional appreciation" and dominated his knowledge that his act was illegal.[31] In another area of disagreement, Dr. Dietz testified that Hinckley had a substantial capacity to conform his conduct to the law: "His ability to wait, when he did not have a clear shot of the President on the President's way into the Hilton is further evidence of his ability to conform his behavior. A man driven, a man out of control, would not have the capacity to wait at that moment for the best shot."[32] On the other hand, Dr. Carpenter testified that "the driven quality to his experiences, the frantic activity that he had become involved in, his determination to end his own life, . . . the lack of anchor[s] potentially holding him somewhat in contact with reality" rendered him substantially unable to conform his conduct to the law.[33] The burden of proof in the District of Columbia was on the prosecution to prove that the defendant was sane at the time of the crime. It failed to satisfy this burden, and the defendant was acquitted by reason of insanity and committed indefinitely to a mental hospital.

Until recently, Hinckley's repeated requests to leave the hospital were rejected by federal judges, despite Hinckley's claims to have "great remorse for the pain I inflicted on so many people [with this] crazy assassination attempt."[34] In December of 2003 a federal judge ruled, over the objections of government officials and Reagan family members, that Hinckley was mentally stable enough to leave the hospital for unsupervised visits with his family, subject to strict conditions.

The Hinckley case is important for several reasons: Had he succeeded in assassinating President Reagan, he might have changed the course of world history. That he came so close to doing so makes this case compelling. Moreover, his acquittal on the grounds of insanity altered the law of insanity in this country. The verdict was so unpopular (and misunderstood) that it resulted in major changes to the law of insanity throughout the country. Indeed, the Reagan administration began a move, followed by many legislatures and courts around the country, to erode and eventually eviscerate the insanity defense altogether. Before the Hinckley acquittal, many states had liberalized the traditional M'Naghten Rule, which required the jury to find, essentially, that the defendant did not know right from wrong. In its place, they had adopted standards that allowed juries to acquit if the government failed to prove beyond a reasonable doubt that the crime was not "a product of mental disease or defect" or that the defendant could not reasonably conform his conduct to the requirements of the law. Since the Hinckley trial, very few defendants have been able to invoke an insanity defense successfully because the criteria for acquittal have become more stringent, harking back to M'Naghten and several variants. A verdict of guilty but mentally ill has made it easier for juries to split the difference and convict without rejecting the psychiatric evidence. Easing, or shifting, the burden of proof has also invited convictions in close cases. This process mirrored one that had taken place in England a century and a half earlier, following the insanity acquittal of a man who had tried to kill Queen Victoria. It clearly continues to this day.

The Trials and Appeal of Claus von Bülow

Date: 1982–85
Location: Newport and Providence, Rhode Island
Defendant: Claus von Bülow
Charge: Assault with intent to kill
Verdict: Guilty at first trial, reversed on appeal; not guilty at second trial
Sentence: Twenty-year sentence

The von Bülow trial was among the first to be covered live on television. The appeal was the first to be televised. The case was covered internationally. Von Bülow's original conviction, its reversal on appeal, and his subsequent acquittal were all front-page news. Nonevents — such as the emergence of witnesses who never testified — became headlines. Even now, almost two decades after its denouement, the von Bülow case is still receiving coverage, despite the fact that Claus von Bülow himself has retired to the obscurity of a very private life in England and his comatose wife remains secluded in a private hospital room.

I have never quite understood why the von Bülow case so captivated the public's imagination and the media's interest. There is nothing extraordinary about the cast of characters, except that they were very rich. Until the case became the focus of media attention, few people had heard of the von Bülows, the von

Auerspergs, or any of the other dramatis personae. Claus von Bülow, a strikingly tall and attractive man with a dry sense of humor and a somewhat mysterious past, lived the life of a quite ordinary rich man, with a low profile. He worked occasionally, but mostly he lived a wealthy, though mundane, life behind the high walls of the family's Newport mansion and the guarded doors of their Fifth Avenue residence. His heiress wife, Sunny, never worked. She simply lived off her inheritance, appeared bored, and, according to acquaintances, *was* boring. Her two children, by a former marriage to a philandering "prince," were, by all accounts, spoiled and vapid. Claus and Sunny's only child, a young teenager at the time of the alleged crimes, was sweet, innocent, and very private.

The "crime" itself — if indeed there was one — was not the stuff of tabloids: There were no axes, bullet-riddled bodies, or even bloodstains. There were simply two comas, one of which left Sunny von Bülow in a permanently vegetative state. The "whodunit" was more of a "was-anything-criminal-done-at-all." It was largely a medical and scientific mystery, which was eventually resolved by experts with fancy degrees and distinguished backgrounds. Sunny's children, and eventually the state of Rhode Island, claimed that Claus had injected his wife with insulin in an attempt to kill her. Claus, and their daughter, Cosima, maintained that Sunny's coma had been caused by illness or was self-induced.

Despite the ultimate jury verdict of not guilty, public opinion is still very much divided. A week does not go by during which some well-meaning admirer does not say to me: "You did a great job in getting that guilty SOB off. He did do it, didn't he?" It would be professionally pleasing for me to believe that it was my legal talent — and that of the other lawyers with whom I worked — that resulted in Claus von Bülow's "reversal of fortune." But I sincerely believe that there was no compelling evidence of any crime. Accordingly, we can claim little credit for the jury's correct verdict at the second trial. Innocent defendants should be acquitted, with or without good lawyers, though it does not always work out that way. But having an innocent client helps a great deal, just as it helps a doctor to have a curable patient.

If Claus von Bülow was innocent, one may be thinking, *then why was he convicted at the first trial?* Therein lies a fascinating tale, which I recount in some detail in my book *Reversal of Fortune.* Suffice it to say that there is evidence to support the following intriguing theory: Certain people believed that Claus von Bülow had injected his wife, but that he was too smart to be caught; thus, they "tampered" with the evidence and "remembered" things that did not happen in an effort to frame a man they believed to be guilty!

If von Bülow was, in fact, framed by someone who honestly, but mistakenly, believed he was guilty, that would constitute one of the most bizarre frame-ups in the annals of crime.

Because the frame-up theory was always hovering, both sides of the case — really all three sides: the prosecution, the defense, and Sunny's family (who paid for much of the investigation) — fought hard to convince the media of the righteousness of their causes. My intimate involvement in one of the most highly publicized criminal cases in American history — including the media aspect of the case — has prompted me to reflect on the interaction between this country's criminal justice system and media.

The media — television, radio, daily newspapers, magazines, and the like — has a profound impact on criminal justice. Everybody within the system understands this fact of life and attempts to manipulate the media to serve the interests of his side of a case. (The media, of course, also tries to use a case to serve its interests.) Yet nearly all the participants in a criminal case go through the charade of pretending that they are not playing to the press.

In the von Bülow case, each side battled openly to convince the Fourth Estate of the righteousness of its cause. The prosecution convened press conferences, leaked stories, and timed its news for maximum coverage. Claus von Bülow's stepchildren, who initiated the investigation against him, made the rounds of national television magazines and talk shows telling the world that they believed he was guilty. The defense, of course, tried to generate a media atmosphere favorable to Mr. von Bülow, though our role was primarily reactive. By the time I became involved (immediately after the conviction at the first trial), the prosecution's view of the case had become the standard media perspective. Part of our job was to change that perspective, so we set out quite deliberately to do precisely that.

Although the jurors who sat in judgment of — and ultimately acquitted — Claus von Bülow were sequestered during the entire trial, most of them came to the task with some knowledge of the case. They obtained that knowledge from the media. Had the defense not counterattacked, the second jury would have known only that Claus von Bülow had been unanimously convicted by one jury, that his conviction had been reversed on legal grounds, and that Rhode Island's attorney general believed there was enough evidence for a second jury to convict him. It was important, therefore, for the defense to respond to this one-sided perception by presenting our side of the story to the public via the media.

This we did by consciously writing briefs and legal memoranda that were not only legally compelling but also media-friendly. We knew that those documents had two distinct audiences: the judges and the media — and ultimately the public as well.

Trial by the press is, of course, no substitute for trial by jury. The jury eventually hears all the relevant and admissible evidence and is instructed to decide the case on that basis alone. But students of psychology understand that people — even people who take the solemn oath of jurors — perceive evidence in light of their predispositions. A juror predisposed against a defendant will hear and see the very same evidence differently from a juror predisposed in favor of that defendant. This is why no vigorous defense lawyer can afford to ignore the prosecutor's efforts to manipulate the media.

In light of recent media cases — such as von Bülow, O. J. Simpson, John DeLorean, Mike Tyson, Scott Peterson, Michael Jackson, Martha Stewart, and Kobe Bryant — critics have proposed that our country adopt the English rule that prohibits the press from reporting about ongoing criminal cases. But such a rule would not be suited to our national style (or Constitution). A press ban of the kind enforced in England would have made Watergate and other triumphs of American investigative reporting impossible, or at least far more difficult. The press performs a critical function in monitoring and exposing all three branches of our government. And the criminal justice system is an important — and a frequently abused — part of our governmental power structure. Indeed, the judiciary is the least thoroughly examined and investigated branch of our government. We need more, rather than less, reporting about criminal cases.

Moreover, the public is entitled to know about interesting cases, even if its interest is less to be informed than titillated. Censorship of any kind requires a higher degree of justification than the English offer in defense of their restriction on the press.

We pay a price for our freedom of the press. That price, however, should not be paid entirely by those accused of crime, as it would be if prosecutors were permitted to announce their accusations in the press with no opportunity for a full response by the defense. We should acknowledge the important role played by the press in our criminal justice system and recognize that the adversary system is not limited to the courtroom itself, but extends as well to the courthouse steps.

The media played a role in Claus von Bülow's first conviction.

It also played a role in his eventual acquittal. The media can distort the criminal justice system in numerous ways. In addition to filtering into the jury box and the judicial chamber, press coverage can also influence the action taken by prosecutors and defense attorneys. After all, the media can make or break a lawyer's career. Whether that lawyer's goal is elective office, more and better-paying clients, a partnership in a big firm, or simply greater public visibility, the press is an important vehicle for such ambitions. The danger, of course, is that the personally ambitious lawyer can place her own agenda before that of the client. This can happen consciously or unconsciously. Sometimes the interests of the client, whether the client is the government or the defendant, are best served by silence. But a lawyer who invokes the shield of "no comment" risks the sword of the media. This is a risk that any lawyer worth his or her salt must take, if that posture will benefit the client.

Before any lawyer decides to try a case in the media — either proactively or reactively — it is essential to consider the impact of media attention on the client's interests. Sometimes even the client does not know what is best. An incident in the von Bülow case illustrates this danger. Claus von Bülow, and his then companion Andrea Reynolds, decided — without telling the lawyers — to pose for a photo spread by German photographer Helmut Newton in the August 1985 issue of *Vanity Fair*. The magazine, which hit the stands while the second trial was in progress, showed von Bülow dressed in leather. It made a dreadful impression. We thanked our lucky stars that Rhode Island jurors do not typically read *Vanity Fair*.

Even if both lawyer and client agree that media coverage will be best for the client, it is important to remember that the media has its own agenda. No lawyer — especially no private lawyer — can hope to control the media. Government lawyers, who maintain ongoing relationships with reporters and become a pipeline for off-the-record information, have greater power to assure that they will not be burned. But reporters seeking a blockbuster story often hurt private lawyers, particularly inexperienced ones. More importantly, their clients suffer because of the press.

Finally, not every good lawyer is adept at presenting the client's best face to the media. Talking to the press is different from talking to a judge or jury. A lawyer has hours to persuade a jury, but a TV sound bite is measured in seconds. The power of the press, especially the print media and nonlive television, to edit can distort a lawyer's presentation beyond recognition. A lawyer must understand the media before putting the client's fate in its fickle hands. But sometimes the rewards are worth the risks, as they were in the von Bülow case. Without the media, there is a significant possibility that despite his innocence, Claus von Bülow might today be serving the twenty-year sentence he originally received for allegedly twice attempting to kill his wife.

Media attention in the von Bülow case has also had an impact on my life and career. It thrust me into the media limelight and resulted in a significant increase in the number of people who ask me for legal assistance. The vast majority of these people are indigent, so the media attention has not enriched me. But it has given me an opportunity to take a number of quite interesting cases that would not otherwise have come my way. Many of the "von Bülow clients" — as my staff refers to them — expect me to publicize their case as well as win it in the courtroom. I try to explain that not every case benefits by this approach, but they almost invariably respond: "You did it for von Bülow, why can't you do it for me?" Well, sometimes you can and sometimes you can't. Sometimes it works, and sometimes it doesn't.

The media is a fact of life in the American criminal justice system. It can be ignored only at great risk to clients. It can be used only at some risk to clients. Lawyers must learn to weigh those risks and decide what is best for the client. The von Bülow litigation is a case study of a modern courtroom drama that was won as much outside the courtroom as inside it.

The von Bülow trials rate inclusion in any list of notable American trials not only because of the enormous public interest they generated, but also because they showed a doubting public that an appellate reversal could result in an innocent defendant being acquitted. At the first trial nearly everyone thought von Bülow was guilty, because the state had suppressed certain notes taken by the lawyer for the victim's family. On appeal, we got the Rhode Island Supreme Court to order production of those notes, which proved that several prosecution witnesses had not told the truth at the first trial. Armed with these notes, and with more sophisticated medical testimony, the defense had little difficulty securing an acquittal from the second jury. Many observers who had previously believed that appellate reversals were based on "legal technicalities" learned that at least in some cases, an appellate reversal can contribute to a search for truth.

The John DeLorean Trial

Date: 1984
Location: Los Angeles, California
Defendant: Automobile magnate John DeLorean
Charges: Drug possession and sale
Verdict: Not guilty (entrapment)

Millions of Americans saw John Z. DeLorean engage in a cocaine deal. Yet a federal court jury unanimously acquitted him.
What is it about the law — and the jury system in particular —
that produces such a verdict? The answer is that the American
jury is more than a simple instrument for finding the facts. It is
the ultimate conscience of the American community. It speaks
for the common morality of the people, rather than for the dry
application of the law to the facts.

In this case, the jurors sent a strong message of disapproval to
the Justice Department concerning the "sting" operation
mounted against DeLorean, which said, in effect: *We don't care
what the law permits you to do, this time you went too far.* The jurors obviously believed at least some of the defense evidence —
evidence that showed a Justice Department "out to get"
DeLorean, evidence of a conniving undercover agent selectively
recording only some conversations, and evidence of a willingness to tamper with records.

There was also evidence that DeLorean willingly agreed to
participate in a huge cocaine deal. DeLorean was charged with

conspiring to obtain and distribute fifty-five pounds of cocaine; the clear motive for the transaction was that, at the time, he was trying to raise thirty million dollars to save his automobile factory from insolvency. On a tape of a meeting on September 4, 1982, the government informer is heard saying: "I mean if you don't want to do it, if you want to stop, you're not compelled to, I won't be mad, I won't be hurt, I won't be anything. If you can get the money somewhere else and it's better circumstances, I'd say do it." DeLorean replies: "Well, I want to proceed."[35] On other tapes, DeLorean volunteers to alter the books of his company to help launder a drug dealer's money, indicates that he has found two million dollars of financing from the Irish Republican Army, and toasts the success of the cocaine deal, referring to the brief- case full of cocaine as "better than gold. Gold weighs more than that, for God's sake."[36] On the basis of these facts and the appli- cable law, the jurors could easily and properly have convicted him. Had they done so, it is extremely unlikely that the higher courts would have reversed the conviction on appeal. The ap- pellate courts, and especially the Supreme Court, have been limiting the entrapment defense and rarely reverse jury verdicts. The only realistic hope for a defendant in an entrapment case these days is the occasionally sympathetic jury, such as the one selected by the lawyers in the DeLorean case.

These jurors obviously chose to focus their attention on the government's conduct rather than DeLorean's. This focus on the sordid behavior of the government is evidenced by the fact that the jury acquitted the defendant despite his unwillingness to take the witness stand to testify on his own behalf — an unusual jury response, to say the least. Although the verdict sent an im- portant message to prosecutors, it was a message of limited im- pact. One jury in one part of the country expressed its collective outrage at the particular sting operation used against DeLorean. This verdict is not a binding precedent for other judges or juries, but it could influence prosecutorial decisions.

Until the DeLorean verdict, the vast majority of juries had approved nearly every sting operation, from Abscam (the bribery operation that sent several members of Congress to prison) to the New York City Police Department's operation of a pornographic bookstore.

But the DeLorean verdict sent a chilling call for restraint to prosecutors planning major entrapment schemes. Jury verdicts in highly publicized cases, though not precedental, have a way of becoming contagious. Jurors in other "scam" cases might have become emboldened by the DeLorean verdict and its generally favorable reception. No prosecutor wants to invest millions of dollars and years of work in a scam operation and the subsequent prosecution only to see a jury nullify, and even condemn, that effort.

Prosecutors should begin to realize that they ignore the basic sense of morality, fair play, and outrage of the American jury at the risk of an occasional acquittal. This is a message to which cost-conscious (and publicity-conscious) prosecutors may have to pay increasing attention. But what message did this verdict send to John DeLorean?

It certainly should not be interpreted as an expression of praise or approval for what he did. The evidence shows DeLorean engaging in conduct that would surely have been criminal if he had been "stung" by anyone but government agents. Had his private creditors or his personal enemies conducted this sting, he doubtlessly would have been convicted.

Indeed, he would not even have been permitted to put forth an entrapment defense. That defense is available only if it is the government involved in entrapment. Despite statements by some of the jurors, the evidence strongly suggested that DeLorean committed all the acts and had all the moral culpability necessary to commit a crime. In that respect, the verdict might well have read: "guilty, but entrapped."

The "scam" has become one of the most frequently used prosecutorial tools in America. Every district attorney's office and police department uses variations on it. This trend will not be halted by a single jury verdict. There are some types of ongoing criminal activity that simply cannot be detected except by means of scams and undercover agents. And as prosecutors are fond of pointing out in justifying the use of unsavory witnesses, "When you prosecute the devil, you've got to go to hell for your witnesses."

The occasional acquittal in a highly publicized case helps strike the balance by sensitizing the American public to the potential abuses of entrapment. As one juror put it: "The way the government agents operated in this case was not appropriate, and I look forward to the future favorable impact [of this decision on the country]." Another juror added, "What they did to John DeLorean they could have done to someone in my family."[37]

Most Americans first heard of "entrapment" during the Abscam prosecutions of several congressmen and a senator, who were "tricked" into accepting bribes from a government agent disguised as an Arab sheik.

"I was entrapped" is now heard almost as often as "I was framed." But being entrapped is different from being framed, and the meaning of the entrapment defense is widely misunderstood. A person who was framed did not commit any crime; those who framed him falsified the evidence against him. He is innocent in every sense of that word. However, a person who was entrapped did commit the criminal act, but she claims that she shouldn't be convicted because the government tricked her — "scammed" her — into doing it. The difference is between the age-old cries of "I didn't do it!" and "It wasn't my fault!"

Simply put, the entrapment defense means this: The government is not permitted to talk you into committing a crime that you would not otherwise have committed. Sound pretty straightforward? It's anything but that. Let's look at the main elements of entrapment.

Only "the government" may entrap a citizen. If your boss, spouse, or enemy — any private person — talks, pressures, or tricks you into committing a crime, no entrapment defense is available. The government may prosecute you (and whoever persuaded you) for the resulting crime.

The government may trick a criminal into a crime she'd commit anyway — but under circumstances in which she can be caught and convicted. For example, if police know John Smith is a drug dealer, it's perfectly proper for an undercover "narc" to pose as a junkie and try to buy drugs from Smith. Smith is willing to sell to a real junkie, but not to an undercover cop. Smith is tricked, but properly. There are, though, some gray areas.

Consider the following scenario: An undercover policeman dresses up as a drunken street bum. He places a wallet stuffed with money in his back pocket. Seeing a teenage kid approaching, he pretends to be asleep with the wallet protruding visibly from his pocket. The kid passes by, noticing the wallet, but does nothing. The policeman loosens the wallet, making it easy to be lifted from his "sleeping" body. This time the kid goes for the bait and is caught.

Was he entrapped? It's a tough question. On the one hand, nobody made the kid do anything; the policeman just put the bait on the hook and waited. A completely honest kid wouldn't have bitten. On the other hand, the police did create a crime: They tempted a kid into committing a criminal act that he did not set out to commit. The basic question is whether it is the proper role of government to conduct periodic tests of honesty.

Nor is this merely an academic issue. Law enforcement authorities throughout the country are busy devising scams of every description. A few examples:

- New York City police ran a pornography bookstore in Times Square and even commissioned and financed the

production of an obscene movie in order to entrap organized crime members who were seeking to monopolize the
industry by extortion.

- The FBI established its own fencing warehouse in Washington, DC, and bought several million dollars' worth of
hot goods. They then turned around and sold the goods at
prices sufficiently cheap to alert the buyers that they were
stolen and arrested the buyers. (A federal prosecutor was
among those arrested for buying stolen goods.)

- The Los Angeles Police Department dressed up two police-
women as prostitutes. They arrested ninety-one customers.

- The U.S. and Russian governments recently scammed an
arms dealer into buying and transporting inoperable
surface-to-air missiles capable of destroying commercial aircraft in flight.

Not all scam operations go as smoothly, however. In one tragic
case, an undercover policeman sold drugs to an undercover
agent for a local vigilante group that was trying to rid the community of heroin. The vigilantes killed the "junkie" cop.

Sometimes the result is pure burlesque: One undercover cop
pretending to be gay arrested another undercover cop pretending
to be a gay prostitute in a Greenwich Village bar.

Other times, a scam can produce a result that seems entirely
just. A dentist is suspected of making sexual advances toward his
anesthetized patients. A policewoman posing as a patient allows
herself to be put under anesthesia as a hidden camera records
the dentist's movements. As soon as she is unconscious, the dentist begins to unbutton her blouse and is arrested.

What is it, then, that distinguishes the "good" scam from the
"bad" scam? The boundaries are hazy, depending on value judgments and matters of degree. That's precisely why it is so dan-

gerous to leave it up to individual policemen or prosecutors. There should be some objective guidelines instructing law enforcement officials as to when a scam is proper.

In Congress, a bill was drafted in the 1980s that would have required a court order — a "scam warrant" — prior to a federal scam. Law enforcement officials, to run a scam, would have to "demonstrate reasonable suspicion that [a crime] has been, is being, or is about to be committed" by the target person.

If enacted, this bill would have severely limited "fishing expeditions" or "honesty tests," but would still have permitted scams to detect ongoing crimes that would otherwise be difficult to prove. A "scam warrant" would give the courts far more control over government agents' activities. It would make it far harder for the government simply, in the words of one member of Congress, "to put out the honey pot and see which flies gather round." To date, that bill has made no progress toward enactment into law, and in the current age of terrorism, there is little likelihood that any law limiting scams will do better.

Flynt v. Falwell

Date: 1983
Location: Roanoke, Virginia; Washington, DC
Plaintiff: The Reverend Jerry Falwell
Defendant: Publisher Larry Flynt
Claims: Libel and emotional distress
Decision: The Supreme Court reversed an initial verdict for
            the plaintiff

Imagine your reaction if you were to open the pages of a nation-
ally circulated magazine to find yourself portrayed as a drunk
having sex with your mother in an outhouse. It is not surprising
that the Reverend Jerry Falwell was outraged when he saw *Hustler* magazine's parody of the popular Campari ad in which he
described "his first time." Nor is it surprising that a Virginia jury
awarded Falwell two hundred thousand dollars for the "emotional distress" he suffered.

What is surprising is that a unanimous Supreme Court — in
an opinion written by its most reactionary member, Chief Justice
William H. Rehnquist — ruled that the First Amendment fully
protects *Hustler's* gross and offensive parody, irrespective of how
much actual distress its publisher intended or caused.[38] Chief
Justice Rehnquist candidly acknowledged that he would have
preferred to find a rule that protected only the sorts of reasonable
political cartoons that appear in our daily newspapers, while condemning the kind of gross distortions *Hustler* publishes. But he

doubted whether a court could devise any standard or rule for distinguishing the reasonable from the gross.

Even more surprising than the result is the broad interpretation Justice Rehnquist gave to the constitutional right of free speech. He declared "the First Amendment recognizes no such thing as a 'false' idea."[39] Nor must the criticism of public figures be limited to "reasoned or moderate" attack; it may include "vehement, caustic, and sometimes unpleasantly sharp attacks."[40] It may also include caricature, satire, exaggeration, hyperbole, mockery, and ridicule. And, finally, the publisher may even be motivated more by "hatred or ill will" than by a genuine wish to improve or reform.

This broad interpretation gives any citizen the right to criticize presidents, governors, and senators. Indeed, Chief Justice Rehnquist cited historical examples of caustic caricatures of some of our most beloved presidents, including George Washington, Abraham Lincoln, and Teddy and Franklin Roosevelt. The interpretation also gives any citizen the right to ridicule public figures, such as the Reverend Falwell, who do not hold elective office but who "by reason of their fame, shape events in areas of concern to society at large."[41]

If hard cases make bad law, as Oliver Wendell Holmes once observed, then this case illustrates the counterpoint—that extreme cases sometimes produce extremely good law. Because the parody in this case was so extreme — so tasteless, so nasty, so personal, so maliciously motivated — only a blanket rule protecting even the most "outrageous" parodies would cover the *Hustler* parody. The *Hustler* case thus took the protection accorded by the first amendment well beyond *New York Times v. Sullivan*[42] or the Pentagon Papers case. Those cases had given broad protection to serious newspaper reports about or commenting on core political issues central to the workings of democracy, so long as material was not false and published with "malice" or "reckless disregard" for its truth. *Hustler* expanded this protection to trashy humor — even maliciously provocative humor — as long as it was clear that it was fictional humor, rather than purported fact. The message to lower courts is, therefore, far clearer than it would have been had the parody at issue been within the mainstream of political cartoons. The rule now is that if the *Hustler* parody is protected, then virtually "anything goes," since it is almost impossible to imagine anything worse.

Perhaps that is what Larry Flynt had in mind in some perverse way. He surely wanted to go farther than anyone had previously gone in insulting a public figure — and he probably succeeded. Of such gross stuff is great constitutional law made.

This case also illustrates an important point that many lawyers fail to understand. Arguing a constitutional case before the Supreme Court is not the reward for having argued — or even won — the case in the lower courts. It takes a special kind of expertise to influence the justices, if they can be influenced at all, especially in areas — such as the First Amendment — where their views are fairly well formed.

The attorney for Falwell, Norman Roy Grutman, did not understand, or did not act on, this point. Grutman was a legal gunslinger for hire. He made his reputation representing *Penthouse* magazine and its publisher, Robert Guccione. Then he switched sides and represented Guccione's archenemies, Jerry Falwell and the Moral Majority. In an earlier case, when he was representing Guccione against Falwell, Grutman referred to his soon-to-be client as "Foulwell."

There may be some virtue in the gun-for-hire approach to lawyering — at least as long as there is no conflict of interest — but there is little virtue in a lawyer not realizing, or acting on, his own professional limitations as an effective advocate.

Grutman simply did not seem to understand how to argue a constitutional case to the High Court. He was trying to seduce the justices with his pretty words, rather than trying to educate them with thoughtful ideas. This may sometimes work in front of a passive jury; it rarely works in front of a "hot" appellate bench that is shooting questions and expecting helpful answers.

Grutman rambled on about "Aristotelian" interpretations of "fact." He talked about "interesting philosophical questions that we could explore endlessly," and he tried to flatter Justice White by suggesting that one of his recent dissents "should become the law of the land," to which White responded, "I doubt it."

Grutman also overargued his position, responding in the affirmative when asked whether humorously "portraying a Baptist minister as having taken a shot or two before he went on to the pulpit"[43] would qualify as the kind of heinous parody that would be beyond constitutional protection.

Grutman also committed the cardinal sin of quarreling with the jury verdict and proposing an interpretation of it that insulted the intelligence of both the jurors and the justices. The jurors were asked to decide whether the *Hustler* parody was intended to describe actual facts, namely that Falwell really had sex with his mother, as distinguished from hurling an insulting epithet at him, namely "Motherf____r."[44] The jury quite understandably concluded that the parody was not intended to be taken literally. But Grutman tried to persuade the justices that the jurors had concluded that the parody was a "statement of fact." This is how Grutman put it in a colloquy with Justice O'Connor:

"Well, Mr. Grutman . . . the jury said this can't be reasonably viewed as making a factual allegation."

"I disagree, Justice O'Connor, and if you'll give me a moment — that is the easy way of looking at it, but that's not what they said. The question they answered is, can this be understood as describing actual — meaning truth — actual facts about the plaintiff or actual events in which the plaintiff participated? And they said no. That to me means that they said this is not a true statement of fact, but it's nonetheless a statement of fact for the purposes of New York Times [v. Sullivan] or for the purposes of this case."[45]

Then Grutman proceeded to his discussion of Aristotelian interpretation of facts and issues that could be explored endlessly. It is one of the least effective answers I have ever read in High Court argument. In the end, Grutman seemed to have no constitutional theory supporting his side of the case. His words sounded more like a bombastic jury summation than a thoughtful appellate argument.

Every lawyer in America who has dreamed of arguing a case before the Supreme Court should read the transcript of this argument. It shows how a dream can become a nightmare if you are not prepared for the very different experience that a High Court argument provides.

Every American who cares about freedom and who enjoys a good laugh at the expense of a politician, a preacher, or a pundit should read the decision in the great outhouse case as well.

The Bernhard Goetz Case

Date: 1987
Location: New York City, New York
Defendant: Bernhard Goetz
Charges: Attempted murder, unlawful gun possession
Verdict: Not guilty of attempted murder; guilty of gun charge
Sentence: Imprisonment for one year

The case of Bernhard Goetz, the New York "subway vigilante," captured the imagination of a society fearful of random urban crime. It had everything from racial conflict, to gun control, to the limits of self-defense, to jury nullification. It was a metaphor for urban life in the 1980s. The Goetz case continues to fascinate even today, even as urban crime appears to be on the decline.

Bernhard Goetz was an angry victim of what he perceived as random black-on-white violence. He told friends that he had been mugged four years before his subway confrontation and had sworn revenge against black street thugs: "Sooner or later, I'm going to get them," he had boasted.[46]

Armed with an illegally possessed pistol, a quick-draw holster, and specially prepared bullets, Goetz entered the New York subway system each day prepared to do battle with the enemy. Inevitably, he got his chance. On the Saturday before Christmas, 1984, just after high noon, Goetz boarded a downtown train and seated himself next to four black teenagers. One of the youths greeted Goetz with, "How are ya?" Another asked — demanded — "Give me five dollars." Instead Goetz pulled out his gun and started shooting at the black men, injuring all four, one of them permanently. Goetz then escaped onto the subway tracks and was not heard from for several days, lending an additional aura of mystery to his vigilantism.

In the meantime, the public began to learn a considerable amount about the four wounded black teenagers. They were obviously up to no good. In their pockets were found screwdrivers; a rumor spread that they were "sharpened" for use against people rather than vending machines. They each had criminal records for offenses ranging from petty theft, to disorderly conduct, to armed robbery. Goetz, of course, could not have known all this simply by looking at them. But it is certainly possible that he correctly perceived their criminal intentions from their aggressive demeanor.

Goetz soon surrendered himself, setting the stage for a courtroom confrontation in which the venerable rules of self-defense would be placed on trial, and in which the jurors (some of them subway riders themselves) would be asked to adapt these rules to the reality of the underground war zone called the New York subway system.

In the beginning, the case was triangular, with three different and conflicting sets of parties, advocates, and perspectives. Bernhard Goetz hired famed New York attorney Barry Slotnick, who was not only his advocate in court but also a firm believer in — and media advocate for — Goetz's brand of vigilante justice. The most seriously injured of the black youths retained the equally famous and equally ideological (though on the opposite side) radical lawyer William Kunstler to sue Goetz and to put pressure on prosecutors to charge him with attempted murder. Finally, there was the district attorney of Manhattan, Robert Morgenthau.

The first time Morgenthau presented the case to a grand jury, the jurors declined to indict Goetz for attempted murder. Although Morgenthau presented a weak case, he denied reports that he had not "pushed" for an indictment. He then added, "We don't ever push a grand jury to return an indictment."[47] Eventually, public opinion pressed Morgenthau to try again. This time the grand jury did indict Goetz on charges of attempted murder and illegal possession of an unregistered handgun.

After a long and contentious trial — in which the defense brilliantly succeeded in re-creating the fears that a subway rider would feel in being confronted by four youths up to no good — the jury returned a verdict of not guilty on charges of attempted murder, and guilty on a charge of criminal possession of a weapon.

Though the verdict reflected a degree of jury nullification, since under the New York law of self-defense it would be difficult to conclude that all the shots were fired defensively, it also reflected a degree of common sense. Goetz was found guilty of the crime that he had committed with full premeditation: namely, carrying an illegally owned gun onto the subway. He was found not guilty of using that gun under the pressures of what he believed was a potentially dangerous assault on him. The jurors were not prepared to second-guess his spontaneous decision to err on the side of disproportionate self-protection during the split second he had to make up his mind on whether to become a victim or an assailant.

Luck, of course, played a major role in the outcome of the Goetz case. Several of the bullets he fired ricocheted after striking or missing their intended targets. If one of those bullets had ended up wounding or killing an innocent bystander, the reaction of the public — and jury — to Goetz's vigilantism would have been entirely different, even though Goetz's acts would have been morally identical, since he had no control over the ricocheting bullets.

The rules of self-defense can never be stated with precision. At bottom, they are only guidelines for jury action. Accordingly, they inevitably invite a wide latitude of jury discretion. In every age and in every place, the specific content of these millennia-old rules will vary with the temper of the community. The Goetz verdict, with its mixed messages about guns and their use, is a keen reflection of the fears and hopes of one metropolis during an age of increasing violence, decreasing faith in law enforcement, and simmering racial tension. It tells us more about life in the American city during the 1980s than about the venerable rules of self-defense.

The McMartin Case

Date: 1983
Location: Manhattan Beach, California
Defendants: Seven members of the McMartin preschool staff,
              age twenty-eight to eighty
Charge: Child sexual abuse
Verdict: Not guilty

The McMartin preschool "child abuse" case was the Salem witch trial of the twentieth century. Hysteria surrounded vague charges of sexual abuse. A lynch mob mentality, encouraged by police and prosecutors, created an atmosphere that made a fair trial nearly impossible. The media contributed to the frenzy. Opportunists — from parents to police to prosecutor to judges to members of the media — tried to take advantage of the climate of fear to promote their own careers. Innocent people suffered immeasurable harm.

There is, however, an important difference between the McMartin case and the Salem witchcraft trials. Sexual molestation of children really does exist. It's an extremely serious problem whose full dimensions are not completely known because many actual cases are not reported, and some that are reported are disbelieved. There have also been numerous fabricated cases, made up either by children or by parents and sometimes encouraged by "mental health professionals" who claim that virtually everyone has been an abuse victim. The net result is that many abusers never get charged, while some innocent people do.

I believe there is no serious crime that has a lower rate of accurate outcomes than child sexual abuse; fewer abusers are convicted and more innocent defendants are falsely accused. It is precisely because of this high level of inaccuracy that our legal system must be scrupulous in safeguarding the rights of all concerned. If we truly believe that it is better for ten guilty people to go free than for even one innocent person to be wrongly convicted, then our legal rules must err on the side of the defendant rather than the accusers, even — perhaps, especially — if the accusers are children. This is a difficult concept for many to accept, but it is central to the way our Constitution strikes the balance between the evil of false acquittals and the even greater evil of false convictions.

Against this background, the McMartin case must be viewed as one of the greatest miscarriages of American justice. To see a miscarriage of justice in a case in which there were no convictions requires us to understand that the failure to convict defendants who spent so much time in jail and so much time under a public presumption of guilt was itself the essence of injustice. Despite the absence of any criminal record and the presence of deep roots in the community, Raymond Buckey spent four years in jail before he was released. He spent additional years in court before the legal proceedings against him were finally terminated.

Much of the blame for the McMartin injustice rests on ambitious prosecutors who saw the case as their ticket to fame, riches, and higher office. They knew that at least one witness they presented was a professional perjurer. George Freeman had a criminal record a mile long and had spent most of his life in prison for crimes ranging from robbery to murder.[48] There was an open murder charge then pending on which a judge had found probable cause. Freeman testified that he had heard Raymond Buckey confess his guilt while they were cellmates. The problem with this testimony is that the prosecutors knew that Freeman had a habit of testifying falsely about alleged confessions made by his cellmates. Indeed, the prosecutors knew that he had been convicted of perjury for having done precisely that. The prosecution knew, moreover, that it was a widespread practice among professional snitches, such as Freeman, to try to get close to high-profile defendants and then make up confessions, especially in cases where the evidence was weak. Freeman admitted under oath that at least one Los Angeles district attorney had "used" him as a witness "after he knew" he had lied. Freeman testified that he was rewarded for his lies by reduced sentences and freedom, though he said that he had been made no promises in this case.[49] None of the prosecutors was punished for suborning perjury. As one experienced criminal defense lawyer put it, "When we break the rules we go to jail. When they break the rules they go to lunch. And maybe get a promotion if they do it right."[50]

In addition to this sordid episode, prosecutors relied on "experts" who were really advocates. These experts had never seen a case of false accusation. They believed that children all tell the truth regardless of how preposterous the allegations are. If the children recanted their accusations, that proved that the original accusations were valid, because abused children often recant. If the children did not recant, that proved they were telling the truth. It was "heads-I-win-tails-you-lose" testimony by witnesses whose expertise was never tested by the scientific method.

There were also numerous instances of deliberate prosecutorial suppression of highly exculpatory information, including the mental illness of the original complaining witness.

The trials ended inconclusively, with acquittals on some counts and deadlocks favoring acquittal on others. But the problems persist. We have not yet learned how to maximize the chances of convicting guilty child abusers without also convicting innocent people who have been falsely accused. The McMartin case is a wake-up call to those who believe that prosecutors and their experts can be trusted to do justice in the emotional context of child abuse. The law must assure that the defense has the fullest opportunity to challenge both child witnesses and the experts who claim to believe them if we are not only to find the real abusers, but to free the falsely accused as well.

The Central Park Jogger Case

Date:	1990; 2002
Location:	New York City, New York
Defendants:	A group of black youths
Charges:	Rape, attempted murder
Verdict:	Guilty of rape; not guilty of attempted murder
Sentence:	Imprisonment; all charges dropped after another man confessed

Can the great Anglo-American experiment with trial by jury survive highly politicized and racially charged trials such as the notorious "Central Park Jogger" case of 1989–90? In these widely publicized trials — there were two separate ones involving different groups of defendants — the evidence seemed overwhelming that a young, white investment banker had been raped, brutalized, and nearly murdered by one or more young minority men who were "wilding" through Central Park on the night of April 19, 1989. Arrests followed quickly and several of the defendants admitted complicity in the crime, while generally minimizing their own roles.

Reasonable observers could have some doubt about whether any of these specific defendants had been directly involved, or what the precise role of any of them might have been. But a person of good faith, with any kind of an open mind, could hardly dispute the unchallengeable reality that this horrible crime was committed by someone in the park that night to whom the jogger was a stranger. Yet despite the overwhelming evidence, some African American "leaders" undertook a crude campaign to persuade their constituency that the real perpetrator was the young woman's white boyfriend.[51] The "evidence" in support of this cruel and preposterous diversion was a semen stain on the jogger's clothing that was said to match her boyfriend's DNA. There was an obvious explanation for the stain (if it was a match): The jogger had had intercourse with her boyfriend a few days before the rape and then jogged in the same outfit right after the consensual sex, and some of her boyfriend's semen leaked from her vagina onto her clothing. Despite this explanation, which was testified to by the jogger and corroborated by the physical evidence, many "supporters" of the defendants persisted in their accusation of the boyfriend and their exculpation of the young wilders. They simply would not believe — or admit — that this crime was committed by a young minority man or men. (Some of the same "leaders" and "lawyers" who perpetrated the Tawana Brawley hoax — that a black teenager was raped by a white assistant district attorney — participated in this attempt to "blame whitey" as well.[52])

Although the verdicts were somewhat inconsistent and — it now turns out — wrong, they did not reflect the kind of racial jury nullification that has characterized some other recent cases.

Although jury nullification has a long history in this country, ranging from John Peter Zenger's free speech acquittal in 1735, to the white racist acquittals of Ku Klux Klan killers in the 1960s, to the Lorena Bobbitt acquittal in the 1990s, it is a double-edged sword that poses considerable dangers to the rule of law.

This, of course, did not trouble radical lawyers such as William Kunstler, who became involved in these cases despite his pledge a year earlier that he would never represent a defendant accused of rape. (He also said he would never represent anyone accused of child molestation and then immediately broke that pledge as well.[53]) Kunstler filed a sparse brief in which he forwent a legitimate argument that one of the trial lawyers was ineffective because, as Kunstler said, "he didn't want to publicly criticize a black lawyer."[54] This decision, if true, placed Kunstler's politics above the interests of his client. But that is often true of political defenses in which "the community," or a part of it, is the real client and the defendant is merely a legal means toward the political end sought to be achieved by the trial and appeal.

Years after these verdicts satisfied most New Yorkers that the perpetrators had been brought to justice, another young minority man, who was in the park that night but was not part of the group of wilders, admitted that he alone had raped and assaulted the woman — a claim corroborated in part by the absence of any DNA evidence linking the other defendants to the rape. He said that the confessions by the others were false. Although they were committing other assaultive crimes that night in the park, the wilders were not involved in this more serious one. The district attorney consented to the convictions being thrown out — years after the defendants had served their sentences — and lawsuits have now been filed. There is plenty of blame to go around. Some of the defendants' lawyers, to whom this was a racial cause rather than an individual case, share the responsibility for looking in the wrong place for the real culprit. But the real message of the trial of the Central Park wilders is that despite confessions and circumstantial evidence, we should never become overconfident about our ability to find the truth. Our system of justice remains imperfect, and we should never regard a case as permanently closed.

The Trial of Mike Tyson

Date: 1992
Location: Indianapolis, Indiana
Defendant: Heavyweight boxing champion Mike Tyson
Charge: Rape
Verdict: Guilty
Sentence: Six years in prison; served three years

Mike Tyson, the former heavyweight boxing champion of the world, was convicted of rape on the basis of testimony by his alleged victim that he forced her to have sex with him after she voluntarily went to his hotel room at two o'clock in the morning. The evidence that convicted Tyson was known to be false and incomplete by the prosecutors. Indeed, the prosecutors themselves — knowingly assisted by the trial judge — played an active role in misleading the jurors and in keeping the true story from them. Had the jurors known what the prosecutors knew all along, they would have acquitted Mike Tyson. Indeed, at least four of the jurors, after learning of the false evidence, urged that Tyson be given a new trial.

As one of the jurors put it: "We [the jurors] felt that a man raped a woman. . . . In hindsight, it [now] looks like a woman raped a man."[55] Another juror now believes that Desiree Washington, a beauty pageant contestant who accused Tyson of raping her, "has committed a crime."[56]

In order to understand why these jurors had second thoughts

about their verdict, we must go back to the trial itself and see how Desiree Washington, the alleged victim, was presented to the jury. During the trial she did not even allow her name or face to be revealed. She was portrayed as a shy, young, inexperienced, religious schoolgirl who wanted nothing more than to put this whole unpleasant tragedy behind her. Her family had hired a lawyer for the express purpose of helping to "ward off the media" because she did not want any publicity.[57] She said she had no plans to sue Tyson and she had certainly not hired a lawyer for that purpose. When she and her family were asked whether they had a "contingency" fee agreement with any lawyer — the kind of agreement traditionally made with lawyers who are contemplating a money suit for damages — they all claimed not even to know what that term meant. When Desiree's mother was asked whether there had ever been any "discussions" with lawyers about fees, she said no, and she swore under oath that there were no "written documents relating to the relationship between you and [the lawyer who was supposed to ward off the media]."

Thus, as one of the jurors later put it: "When she [Washington] said she wasn't looking to get any money, I believed her and thought then that we made the right decision."[58] Another juror agreed, saying that at the trial, "she was very, very credible,"[59] because she had no motive to lie, since she was not intending to collect any money or benefit in any way from Tyson's conviction.

In addition to portraying herself as an altruistic victim whose only goal was to see to it that Mike Tyson received the treatment he needed, Desiree Washington also pretended — with the complicity of the prosecutor — that she was an inexperienced virgin before she met Tyson. She testified that she was "a good Christian girl,"[60] and the prosecutor told the jury that she expected to go home after her date with Tyson "the same girl" that she was before her date, namely a virgin. She was an "innocent, almost naive" girl, according to the prosecutor. She knew how to "handle the hometown boys" if they even dared to try to cop a "quick feel," thus suggesting that she did not even neck or pet. As a waitress in Washington's hometown put it: "America thought this girl was a blushing, virginal type."[61]

The prosecutor also argued to the jurors a variation on the "dressed-for-sex" theory that has been rejected by most courts. He told them that Washington went to meet Tyson wearing "little pink polka dot panties," rather than "Fredericks of Hollywood underwear," thus showing that she did not wear the kind of sexy underclothes that women wear when they are out to have sex. (As an example of just how tricky and unfair the prosecutor was, even his "dressed-for-no-sex" argument was based on misleading information: The fact is that Desiree's sexy underwear was all still wet from having been washed; her only pair that was dry — when she went to meet Tyson at two o'clock in the morning — was the one with polka dots.)

Finally, Desiree Washington solidified her image as a totally nonsexual platonic date who only wanted to go sightseeing with Tyson at two o'clock in the morning by describing to the jury how she responded when Mike tried to kiss her as she entered his limousine for the ride to his hotel: "he went to kiss me and I just kind of jumped back."

Thus, the jury and the world at large were presented with the picture of a zealously religious, young, naive "virginal type" girl who did not kiss, neck, or wear sexy underwear, and for whom a lawsuit or media attention were the farthest thing from her altruistic mind. This public image was capped when Desiree Washington publicly stated that if Mike Tyson had simply apologized to her, she would have been satisfied and would not have pressed criminal charges.

No wonder the jurors believed her testimony, in what was a classic "she-said, he-said" credibility contest. As the trial judge instructed them, "You should not disregard the testimony of any witness without a reason and without careful consideration."

There was no reason — at least not any then known to the jury or the public — for not believing Desiree Washington at that time.

It now turns out that the Washington family did not hire a lawyer to "ward off the media," as they claimed, but rather to do precisely the opposite — namely, to sell Desiree's story to the media for huge sums of money. Donald Washington, Desiree's father, has now publicly acknowledged that he discussed movie rights with the very lawyer whom he falsely told the jury he had hired solely to "ward off the media." The tape of an interview he gave after the trial contains the following important admission: "I expected to get money from movie rights, that's where the money is."

It also now turns out that the trial testimony denying any "contingency" fee agreement and any "written document" between the Washingtons and the lawyer concerning a planned money damage suit against Tyson was totally false. Immediately after Desiree Washington's sexual encounter with Mike Tyson, the Washington family went to see a high-powered money lawyer in their home state of Rhode Island. He brought in another high-powered lawyer, and the discussion turned instantly to how the Washington family could parlay Desiree's date with Tyson into big bucks. They talked about movie rights, book deals, and multimillion-dollar lawsuits. The lawyer carefully explained what a contingency fee agreement was — that he would charge a percentage, usually one-third of whatever the family collected from the lawsuits. The family agreed to this arrangement and Desiree signed a contingency fee agreement, which her father and mother officially witnessed. The family was given a copy of this written document to keep.[62]

It was only a few short months after Desiree signed this contingency fee agreement that she and her family were asked, under oath, whether they had a contingency fee arrangement or "any written document" with the lawyer. They denied any such arrangement or document, despite having explicitly asked for the arrangement and having actual possession of the document.

At the time of these denials (and the subsequent ones at the trial itself), the prosecutor was aware of the relationship between the Washingtons and their lawyer. Indeed, during the prosecutors' "rehearsal" cross-examination of Desiree Washington, in preparation for her actual in-court cross-examination by Tyson's trial lawyer, the issue of the contingency fee agreement was explicitly raised. Yet the prosecutor did everything in his power to keep the truth from coming out. He objected, on frivolous grounds, when Tyson's trial lawyer tried to ask about a contingency fee agreement, and tried desperately — but unsuccessfully — to obtain a ruling that any evidence about contemplated civil suits would be inadmissible. He then arranged for the Washington family to take the courtroom pass away from their lawyer, so that he could not attend the trial. It now appears, in retrospect, that the prosecutor wanted the lawyer out of the courtroom while his clients testified, so that the lawyer would not feel ethically compelled to stand up and correct the Washingtons' testimony when they falsely denied any contingency fee or written agreement with him.

The ploy worked — at least for a while. But the lawyer soon learned that his clients were not being straight with the jury. He began to worry that he might have an ethical obligation to blow the whistle on his clients, as lawyers do when their clients are committing perjury. So the lawyer went to the Rhode Island disciplinary counsel — the attorney in charge of enforcing the ethical rules that govern lawyers — to obtain guidance about what his ethical obligations were in light of the Washingtons' testimony. Disciplinary counsel advised the lawyer to get a copy of the trial transcript. In the meantime, the trial ended with Tyson's conviction. After the verdict, disciplinary counsel reviewed the transcript herself and concluded "that the attorney had an obligation to report to the [Indiana] trial judge the fact of his contingent fee agreement." She also asked the Rhode Island Supreme Court for guidance.

After reviewing the materials from disciplinary counsel, and after questioning the attorney face-to-face, the Rhode Island Supreme Court issued an unprecedented opinion concluding that "the attorney had an obligation to disclose the existence of his contingent fee agreement to the [Indiana] criminal trial court."[63] The state's highest court found that the agreement's "existence might well have had a bearing upon the jury's determination."[64] The Rhode Island court then directed the attorney to disclose to the Indiana court the information that the Washingtons had withheld. He did so, but the Indiana trial judge refused to make the contingency fee agreement available to Tyson's legal team, despite its obvious relevance and despite the conclusion of the Rhode Island Supreme Court that it might well have affected the jury's verdict. Indeed, what could be more important than the fact — unbeknownst to the jury — that Desiree Washington had lied in denying that she had millions of dollars riding on whether Mike Tyson was convicted or acquitted, since without a conviction it would have been difficult for her to collect monetary damages or sell her story to the media?

Other important information was kept from the jury about Desiree Washington's background and her activities on the night in question. It now turns out that Desiree was hardly a naive virgin. Numerous witnesses have confirmed that Desiree Washington was a sexually active young woman who hung out in nightclubs. Indeed, her new lawyer — who received a megabuck settlement from Tyson — implied to the media that Washington had been examined for venereal disease a month before she had sex with Tyson and that she was "not sexually active" during that brief period. He provided this information in order to show that Washington could not have had venereal disease before she had sex with Tyson. But her lawyer did not explain why a young virgin should have been examined for venereal disease before she had sex with Tyson.

Not only were the jury members misinformed about Desiree Washington's general sexual proclivities, but they were also denied the most crucial eyewitness testimony of what she was doing just minutes before she went to Tyson's hotel room. Remember that she denied necking with Tyson in the limo on the way to the hotel. Indeed, she testified that she rebuffed his attempt to kiss her and "jumped back," and that Tyson reacted by saying, "Oh, you're not like these city girls. You're a nice Christian girl." Tyson's testimony was precisely the opposite. He swore that when he kissed her, "she kissed me," and that on the drive to his hotel, he and Washington were "kissing, touching." The jury obviously believed Desiree's testimony because Tyson's was uncorroborated and self-serving.

But it turns out that there were three eyewitnesses — disinterested outsiders who happened to be in front of the hotel when the limo pulled up — who saw what was going on inside and outside the limo just before Tyson and Washington left it to go to his hotel room. They saw the couple necking — "they were all over each other" — and holding hands on the way to the hotel (Desiree denied both necking and holding hands).[65]

Of course, the fact that they were necking and holding hands doesn't preclude the possibility that Desiree may have said no when it came to intercourse. Nor does it mean that a woman who engages in sexual foreplay may not refuse further sex at any point. Of course she may, and if the man then forces her to have sex, it is rape. But the testimony of these eyewitnesses shows three important facts: The first is that Washington was lying when she denied necking with Tyson; the second is that Tyson was telling the truth when he testified that they were necking; and third is that just moments before the hotel door closed behind them, Washington was involved in sexual foreplay with Tyson.

Despite the importance of this eyewitness testimony by three disinterested witnesses in an otherwise uncorroborated "she-said, he-said" credibility contest, the trial judge refused to allow the jury to hear the evidence of the three eyewitnesses. She ruled that the prosecution — which admitted that the testimony was "pivotal"— would have been prejudiced by its late disclosure. (The eyewitnesses had come forward near the end of the prosecutor's case — after learning that Desiree Washington had denied necking with Tyson but before the defense case began.) The jury never learned, therefore, the truth about what Desiree was doing in the limo moments before she went to Tyson's hotel room.

It should come as no surprise that the trial judge made such a bizarre and unprecedented ruling excluding such relevant and exculpatory evidence. This judge, Patricia Gifford, was previously a full-time professional rape prosecutor, who had prosecuted more than fifty rape cases and counseled dozens of rape victims. She has extremely strong personal feelings about rape, especially what has come to be called "date rape." She apparently does not believe there is any difference between a stranger who rapes a woman at gunpoint and a misunderstanding about consent between a dating couple at two o'clock in the morning after a couple of drinks. Indeed, she lectured the lawyers against even using the term *date rape* in her courtroom and refused to give the traditional "date rape" instruction, which requires acquittal if the jury concludes that the defendant reasonably believed the woman consented, even if she did not intend to consent.

In light of Judge Gifford's attitudes and professional background in regard to rape, it might be wondered how the prosecution got so lucky as to have her as the judge in the Tyson case. Luck played no part in the selection. Under Indiana law and practice, the prosecutor gets to pick the judge who will try a criminal case. Almost nowhere else in the free world does the prosecutor have this prerogative other than in the Hoosier State. And the prosecutor picked wisely, if not fairly. Judge Gifford made virtually every important ruling in the prosecutor's favor, including the exclusion of those three "pivotal" witnesses who would have won the case for Tyson.

Tyson was denied bail pending appeal, on the grounds that any appeal would be "frivolous." Gifford then convened a press conference — in clear violation of the Code of Judicial Conduct — and "expressed some worries about having her rulings overturned, especially in an internationally publicized case in which prosecution costs alone reached $150,000,"[66] commenting on "the enormousness of the reversal of a case that would have to be tried again like this." She should have been removed from the bench for becoming an advocate — and an unfair one at that — but instead she was promoted! That's Indiana justice.

Judge Gifford's one-sided rulings shifted the balance against Tyson in what otherwise was a very close case. Indeed, even without all this exculpatory evidence, the initial jury vote was 6–6. Eventually the six who voted for conviction were able to persuade the six who voted for acquittal that there was no reason to disbelieve Desiree Washington's account.

What then was Desiree Washington's account of what happened that night? She acknowledges that she led him on and that she behaved as a groupie would behave. She sat in his lap and hugged him during the pageant rehearsal when they first met. She showed him a picture of herself in a bathing suit, gave him her hotel room number, and agreed to go out with him. She took his call at one forty-five in the morning and agreed to come down to meet him in his limo. She then went into her bathroom and put on a panty liner to keep her expensive borrowed dress from becoming stained by the beginning of her menstrual flow during the partying and sightseeing she said she expected to do over the next several hours. Yet shortly after going to Tyson's hotel room and sitting with him on his bed, she testified that she went to the bathroom again and *removed her panty liner* without replacing it. How did she expect to prevent her borrowed three-hundred-dollar outfit from becoming stained over the next several hours of anticipated partying and sightseeing? The only plausible explanation for the removal and nonreplacement of the panty liner was that it was done in anticipation of consensual sex.

Moreover, if she did not want to have sex, she could easily have locked herself in the bathroom and called for help from the bathroom phone. The bathroom had a working lock and a phone. Instead, she willingly came out of the bathroom, passed a door leading to the outside corridor, and went back to Tyson's bedroom. According to Washington's own testimony, Tyson asked her — during their sexual encounter — whether she wanted to "get on top" and she responded "yeah"; she presumably continued to have sex with Tyson while on top of him. After the sex was over, he asked her, "Now do you love me?"

No one except Tyson and Washington knows exactly what went on behind the closed doors of his hotel room. There was no videotape. Nor was there any physical evidence to corroborate Washington's unlikely story. Indeed, the available physical evidence completely undercut her story. She was wearing a sequin-studded outfit, which she claims Tyson "yanked" off her as he "slammed [her] down on the bed." If that had happened, there would have been sequins all over the hotel room. Indeed, at the trial, when the dress was gingerly introduced into evidence, sequins fell off in the courtroom. But only one sequin was found in Tyson's hotel room after the allegedly forcible rape.

Nor were there any bruises — external or internal — found on Ms. Washington that were consistent with her account of how Tyson had "forced" her to have sex. She testified that Tyson "slammed [her] down on the bed,"[67] got on top of her, held her down with his forearm across her chest, and forced himself inside her.

Had the 230-pound, muscular Tyson done that to the 105-pound, slight Washington, there would have been bruises, welts, contusions, and even broken ribs. Yet there was not even the slightest bruise on Washington's body when she went to the hospital just hours after the sexual encounter. The doctors found only two tiny microscopic abrasions, which, according to leading experts, are perfectly consistent with consensual sex — especially if the man has a larger-than-average penis or the woman a smaller-than-average vagina. Such tiny abrasions are also more likely when two people have consensual sex with each other for the first time and are not used to one another's sexual movements and desires. Mike Tyson's account of what occurred was entirely consistent with the physical evidence and with what is widely known about the world of athletes and "groupies" in general and about Mike Tyson in particular.

Desiree Washington presented herself to Mike as a "groupie." Indeed, the pageant director herself criticized Washington for behaving like a groupie. The "rules" of groupie sex are well known to both groupies and athletes. The groupies want sex with superstars in exchange for bragging rights that they slept with the "high-scorer," the "champ," or the "star." Some, like Washington, hope that the star will fall for her and make her rich and famous. Indeed, several other contestants — friends of Desiree — testified that after meeting Mike Tyson, Desiree bragged to her friend that she was going out with him because "this is Mike Tyson. He's got a lot of money. He's dumb. You see what Robin Givens got out of him." She told another friend that "Robin Givens had him. I can have him too. . . . He's dumb anyway." To her roommate, she said: "Mike doesn't have to know how to speak well. He'll make all the money and I'll do the talking."

Tyson testified that he was blunt, direct, and unambiguous about what he wanted from Washington. When he asked her out — in front of a witness — she suggested a movie or dinner.

But he said no: "That's not what I [have] in mind . . . I want you. I want to fuck you." The witness — Johnny Gill, a singer — testified that Tyson said, "I want to fuck." Gill later asked Tyson how he could be so straightforward with women, and Tyson explained that he is used to saying what is on his mind.

Everyone who knows Mike Tyson will tell you that this is characteristic of the former champ. He always says exactly what is on his mind and asks for precisely what he wants. Indeed, several years before his encounter with Washington, Tyson was being deposed by a woman lawyer who was a former student of mine. In the middle of the deposition, he leaned over and asked her if she wanted to fuck him. She said no, and that ended the matter. Even though this lawyer was on the opposite side of the case from Tyson and doesn't like him one bit, she has no doubt that he told Desiree Washington that he wanted to "fuck" her. That's just the way he does things.

Desiree Washington knew full well that Mike wanted to have sex with her when she went to his hotel room at two o'clock in the morning. Yet she testified that she had no idea that Tyson had any interest in having sex in his hotel room at 2 AM. How any rational person could believe that, especially in light of what is now known about Washington, is mind-boggling. She was obviously disappointed and hurt when he treated her like a groupie — a one-night stand — rather than as a continuing romantic interest. She realized that she could not exploit his sexual interest in her the way Robin Givens had done, and she was afraid of the reaction of her friends and family when it became known that she had indulged in a one-night stand with Tyson. According to a post-trial press account, a friend of hers says that Desiree "only cried rape" after her furious father found out she'd had sex with Tyson.[68] It turns out that once before she had had consensual sex with an athlete — the high school football hero — and when her father found out about it and threatened to beat her, she lied to him and told him she had been raped. In order to avoid his fury once again, she decided to cry rape once again. At first, she said that he had "tried" to rape her. She initially denied having sex with Tyson. Then she said they had sex "on the floor." She told the female chaplain at the hospital that there had been some "participation" and consensual physical involvement on her part, before he forced her. Finally, she settled on the account she gave at trial: that he had raped her on the bed with no prior consensual involvement on her part. To provide "evidence" of that account, she contrived with her mother to place a phone call to the 911 operator a full day after the event, and — after ascertaining that the call was being recorded — told the 911 operator the story she eventually recounted at the trial. That contrived recording became the corroboration for her testimony.

Despite the absence of physical evidence to corroborate Desiree Washington's story, the jury eventually believed her because there was no compelling reason to disbelieve the testimony of a young, religious, sexually inexperienced "girl" who had no possible motive to put herself through the agony of a rape trial. But it turns out that there are very good reasons for not believing her. As one juror recently put it: "She was very, very credible [at the trial], but now she's not credible at all. Right now, I wouldn't believe anything she said. I would sign an affidavit that if we had known about the money, I couldn't have voted to convict him. Mike Tyson deserves a new trial."[69]

I was Tyson's appellate lawyer. Of all the appeals I have argued, this should have been the easiest one to win. The law clearly required a reversal of the conviction and a new trial. I am convinced — and I think most observers were convinced — that at a second trial, with all the new evidence before the jury, Tyson would have been acquitted. But this was Indiana. They had a trophy in Tyson. The conviction was affirmed on a 2–2 tie vote by the Indiana Supreme Court, with the chief justice disqualifying himself from participation in the decision on a phony pretext. I believe that the real reason he disqualified himself was that his own previous decisions would have required him to vote for reversal, and if he did, the public would be reminded that he himself had been accused of sexual impropriety by a fellow judge. In my forty years of practicing law throughout the world, I have never encountered a more thoroughly corrupt legal system than I did in 1992 in Indiana and a less fair trial than the one accorded Mike Tyson. If hard cases make bad law, then the Tyson case proves that unpopular defendants often receive bad justice.

The Two Trials for the Beating of Rodney King

Dates: 1992; 1993
Locations: Simi Valley, California; Los Angeles Federal District Court
Defendants: LAPD officers Stacey Koon, Theodore Briseno, Laurence Powell, and Timothy Wind
Charges: Police brutality and assault with a deadly weapon; depriving Rodney King of his federal civil rights
Verdict: Not guilty; guilty (Koon and Powell), not guilty (Briseno and Wind)
Sentence: Thirty months' imprisonment

It is rare to see two criminal trials, based on essentially the same evidence, that produce dramatically opposing verdicts.[70] It is rarer still when the key piece of evidence is a videotape seen by millions of people. Yet that is what happened in the notorious case involving the beating of black motorist Rodney King by Los Angeles police officers.

The King beating was captured on home video by a man named George Holliday and viewed around the world countless times before the first trial ever began. The videotape became a Rorschach test for different segments of the community. Most African Americans and many whites responded with outrage at the fifty-six visible baton lashes landed on King's body in the eighty-one seconds of tape. In the race-charged atmosphere of the early 1990s — when controversial urban rap albums leveled obscenities and death threats at the much-maligned Los Angeles police — this videotape was seen by some as a vindication of the claims of many inner-city residents that racially motivated violence and abuse at the hands of the LAPD had become routine.

To most police officers, and those who support tough law enforcement, the video showed hardworking police trying to subdue a drug-crazed criminal who repeatedly refused to submit to the lawful authority of the police. The all-white jury that first tried the officers apparently viewed the tape in this latter way.

The first trial — conducted in state court — was controversial from the start. The venue of the trial was changed from downtown Los Angeles, with its racially diverse jury pool, to suburban Simi Valley, where the racial makeup of the prospective jury pool was almost entirely white. Moreover, Simi Valley was a place that attracted many retired police officers seeking escape from the heterogeneity of LA. The all-white jury that eventually sat on the case watched George Holliday's home videotape broken down into split-second bits, with defense attorneys pointing out every flinch and flicker in King's body and arguing that these were potentially threatening movements to which the police were responding. The jurors were also told that, before the camera captured some of the events on tape, King had led California Highway Patrol and the LAPD on a high-speed chase at speeds of more than eighty miles per hour on the freeway and downtown city streets. The police also testified that King shook off all four officers when they attempted to restrain his arms and legs, and that they believed at the time that he was "dusted" (taking PCP). The videotape that so many had found so disturbing thus looked somewhat less incriminating to this unrepresentative suburban jury.

In fact, the totality of the evidence in the Rodney King beating trial was not nearly as conclusively incriminating as a viewing of the infamous videotape made it seem to many. King was very drunk — almost twice the legal limit. The two other people in his car followed police instructions and went unharmed; King failed to comply with the police order to lie facedown on the ground, shook off the officers who tried to restrain him, and behaved erratically. He had led police, who were not able immediately to search him and verify that he did not have a weapon, on a reckless high-speed chase through city streets. Not only had he shaken off four cops trying to handcuff him, but he also had continued to resist after being shocked with a taser, leading the police to believe that his unusual strength and resistance reflected the influence of a dangerous drug. It might have been anticipated, in these circumstances, that even a more representative jury might have a reasonable doubt about the guilt of the arresting officers, believing that they feared for their safety during this particularly difficult arrest.

There was also considerable evidence from which a reasonable jury could have concluded that at least some of the officers overreacted and may have been motivated by racial bias. It appeared on the tape that one of the officers, Laurence Powell, deliberately struck King *in the face* with his baton — which, if true, would certainly be an unjustifiable and malicious use of force. Moreover, Powell had sent an electronic message to another member of the LAPD twenty minutes before the incident referring to a domestic dispute between two African Americans as "right out of *Gorillas in the Mist*," and soon after the incident sent another message saying, "Oops, I haven't beaten anyone that bad in a long time." These messages were offered by the prosecution to show first an element of racial animus in the officers, and second a state of mind that trivialized the abuse of a civilian. In addition, the fifty-six blows, which included thirty from Powell, could easily be seen as excessive, especially when one expert witness on the use of force testified that one *single* blow behind the knee should generally be sufficient to immobilize almost any suspect.

The primary issue at the first trial was not whether the police *did* beat Rodney King to a pulp, but rather whether their actions were excessive considering the surrounding circumstances. In that respect, the case required a judgment call on the part of the jury, whose primary job was not to find the external facts the way a jury usually does, but rather to decide whether the actions of the police were reasonable. In other words, if the jurors had a reasonable doubt about whether the police acted reasonably, they were to acquit. If they had no such doubt, they were to convict. Reasonableness is, of course, in the eyes and experiences of the beholder. That is why the racial and experiential makeup of the jury in this case was so important. The decision to acquit amounted to a judgment, on the part of twelve white people, that it may have been reasonable for four white police officers to strike fifty-six heavy nightstick blows on a black motorist in order to subdue him while he was resisting arrest for a speeding infraction.

The reaction to the verdict was immediate and violent. Los Angeles burned for three days, with looting and rioting resulting in millions of dollars' worth of damages, as well as deaths and injuries. The jurors were branded as racists, and race relations reached a nadir unknown since the civil rights movement. After considerable pressure from civil rights groups, George Bush's Department of Justice decided to try the four officers *again*, this time on *federal* charges of willfully violating King's federally protected civil rights. In 1993, Officers Koon, Powell, Briseno, and Wind went on trial a second time, in federal court, and this time two of them were found guilty beyond a reasonable doubt.

The two trials constituted a kind of controlled experiment in American trial justice. Not very much changed by way of evidence between the state trial and the federal trial. Tactics might have changed — the videotape was not shown as many times by

the prosecution, and Rodney King did testify for the first time —
but in general, the facts presented to the jury remained almost
entirely the same. Two major factors account for the different
outcome at the second trial, where Koon and Powell were found
guilty. The first is that the racial makeup of the second jury was
likely more diverse in Los Angeles Federal District Court than it
had been in Simi Valley (although no one knows the makeup of
the jury for sure because the jurors were kept anonymous for
their own protection). The second is the riot that followed the acquittal at the first trial. That riot left a deep scar on the American
race conscience, and could certainly have influenced the way
the jurors in the second trial saw the case and their own role in
American history.

I have said that great trials are worth reviewing and investigating because they show us something of the passions of their time.
The Rodney King beating trials teach us that passions can
quickly change — from one year to another, and from one jury to
the next. The trials remind us that a criminal jury is a unique
group of twelve (in some states fewer) people, who come into existence as an instrument of justice for one trial, of one crime, in
one time and one place. A different set of people, in a different
historical context, will have a different opinion of what happened to Rodney King, even if they are looking at the same
videotape. That is why the same event could be viewed as an act
of self-defense by twelve white jurors in Simi Valley in 1992, and
then seen as a savage act of police brutality by a different panel
in federal district court in 1993. Times change, juries change,
people change, and passions change, making the same verdict
anything but certain, even in a case based on a single videotape.

Perhaps that is why the framers of our Bill of Rights included
the protection against double jeopardy within the Fifth Amendment. Prosecutors should get only one opportunity to prove their
case against a defendant. Allowing them to place a defendant on
trial again and again before different juries for the same crime

seemed unfair to our Founding Fathers. In any given case, like this one, where the initial verdict seemed so wrong to so many, it is understandable that the victim and his supporters would want another shot in front of a different jury. But as a general proposition, it would seem fairer to limit the prosecution to one trial, even if the outcome of that trial is less than satisfying. That *one* trial should take place in a location, and before a jury, that best assures justice to both sides; but the response to one injustice should not be another injustice in the form of a second trial on essentially the same evidence. Today, the double jeopardy clause is easily circumvented by trying defendants in federal court after they have been acquitted in state court. The Supreme Court has approved this growing trend, ruling that a federal offense is different from a state offense even if all the factual elements are identical. The reality is, however, that a second criminal trial in any court based on essentially the same facts plainly violates the spirit, if not the letter, of the constitutional protection against double jeopardy.

Even those of us who cannot sympathize with Laurence Powell — who seems, by any account of the evidence, to be both a racist person and a reckless policeman — must sense the injustice in double jeopardy and be willing to learn the hard lessons of this case. The answer to a dubious acquittal by an unrepresentative jury simply cannot be to go out and find a new jury — this is manifestly unfair to defendants, it undermines the power of the jury while magnifying the power of the government, and it will eventually result in innocent people being convicted of crimes they did not commit. The real answer is instead to tread carefully when finding a venue and constructing a jury for a case as controversial as the Rodney King trials. The jury must reflect a broad cross section of the community whose voice and conscience the verdict is supposed to reflect. In fact, forcing the government to win its *one and only* shot at a defendant will likely help ensure that an appropriate jury is picked the first time around. Justice demands a fair procedure, not the "right" result, and the Rodney King case should reinforce our commitment to the principle of protecting all defendants against double jeopardy and getting a fair jury the first time rather than by "trial" and error.

The O. J. Simpson Trial

Date: 1994–97
Location: Los Angeles, California
Defendant: Former football star O. J. Simpson
Charge: Double murder
Verdict: Not guilty in criminal case; liable in civil case

The world seemed to stand still for a moment in time. Everyone would remember where they were when the verdict was announced in the case of *The People of the State of California v. Orenthal James Simpson*. They were either watching television or listening to the radio. As one prominent media executive put it: "You have to look back to when Kennedy was shot to find another media event that virtually everyone saw during the day." But the reading of the Simpson verdict was different from the Kennedy assassination, the Japanese attack on Pearl Harbor, or the death of Franklin D. Roosevelt. Those were unexpected events, which came out of the blue like bolts of lightning on a clear summer day. What people watched or listened to was not live coverage of the actual event, but rather replays of coverage or the subsequent actions, such as the shooting of Oswald by Ruby. In the Simpson case, the public waited for and watched the actual, live reading of the verdict. Judge Lance Ito, who presided over the trial, had carefully scheduled the announcement of the Simpson verdict. Although the bell from the jury room signaling that a verdict had been reached after only four hours of collective deliberation sounded just before 3 PM Pacific time on October 2, 1995, Judge Ito decided to withhold announcement of the verdict until 10 AM the following day, so that the lawyers, the media, and the police could prepare for the unknown outcome of the most closely followed criminal case in history. On that day, a worldwide audience estimated at more than one hundred million would stop what they were doing to see or hear for themselves whether the Los Angeles jury of nine African Americans (eight of whom were women), two whites, and one Hispanic had rendered justice.

Hours before the verdict was to be announced, President Bill Clinton was briefed on nationwide security measures in the event of possible rioting. The Los Angeles Police Department was on full alert. As the witching hour approached, long-distance telephone calls dropped by 58 percent. There was a surge in electrical consumption as millions of Americans turned on television sets. Water usage decreased as fewer people used the bathroom between 10 and 10:15 AM Pacific time. Trading volume plummeted 41 percent on the New York Stock Exchange. A meeting between the secretary of state and the director of the CIA was put off for several minutes. The president left the Oval Office to join staffers watching television. Another presidential hopeful, scheduled at 10 AM Eastern time to announce whether he would seek the nomination, postponed the announcement until after the verdict. Arrangements were made to pass notes to the justices of the Supreme Court sitting on the bench, telling them the verdict. Exercise stopped in gyms around the country. Work ceased in factories, in post offices, and in the surgical suites of hospitals. It was the most unproductive half hour in U.S. business history, costing an estimated $480 million in lost output. Even in Israel, where the Yom Kippur holiday had already begun and where most televisions were dark in commemoration of this holiest of days, thousands of Jews tuned in to Jordanian television to watch the verdict.[71]

Never before in history had so many people waited in anticipation to learn what twelve of their "peers" had decided in secret the day before. No one, aside from those twelve ordinary people, knew what their verdict sheet contained — not the judge, not the defendant, not the lawyers, not the police, not the president of the United States. *Time* magazine described it as "the single most suspenseful moment in television history."

Nearly everyone had an opinion of how the case should or would be decided. During the night and morning before the verdict was announced, the media was overloaded with "informed speculation" about the likely outcome. Tea leaves were read, crystal balls gazed into, and tarot cards turned over. Trial lawyers, with long experience in "reading" juries, offered their interpretations of the brevity of the deliberations, the unwillingness of jurors to look the defendant in the eye, and the significance of the one portion of the trial transcript they asked to have reviewed.

In an effort to obtain inside information, a television crew beamed a parabolic microphone at the windows of my home in Cambridge, hoping that I knew what the verdict would be and that they could pick up my conversations. I had no more information, however, than anyone else.

At 1 PM Eastern time — 10 AM Pacific time — my office at Harvard Law School was bursting at the seams with students, journalists, TV cameras, and assorted friends and colleagues. When the word had come late the previous afternoon that there was a verdict, I was invited by the defense team to fly to Los Angeles to be in the courtroom when it was read. But it was the day before Yom Kippur, and I wanted to remain in Cambridge to attend the Kol Nidre service with my family. I also thought I would have to begin preparing for an appeal. Indeed, from the moment I learned that the jurors had reached their verdict, I began to outline the likely issues for the appeal. I focused on the questionable search of Simpson's premises hours after the killings; on the trial court's refusal to allow the defense to play the Mark Fuhrman tapes in which he had repeatedly used the "n" word, having sworn he had not; and on the possible planting of blood evidence on the sock found in Simpson's bedroom.[72]

As an appellate lawyer, I am programmed to be a pessimist. My job is to prepare for the worst, to provide a parachute in the event of a conviction. That is why O. J. Simpson always referred to me as his "God forbid" lawyer — "God forbid there should be a conviction, you've got to get it reversed on appeal." My own mind, therefore, is always on the likelihood of conviction — a likelihood that comes to pass in approximately 75 percent to 80 percent of contested criminal cases. I was prepared for that possibility as I watched Judge Ito call the hushed courtroom to order at precisely 10 AM. A few quick formalities, and then came the critical words, uttered in the halting voice of a court clerk, which almost succeeded in blunting the drama of the moment. But there was no mistaking the jury's verdict: not guilty.

There was silence in my office. No one cheered. No one laughed. I turned to the television set on my desk, reached out my hand, and touched the screen. No one in the office understood the gesture, because they had not accompanied me on my numerous visits to O. J. Simpson in prison. When we met, he was always on the opposite side of a thick glass partition. We would extend a hand and "touch" through the glass — the prison handshake, as criminal lawyers and their clients know it. At the moment of the verdict, I shook hands with O. J. Simpson through the television set.

It was not a moment for celebration. There were two victims, brutally murdered. There were children who would never again be comforted by their mother; parents, sisters, and friends who would never again hug their loved ones. There was a man who had spent sixteen months in jail accused of a crime of which a jury had just ruled he was not legally guilty, but of which most Americans thought he was factually guilty. It was a moment for introspection and quiet professional satisfaction among the members of my team of student assistants.

The muted reaction to the verdict in my office was not typical of reactions around the country, which ranged from anger and outrage to jubilation. At predominantly black Howard University Law School, "students crossed their fingers, held hands, and when the clerk read the verdicts, the room erupted with a chorus of cheers. Many cried and hugged."[73] At a battered women's shelter, women also cried and hugged — but not for joy. "It hurt my gut," one said. "I just had to leave."[74] At Benjamin's Deli in a Jewish neighborhood of Milwaukee, "a dull groan" rolled through the restaurant as the verdict was read. At Clancy's Pub in Omaha, "people in the bar gasped."[75] At the University of Nebraska, a white student shook his head, saying, "It's a payback for Rodney King."[76] At a sports bar in Atlanta, rage was expressed. "As far as I'm concerned Cochran and Shapiro are accessories to murder!"[77] one man shouted. Some booed. Others stood in stunned silence. A black woman on a District of Columbia street corner shouted, "We won!" Another thanked Jesus. A white man yelled, "Jesus!" but not in praise.

Many whites, convinced of Simpson's guilt, complained that the criminal justice system had failed them. But angry whites did not riot as blacks had rioted following the initial acquittal of the police officers who beat Rodney King. Writer Ben Stein predicted that "the whites will riot the way we whites do: leave the cities, go to Idaho or Oregon or Arizona, vote for Gingrich . . . and punish the blacks by closing their day-care programs and cutting off their Medicaid." Some whites also "rioted" by sending me racist hate letters. Dr. John S. Blankfort, an orthodontist from San Francisco, wrote the following on his prescription pad: "Congratulations — a murdering butcher is on the street. [I]f the 'nigger' is so innocent, then he should have no problem speaking — may you catch cancer." Another letter read: "The homicidal 'nigger' (an epithet I've shunned all my life, but shall use from now on, having witnessed black America's reaction to the verdict) did it, and you know it!" A woman at a concert in Boston's Symphony Hall tried to attack me physically, and a man spit at me in front of my daughter while we were walking in Harvard Square. Even my mother received hate mail.

The content of these letters, and the hundreds like them I received, were not necessarily typical of the white reaction to the jury's unpopular verdict. But the passions reflected in them and in the immediate response to the verdict were representative of the very personal manner in which many people had viewed the case. It was a verdict that was not only heard throughout the world but also felt throughout the world, especially in every corner of the United States. As one woman who had followed the case closely told me, "The acquittal was like a swift kick to my stomach. I felt nauseated, pained, frightened — even violated — when I heard the words 'not guilty.'"[78]

Why this extraordinary personal reaction by so many to whom Nicole Brown, Ronald Goldman, and O. J. Simpson were complete strangers? Why the fascination with this murder in an age when, tragically, murders are all too commonplace? Why did this busy nation stand transfixed in front of millions of television sets during a working day to watch twelve people deliver their collective opinion on an issue about which most Americans had already made up their minds? Why has the Simpson case become for so many the preeminent symbol of what is wrong with the American criminal justice system — and, indeed, with America? Or as one commentator put it, "For many Americans, the O. J. Simpson trial has become the criminal justice system's Vietnam — an event of sickening revelation."[79] Why?

At a superficial level, the answers come easily. O. J. Simpson is the most famous American ever to stand trial for murder. His trial took place at a time of instant communications in a place that is the media capital of the world. Anyone with access to a television set could watch as the drama unfolded. Then the audience could read about what they had seen and hear experts analyze what had occurred and predict what would happen the next day. The Simpson case was the first and most pyrotechnic multiple car crash on the information superhighway, and the cars were all Mercedes, Bentleys, and Rolls-Royces. There was wealth and celebrity, "the beautiful people," an interracial marriage, a vicious double murder, a charismatic defendant, the high drama of a car chase, and a criminal trial — all the ingredients of a fictional whodunit, and they were true.

This surface analysis may explain the obvious fascination with the case and even with the verdict itself. But it does not begin to explain why so many serious people who would not be caught dead reading the tabloids or watching *Hard Copy* were caught up in the Simpson trial and its aftermath. The trial was not merely entertainment for a voyeuristic world obsessed with celebrity and a fall from grace. It became a morality play for Americans concerned about race, gender, violence, equality, and the wide range of other issues that permeated the last decade of the millennium. The Simpson case — like the Sacco-Vanzetti, Scopes, Lindbergh, Rosenberg, Ruby, von Bülow, and other paradigmatic cases before it — touched upon the eternal themes of passion and revenge, but also on the pressing contemporary questions of equality and the perceived ineffectiveness of our criminal justice system.

There was nothing about the trial itself that made it notable or great. The prosecuting attorneys were mediocre. The defense "dream team" was a mixed bag of mostly good lawyers. The legal issues were mundane. The factual issues were typical of modern-day forensic disputes. A really good prosecutor might well have won a conviction, based on the evidence. A bad defense team could easily have lost. Race clearly played a role, but not the role assumed by many critics. Black jurors were probably more receptive to defense claims of police perjury and evidence tampering than an all-white jury would have been. And though the jury did consist predominantly of black women, there were two whites and one Hispanic — all of whom eventually voted to acquit.

What made this case notable was little more than its notoriety, its fascination to the public, and its racially divisive verdict. Among my own cases, it ranks near the bottom of the list of important ones. Still, it was a major event in the history of television and in the American *public's* experience with trial law, and thus must be noted as one of the great trials in our nation's history.

The Clinton Impeachment Trial

Date: 1997–98
Location: District of Columbia
Defendant: President Bill Clinton
Charges: Perjury and obstruction of justice
Verdict: Impeached but not removed

The framers of our Constitution could hardly have imagined that the extraordinary power to impeach a duly elected president would have been invoked in response to a sex fib told under oath by that president in an unsuccessful effort to keep secret an improper sexual relationship. Because the improper invocation of the impeachment power threatened to produce a constitutional crisis, I became interested in various aspects of the matter from the very beginning.

At first I was supportive of the appointment of an independent counsel to investigate Whitewater, Filegate, and the travel office. I also supported the continuation of the Paula Jones civil lawsuit. I began to worry when Kenneth Starr replaced Robert Fiske as independent counsel. My concern grew when Starr managed to persuade both Janet Reno and the court to expand his jurisdiction into the Monica Lewinsky matter. Though the justification put forward for expanding the investigation dealt with buying the silence of witnesses, I immediately suspected that the vague connection between Whitewater and Lewinsky was merely a pretext for what I began to call "sexual

McCarthyism" — a term that has now been used widely to characterize the danger of Starr's inquisition into Clinton's sex life. There is a compelling analogy to what Joseph McCarthy, Roy Cohn, and J. Edgar Hoover did back in the 1950s: They investigated the private sexual behavior of public figures in an effort to influence their public actions.

At bottom this is a story of how two men who were obsessed with forbidden sex — Clinton about engaging in it and Starr about exposing it — managed to turn a tawdry series of Oval Office sexual encounters into a constitutional crisis. Clinton and his advisers made mistake after mistake in a futile effort to keep his embarrassing little secret from becoming public. Starr and his staff overreached, overreacted, exaggerated, and pressed every issue to the limits of its logic to expose the secret and embarrass the president. The result was a highly unlikely combination of factors — an almost perfect storm — that led the nation to where almost no one (except the extreme right) wanted to go: to the brink of a constitutional crisis with international implications.

It is also a story about lawyers and their unprecedented influence on matters of governance. The two alleged crimes that are at the core of what Starr believed were impeachable offenses were committed by Clinton (a lawyer) in the presence of his lawyers and were based on answers he gave to questions asked by other lawyers. Lawyers debated the legal niceties of whether the president's statements constituted the highly technical crime of perjury — as well as whether they were impeachable offenses under the Constitution. Many Americans, both in and out of Congress, were outraged at the legalisms employed by the president and his lawyers. They asked, "Why can't the president just admit he lied?" The answer inheres in the nature of the legal and constitutional system under which we live. The virtue of the rule of law (over the fiat of man and woman) is that it is — at least in theory — predictable because it is written down in precise language that gives fair warning to all. The vice of the rule of law is that precise language encourages precisely the kind of hairsplitting legalisms that so many deplore.

Doctors conduct autopsies on patients who die, business schools do postmortems on companies that failed, coaches watch videos of games in which they are beaten, and lawyers analyze cases they lost. The purpose is to learn from mistakes. As Santayana said, "Those who cannot remember the past are condemned to repeat it." (Sometimes I think that those who have heard this Santayana bon mot "are condemned to repeat it.")

It is in the spirit of Santayana that I look back at the history of mistakes, misjudgments, blunders, and lost opportunities that led President Clinton to the uncomfortable place in which he found himself. It does not take a Monday-morning quarterback to identify the worst of the errors. They were obvious at the time to any discerning eye. Indeed, Clinton was warned in advance about virtually every one of them. He chose to ignore the warnings and listen to those who called for short-term solutions — quick fixes — to what became long-term problems.

In my forty years of practicing and teaching law, I have seen this pattern repeated by people who eventually get into trouble. They mortgage their future to obtain immediate gratification — political, economic, or sexual. They believe that when the future finally arrives, there will be new quick fixes. And usually they are right. It generally requires a combination of unlikely factors to produce disaster, and most successful people are good at reducing risks. But even the most successful people are subject to probabilities, and eventually — if they persist in their reckless behavior — statistics will catch up with them.

There is not enough space here to review each of the crucial decisions along the road to disaster. At every point, the president and his advisers opted for the short-term political tactic that helped them avoid worse headlines and poll results, rather than the longer-term strategy that might have prevented an entirely lawful sexual indiscretion from turning into a possible crime, and also prevented an impeachment crisis.

The first and most important point was the president's foolhardy decision to engage in a surreptitious sexual relationship with a White House intern at a time when he knew he was under intense investigation by a puritanical prosecutor and was subject to a lawsuit for sexual harassment by a vindictive woman who was represented by politically motivated lawyers.

If there was indeed a "right-wing conspiracy" out there waiting to "get" the president, it is difficult to imagine any action more reckless than Oval Office sex with a young blabbermouth whose goal was probably as much to brag about her conquest of the president as to engage in an intimate relationship. She really did want oral sex: She wanted to talk about it. And talk she did — to more than a dozen people. The president achieved immediate gratification while risking long-term consequences to his marriage, his daughter, his presidency, and above all the nation's stability. At the time he began his sexual encounter with Lewinsky, Clinton knew that he might possibly have to testify under oath about his sex life. He knew that two sets of enemies had the powerful legal weapon of subpoena power aimed directly at his heart — and perhaps other parts of his anatomy. That is probably why he was reluctant to engage in sexual intercourse. He wanted sex with deniability.

Because our system of prosecution has become so politicized and because the role of attorney general of the United States merges the political with the prosecutorial, it has become necessary to create the office of independent counsel. When evidence of improprieties surrounding Whitewater began to emerge, it became evident that an independent counsel would have to be appointed.

The Independent Counsel Law — which vests the selection in a panel of judges — having lapsed when the Lewinsky matter surfaced, Attorney General Janet Reno at first decided that she would have to appoint a special prosecutor to investigate President Clinton. She appointed a moderate Republican named Robert Fiske, who had long experience as both a federal prosecutor and a private lawyer. But Republican senators conspired with a Republican judge to remove Fiske and have Kenneth Starr appointed. Although Starr's reputation as a right-wing ideologue and ambitious Republican politician was well known, White House counsel Abner Mikva — who had served as an appellate judge alongside Starr — assured President Clinton that Starr would be fair. The White House accepted the appointment without challenge. The stage was thus set for a clash between two men who shared different obsessions about the same subject — forbidden sex. But before any of the president's private sexual activities could become the subject of Starr's prosecutorial agenda, the president had to give Starr one of the greatest gifts anyone can give an overzealous prosecutor — a deposition under oath about his sex life.

It is unlikely that Bill Clinton confided the full truth of his relationship with Monica Lewinsky to any of his lawyers. He couldn't, because David Kendall was representing both him and his wife. Robert Bennett, though representing only President Clinton, was sharing information with Kendall. Thus if President Clinton did not want his wife to find out about Lewinsky, he could not tell either Bennett or Kendall, who would be obliged to share this privileged information with their other client. His lawyers must have suspected the possibility that there was some truth to the rumors that something untoward had occurred between Bill Clinton and Monica Lewinsky. After all, Clinton did tell his lawyers — and did testify — that he engaged in adulterous sex with Gennifer Flowers, despite his previous public denial. Moreover, his reputation as a womanizer was well known. Any lawyer worth his salt should have based decisions regarding the president's testimony on the assumption that he may well have engaged in a sexual relationship with Lewinsky. A good lawyer should also have assumed that a twenty-two-year-old intern who had engaged in a sexual relationship with the president would talk about it.

Robert Bennett was on notice that the president was going to be asked about Lewinsky. If he had conducted any kind of investigation to determine the nature of their relationship, he would surely have uncovered the widespread concern around the White House over Monica Lewinsky's unusual access to the president. At the very least he should have interviewed Lewinsky, confronted her with the concerns, and asked her direct questions. He should also have interviewed those White House officials who had expressed concern. Yet on the basis of little more than an assurance from the president, he allowed an affidavit to be submitted by Lewinsky denying any sexual relationship. Putting aside the ethical issues arising from relying on an affidavit that he was on notice might well be false, and having his client testify to facts that he had to suspect might be false, it is difficult to understand the tactical considerations that led the president's lawyers to allow him to testify about his sex life. It is not as if Bennett had not been cautioned about the risks of having the president testify about his sex life at the Jones deposition. On May 27, 1997, six months before President Clinton testified at a deposition in the Paula Jones lawsuit, I said on the *Geraldo Rivera Show*, "This case never should have gotten this far. It should have been settled early when he could have settled it easily. . . . Remember, depositions are very broad in latitude. . . . I think the president could win if it actually went to trial, but it won't go to trial."

The president had three options, but he was aware of only two of them. He knew that he could litigate and try to win — as he ended up doing. He also knew that he could try to settle the case, which would have avoided the necessity of testifying at the deposition or trial. A settlement requires both sides to agree. In the Jones case, the president reportedly offered to pay Jones seven hundred thousand dollars to settle. Jones insisted on an apology, and the settlement talks eventually broke down.

The third option, of which the president was unaware, was to default the Jones case. Every litigant in a civil case has the right to default — which means, essentially, to settle the case unilaterally by simply refusing to contest the allegations in the complaint. Little stigma is attached to defaulting a case. It does not even necessarily entail an admission of liability. It represents a practical assessment of the costs and benefits of litigating and not litigating, just as a settlement does.

Robert Bennett never told President Clinton that he could have defaulted and paid Jones the seven hundred thousand dollars demanded by her — without making any apology. Nor did he tell the president that he could have used the threat of defaulting to increase the chances of securing a settlement. Bennett could have approached the Jones lawyers and told them that under no circumstances would there be a trial: The only options were default or settlement. Moreover there would be no apology of any kind. To the contrary, the president would assert his absolute innocence and release a statement explaining why he had no choice but to default, since litigation would take too much valuable time from his presidential duties.

Faced with these options, it is likely that the Jones lawyers would have accepted a settlement and Clinton would never have had to testify about his sex life in any proceedings. Perhaps the Lewinsky story would have leaked, but the president would not have had to dignify a rumor with a response. It was the entirely avoidable decision to have him testify under oath not once but twice that turned a sex rumor into a possibly impeachable offense. How do I know that Robert Bennett never told President Clinton of the default option? Because both men personally told me. Here is the story:

On January 17, 1998, President Clinton was deposed in the Paula Jones lawsuit and was asked questions about his relationship with Monica Lewinsky. He denied that there was one. Shortly thereafter, reports began to appear of tape-recorded conversations between Linda Tripp and Monica Lewinsky suggesting that there had been a sexual relationship of some kind between the president and Monica Lewinsky.

On January 23, 1998, I appeared on the MSNBC program *Internight* and criticized Bennett for allowing the president to walk into a perjury trap and a swearing contest. I urged the president to "get out in front of this story. He has to tell the truth, and if the truth is inculpatory he has to tell it." I recommended that the president "get a new lawyer, tell him the truth, sit down with your new lawyer . . . and [have him give you] the straight poop." The lawyer has to be someone "who doesn't care what the president thinks of him. His obligation is to tell the president what he doesn't want to hear."

On January 27, 1998, Robert Bennett called me to complain about what I said on television. Bennett kept me on the phone for nearly half an hour telling me that I did not understand his "strategy" in the case and accusing me of "Monday-morning quarterbacking" his decisions.

I asked Bennett a direct question: "Did you ever advise the president that in addition to the option of settling the Jones case, he could simply default on the liability phase of the case?"

Bennett replied that defaulting would have been "ridiculous" and "a stupid idea" and that he would never recommend it. He also told me that it was the president who did not want to settle the case and that he would never agree to default because other women would "come out of the woodwork."

I asked Bennett what kind of an investigation he had conducted of the Lewinsky matter before he allowed the president to be deposed, and he acknowledged that he simply accepted the president's word, since it was supported by Lewinsky's affidavit. I asked him whether he had ever questioned Lewinsky, and he gave a vague response. He did say that he was surprised about the questions asked concerning Lewinsky at the deposition.

I told Bennett that I strongly believed he had made a mistake by walking his client into a perjury trap and allowing him to get into a swearing contest about his sex life. He assured me that he knew what he was doing and that it would all work to the advantage of his client. I told him I hoped he was right, but that I still thought he had made a mistake.

In August 1998, in the presence of a dozen people on Martha's Vineyard, I asked the president if Bennett had ever told him that he had the option of defaulting rather than testifying about his sex life. He said, "Nobody ever told me I could default instead of testifying. I thought I had to testify. Nobody told me about defaulting until just now."

Defaulting the Jones case would have resulted in bad headlines the next day — and perhaps for an additional week. But testifying about his sex life resulted in a dangerous threat to the Clinton presidency — a threat that would not materialize for several months.

On January 26, the president, with the assistance of Hollywood producer Harry Thomason, decided to make a public statement denying a sexual relationship with Monica Lewinsky.[80] Pointing his finger at the TV camera for emphasis, he said, "I did not have sexual relations with that woman, Miss Lewinsky." This statement, made directly to the American public and not under oath, came back to haunt Clinton. Why did he make it? He was under no legal obligation to make any statement. He could easily have said, as so many others have said, "Since the matter is now the subject of a legal proceeding, my lawyers have advised me to make no public comment about it. I'm sure you understand."

Once again, the president and his advisers opted for the quick fix. They felt that it was necessary to put out the political brushfire that was burning around them. By issuing a firm denial, the president could postpone — perhaps forever — the longer-term consequences of his improper sex and his misleading testimony. At the time he made the statement, the president was probably not aware that Lewinsky had saved the semen-stained dress that would eventually force him to change his story.

On July 28, 1998, Monica Lewinsky's new lawyers struck a deal with Starr under which she was given total immunity in exchange for her cooperation and testimony. On July 29, the president's lawyer, David Kendall, announced that an agreement had been reached with the independent counsel regarding the president's subpoenaed grand jury testimony. The subpoena would be withdrawn, and the president would submit voluntarily to four hours of questioning in the White House, in the presence of his own lawyers.

In reaching this agreement, the president withdrew his constitutional challenge to the power of a grand jury to compel his testimony. I doubt that his lawyers wanted him to testify, especially since he was not prepared to come completely clean. What I don't know is whether at the time the president made the decision to testify, he knew of the existence of the semen-stained dress. What we do know is that the decision to testify before the Starr grand jury gave the prosecutor an opportunity to trap the president once again into committing perjury — this time not in a live deposition in a dismissed case where the testimony was only marginally relevant but in a grand jury proceeding where the testimony was central. It also gave the prosecutor an unprecedented opportunity to videotape the interrogation so that Congress and the public could see it.

Some critics believe that Clinton and Starr deserved each other. But we the people did not deserve to see our delicate system of checks and balances endangered by the reckless actions of these two men. The question therefore remains: What kinds of offenses warrant the extraordinary remedy of legislative removal of a president? The answer must be an offense that poses a clear and present danger to our body politic — a high public violation of official duty, not a low, private sex scandal, even if it may have included acts that might technically be criminal (though almost never prosecuted).

The constitutional remedy of removal of a duly elected president is extraordinary. It is intended to be invoked only as a last resort, after all other checks and balances have been exhausted. It is like the fire alarm or the ax behind the glass that must not be broken except in case of a dire emergency. Just how extraordinary the removal of a president — as distinguished from a judge or other individual — was intended to be may be gleaned from the text of the Constitution itself: "when the President of the United States is tried [by the Senate], the Chief Justice shall preside." This means that the judicial branch must also be involved in the grave act of undoing a presidential election.

In this case, the chief justice did preside over the trial in the Senate. It was a great trial, because any trial that could result in the removal of a president is necessarily a central event in our history. But it was a political trial, not a legal trial. Its outcome was determined not by the evidence, or even the legal rulings, but rather by the fact that there were not enough Republicans to garner the necessary sixty-seven votes for removal. The outcome of the Senate trial was known with virtual certainty even before a single witness was called. Only an incredible blunder by the Clinton defense team could have changed the result, but by this time, President Clinton was no longer relying on the lawyer who had helped him get impeached. His Senate legal team did a commendable job.

The impeachment of President Clinton was an abuse of power by the Republican-controlled House of Representatives. The Republican-controlled Senate saved the nation from a constitutional crisis by refusing to remove Clinton, though most Republicans voted for removal. Our system of checks and balances worked, though not without some damage to our Constitution.

1. Richard L. Fox and Robert W. Van Sickel, *Tabloid Justice: Criminal Justice in an Age of Media Frenzy* (Boulder, CO: Lynne Rienner Publishers, 2001).

2. Benjamin G. Rader, "Television," in *Encyclopedia of American Social History*, vol. 3, ed. Mary Kupiec Cayton, Elliot J. Gorn, and Peter W. Williams (New York: Charles Scribner's Sons, 1993), p. 1847.

3. General Social Survey, Rober Center, University of Connecticut (Chances in News and Information Dissemination Since 1970).

4. Fox and Van Sickel, p. 69.

5. *Ibid.*

6. Richard Turner, "A Tabloid Shocker," *Newsweek*, Oct. 12, 1998.

7. Rader, p. 1847.

8. Fox and Van Sickel, p. 130.

9. Gary W. McDonough, Robert Gregg, and Cindy H. Wong, eds., *Encyclopedia of Contemporary American Culture* (New York: Routledge, 2001), p. 124.

10. Alan Dershowitz, *Reversal of Fortune* (New York: Random House, 1986), p. xvii.

11. Fox and Van Sickel, p. 2.

12. Steve Chapman, "Could 2000 Be the Real Year of the Woman?" *Chicago Tribune*, Jan. 7, 1999.

13. Ray Surette, *Media, Crime, and Criminal Justice: Images and Realities*, 2nd ed. (Belmont, CA: Wadsworth Publishing, 1998), p. 72.

14. Fox and Van Sickel, p. 23.

15. *Ibid.*, pp. 35–39.

16. *Ibid.*, p. 133; Robert Giles and Robert W. Snyder, eds., *Covering the Courts* (New Brunswick, NJ: Transaction Publishers, 1999), p. 111.

17. Jonathan Alter, "In the Time of the Tabs," *Newsweek*, June 2, 1997.

18. Denise Noe, "The Jean Harris Case," in *Court TV Crime Library*, http://www.crimelibrary.com/notorious_murders/women/harris/l.html?sect=11.

19. Shana Alexander, *Very Much a Lady: The Untold Story of Jean Harris and Dr. Herman Tarnower* (Boston: Little, Brown and Co., 1983), pp. 199–200.

20. Comment by friend Peg Cullman upon hearing the news, quoted in Alexander, p. 214.

21. Alexander, p. 192.

22. *Ibid.*, p. 262.

23. See, generally, Noe.

24. Quoted in Alexander, p. 259.

25. *Ibid.*, p. 265.

26. See Noe.

27. See Alexander, p. 271 (quoting from trial transcript of Mar. 20, 1981, p. 9729).

28. Joan Mower, "Wounds Still Healing from Assassin's Shot," *Houston Chronicle*, Mar. 30, 1986.

29. *Ibid.*

30. Richard Bonnie, John Jeffries, and Peter Low, *A Case Study in the Insanity Defense: The Trial of John W. Hinckley, Jr.*, 2nd ed. (New York: Foundation Press, 2000), p. 64.

31. *Ibid.*, p. 56.

32. *Ibid.*, p. 84.

33. *Ibid.*, p. 67.

34. Associated Press, "Hinckley Tells of 'Great Remorse' Over His Attempt to Kill Reagan," *Washington Post*, Mar. 22, 1984.

35. Judith Cummings, "DeLorean Is Freed of Cocaine Charge by a Federal Jury," *New York Times*, Aug. 17, 1984.

36. Jay Matthews, "DeLorean Acquitted of All Eight Charges in Drug-Scheme Trial," *Washington Post*, Aug. 17, 1984.

37. Alan Dershowitz, "The DeLorean Verdict: Guilty, but Entrapped," *Boston Herald*, Aug. 19, 1984.

38. *Hustler Magazine and Larry C. Flynt, Petitioners v. Jerry Falwell*, 108 S. Ct. 876 (1988).

39. *Ibid.*, p. 879.

40. *Ibid.*, p. 880.

41. *Ibid.*

42. The Sullivan case ruled that newspapers may report on public figures without fear of defamation lawsuits, so long as they do not act in "reckless disregard" of the truth. In other words, they have the constitutional right to be wrong — so long as their mistakes are honest and reasonable ones.

43. *Flynt v. Falwell*, p. 283.

44. *Ibid.*, pp. 280–83.

45. *Ibid.*, pp. 284–85.

46. George P. Fletcher, *A Crime of Self-Defense: Bernhard Goetz and the Law on Trial* (New York: The Free Press, 1988).

47. *Ibid.*

48. James Raine, "Defense Will File Complaints Against McMartin Prosecutor," *Los Angeles Times*, Jan. 27, 1990.

49. Paul Eberle and Shirley Eberle, *The Abuse of Innocence: The McMartin Preschool Trial* (Buffalo: Prometheus Books, 1993), p. 207.

50. *Ibid.*, p. 105.

51. Emily Sachar, "Lawyers Make Final Defense in Jogger Case," *Newsday*, Aug. 8, 1990.

52. *Ibid.*

53. Timothy Sullivan, *Unequal Verdicts: The Central Park Jogger Trials* (New York: The Notable Trials Library, 1994), p. 223.

54. *Ibid.*, p. 316.

55. Alan Dershowitz, "The Rape of Mike Tyson," *Penthouse*, June 1993, p. 59.

56. *Ibid.*

57. *Ibid.*, p. 60.

58. *Ibid.*

59. *Ibid.*

60. *Ibid.*

61. *Ibid.*, p. 65.

62. *Ibid.*, pp. 63–65.

63. *Ibid.*, pp. 64–65.

64. *Ibid.*

65. *Ibid.*

66. *Ibid.*

67. *Ibid.*, p. 66.

68. *Ibid.*, p. 68.

69. *Ibid.*

70. In the O. J. Simpson case, only the first trial, which resulted in an acquittal, was a criminal trial, whereas the second trial was a civil suit with a lower burden of proof.

71. See, generally, Alan Dershowitz, *Reasonable Doubts* (New York: Simon and Schuster, 1996).

72. For an elaboration of these issues, see Dershowitz, *Reasonable Doubts.*

73. Dershowitz, *Reasonable Doubts*, p. 14.

74. *Ibid.*

75. *Ibid.*

76. *Ibid.*

77. *Ibid.*

78. *Ibid.*, p. 15.

79. *Ibid.*

80. Merrill McLoughlin, ed., *The Impeachment and Trial of President Clinton* (Delanco, NJ: The Notable Trials Library, 2001), pp. 15; see generally Alan Dershowitz, *Sexual McCarthyism* (New York: Basic Books, 1998).

PART XIV

The New Millennium and the Future

THE TWENTY-FIRST CENTURY began with one of the worst legal events in the history of our country — the Supreme Court's utterly corrupt and partisan decision to stop the recount in Florida, thus assuring the election of George W. Bush as president. The Supreme Court placed its own legitimacy in question, as well as the legitimacy of the new president. The nation was deeply divided over the manner by which the High Court injected itself into a political decision. This discussion ended abruptly on September 11, 2001 — just eighteen months into the Bush presidency — when terrorists attacked our nation.

The attacks of September 11 gave rise to many legal cases. At this point none have yet become great trials, but I predict that the great trials of this decade will include several terrorism prosecutions. The other divisive issues that will probably generate great trials in this decade relate to the separation of church and state, and the efforts of the religious right to impose its puritanical religious morality on all Americans. The trial — and Supreme Court appeal — of two gay men in Texas for violating the state's anti-homosexual sodomy law is the second great case of the twenty-first century. It qualifies as great because the Supreme Court's broad decision in favor of sexual liberty not only is important to gay men and women, but also marks an important step forward for all Americans who love liberty and believe in limited governmental power. Still, no book about great American trials throughout history can end on so optimistic a note, especially in this age of terrorism. Many courts seem to be abdicating their constitutional role to enforce the rule of law even during those times of crisis that test not only the souls of citizens, but also the courage of judges. It remains to be seen whether our courts will live up to their responsibilities as guardians of our rights, or whether they will do as so many courts in previous generations have done: submit to popular passions rather than insisting on applying the Constitution in the face of political pressures.

As this book went to press, a front-page story in the *New York Times* carried the following headline: "Justices face decision on accepting 9/11 cases." The story began: "With cases generated by the Bush administration's response to the terrorist attacks of Sept. 11, 2001, now reaching the Supreme Court in substantial numbers, the court faces a basic decision apart from the merits of any individual case: whether to become a player in the debate over where to set the balance between individual liberty and national security."[1] Whether the High Court decides to become a player in this critical debate may determine the future of our civil liberties and the nature of the great trials of the twenty-first century.

Bush v. Gore

Date:	*November–December 2000*
Location:	*Florida, District of Columbia*
Litigants:	*The Democratic and Republican nominees for president*
Issue:	*Who won Florida's electoral votes*
Decision:	*The U.S. Supreme Court reversed the Florida Supreme Court, which had ordered a statewide recount*

The critical question raised by *Bush v. Gore*[2] is whether we can trust the U.S. Supreme Court to administer justice fairly and apolitically when the stakes are high. This is an even more important question after September 11, 2001, than it was before. If history teaches us anything, it teaches us that in times of national emergency, many of the most difficult questions eventually make their way up to the Supreme Court — which makes the ultimate decision whether to answer them or leave them to other branches of government or to the lower courts. More than any other institution in our tripartite system of checks and balances, it is the High Court that must strike the appropriate balance between security and liberty.

In *Bush v. Gore*, a majority of the Supreme Court believed it was deciding the presidency of the United States. Subsequent recounts by various media organizations suggest that the majority's decision may not have changed the outcome — that George W.

Bush might have been elected even if the Supreme Court had stayed out of the matter. It turns out that under most plausible scenarios Bush would have won, though under some Gore might have won. Since my criticism relates to *the integrity* of the Supreme Court, it matters not at all what the outcome of the election would have been without its intervention. The critical question is what the majority of justices *believed* at the time they issued their unprecedented stay, thereby stopping the recount, and their final decision making the stay permanent, thereby ending the election. In my book *Supreme Injustice,* I demonstrate that the majority believed that Gore might well have won the recount, if it were allowed to continue. I also prove that the five justices cheated — that is, they violated their oath of office, which requires them to administer justice "without respect to persons." If the shoe had been on the other foot — if it had been Bush who needed the recount to win — these same five justices would not have stopped the recount. That constitutes cheating under the rule of law.

Prior to September 11, Judge Richard Posner predicted that the Supreme Court's decision in *Bush v. Gore* would be judged "on the success of Bush's presidency." This is the wrong criterion for testing the integrity of a Supreme Court decision. Even corrupt decisions sometimes bring about positive results. Judge Posner was right, however, in one respect: Following September 11, and the important role President George W. Bush has played in rallying Americans around the war against terrorism, few Americans want to think about the ignoble role played by the Supreme Court in Election 2000. Following the inauguration, and especially after the events of September 11, 2001, a significant majority of Americans decided that George Bush was a better president than Al Gore would have been (whether that perception persists, of course, remains to be seen). But the "success" of the Bush presidency must not mask the failure of the Supreme Court.

In the months and years to come, the focus will once again shift to the U.S. Supreme Court. There will be vacancies, and nominations to fill these vacancies. It is possible that one of the five majority justices will be considered to fill the vacancy in the chief justiceship that is likely to occur. This will renew debate about the Supreme Court's role in *Bush v. Gore.*

Equally important will be the post–September 11 cases that will inevitably be decided by the Supreme Court. This is an important time for the justices, and the emergency we are in — and will likely remain in for a long time — should not in any way diminish appropriate criticism of the Supreme Court. During times of emergency, the public serves as an important additional check on the three branches of government. An informed public, knowledgeable about the inner workings of our institutions — including the most secretive of our institutions, the Supreme Court — is essential to the proper workings of democracy.

The five justices who ended Election 2000 by stopping the Florida hand count may have permanently damaged the credibility of the Supreme Court. The lawless decision in *Bush v. Gore* promises to have a more enduring impact on Americans than the *outcome* of the election itself. The nation has accepted the election of George W. Bush, as it must under the rule of law. The citizens always will have an opportunity to reassess the outcome of any election in subsequent elections. But the unprecedented decision of the five justices to substitute their political judgments for those of the people threatens to undermine the moral authority of the High Court for generations to come.

Because it lacks the legitimacy and accountability that come with election and the power that derives from the sword and the purse, the Supreme Court's authority rests on public acceptance of its status as a nonpartisan arbiter of the law. This moral authority is essential to its continued effectiveness as an important guarantor of our constitutional liberties. Unless steps are taken to mitigate the damage caused by the wound inflicted on the Court by the five justices, the balance struck by our Constitution between popular democracy and judicial oligarchy will remain askew. Preserving this delicate balance is essential to our liberties and to our system of checks and balances.

The majority ruling in *Bush v. Gore* marked a number of significant firsts. Never before in American history has a presidential election been decided by the Supreme Court.[3] Never before in American history have so many law professors, historians, political scientists, Supreme Court litigators, journalists who cover the High Court, and other experts — at all points along the political spectrum — been in agreement that the majority decision of the Court was not only "bad constitutional law," but also "lawless,"[4] "illegitimate,"[5] "unprincipled," "partisan," "fraudulent," "disingenuous," and motivated by improper considerations. In addition to the remarkable expert consensus regarding this case, there is also widespread popular outrage at what the High Court did. Though the level of this outrage tends to mirror party affiliation, it is safe to say that the level of confusion over what actually happened is not limited to one party. There are millions of Americans who do not strongly identify with the Democratic party — indeed, even some who voted for George W. Bush — who cannot understand how five justices could determine the outcome of a presidential election. Moreover, the outrage within the Supreme Court itself — among justices and law clerks — is unprecedented in the annals of this usually harmonious institution.

In light of these factors, many Americans who believed that the Court was an institution that could be trusted to remain above partisan politics are now experiencing a genuine loss of confidence in the impartiality of the judicial branch of our government. This widespread loss of confidence, reaching to the pinnacle of our judiciary, should be the concern of all Americans, because the Supreme Court has played such a critical role in the history of our nation. Without its moral authority, we would be a less tolerant, less vibrant, and less free democracy. The High Court, throughout its long and distinguished history, has helped us — not always perfectly or swiftly — through crises of institutional racism, religious intolerance, McCarthyism, systematic malapportionment, presidents who deemed themselves above the law, and governors who defied the Constitution. The Court stepped in when the other branches of government were unwilling or unable to enforce the constitutional rights of unpopular minorities. The justices were always at their greatest when they could act unanimously and on principles that could easily be justified and widely accepted. When they have acted in an unprincipled and partisan manner — as they did in *Bush v. Gore* — they have lost respect and frittered away the moral capital accumulated by their predecessors over the generations. That is what Justice Stephen Breyer was referring to when he wrote in his dissent in *Bush v. Gore*: "in this highly politicized matter, the appearance of a split decision runs the risk of undermining the public's confidence in the Court itself. That confidence is a public treasure. It has been built slowly over many years. . . . It is a vitally necessary ingredient of any successful effort to protect basic liberty and, indeed, the rule of law itself. [We] risk a self-inflicted wound — a wound that may harm not just the Court, but the Nation." That is why all Americans must care about this case and must derive the appropriate lessons from it. The Supreme Court's moral capital will certainly again be needed in our future, and so it is a tragedy that it has been dissipated for short-term partisan gain in a case in which the Supreme Court had no proper role.

The Constitution, after all, places the power to elect our president in every institution of government but the judiciary. The *people* vote for electors.[6] The *electors* vote for the president. If this process produces no clear winner, then the Constitution (and the laws enacted pursuant to it) assigns varying roles to the

Senate, the House of Representatives, the state legislatures, and even the governors.[7] No role, however, is explicitly given to the Supreme Court. James Madison, in recording his own views of the constitutional debates as to how the president should be elected, dismissed selection by the appointed "judiciary" as "out of the question."[8]

Indeed, the justices themselves seemed to initially recognize the absence of a judicial role when they unanimously remanded *Bush v. Gore* back to the Florida Supreme Court for that court to explain whether it had improperly changed the election law as enacted by the Florida legislature. The High Court suggested that if the court had changed duly enacted state legislation, then it may have violated Article II of the Constitution, which vests authority in the legislature for selecting the manner by which electors should be chosen. It seems ironic that the U.S. Supreme Court would take upon itself a judicial function nowhere speci-fied in the Constitution — effectively deciding a presidential election — while seeming to deny to the Supreme Court of Florida its traditional role in interpreting and reconciling con-flicting statutes.

Some of the Court's defenders have argued that since, in their view, the Florida Supreme Court engaged in partisan judicial ac-tivism in support of Gore, it was permissible for the Supreme Court — as the nation's highest court — to "correct" the "lower court" and undo the harm it had done. Indeed, I am reliably in-formed that the majority of justices were outraged at what they believed was crass partisanship by the Florida justices. I have been told that one of the dissenting U.S. Supreme Court justices characterized the mind-set of some of the majority justices as fol-lows: "If the Florida Supreme Court is going to act like a bunch of Democratic political hacks, well, by God, we will act like a bunch of Republican political hacks." Even if it were true that some Florida justices may have acted in a partisan manner, this would not justify a retaliatory partisan decision by U.S. Supreme

Court justices. Two partisan wrongs do not make a judicial right. Moreover, under the U.S. Constitution, a state court has the right to be wrong on matters of state law, and the Supreme Court has no power to correct it unless its mistake is a matter of federal constitutional or statutory law. Even then, the Supreme Court does not traditionally correct every error a state court may make. Citing death penalty cases, Justice Ruth Bader Ginsburg, in her dissenting opinion in *Bush v. Gore,* reminded her colleagues: "Not uncommonly, we let stand state-court interpretations of federal law with which we might disagree." During oral argument, she put it even more directly to Bush's lawyer: "'I do not know of any case where we have impugned a state supreme court the way you are doing in this case,' Ginsburg scolded Olson. Florida's seven justices 'may have been wrong; we might have interpreted it differently, but we are not the arbiters — they are.'"[9] The very justices who typically allow state prisoners to be executed even if their conviction was based on a mistaken reading of federal constitutional law[10] jumped into this case on the ground that the Florida Supreme Court's decision violated the equal protection clause of the U.S. Constitution in a manner never before suggested by any court. Even some scholars who voted for Bush — Robert Bork, Harvey Mansfield, Richard Posner, Michael McConnell, and Richard Epstein, among others — have found this conclusion unconvincing, troublesome, and "wrongheaded."[11]

It also seemed baffling to many that these five justices, whose record on the High Court showed them to be the least sensitive to claims of equal protection and most beholden to claims of states' rights, determined a presidential election on such doubtful equal protection grounds. *New York Times* reporter Linda Greenhouse, quoting experts to the effect that the majority chose their politics over their jurisprudence, concluded that the decision left the Supreme Court diminished, if not actually tarnished.[12]

These and many other questions have led many Americans to wonder about whether the black-robed justices are really any less politically partisan than elected politicians. When Antonin Scalia — one of the architects of the majority decision — was still a law professor, he made an observation that aptly characterized the feelings of many scholars in regard to this decision: "It is increasingly difficult to pretend to one's students that the decisions of the Supreme Court are tied together by threads of logic and analysis as opposed to what seems to be the fact that the decisions of each of the Justices on the Court are tied together by threads of social preference and predisposition."[13]

In dissenting from the Supreme Court's decision ending the hand count, Justice John Paul Stevens, the court's senior associate justice, echoed Professor Scalia in strong words that will be long remembered and often quoted by those who follow the Court. He warned that the majority's position "can only lend credence to the most cynical appraisal of the work of judges throughout the land. It is," said Justice Stevens, "confidence in the men and women who administer the judicial system that is the true backbone of the rule of law. Time will one day heal the wound to that confidence that will be inflicted by today's decision. One thing, however, is certain. Although we may never know with complete certainty the identity of the winner of the 2000 presidential election, the identity of the loser is perfectly clear. It is the nation's confidence in the judge as an impartial guardian of the rule of law."[14]

Justice Stevens is wrong in only one respect: Time will never heal this wound, so long as the source of the illness remains untreated. There are few things worse than a healed wound that still contains an infection. Only the strong disinfectant of sunlight will allow this wound to heal properly. And heal it must, if our system of checks and balances, with the unique role our Supreme Court has played throughout our history, is to remain strong.

A significant diminution of confidence in our Supreme Court, based on legitimate concerns, should not be covered up or minimized in the false hope that it will be forgotten over time. Nor should well-intentioned defenders of the justices hold back their criticism out of fear that those who would weaken the Supreme Court as an institution will misuse it. Well-founded criticism, if it leads to proper healing, can only strengthen the Court.

It will come as no surprise that I, too, was a partisan in this election and in the postelection legal and political dispute. I am a Democrat (who occasionally votes for Republicans) who in this election voted for Al Gore. A few days after the election, two groups of voters in Palm Beach County asked me to represent them on a pro bono basis to oppose the Bush efforts to stop the mandatory hand recount requested by Gore and to obtain other legal relief. I appeared in court once on behalf of one of these groups and continued to maintain an interest throughout the litigation. I also appeared frequently in the media, not as a spokesman for the Democratic party — indeed, I disagreed strongly with some of its tactics[15] — but rather as a supporter of a statewide hand count done by categories. (Shortly after Election Day, I proposed that an objective body conduct the count and catalog every disputed ballot by its salient characteristics: how many were fully punched through; how many had one, two, or three hanging chads; how many were pierced, dimpled, and so forth.) I am also an academic who has practiced before the Supreme Court for many years and who has taught courses for even more years dealing extensively with Supreme Court decisions. I served as a law clerk to the late Justice Arthur Goldberg during the 1963–64 term of the Supreme Court. I think I understand the important and unique role our High Court plays in our system of governance and I revere it as an institution, though I have often been critical of its work.

I wanted Al Gore to be elected president, but it was not Gore's loss or Bush's win that animates my criticism. I care much more about the enduring impact of this case on the credibility of the Supreme Court than on the transient effects of a single presidential election. I am angry with the Supreme Court not so much because of *whom* it elected, but because it took it upon itself to elect anyone at all.

The Texas Sodomy Trial and Appeal

Date:	2000–03
Location:	Houston, Texas; District of Columbia
Defendants:	John Geddes Lawrence and Tyron Gardner
Charge:	Homosexual sodomy
Verdict:	Guilty at trial; conviction reversed on appeal, and statute declared unconstitutional
Sentence:	Two-hundred-dollar fine; overturned on appeal

The trial of John Geddes Lawrence and Tyron Gardner was not about disputed facts; it was about disputed constitutional law. Everyone agreed that two men were engaged in homosexual sodomy when the police broke into Lawrence's apartment, and that sodomy between people of the same sex is a violation of Texas law. The police were allegedly responding to a reported "weapons disturbance," but it is widely believed the call had come from someone who objected to what the two adult men were doing in the privacy of Lawrence's bedroom. The caller could not get the police to enter based on a report that the men were committing the Texas misdemeanor of sodomy, since suspicion of a misdemeanor does not generally justify a house search. So the caller reported the felony of a weapons disturbance, and what police found was the two men engaging in sodomy.

In Texas, a man and a woman may lawfully engage in sodomy — which is defined as contact between "the genitals" of one person and "the mouth or anus" of another person — but two people of the same sex who do the same thing are criminals. Several other states have criminalized all sodomy, including oral–genital contact between a man and woman — even a married couple.

Obviously these laws are sporadically enforced, precisely because it would be a rare case, such as this one, in which the police had a legitimate basis for entering anyone's home to arrest a person for private sexual behavior. Moreover, if every couple — married, unmarried, gay, or straight — who engaged in oral sex were prosecuted, our nation would become a virtual prison, since polls show that tens of millions of Americans routinely engage in this increasingly common sexual activity.

In this case, all the elements coalesced to make the perfect test case. The defendants admitted — proclaimed — that they had committed the prohibited act, and they challenged the Texas law under the equal protection and due process clauses of the Constitution. They lost, were convicted, and were sentenced to pay a two-hundred-dollar fine. The trial itself (in which the defendants admitted the facts but challenged the law) simply laid the foundation for the real conflict — which would be fought in the appellate courts. The Texas appellate court affirmed the conviction, relying on the U.S. Supreme Court's 1986 decision in *Bowers v. Hardwick*, which had upheld Georgia's sodomy law on the ground that homosexual activity is not a "fundamental right" and that sodomy has been prohibited since ancient times.

The Supreme Court used the Texas case as an opportunity to overrule *Bowers v. Hardwick* and to declare that "*Bowers* was not correct when it was decided, and it is not correct today."

Court watchers were not surprised at the outcome of the case. The *Bowers* decision was decided by a closely divided Court, and the swing justice — the late Lewis Powell — had said, after his retirement from the Court, that he regretted his vote. What surprised nearly everyone was the extraordinary breadth of the majority opinion, written by moderate conservative Justice Anthony Kennedy, and the even more extraordinary potential reach of the dissenting opinion written by Justice Antonin Scalia, the Court's reigning political and religious reactionary.

The majority opinion opened with the following paragraph that could have been penned by John Stuart Mill:

> Liberty protects the person from unwarranted government intrusions into a dwelling or other private places. In our tradition the State is not omnipresent in the home. And there are other spheres of our lives and existence, outside the home, where the State should not be a dominant presence. Freedom extends beyond spatial bounds. Liberty presumes an autonomy of self that includes freedom of thought, belief, expression and certain intimate conduct. The instant case involves liberty of the person both in its spatial and more transcendent dimensions.

It then proceeded to articulate a "general rule" that counsels against

> . . . attempts by the State, or a court, to define the meaning of the relationship or to set its boundaries absent injury to a person or abuse of an institution the law protects. It suffices for us to acknowledge that adults may choose to enter upon this relationship in the confines of their homes and their own private lives and still retain their dignity as free persons. When sexuality finds overt expression in intimate conduct with another person, the conduct can be but one element in a personal bond that is more enduring. The liberty protected by the Constitution allows homosexual persons the right to make this choice.

Finally, the majority concluded that in cases such as this one, the state has no legitimate interest in intruding on the privacy of adult individuals:

The present case does not involve minors. It does not involve persons who might be injured or coerced or who are situated in relationships where consent might not easily be refused. It does not involve public conduct or prostitution. It does not involve whether the government must give formal recognition to any relationship that homosexual persons seek to enter. The case does involve two adults who, with full and mutual consent from each other, engaged in sexual practices common to a homosexual lifestyle. The petitioners are entitled to respect for their private lives. The State cannot demean their existence or control their destiny by making their private sexual conduct a crime. Their right to liberty under the Due Process Clause gives them the full right to engage in their conduct without intervention of the government. "It is a promise of the Constitution that there is a realm of personal liberty which the government may not enter." The Texas statute furthers no legitimate state interest which can justify its intrusion into the personal and private life of the individual.

Had those who drew and ratified the Due Process Clauses of the Fifth Amendment or the Fourteenth Amendment known the components of liberty in its manifold possibilities, they might have been more specific. They did not presume to have this insight. They knew times can blind us to certain truths and later generations can see that laws once thought necessary and proper in fact serve only to oppress. As the Constitution endures, persons in every generation can invoke its principles in their own search for greater freedom.

The convictions of Lawrence and Gardner were reversed, and they were constitutionally entitled to continue to engage in sodomy. It was a Magna Carta for gay Americans — indeed for all Americans who value privacy and autonomy.

Justice Scalia wrote a scathing dissent, characterizing the majority decision as a "result oriented expedient." (Considering Scalia's own result-oriented expedient vote in *Bush v. Gore*, there is an element of the kettle calling the pot black here.) Scalia then proceeded to parade the horribles that would follow if this decision were to be taken to its logical conclusion: "State laws against bigamy, same-sex marriage, adult incest, prostitution, masturbation, adultery, fornication, bestiality, and obscenity are likewise sustainable only in light of *Bowers'* validation of laws based on moral choices. Every single one of these laws is called into question by today's decision."

Imagine, striking down laws against "masturbation"! Surely the pillars will crumble (or at least more people will go blind or grow hair on the palms of their hands, as my rabbis warned). At another point, Scalia wondered whether a state would still be able to prohibit nudity. Since he says, "I do not know what 'acting in private' means," perhaps the Scalian state could prohibit nudity in the privacy of one's home, as he believes it should be able to criminalize "fornication" — that is, consensual heterosexual contact between unmarried adults.

Scalia would uphold state laws prohibiting masturbation, fornication, and nudity for one simple reason: Some states prohibited such conduct in the eighteenth century, when our Constitution and Bill of Rights were adopted. (States also prohibited friendly games of poker for money, a vice in which Scalia has reportedly engaged with lawyers who argue cases before the Court.) Scalia has rejected, as a "constitutional fallacy," the idea that the "Constitution is a living document" — that is, a text whose meaning may change with time and experience. He has proclaimed that the Constitution is a "dead" document, whose words mean precisely what they "meant when it was adopted."[16] And Scalia believes that the Constitution authorizes the states to

criminalize conduct that hurts no one but that merely offends
the morality, including the purely religious morality, or theology,
of a majority of the citizens (or legislators).[17] The "promotion of
majoritarian sexual morality" is, according to Scalia, enough of
a justification to permit the state to imprison people whose private sexual conduct is deemed "immoral and unacceptable,"
even though it has no impact on anyone else.

According to this view, a state could not only require us all to
practice sex as it was practiced (or at least *said* to be practiced)
two hundred years ago — between a husband and wife, in the
missionary position, and for procreative purposes only — but also
prohibit blasphemy, require church attendance, and censor
newspapers. The federal government could not do all of these
things because the First Amendment prohibits "*Congress* from
making any law respecting an establishment of religion" (emphasis added) or abridging the freedom of speech or press. But
nothing in the Constitution or Bill of Rights explicitly prohibits
the states from enacting such laws.

Scalia has claimed he has no choice but to consider the Constitution "dead," since he believes that a dead Constitution was
the original intent of its framers. He also believes that interpreting the Constitution as a living document, whose words can
change with time, merely empowers Supreme Court justices to
"pursue their own objectives and desires." A "dead" Constitution, on the other hand, limits the power of judges to interpreting its words as they were used by its eighteenth-century authors.
Scalia claims that he does not "want to impose on the society"
the "most deeply felt beliefs of Scalia."[18] But the reality is that
Scalia's dead Constitution, with its eighteenth-century view of
the world, just happens to coincide largely with the "most deeply
felt beliefs of Scalia." And when it doesn't — as it didn't in *Bush
v. Gore* — Scalia conveniently resurrects the "dead" Constitution,
bringing it to life in his own image. In *Bush v. Gore*, Scalia was
willing to stop a state recount by employing an unprecedented

and extremely creative — "live" — twenty-first-century view of the "equal protection clause" in order to assure that his "deeply felt belief" that Bush should be president was implemented. [19]

For the most part, Scalia seems at home with an eighteenth-century view of the world. He believes that the state derives its moral authority from God and speaks dismissively of "the emergence of democracy" and of "post-Christian Europe." He bemoans "the tendency of democracy to obscure the divine authority behind government," and calls on "people of faith" "to combat" this tendency "as effectively as possible," by keeping God visible in our public lives. In this way, people will be more likely to accept Saint Paul's view "that government carries the sword" as "the minister of God," to "execute wrath" upon "the evildoer."[20] He is a deeply religious fundamentalist who once told a prayer breakfast that "we are fools for Christ's sake. We must pray for the courage to endure the scorn of the sophisticated world."[21] He reads the Bible as he reads the Constitution: as a never-changing dead document.[22] He has described himself as a "Roman Catholic" who is "unable to jump out of his skin" and would never become part of any state "machinery" that produced results contrary to binding church morality. For example, he "could not participate" in that process of imposing or affirming a death penalty if he believed "what was being done to be immoral."[23] Fortunately for him, he regards the death penalty as both moral and in line with "the long and consistent Christian tradition." Part of the reason he regards the death penalty as moral is that — in Scalia's words — "for the believing Christian, death is no big deal." (As an avid hunter — who once hunted with Vice President Richard Cheney while Cheney was a defendant in a case before the Supreme Court — Scalia obviously believes that killing animals is also "no big deal.") Scalia dismisses the current Vatican opposition to the death penalty — which he derides as "the latest hot-off-the-presses version of the catechism" — as nonbinding and dead wrong.[24] His views of when Catholic doctrine is binding, like his views of when Constitutional doctrine is binding, generally coincide precisely with his personal and political views. How convenient! How transparent! How hypocritical!

Yet Justice Scalia, along with Justice Thomas, is President Bush's favorite justice — his model for future appointments. This is why the Texas sodomy case may mark an important watershed in our history. Its majority opinion points to a future in which men and women retain considerable "liberty . . . from unwarranted government intrusions." Its minority opinions point to a future in which religiously inspired state inquisitors may — in the name of enforcing a uniform morality — regulate the most intimate aspects of our private lives. Which future will be ours may depend — at least in part — on who sits on the Supreme Court and on our lower courts. The great trials of the future may not be so different from the great trials of the past. The liberties for which John Peter Zenger, Susan. B. Anthony, John Scopes, and others struggled can never be taken for granted. There are always Scalias and Thomases — some on the right, others on the left — eager to take them away in the name of "morality," "God," "political correctness," or some other "truth" of which they are certain. The struggle for liberty never stays won. The trials of the future will help strike the inevitable balance between the liberty of the individual and the authority of government in much the same way that great trials have always done — though the stakes may be higher in this age where criminals and terrorists seem especially dangerous because of weapons of mass destruction and unlimited technological power.

The Cases of the Terrorist Detainees—in Guantanamo, on the U.S. Mainland, and in Unknown Places Around the World

Date: 2004–
Locations: *Virginia, District of Columbia, San Francisco, New York, and places unknown*
Defendants: *Jose Padilla, Yaser Esam Hamdi, Khaled A. F. Al Odah, Falen Gherebi, and others*
Charges: *Association with terrorism*
Verdict: *Some detained, some ordered released*
Appeals: *Pending*

Cataclysmic historical events often produce great cases. The terrorist attacks on America of September 11, 2001, have not yet led directly to a trial, since the actual perpetrators all died in the plane crashes. But these terrible events have led indirectly to a plethora of cases that together constitute a major legal event of the twenty-first century.

As this book goes to press, there have been plea bargains and accusations, but no notable trials. The absence of any criminal trials is itself notable and may suggest a dangerous trend in our nation's approach to terrorism. Despite the absence of trials, however, the courts have not been silent.

Four major terrorist cases have divided the United States Courts of Appeals and roiled the nation. The Supreme Court has agreed to review two of them and may decide to review others as well. Potentially the most far-reaching of these cases involves the so-called "dirty bomber," an alleged Al Qaeda terrorist named Jose Padilla, who was arrested in Chicago and initially held as "a material witness." Subsequently, President Bush designated Padilla — who is an American citizen — "an enemy combatant" and directed that he be held in the custody of the military. He had been detained for a year and a half in the brig at Charleston with no access to his lawyer, his family, or his friends. He is undergoing "ongoing questioning regarding the Al Qaeda network and its terrorist activities in an effort to obtain intelligence."[25]

The government has alleged that Padilla, who was born in New York and convicted of murder in 1983, moved to Egypt in 1998 and traveled to Afghanistan in 2001, where he became associated with an Al Qaeda "plan to build and detonate a 'dirty bomb' within the United States." The government does not allege that he became "a member of Al Qaeda" — whatever that means — but it does claim that "he was closely associated with known members and leaders" of that terrorist group. It apparently prefers not to put him on trial for conspiracy to detonate a dirty bomb, because the sources of its information remain confidential. It is content to hold him, perhaps indefinitely, as an enemy combatant. It cites as authority for this power "the President's authority, settled by *ex parte Quirin*, 317 U.S. 1 (1942) to detain enemy combatants in wartime — authority that is argued to encompass the detention of United States citizens on United States soil." The Quirin case, you will remember, involved Nazi saboteurs — including at least one U.S. citizen — who landed by submarine on Long Island during World War II, were quickly caught, tried by a military tribunal, and executed, with the hasty approval of the Supreme Court.

The Court of Appeals for the Second Circuit (located in New York) limited its analysis to "the case of an American citizen arrested in the United States, not on a foreign battlefield or while actively engaged in armed conflict against the United States." It distinguished this case from another one that also involved an American citizen, this one named Yaser Esam Hamdi, who was captured by American troops on a battlefield in Afghanistan. It agreed with a statement by a judge of the United States Court of Appeals for the Fourth Circuit (located in Virginia) that "to compare this battlefield capture [of Hamdi] to the domestic arrest [of Padilla] is to compare apples and oranges." The Fourth Circuit had affirmed Hamdi's detention, focusing on the fact that he was captured by American soldiers on a foreign battlefield.

The Second Circuit reversed Padilla's detention, ruling that "the President lacks inherent constitutional authority as Commander-in-Chief to detain American citizens on American soil outside a zone of combat." It distinguished the *Quirin* precedent on the ground that during World War II Congress had authorized the use of military tribunals to try combatants who had violated the laws of war, whereas Congress has never authorized the president to detain American citizens arrested here, indefinitely and without any semblance of a trial.

The court ordered Padilla's release within thirty days unless the government should transfer him to civilian authorities for a criminal trial or detain him "as a material witness in connection with grand jury proceedings" (a loophole through which a Sherman tank could be driven). The government has appealed the *Padilla* decision to the Supreme Court, seeking an "expedited" hearing. The lawyer for Hamdi has sought review by the Supreme Court, arguing that the *Padilla* decision, ordering the detainee's release, "clearly conflicts" with the *Hamdi* decision ordering his continued detention. On January 9, 2004, the justices agreed to review the Hamdi case. One prominent law professor has noted that the Hamdi case had become "the rallying cry for all those people concerned about how far the president can go." He characterized the Hamdi case as "the case that goes to the very heart of the nationwide debate about whether the administration has gone too far."[26] It is uncertain, of course, how the Supreme Court will decide *Hamdi*, or whether the High Court will regard the Padilla and Hamdi cases as "apples and oranges" because Padilla was arrested here and Hamdi on a foreign battlefield, or whether it will regard them both as "fruits" because they both involve American citizens. What does seem likely is that the justices will consider the issues raised in both *Padilla* and *Hamdi* and will decide whether a detainee's status as an American citizen, as well as the place of his original capture, determines how he is to be treated by the American legal system.[27]

The justices will also decide another important issue involving hundreds of detainees currently being held at Guantanamo. The Supreme Court has already decided to hear the narrow issue of whether "United States' courts lack jurisdiction to consider challenges to the legality of the detention of foreign nationals captured abroad in connection with hostilities and incarcerated at the Guantanamo Bay Naval Base, Cuba."[28] The Court of Appeals for the District of Columbia circuit ruled that "Cuba — not the United States — has sovereignty over Guantanamo Bay," and therefore U.S. courts have no authority over foreign detainees being held there. The U.S. Court of Appeals for the Ninth Circuit (located in California) came to the opposite conclusion, ruling that the United States had exercised complete jurisdiction over Guantanamo for more than a century, had acted as if it intended to retain Guantanamo permanently, and had exercised the exclusive, unlimited right to use it as it wished. The United States also subjects persons who commit crimes at Guantanamo to trial in its courts. These legalistic formulations mask some of the most divisive and fundamental issues that confront our nation. Does the Constitution follow the flag and require all American officials, wherever they be and whomever they are detaining or interrogating, to comply with the restrictions of the Bill of Rights? Do foreign combatants captured and detained outside of our nation have any rights? And, most important, will the current Supreme Court rise to the occasion and do its job of checking and balancing the Bush administration's otherwise unchecked and unbalanced approach to combating terrorism?

If the Bush-Ashcroft-Rumsfeld crowd were to have its way, the courts would simply take a hands-off approach, leaving it to the executive and the military to fight the war against terrorism by any means that they deem effective, without regard to the protections afforded by the Constitution. They cite the actions of previous great presidents — especially Lincoln and Roosevelt — as precedents for the need for strong and unchecked executive action in time of war. It is true that Lincoln suspended the writ of habeas corpus during the Civil War and that Roosevelt during World War II ordered the detention of more than 100,000 Americans of Japanese origin, as well as the military trial and quick execution of the German saboteurs — and that both men acted with little interference from the Supreme Court. But it was not these lawless actions that made Lincoln and Roosevelt great. Indeed, these aberrations from compliance with the rule of law diminished the greatness of their presidencies in the estimation of many historians. These high-handed actions were certainly not among their finest hours. Nor is there any evidence that our nation's war aims would have been compromised had the Constitution been followed faithfully.

There will probably be no single substantive resolution to the myriad issues currently dividing our nation. The Supreme Court will almost certainly decide that an American citizen has greater access to our courts than a total stranger whose only connection to America is his intent to inflict harm on its national interests. It is unlikely that the Court will rule that the Constitution follows the flag — that is, that American soldiers are bound by all constitutional restraints wherever they may be and whomever they may be detaining or interrogating. But it is possible that it will rule that Guantanamo, which is leased from Cuba on a long-term basis and is home to a large U.S. military base, is functionally part of our country. Whatever the justices decide, new law will be made, because new circumstances have arisen in the never-ending war against terrorism.

Indeed, new law is sorely needed, because the post–World War II body of international law has become dangerously anachronistic in the new age of warfare. Consider for example, the legal status of the captured Iraqi dictator Saddam Hussein.

On January 9, 2004, the Defense Department officially designated Saddam Hussein a "prisoner of war." The POW status guarantees the captured dictator certain rights under international law. It is somewhat ironic that, under the Defense Department's approach, this mass murderer, who is directly responsible for numerous war crimes against his own people as well as against foreign civilians, will be treated far better than a foot soldier of the Taliban captured in the battlefields of Afghanistan. This only goes to show how dangerously anachronistic current international law has become in the age of terrorism.

It is far from certain whether the High Court will soon agree to take additional cases, and, if so, how many and of which kind. The decision not to decide can sometimes be the most significant decision the justices make, because it gives the final word to the lower courts or to the executive branch. Since some of the lower courts have ruled in favor of the government, and since the government has considerable power to direct cases toward these favorable courts, a decision by the High Court to not decide would be a practical victory for the Bush administration.

Our system of checks and balances also includes the legislative branch, but the Senate and the House of Representatives have generally been silent in the face of executive overreaching in the war against terrorism. No elected official has ever lost an election for being too tough on terrorism. Only unelected federal judges, and especially the justices of the Supreme Court, can effectively check the abuses of the executive. The war against terrorism will provide an important test for whether this Supreme Court is up to the job.

The terrorism cases now pending in our courts may point our legal system in a different and dangerous direction. Criminal trials in terrorism cases may become a thing of the past as military justice takes over. But as one wag put it, "military justice is to justice, as military music is to music." If the Supreme Court grants the president a license to dispense with basic constitutional protections in waging the war against terrorism, this license may endure beyond any previously given during wartime — because, unlike previous wars, which ended on specific dates, the war against terrorism will continue indefinitely. It is appropriate, therefore, to end this book with the powerful warning issued by an earlier Supreme Court following the Civil War:

> [Our Constitution] foresaw that troublous times would arise, when rulers and people would become restive under restraint and seek by sharp and decisive measures to accomplish ends deemed just and proper; and that the principles of constitutional liberty would be in peril, unless established by irrepealable law. . . .
>
> This nation . . . has no right to expect that it will always have wise and humane rulers, sincerely attached to the principles of the Constitution. Wicked men, ambitious of power,

with hatred of liberty and contempt of law, may fill the place once occupied by Washington and Lincoln, and if this right [to suspend provisions of the Constitution during the great exigencies of government] is conceded, and the calamities of war again befall us, the dangers to human liberty are frightful to contemplate.[29]

1. Linda Greenhouse, "Justices face decision on accepting 9/11 cases," *New York Times*, Nov. 3, 2003, p. A1.

2. 121 S. Ct., p. 525 (2000). See generally Alan Dershowitz, *Supreme Injustice* (Boston: Little, Brown and Company, 2002).

3. A single justice decided the Tilden-Hayes election, but he was serving as a member of a bipartisan electoral commission, which had been established by Congress to decide the disputed presidential election of 1876. See William Bennett Munro, *The Government of the United States*, 5th ed. (New York: Macmillan, 1946), pp. 151–52; C. Vann Woodward, *Reunion and Reaction: The Compromise of 1877 and the End of Reconstruction*, 2nd ed. (Garden City, NY: Doubleday, 1956), pp. 161–62; Sidney I. Pomerantz, "Election of 1876," in *History of American Presidential Elections, 1789–1968*, ed. Arthur M. Schlesinger Jr. (New York: Chelsea House, 1971); www.elections.harpweek.com/4Overview/overview-1876-2.htm.

4. Cass Sunstein and Richard Epstein, ed., *The Vote: Bush, Gore and the Supreme Court* (Chicago: University of Chicago Press, 2001), p. 340.

5. *Ibid.*

6. Under the Constitution, the people can actually be denied the right to vote for electors, but every state grants them that right.

7. "An 1887 law states that if there are two slates of electors, the one certified by the governor should be counted. But the meaning of the statute is not clear." *New York Times*, Dec. 9, 2000.

8. Quoted in Sunstein and Epstein, p. 318.

9. The *Washington Post* Political Staff, *Deadlock: The Inside Story of America's Closest Election* (New York: Public Affairs, 2001), p. 171.

10. See, e.g., *Coleman v. Thompson*, 501 U.S. 722 (1991) (opinion by O'Connor, J., in which Rehnquist, C. J., White, Scalia, Kennedy, and Souter, J. J. joined) (holding that federal habeas courts generally may not review a state court's denial of a state prisoner's federal constitutional claim if the court's decision rests on a state procedural default that is independent of the federal question and adequate to support the prisoner's continued custody); *Castille v. Peoples*, 489 U.S. 346 (1989) (opinion by Scalia, J., for a unanimous Court) (holding that a state's prisoner's federal habeas petition should be dismissed if the prisoner has not exhausted available state remedies as to any of his federal claims); *Wainwright v. Sykes* (1977) (opinion by Rehnquist, J.) (holding that a convicted man's failure to make timely objection to the admission of his inculpatory statements in state court proceeding barred federal habeas corpus review of his *Miranda* claim).

11. See, e.g., Robert Bork, Introductory Remarks, American Enterprise Institute Annual Dinner and Francis Boyer Lecture, Feb. 13, 2001. ("The per curiam opinion joined by five Justices does have major problems.")

12. Sunstein and Epstein, pp. 297–98.

13. Antonin Scalia, "Commentary," *Washington University Law Quarterly* 147 (1979).

14. Some conservative commentators have condemned the dissenters for "fouling their own nest." In doing so, they have failed to understand the inaptness of this scatological metaphor. The dissenters are merely calling attention to the fouling done by their majority brothers and sisters.

15. I strongly opposed the tactic of seeking to change the statutory date on which the election was to be certified and urged the Democrats to do everything in their power to have the ballots immediately counted "by categories" in order "to establish the facts on the ground."

16. Antonin Scalia, "God's Justice and Ours," *First Things* 123, May 2002, pp. 17–21.

17. For example, the Ten Commandments contain both moral and theological directive. Do not murder is a moral directive, but the injunctions against making a graven image or worshipping another god are purely theological.

18. Quoted in Tinsley Yarbrough, *The Rehnquist Court and the Constitution* (Oxford: Oxford University Press, 2000), p. 14.

19. He also supported a living view of Article II. See Dershowitz, *Supreme Injustice*.

20. Scalia, "God's Justice and Ours," pp. 17–21.

21. Quoted in Maureen Dowd, "Nino's Opéra Bouffe," *New York Times*, June 29, 2003.

22. Scalia, "God's Justice and Ours," pp. 17–21.

23. *Ibid.*

24. *Ibid.*

25. All quotes relating to the Padilla case are from the Court of Appeals decision at 2003 U.S. App. Lexis 25616.

26. *New York Times*, Jan. 10, 2004, p. A11.

27. On February 20, 2004, the Supreme Court agreed to hear the Padilla case. His release has been stayed pending the Supreme Court decision.

28. *Al Odah v. United States*, 124 S. Ct., p. 534 (2003).

29. *Ex parte Milligan*, 71 U.S. 2, 18 L.Ed., p. 281 (1866).

Index

Buckey, Raymond, 487
Burger, Chief Justice Warren, 40,
    41, 403, 408
Burns, Sleepy Bill, 238
Burr, Aaron, 75–77
    fatal duel with Hamilton, 75,
        76–77
    trial of, xix, 67, 75, 77–80
Burton, Mary, 51
Bush v. Gore, xv, xix, 541–50, 555,
    556, 568n. 15
    dissent, 545, 546, 547, 548, 567n.
        14
    election of 1876, parallels, 167–68
Butler, Benjamin, 172

Calley, William L. Jr., 395–99
capital cases
    American colonies, 29, 31
    anti-capital-punishment
        movement, 24–25
    challenges to death penalty,
        248–49
    courtroom verdict vs. historical,
        254–55
    degrees of murder and, 86
    execution of children, and
        Darrow's arguments, 260
    flawed process in, 278–79
    innocenceproject.org, 281n. 61
    innocent defendant, Hauptmann
        cited as, 272, 274–75
    kidnapping across state lines, 249
    reconsideration of death penalty
        and lessons of Scottsboro trials,
        276–79
    Supreme Court decisions on state
        procedural errors, 547, 567n. 10
    "worth" of victim and, 432–33
    See also Leopold and Loeb
        murder trial
Castille v. Peoples, 567n. 10
censorship, 13

colonial America, 29, 44–48
early American republic, 70
Trading with the Enemy Act of
    1917, 200
See also Alien and Sedition Act;
    freedom of speech and the press
Central Park Jogger case, xvi, 10,
    490–92
Chafee, Zechariah, 229, 232
Chambers, Whittaker, 308, 313,
    316, 317
Chandler, A. B. "Happy," 239
Charles I, King of England, 20, 21
Chase, Chief Justice Salmon, 165
Chicago Seven case, xv, 378,
    390–94
Chipman, N. P., 149–50
civil rights
    Brown v. Board of Education,
        340–41, 346–55
    end of Reconstruction and end to
        black voting rights in the South,
        168
    execution of black soldiers by the
        South, 135–36
    legislation under President
        Lyndon Johnson, 344–45
    Martin Luther King, Jr., and
        nonviolent protest, 307, 341–45
    racism and bigotry, American
        South and, 163, 199–200,
        218–26
    Walker v. Birmingham, 356–60
Civil War
    Andersonville Prison, 135–36,
        146–51
    Dred Scott case as prelude to, 111,
        112, 114, 117–23
    execution of black soldiers by the
        South, 135–36
    Fugitive Slave Act and, 111
    habeas corpus suspended, 285,
        563

truth as no defense to libel
charges, 45–46, 70
See also censorship; media
coverage of trials; Zenger, John
Peter
Frémont, John C., 111
Fugitive Slave Act, 111, 112

Galileo Galilei, trial, xvii, xix, 1,
13–15
plea bargain in, 14
Gardner, Tyron, 551–58
Garfield, James A., 168
assassination of, 168, 169
trial of assassin Guiteau, 183–86,
193n. 48
Genesis of Justice (Dershowitz), 3
genocide, 294–95, 296
German saboteurs, secret trials of,
287–88, 560–61
Gideon v. Wainwright, 340, 345,
361–68
defendant, Clarence Earl Gideon,
361, 362, 364
Gideon's Trumpet (Lewis), 364–66,
367
Gifford, Judge Patricia, 500–501
Ginsberg, Allen, 391
Ginsberg, Ruth Bader, 547
"God card," 57–59
Goetz, Bernhard, "subway vigilante"
case, 450, 482–85
Goldberg, Justice Arthur, 363, 549
Goldstein, Max, 225
Göring, Hermann, 290, 292
Grant, Ulysses S., 164, 165–66
Gratz v. Bollinger, 426–27
Greek law, 6–8
American law and, 1, 6
Draconian, 6
Euphiletus, trial of, 7
Helos, trial of, 7
Socrates, trial of, xvii, xix, 6, 8

Solonic, 6, 7, 8
Greeley, Horace, 165
Grier, Robert, 112
Griswold, Erwin, 401–2
Griswold v. Connecticut, 340
Gruter v. Bollinger, 426–27
Grutman, Norman Roy, 479–81
Guantanamo detainees, case of,
562–64
Guiteau, Charles, 168, 169, 183–86,
193n. 48

habeas corpus
Johnson suspends writ of, 157
Lincoln suspends writ of, 285, 563
review of capital cases and, 567n.
10
Susan B. Anthony case and, 166
Halberstam, David, 312
Hamdi, Yaser Esam, 561–62
Hamilton, Alexander (attorney in
Zenger trial), 45–48
Hamilton, Alexander (Founding
Father), 20, 33, 66–67, 75,
76–77
Hand, Justice Learned, 42–43, 228,
232, 333, 334
Harding, Warren, 249
Harlan, Justice John Marshall, 403
Harris, Jean, 449, 452–57, 533n. 20
Harrison, Benjamin, 169
Harvard Medical School murder,
101–6
Hauptmann, Bruno Richard,
248–49, 272–75
Havel, Václav, 13
Hay, George, 76
Hayes, Rutherford B., 167–68
Haywood, "Big Bill," 198, 208,
209–12
Herold, David, 155
Herrin, Richard, murder case,
380–81, 428–33

INDEX

585

Desiree Washington, lies and
fabrications, 494–505
prosecutors and trial judge,
misleading of jury by, 493–501
rape trial, 493–505

United States Constitution, xvii,
65–66
Bill of Rights, addition of, 65
Bill of Rights, protection of the
guilty and, 321–22
Constitutional Convention, 19, 20
double jeopardy, 507–13
Dred Scott decision and, 118–21
equal protection clause, 122
"facially unconstitutional," 374n.
41
First Amendment, 12–13, 59, 71,
200–201, 227–32, 378–79,
400–404, 477–81, 534n. 42, 556
Greek law and, 6
impeachment, 19–20, 170–71,
170, 173, 532
limits on police and prosecution
tactics, 340
"originalists," 122, 355
principles of British law and, 29
protections in time of war, 565–66
ratification, 65, 66
Sixth Amendment, 361
Socrates, trial of, and Bill of
Rights, 8
Thirteenth, Fourteenth, and
Fifteen Amendments, 122, 123,
163, 164, 166, 174
Twenty-fifth Amendment, 170
See also freedom of speech
*University of California Regents v.
Bakke*, 380, 419–27
Ury, John, 52

Van de Kamp, John, 383, 386
Vietnam War, 377–79

Benjamin Spock antiwar
conspiracy case, xv, 378, 382–89
Chicago Seven case, 390–94
My Lai massacre, 378, 395–99
Pentagon Papers case, 378–79,
400–404
protests and prosecutions of
protestors, 378, 382–94
Vinson, Chief Justice Fred, 327
von Bülow, Claus, murder case, xv,
449, 462–69

Wainwright v. Sykes, 567n. 10
Walker v. Birmingham, 356–60
Wall, John, 385
Waltz, Jon R., 370, 371–72
Warren, Chief Justice Earl, 340–41,
352, 354, 361
Washington, George, 19, 67, 70, 73
Watergate scandal, 400–401
Watson, Thomas, 221
Webster, John White, 102–6
Weddington, Sarah, 407–8
Weinglass, Len, 391
Weinstein, Allen, 314–15, 316,
317–18
Welch, Joseph, 312
Whelan, Rev. Peter, 150
White, Justice Byron, 402, 403, 407,
480
White, Sanford, 197, 203–7
Wigmore, Dean, 190
Williams, Lefty, 238
Williams, Robert Anthony, 363
Wilson, Woodrow, 201
Wind, Timothy, 507–13
Wirt, William, 76
Wirz, Henry, 135, 146–51
Wise, Henry, 113
women
abortion and *Roe v. Wade*, 379,
405–11
"abuse excuse" or "battered
woman syndrome," 203, 242n.
32, 452–57